THE MONGOL EMPIRE

Craig Benjamin, PhD

THE GREAT COURSES®

4840 Westfields Boulevard | Suite 500 | Chantilly, Virginia | 20151-2299
[PHONE] 1.800.832.2412 | [FAX] 703.378.3819 | [WEB] www.thegreatcourses.com

Copyright © The Teaching Company, 2020

Printed in the United States of America

Craig Benjamin, PhD

Professor of History
Grand Valley State University

Craig Benjamin is a Professor of History in the Frederik Meijer Honors College at Grand Valley State University, where he teaches big history and ancient Inner Eurasian history to undergraduate honors students. He has been awarded virtually every teaching and research award that his university has to offer. Professor Benjamin earned his PhD from Macquarie University in Sydney for a dissertation on the Yuezhi, an ancient pastoral nomadic confederation whose migration from China to Afghanistan had major ramifications for ancient Eurasia and the Silk Roads. He is the author or editor of nine books and more than 50 published chapters and articles on ancient Central Asian history, big history, and world history, including *Big History: Between Nothing and Everything*; *The Cambridge World History: Volume IV—A World with States, Empires, and Networks, 1200 BCE–900 CE*; *Empires of Ancient Eurasia: The First Silk Roads Era, 100 BCE–250 CE*; *The Routledge Companion to Big History*; and *Traditions & Encounters: A Global Perspective on the Past* (6th edition).

Professor Benjamin is also a frequent presenter and plenary speaker at conferences and symposia worldwide. He has recorded numerous programs for HISTORY and the Discovery Channel in the US and Canada. Additionally, Professor Benjamin is an in-demand destination speaker on cruises all over the world, including for *Scientific American* and *New York Times Journeys*. He has worked as a guide lecturer for Archaeological Tours, leading parties to Xinjiang in western China, Mongolia, Kazakhstan, Kyrgyzstan, Uzbekistan, and Turkmenistan.

Professor Benjamin was employed for several years as a consultant by the College Board, serving as a member and chair of the Test Development Committees for both the AP World History exam and the SAT World History Subject Test. He is a Past President of the World History Association and served as an officer on the board of the International Big History Association.

Before becoming a historian, Professor Benjamin was a professional jazz musician in his native Australia for 25 years; he continues to perform publicly on flute and saxophone. He has also been an adventurer for much of his life and has trekked and climbed in most of the great mountain ranges on the planet.

Professor Benjamin's other Great Courses are *The Foundations of Eastern Civilization* and *The Big History of Civilizations*. ∎

TABLE OF CONTENTS

INTRODUCTION

GUIDES

SUPPLEMENTARY MATERIAL

THE MONGOL EMPIRE

COURSE SCOPE

This is a course about the Mongols, who, in the 13th and 14th centuries, constructed the largest contiguous empire in the history of the world. By the time they had finished their campaigns, Chinggis Khan and his successors ruled over roughly one-sixth of the world's land surface.

This course follows the story of the Mongols from their origins as just one of many fragmented tribal groups dwelling on the steppe north of China through their consolidation into a unified confederation under Chinggis Khan. It covers their construction of one of the most effective military forces ever seen as well as the collapse of the Mongol empire and the rise of Timur, the last nomadic conqueror in history.

Early lectures consider the environment of the steppe and its impact on the social structures and lifeways of the region's pastoral nomadic communities. They also consider the various militarized confederations that preceded the Mongols, including the powerful Xiongnu and Turks. It follows the rise of Chinggis Khan from his birth as Temujin, his years of exile, and his gradual rise to power until the assembled Mongol clans proclaimed him ruler in 1206.

Chinggis then used the formidable cavalry he had assembled to launch campaigns of conquest south into China and west into central Asia and Persia, the latter resulting the destruction of many of the great cities of ancient inner Eurasia. The course also considers the political and legal institutions created by Chinggis Khan that would lead eventually to the creation of the modern nation of Mongolia.

The next group of lectures follows the continuing expansion of the empire under various khans, despite a decade-long pause in campaigning because of internal squabbling among Mongol elites. The course follows Mongol fortunes in the four khanates that emerged after the death of Mongke Khan in 1259.

The establishment of the Mongol empire, despite its division into four khanates, created secure conditions that allowed for hundreds of adventurers, merchants, and missionaries to travel in safety from one end of Eurasia to the other. The course takes time to follow some of these extraordinary long-distance travelers, including Marco Polo. Later lectures follow the demise of the Mongol empire and the rise of Timur, the Turkic-Mongol conqueror who set out to emulate his hero Chinggis Khan.

The course concludes by returning to the question of how best to sum up the impact of the Mongols on subsequent world history, including their role in facilitating trade and technological exchanges across Eurasia. Historians have struggled to reconcile the undoubted ferocity of the Mongols and Timurids with their more positive impacts, such as their religious tolerance, support of commerce, patronage of artists and architects, and their maintenance of relative peace within their empire during the century-long Pax Mongolica. Finally, the course briefly considers the history of Mongolia after the demise of the Mongols, including the arrival of Buddhism, the influence of China and the Soviet Union, and the emergence of an independent democratic nation in the 1990s. ∎

THE MONGOLS' PLACE IN WORLD HISTORY

Early in the 13th century, Mongol armies began to move out from their homeland on the grasslands of Mongolia to eventually conquer all of China, Korea, central Asia, Persia, the Middle East, Georgia, Armenia, Russia and much of eastern Europe, establishing the largest empire ever seen. However, as surprising and shocking as their sudden appearance clearly was to those they conquered, the Mongols were just the latest in a long line of militarized pastoral nomads who had been raiding and invading even the most powerful sedentary states of Eurasia for a very long time.

The Impact of the Mongols

Chinggis Khan, who claimed a mandate from heaven to rule the world, was singly responsible for creating the Mongol Empire. Once Chinggis and his successors had created the vast Mongol Empire, east and west Eurasia were linked together as never before. This made possible the diffusion of east Asian ideas and technologies that would eventually galvanize Europeans to step out of their parochial kingdoms to explore (and eventually colonize) the world around them. It is because of this unifying effect that some historians claim the Mongols as one of the principal architects of the modern world, although certainly not all agree.

Despite these many positive effects, it is necessary to acknowledge that the Mongols were horrendously destructive. They killed millions of people and destroyed dozens of the greatest cities of the ancient world, along with the agricultural infrastructure that had sustained them for millennia. But we must weigh this against the fact that the Mongols facilitated intensified levels of trade and exchange between east and west, patronized the finest artisans and craftsmen, promoted religious tolerance, and provided sufficient security across Eurasia to allow travelers like Marco Polo to undertake extraordinary journeys from one end of their empire to the other.

Although the Mongols distinguished themselves from those they conquered by their formidable military skill, they also enjoyed a more egalitarian social structure than all the sedentary states they interacted with. As with all other nomadic pastoralist confederations, in the Mongol world decisions were made by a council of political and military elites, including the decision as to who would be elected great khan. Mongol women also enjoyed considerable freedom, respect, and influence, particularly when compared to the status of women in most contemporary sedentary societies.

Chinggis Khan

The man who became Chinggis Khan was likely born in the year 1162 as Temujin, the son of a minor Mongol chief. Over the next four decades, he made many allies and enemies as he slowly clawed his way to the top of the Mongol world, until in 1206 at the age of 44 he was proclaimed Chinggis Khan, meaning the Universal Ruler or the Strong Ruler. For the next five years, Chinggis consolidated his position by bringing various Turkic tribes into his coalition and by waging war against the Xi Xia tribes that controlled parts of western China and Tibet.

In 1211, Chinggis Khan launched his first assault on northern China, then under the control of the Jin dynasty. After capturing the capital of Zhongdu, Chinggis tried to establish commercial relations with the shah of Khwarazmia—a huge Islamic state to the west that stretched from the western edge of China to Persia. The shah treated Chinggis's envoys badly, and Chinggis declared war. The brutal Khwarazmian campaign that followed lasted five years, and by the end many of the great Silk Roads cities of central Asia were in ruins.

After Chinggis Khan

Chinggis died in 1227 at the age of 65 in the midst of yet another campaign, this time against the Xi Xia in western China. Chinggis's successor as Khan was his third son, Ogedai, who was elected in 1229. Ogedai inherited an empire some 9 million square miles in area, already four times the size of the Roman Empire.

Under Ogedai, the war in northern China resumed and successfully concluded with the collapse of the Jin. Korea was also conquered. Far to the west, Mongol armies invaded Armenia, Georgia, and Russia before destroying the flower of European knighthood in major battles in Poland and Hungary. There is every reason to believe that western Europe was only saved from Mongol devastation by the death of Ogedai in 1241.

The decade between 1241 and 1251 gave Eurasia breathing space as disagreements over succession led to an eruption of internal disputes between the families of Chinggis's four sons. That ended in 1251 with the succession of Khan Mongke Khan, the son of Chinggis's youngest son, Tolui.

Upon coming to power, Mongke staged a revolution that destroyed the power of rival lineages. He then dispatched his brothers Qubilai and Hulagu on new campaigns of conquest to China and the Middle East, respectively. Qubilai was intent upon destroying the Southern Song dynasty, while Hulagu's capture of Baghdad in 1258 brought to an end the Golden Age of Islam.

By the mid-13th century, tensions were running so high that there was no longer any possibility of reunifying the Mongol empire, which now devolved into four autonomous khanates. The Yuan dynasty ruled China and East Asia, the Chagatayid *ulus* (or khanate) controlled central Asia, the Ilkhanate ruled in Persia and the Middle East, and the Golden Horde controlled the steppes of southern Russia.

Mongke's death in 1259 led to civil war between various factions, which further entrenched the divisions between the khanates. Qubilai was eventually elected great khan in 1260, but his position was by no means universally accepted. He finally completed the conquest of China in 1274, 63 years after Chinggis Khan had launched his initial assault on the Jin Dynasty back in 1211.

For the remainder of his life, Qubilai worked to expand his domain throughout much of east Asia, although his invasions of Japan and Vietnam both failed. He died in 1294, as nominal ruler of something like one sixth of the land surface of the earth.

After Qubilai Khan

The Ilkhanate in Persia collapsed in 1335, and the Yuan dynasty was eventually destroyed by the Chinese Ming dynasty in 1368. The Chagatayid *ulus* in central Asia suffered a much more gradual disintegration and eventually morphed into the heartland of the Timurid Empire, while the Golden Horde in Russia maintained some degree of power and prestige in the region for almost another four centuries.

Another notable figure was the conqueror Timur. Timur, who was of Turkic-Mongol heritage, was born in modern Uzbekistan probably in the 1320s. Like his hero Chinggis Khan, he gradually rose to power through diplomacy and inter-tribal warfare. Timur was badly wounded in a battle in the 1360s and acquired a limp for the rest of his life. This gave him the name by which he is better known in the West: Timur the Lame, or Tamerlane.

Timur was the last great nomadic conqueror in world history, and in a series of major campaigns all over Eurasia, he created his own enormous empire. After his death in 1405, his sons and grandsons ruled the remnants of that empire through to the early 16th century. One descendant, Babur, would create the Mughal Empire in India that would rule until the British arrival in the 18th century.

THE MONGOLS' PLACE IN WORLD HISTORY

LECTURE 1 TRANSCRIPT

One morning in February of 1220, the residents of the fabled Silk Roads city of Bukhara looked out from their battlements to find Chinggis Khan, his youngest son Tolui, and a formidable Mongol army camped right in front of the city walls. "Chinggis," by the way, is the preferred way of pronouncing the great khan's name by Mongol specialists today. It is a more accurate rendering of his written name than "Genghis." This was hundreds of miles from the last reported sighting of Chinggis, and their unexpected appearance at Bukhara was a testament to the stamina of the Mongol army, which had ridden surreptitiously across the harsh Kyzylkum Desert, and of course to the strategic brilliance of its leadership.

Ata Malik-Juvaini, a Persian scholar whose *History of the World Conqueror* will be one of the key eyewitness accounts we rely on to tell our story in this course, had this to say about the reaction of the citizens of Bukhara that fateful morning: "When the inhabitants … beheld the surrounding countryside choked with horseman and the air black as night with the dust of cavalry, fright and panic overcame them, and fear and dread prevailed."

Three years later, another Mongol army under the command of generals Subedei and Jebe surprised a massive Kievan Rus army of 80,000 men on the banks of the Kalka River and, despite being greatly outnumbered, utterly destroyed it. This was the culmination of a brief period of devastation unleashed without warning on the peoples of Armenia, Georgia, and Russia, but to the Mongols, it was just a sideshow to the main campaign against the Khwarazm-Shah.

As Subedei and Jebe turned east and headed back to Khwarazmia to continue the war, a Russian chronicler living in the city of Novgorod wrote: "The Tatars turned back from the Dnieper River and we know not whence they came, nor where they hid themselves again; only God knows whence he fetched them against us for our sins." A Muslim author and contemporary to all these events, Ibn al-Athir was so overwhelmed by the unexpected devastation caused by the Mongols' Khwarazmian campaign that he lamented "it may well be that the world from now until its end … will not experience the like of it again."

Hello, and welcome to this course on the Mongols and how their conquests of enormous regions of Eurasia changed the course of human history. Early in the 13th century, Mongol armies began to move out from their homeland on the grasslands of Mongolia to eventually conquer all of China, Korea, central Asia, Persia, the Middle East, Georgia, Armenia, Russia, and much of eastern Europe, establishing the largest empire ever seen.

And yet, as surprising and shocking as their sudden appearance clearly was to those they conquered, the Mongols were just the latest in a long line of militarized pastoral nomads who had been raiding and invading even the most powerful sedentary states of Eurasia for a very long time.

We will explore some of these predecessors in detail in lecture 3, but it's worth mentioning them here: the Xiongnu, Xianbei, the Turks, Uyghurs, the Khitan, and the Jurchen. Each of these were formidable militarized confederations of highly skilled mounted archers under inspired leadership, and each had a devastating impact on the peoples around them. It was the Chinese who bore the brunt of many of these nomadic incursions, which is why they built a Great Wall to help protect them. So the Chinese were far less surprised by the appearance of the Mongols than other states further to the west.

The Mongols and the Timurids were destined to be the last in this long line. They created the most influential of all the empires of the steppe, empires that acted as a bridge between the medieval world and the early-modern one that would follow.

Chinggis Khan, who claimed a mandate from heaven to rule the world, was singly responsible for creating the Mongol Empire. Once Chinggis and his successors had created the vast Mongol Empire, east and west Eurasia were linked together as never before. This made possible the diffusion westwards of all manner of east Asian ideas and technologies that eventually galvanized Europeans to step out of their parochial kingdoms and begin to explore and soon colonize the world around them.

It is because of this unifying effect that some historians claim the Mongols as one of the principal architects of the modern world, although certainly not all agree. We will return to this assessment many times in the lectures ahead and try and reach some sort of a conclusion by the end of the course on whether the Mongols deserve this mantle.

Despite these many positive effects, we must of course acknowledge that the Mongols were horrendously destructive. They killed millions of people and destroyed dozens of the greatest cities of the ancient world along with the agricultural infrastructure that had sustained them for millennia. But we must weigh this against the fact that the Mongols facilitated intensified levels of trade and exchange between east and west, patronized the finest artisans and craftsmen, promoted religious tolerance, and provided sufficient security across Eurasia to allow travelers like Marco Polo to undertake in safety extraordinary journeys from one end of their empire to the other.

Although the Mongols distinguished themselves from those they conquered by their formidable military skill, they also enjoyed a more egalitarian social structure than all the sedentary states they interacted with. As with all other nomadic pastoralist confederations, in the Mongol world, decisions were made by a council of political and military elites, including the decision as to who would be elected Great Khan. This meant that although the Khans had great power and prestige, they were still regarded as first amongst equals.

Mongol women also enjoyed considerable freedom, respect, and influence, particularly when compared to the status of women in most contemporary sedentary societies. There are several examples known to us of Mongol women who gained great political power, and we shall also meet some of these formidable Mongol queens in our course.

It was partly because of these more egalitarian social and political structures, and the lifeway of pastoral nomadism itself, that the Mongols held a decided military advantage over even the best equipped and trained sedentary armies. These advantages included advanced cavalry tactics and supreme horse-riding skills, enhanced mobility and field craft skills, and their extraordinary prowess with the composite bow and arrow. The Mongols were rarely beaten in the field, and uniquely amongst their nomadic cousins, they also acquired the skills of siege craft so well they were rarely thwarted in their attempts to capture cities. We will have much to say about these political, social, and military innovations in the lectures that follow.

Let me offer you a brief timeline of the events we unfold in this course, which focuses on a period of just over 300 years, from the late 12th to the early 16th centuries. The man who became Chinggis Khan was born probably in the year 1162 as Temujin, the son of a minor Mongol chief. Over the next four decades, he made many allies and just as many enemies as he slowly clawed his way to the top of the Mongol world, until in 1206, at the age of 44, he was proclaimed Chinggis Khan: the Universal Ruler, the Strong Ruler. For the next five years, Chinggis consolidated his position by bringing various Turkic tribes into his coalition and also by waging war against the Xi Xia tribes that controlled parts of western China and Tibet.

Then, in 1211, Chinggis launched his first assault on northern China, which was under the control of the Jin Dynasty. Eventually capturing its northern capital of Zhongdu, Chinggis then tried to establish friendly commercial relations with the Shah of Khwarazmia to the west, a huge Islamic state that stretched from the western edge of China to Persia. But the Shah treated Chinggis's envoys so shamefully that Chinggis had no option other than to declare war. The brutal Khwarazmian campaign that followed lasted five years, and by the end, many of the great Silk Roads cities of central Asia were in ruins. After concluding this brutal masterpiece of warfare, Chinggis died in 1227 at the age of 65, in the midst of yet another campaign, this time against the Xi Xia in western China.

Chinggis's successor as khan was his third son, Ogedai, who was elected in 1229. Ogedai inherited an empire some 9 million square miles in area, already four times the size of the Roman Empire, but this was by no means the end of Mongol expansion. Under Ogedai, the war in northern China was resumed and successfully concluded with the collapse of the Jin. Korea was also conquered, and far to the west, Mongol armies invaded Armenia, Georgia, and Russia before destroying the flower of European knighthood in major battles in Poland and Hungary. There is every reason to believe that western Europe was only saved from Mongol devastation by the death of Khan Ogedai in 1241.

The decade between 1241 and 1251 gave Eurasia breathing space as disagreements over succession led to an eruption of internal disputes between the families of Chinggis's four sons. This had the effect of turning the attention of Mongol elites inwards and away from further expansion. But that ended in 1251 with the succession of Khan Mongke, the son of Chinggis's youngest son, Tolui. Upon coming to power, Mongke staged a Toluid revolution that destroyed the power of rival lineages. He then dispatched his brothers Qubilai and Hulagu on new campaigns of conquest to China and the Middle East, respectively. Qubilai was intent upon destroying the Southern Song Dynasty, while Hulagu's capture of Baghdad in 1258 brought to an end the Golden Age of Islam.

By the mid-13th century, tensions were running so high amongst the Chinggisids that there was no longer any possibility of reunifying the Mongol Empire, which now devolved into four autonomous khanates. The Yuan Dynasty ruled China and east Asia, the Chagatayid Ulus controlled central Asia, the Ilkhanate ruled in Persia and the Middle East, and the Golden Horde controlled the steppes of southern Russia.

Mongke's death in 1259 led to civil war between various factions, which further entrenched the divisions between the khanates. Qubilai was eventually elected Great Khan in 1260, but his position was by no means universally accepted. Qubilai finally completed the conquest of China in 1274, 63 years after Chinggis Khan had launched his initial assault on the Jin Dynasty way back in 1211. For the remainder of his life, Qubilai worked to expand his domain throughout much of east Asia, although his invasions of Japan and Vietnam both failed. Qubilai died in 1294 as nominal ruler of something like one-sixth of the land surface of the earth.

But such a massive empire riven with so many factions and internal disputes could never last, and so gradually the Mongol khanates fell apart. The Ilkhanate in Persia collapsed in 1335, and the Yuan Dynasty was eventually destroyed by the Chinese Ming Dynasty in 1368. The Chagatayid Ulus in central Asia suffered a much more gradual disintegration and eventually morphed into the heartland of the Timurid Empire, while the Golden Horde in Russia maintained some degree of power and prestige in the region for almost another four centuries.

The final part of our course is focused on the conqueror Timur and his successors. Timur, who was of Turkic-Mongol heritage, was born in modern Uzbekistan, probably in the 1320s, and like his hero Chinggis Khan, he gradually rose to power through diplomacy and inter-tribal warfare. Timur was badly wounded in a battle in the 1360s and acquired a limp for the rest of his life, hence the name by which he is better known in the West, Timur the Lame, or Tamerlane.

Timur was the last great nomadic conqueror in world history, and in a series of major campaigns all over Eurasia, he created his own enormous empire. After his death in 1405, his sons and grandsons ruled the remnants of empire through to the early 16th century, with one descendant, Babur, creating the Mughal Empire in India that would rule there until the British turned up in the 18th century.

This then is the epic tale we unfold in this course—frankly one of the most extraordinary stories in the long annals of world history. In the next two lectures, we'll explore the environmental context in which the lifeway of militarized nomadism emerged and the formidable steppe predecessors to the Mongols, beginning with the mighty Xiongnu.

But in what remains of this first lecture, I thought it might be helpful to try and paint a picture of the larger geopolitical context for the emergence of the Mongols by outlining some of the key developments in Eurasian history over the centuries leading up to the birth of Chinggis Khan. Practitioners in the fields of world history and big history, amongst whom I include myself, believe that individual stories, even ones as epic as the Mongols, make so much more sense when situated in both the environmental and geopolitical context in which they play out.

So let's pick up the story of Eurasian history back in the 3rd century of the Common Era, at a moment when all the imperial states of Afro-Eurasia were facing serious problems. In China, the Han Dynasty collapsed in 220 after decades of poor leadership and internal division. For the next 350 years, China was divided into a variety of kingdoms and small dynasties, with warlords vying for power with nomadic invaders. Late in the 6th century, the Buddhist Sui Dynasty ended this age of disunity, restoring strong central government and building impressive infrastructure works like the Grand Canal. But these put such a strain on conscripted peasant labor that the Sui Dynasty collapsed quickly early in the 7th century.

Their successors, the Tang Dynasty, ruled for the next three centuries until 907 of the Common Era, turning China into what was undoubtedly the wealthiest and most powerful civilization on the planet. Under the Tang, China became a major imperial power again, incorporating Manchuria, Vietnam, much of Tibet, and large regions of central Asia into the Tang Empire. Farming became more efficient, and China's population approached 100 million.

By the 10th century, Tang China was the most urbanized society on the planet, with the capital, Chang'an, home to 2 million residents. Innovation and commerce flourished in the workshops of the many great Tang cities, including in porcelain, iron and steel, silk, gunpowder, and printing. The Silk Roads were revived, and foreign merchants established such a presence in Tang cities that virtually every religion of Afro-Eurasia was practiced somewhere in the country.

The Tang collapsed early in the 10th century, and this led to another period of fragmentation, but this lasted for only 50 years before the Song Dynasty restored order. However, the Song were forced to deal with powerful and restive militarized nomads on their northern border, and eventually the northern half of China was overrun by the Jurchen, who established their own Chinese-style Jin Dynasty. South of an uneasy border, more or less midway between the Huang He (the Yellow River) and the Yangtze River, the Southern Song ruled a dynamic commercial state from their capital of Lin'an, the modern city of Hangzhou. This was the geopolitical situation in east Asia that the Mongols faced when Chinggis Khan launched his initial raids on Jin China in 1211.

In central Asia, meanwhile, the Parthian and Kushan Empires were both overrun by the Sasanians at exactly the same time that the Han Dynasty was collapsing in China. The Sasanians went on to create their own impressive empire that lasted for more than 400 years. At its peak, the Sasanian Empire stretched from Afghanistan to the headwaters of the Tigris and Euphrates, which led to conflict with the Romans. The founder of the Sasanian state, Ardashir I, was a brilliant military leader who fought the Roman emperor Alexander Severus for control of Mesopotamia, and the Euphrates River became a sort of fortified border between the two empires.

The second Sasanian ruler, Shapur I, triumphed over three successive Roman emperors, defeating one, killing the next, and capturing the third. The Silk Roads remained a major land trade route during the Sasanian Era, although maritime routes became more important because these incessant wars between the Sasanians and the Romans disrupted land-based trade.

The Sasanians maintained successful commercial relationships with the Tang Chinese and with the Byzantines, and between them, these three imperial powers controlled much of Eurasia, from the Yellow Sea to the Mediterranean Sea. In the mid-7th century, however, this Eurasian system was upturned by the appearance of another new power, the Muslims, who destroyed the Sasanians and ushered in a brand-new chapter in the history of Afro-Eurasia.

From the 8th century through to the arrival of the Mongols in the early 13th century, the histories of many of the states and cultures of inner Eurasia became interconnected by the expansion of Islam. Created by Muslim warriors, merchants, missionaries, and administrators, the vast Dar al-Islam—the Abode, or the Realm of Islam—became one of the most important economic, intellectual, and cultural structures in the world, dominating the western half of Afro-Eurasia in the same way that the Tang Dynasty dominated the eastern.

The lightning-fast expansion of the Dar al-Islam was unprecedented. By 637, just five years after Muhammad's death, much of Syria, Palestine, and all of Mesopotamia had become part of the Muslim world. In the 640s, much of North Africa was incorporated, and by the time the Sasanian Empire fell to the Muslims in 651, the Dar al-Islam already stretched from the Mediterranean to Afghanistan.

After a period of political consolidation, Islamic armies resumed the jihad early in the 8th century. Parts of northern India were conquered in 711, and Muslim hegemony in North Africa was extended to Morocco, and then across the Strait of Gibraltar and into Spain by 718. In less than a century, the Islamic realm had expanded to become the largest civilization the world had ever seen.

Early Muslim rulers established an administrative structure known as a caliphate that achieved stability under the Umayyad Dynasty, which ruled from 661 to 750. The Umayyads were wealthy Meccan merchants who ruled the caliphate from the Syrian commercial city of Damascus. Initially, the Umayyads provided capable administrators, but during the 8th century, they became increasingly aloof, and they were overthrown by the Abbasids in 750. The Abbasid Dynasty then ruled the Islamic world from their purpose-built capital of Baghdad until it, and they, were destroyed by the Mongols in 1258.

The Abbasids learned from the cultural exclusivity of the Umayyads and instituted a more cosmopolitan form of government in which power and administrative responsibilities were shared more equitably amongst Arabs, Persians, Egyptians, and Mesopotamians. With a steady flow of tributary revenue coming in from all over the Islamic world, Baghdad was beautified with magnificent buildings, mosques, and squares, and became one of the great commercial, financial, industrial, and intellectual cities of the world.

Under the Abbasids, millions converted to Islam and enriched the Islamic realm by bringing into it their own cultural traditions. This cultural and linguistic synthesis resulted in an explosion of intellectual activity throughout the Muslim world, in a period historian Frederick Starr has called the Lost Enlightenment.

With all of central Asia and the Middle East now under control of the Muslims, regions that for centuries had been divided amongst different political powers, an economic golden age also ensued. Under the Abbasids, agriculture thrived in Egypt, Syria, and Mesopotamia during a period sometimes called the medieval green revolution. It was an era of increased productivity and population growth that stimulated the economy of the region like never before. Increased agricultural output was achieved by the expansion and better maintenance of the ancient irrigation canal systems, some of which had been in place in Mesopotamia for 4,000 years by this stage, and also by the introduction of new methods of fertilization and crop rotation.

Commercial activity also flourished across the Islamic world. Remember, Muhammad himself had been a merchant, and under the Abbasids, elaborate trade networks linked all the regions of the Dar al-Islam together, connecting them to an even larger Afro-Eurasian-wide network. Camel caravans facilitated this, leading to the construction of thousands of new caravanserais. And of course, maritime trade became even more prosperous after Islamic sailors adopted Chinese innovations like the compass. Muslim sailors and their ships linked east and southeast Asia to the Indian Ocean, the Persian Gulf, and the coast of east Africa in a thriving commercial network.

It was inevitable that the expansive worlds of Islam and Tang China would eventually need to confront each other. The Tang had reached deep into central Asia in constructing its massive tributary empire, just as the realm of Islam was expanding into the same region from the opposite direction.

An important battle was fought in 751 between Islamic and Tang Chinese forces, deep in the heart of central Asia. During the five-day Battle of Talas, a large Muslim force initially struggled to overcome a smaller Chinese army for control of the important Syr Darya valley. The Chinese forces were eventually overwhelmed, marking the end of westward Tang expansion and opening up much of central Asia to Muslim penetration, leading to the further spread of Islam amongst the Turkic peoples living in the region. Legend has it that amongst the Chinese captives were two paper makers, and this is how the craft of papermaking was introduced into the Islamic world.

Over the centuries that followed, Abbasid control of the caliphate became increasingly compromised as more and more regional Islamic states claimed autonomy and even stopped paying their taxes to Baghdad. New regional powers like the Tahirids and the Samanids effectively ended any semblance of an all-powerful caliph in Baghdad. In the 10th century, Persian aristocrats took over the Abbasid throne, and during the following century, power passed into the hands of the Seljuqs, a group of militarized Turks who had converted to Islam and now occupied much of the caliphate. We'll talk more about the expansion of the Turks in a later lecture.

But even though the Abbasid Caliphate was fragmenting, we need to acknowledge that for about 700 years before the Mongols appeared, Muslim administrators maintained a connected zone of trade, exchange, and communication that stretched from India and central Asia all the way to the Pyrenees. Intellectual activity flourished, and new crops, agricultural technologies, and manufactured goods were spread by merchants across an enormous region of Afro-Eurasia, stimulating that world zone as never before. Any hope that this Golden Age of Islam could be maintained was destroyed in the 13th century by the Mongols, as we shall see.

Finally, let's consider the situation in Europe following the disintegration of the Roman Empire. During the 5th century, the western Roman Empire fragmented into a series of fortified estates and competitive regional kingdoms, but the eastern half remained unified and strong as the Byzantine Empire, which lasted for another thousand years. Constantinople withstood sieges by Islamic armies in the 7th and 8th centuries, although large regions of the empire were lost to the Muslims. The core empire survived, however, and used its strategic position to remain unconquered and wealthy through trade and innovative manufacturing until 1453, when Constantinople was finally sacked by the Ottoman Turks.

Further west, regions of the former Roman Empire gradually lost the ability to collect taxes or maintain a professional army. This led to political fragmentation and a new balance of power between monarchs, wealthy landholders, and the Christian church, which now began to play an increasingly important role in medieval western Europe. The collapse of the Roman taxation and administration system made it difficult to maintain many of the Roman cities of the west. Some disappeared completely, while others broke up into areas of smaller settlements, separated by ruins and spaces converted into market gardens and vineyards.

The Franks were the first in a series of Germanic-speaking dynasties to establish successful states in western Europe. Under King Clovis, who reigned from 481 to 511 and who converted to Christianity, rival Frankish subgroups were consolidated under a strong monarchy that took control of much of Gaul as far as the Rhine River. Renewed Frankish expansion commenced late in the 7th century under a new family of Carolingian leaders, including Pepin II and his son Charles Martel, who stopped the Muslim invasion of Europe at Poitiers in 732 of the Common Era.

The Frankish kingdom reached its height under Charlemagne, whose imperial state included all of modern France, parts of northern Spain, the territory between the Rhine and the Elbe, northern Italy, and much of the middle Danube Basin. Yet Charlemagne's empire was fleeting, and by the late 9th century, power had reverted to a series of local princes who lived in rural palaces in the heartlands of their kingdoms, where their own lands and followers were concentrated.

In Italy, the Germanic Lombards lived in cities like Milan and Venice, which by the 9th century had already developed into a major commercial port. Rome remained the largest city in the west, with a population of perhaps 25,000 in the 8th century. In Spain, the destruction of the Visigothic kingdom by the Muslims in 711 led to wholesale economic collapse, although by the end of the 8th century, the unification of the territory that became known as al-Andalus under the Arab Umayyad emirate led to a gradual recovery.

In Britain, many centuries of Roman occupation had increased the prosperity of a small class of villa owners. But by the mid-5th century, the breakdown of Roman control exposed these Romano-British to regular raids by Picts and Scots, and by Anglo-Saxons from the mainland. By the early 7th century, 10 or more small Anglo-Saxon kingdoms had been established in England.

Further north, trading and raiding in the later 8th and early 9th centuries brought Scandinavian peoples into close contact with communities in both western Europe and Russia. Political instability in Denmark resulted in expeditions by armed bands of Vikings out of Scandinavia in the mid-9th century and to their raiding and eventual settlement in Britain, France, and Russia. Wealthy monasteries were particularly subject to Viking attacks, both on the coasts and in the interior, as the raiders used rivers to move inland.

Vikings looted Paris in 845 and in the decades that followed conquered Anglo-Saxon kingdoms in Britain. In 878, King Alfred of Wessex defeated Viking forces at the Battle of Edington, after which the Danish king Guthrum accepted baptism, and the Scandinavian presence in England was officially recognized as the Danelaw. In France, land around the city of Rouen was granted in the year 911 to a Viking leader named Rollo—land that eventually evolved into the Duchy of Normandy.

Scandinavian peoples also played a critical role in the emergence of the first Russian state. Vikings established commercial bases in Ukraine and Russia and took control of regional exchange networks, establishing themselves as a new elite that would evolve into rulers of the first Russian state, Kievan Rus. The development of Russia was tied to the emergence of another group destined to play an important role in the future history of both Europe and Russia, the Slavs, who eventually occupied a wide region stretching from the Balkans to Russia, setting up a contest for their conversion between the pope in Rome and the patriarch in Constantinople.

By the mid-12th century, then, huge civilizations controlled substantial regions of Eurasia, including the Song and Jin Dynasties in east Asia, the Abbasid Caliphate and its regional affiliates in central and west Asia, and the Byzantines in the Balkans. But in Russia and western Europe, a series of small city-states and kingdoms had emerged that traded and fought vigorously with each other.

With the exception of the Jin and the Song, few of these great powers would have even been aware of the quiet steppe grasslands of Mongolia, nor of the Mongols who were just one of several pastoral nomadic tribes that resided there. But that was all about to change with the birth of an infant named Temujin in the year 1162—an infant born clutching a clot of blood in his tiny hand, a sure sign of destined greatness.

THE ORIGINS OF EURASIAN STEPPE NOMADISM

Flowing through the heart of the modern nation of Mongolia is the beautiful Orkhon River, part of the extensive Selenge River system that empties eventually into Lake Baikal in Siberia. The central valley of the Orkhon River has been a sacred space for all of the militarized nomadic confederations that constructed their vast empires of the steppe, including the Mongols.

Pastoralism

The Mongols, like their predecessors who made the Orkhon Valley home, were a product of the dynamic lifeway of pastoralism, which first emerged many thousands of years before they burst their way on to the world stage. This new lifeway was a revolution. Humans have been on the planet for roughly 250,000 years, and for 95 percent of that time, our ancestors survived by foraging and hunting.

This started to change at the end of the last Ice Age, around 11,000 years ago, when some human communities transitioned from foraging to farming. This transition was made possible because of the warming of the planet that followed the end of the Ice Age and the availability of new species of plants and animals that could be domesticated.

But the adoption of agriculture was not a universal phenomenon. Even as sedentary farming communities appeared in places like the Fertile Crescent, humans continued to live as nomadic foragers in many other parts of the world.

Eventually, a third option emerged: pastoralism, which is essentially nomadic livestock herding. Archaeological evidence reveals that some 7,000 years ago scattered communities living in the grasslands of Eurasia learned to exploit their domesticated animals in more efficient and sustainable ways rather than just slaughtering them for meat and hides.

This was a result of what archaeologist Andrew Sherratt calls the secondary products revolution. Sometime in the 4th millennium BCE, these communities figured out how to use the secondary products of animals while they were alive, such as their wool, their milk and blood, and their hauling and transportation abilities.

Most of the animal species pastoralists came to depend on—sheep, goats, and cattle, for example—had all been domesticated thousands of years earlier during the transition to agriculture. However, it seems to have taken humans a long time to learn how to utilize the secondary products of these species.

The lifeway of pastoralism is at least seminomadic, and in many cases fully nomadic. Pastoralists did practice farming when the environment was favorable to this, but it was their mobility that explains their impact on world history. Efficient pastoralists were now able to take their food, clothing, tools, and dwelling materials with them as they migrated across the landscape, which meant they could move into and eventually colonize the vast steppe and desert regions of Africa and Eurasia.

The Eurasian Steppe

The vast grasslands of the Eurasian steppe were fundamental to the sustainability of the pastoral lifeway. Limited agriculture is possible in some places in the steppe, but it is far more conducive to grazing large numbers of animals, which allowed the pastoralists to tap into an otherwise unusable environment and energy source.

The Eurasian steppe is essentially a massive expanse of grassland that stretches 5,000 miles from Eastern Europe through central Asia to Manchuria. It is bounded in the north by Siberian taiga (a region of swampy coniferous forest) and in the south by large mountain ranges. The sheer size of the steppe explains why some of the empires constructed by militarized pastoralists were so huge.

The steppe does not consist only of grassland; at various places, it is interrupted by mountain ranges, rivers like the Orkhon, or by deserts and other geographical features. Few of these features ever proved to be significant barriers to mobile pastoralists, however.

The environment of the modern nation of Mongolia, the heartland not just of the mighty Mongol empire but of the five great nomadic empires that preceded them, is a quintessential example of the importance of the steppe to the construction of these vast empires. Mongolia is a landlocked country, dominated by vast rolling plateaus of grassland along with some important mountains, lakes, and rivers.

The land slopes from the high Altai Mountains in the west and north to much lower elevation steppe in the east and south. Its climate is cold and dry, with an average of almost 260 cloudless days per year. Less than one percent of the land is arable, perhaps 10 percent is forest, and almost all the rest is pastureland, which explains why pastoralism was a far more viable lifeway here than farming.

So as not to overgraze the steppe, pastoralist families lived by themselves or in small clusters of relatives, along with their flocks and herds. They also practiced transhumance pastoralism by rotating their pastures with the season. This is visible in Mongolia today: huge areas of grassland occupied by just a few family clusters living in ger camps, with thousands of animals grazing all around them. A ger, alternatively known as a yurt, is a portable dwelling that can be set up or packed away quickly. These are round, tent-like shelters traditionally constructed of wooden lattice walls covered by sheets of felt. They are still widely used all over Mongolia today.

Sustaining Society

The pastoralist diet consisted mostly of dairy products. There was also meat, which came from domesticated animals and hunting. Despite the efficiency of pastoral nomads in utilizing the secondary products of their animals to live and live well, there were some needs that could not be met by their herds and flocks. Because of this, the nomads were never completely self-sufficient, which meant they simply had to interact with contiguous sedentary societies from the beginning.

This interaction might come in the form of trading, or if that didn't work, by raiding. All over Eurasia, archaeological evidence reveals the emergence of a type of symbiotic relationship between pastoralists and neighboring sedentary farming societies. Pastoralists had valuable goods to trade. In return, they wanted textiles like silk, grains, and other foodstuffs not available on the steppe; various metal weapons and tools; and some other luxury items that were produced by artisans in sedentary societies. (Many nomadic confederations also possessed superb artisans.)

Pastoralists needed to live in small, sustainable household communities on the steppe, and this influenced the types of social structures that emerged. Everyone had an important role to play in ensuring the survival of the community—men, women and children—so the type of social structure that emerged was much more egalitarian than that which evolved in sedentary societies.

The transition to farming that many communities made during the Neolithic Era gradually changed women's role from equal partners in foraging societies to child rearers and household managers in agricultural communities. This left men freer to take on public roles such as rulers, warriors, or religious leaders. Eventually, this meant that some form of patriarchy was enshrined in virtually every single secular and religious law codes produced by agrarian civilizations. The pastoralists had no such gender-defining luxury: Every member of the family was vital to the family's survival, so women and women's work were valued as being equal to that of men.

Migrations

So as not to overgraze the steppe, pastoralists needed to become increasingly nomadic and graze their herds seasonally over larger ecological regions. Often this resulted in large-scale migrations as multiple groups of pastoralists moved together across the steppe.

Archaeologists give names to some of these migrating pastoralist cultures, often based on the modern name of the place where evidence for the arrival of these groups was first discovered. One of the earliest of these is the Yamnaya pastoralist culture, which dates from the late 4th millennium BCE. They were dispersed across the Caucasus region north of the Black and Caspian Seas. Yamnaya artifacts include horse-riding equipment and wheeled vehicles that were probably used to facilitate migration across the steppe. Weapons have also been discovered—daggers, maces, axes—that had been obtained from early sedentary societies, probably through trade.

Formidable Armies

Archaeological evidence suggests that it was not until quite late in the history of the pastoralists—sometime in the early 1st millennium BCE— that formidable armies of mounted archers first appear. We also have excellent literary evidence of the activities of some of the most powerful of these early militarized groups, such as the ancient Greek historian Herodotus's account of the Scythians or Saka and ancient Chinese historian Sima Qian's account of the activities of the Xiongnu, Wusun, and Yuezhi. Each of these groups would use their military prowess to establish empires of the steppe.

Several factors help explain the success of these steppe empires, but fundamental to all of them were the supreme horse-riding skills of the cavalry and their effective use of the composite bow and arrows. By the 5th millennium BCE, large numbers of wild horses were flourishing in various regions of Inner Eurasia.

Eventually, human communities living at places like Dereivka learned to domesticate some of these horses. The process of domestication then spread outward from some focal point. This likely took place in many areas and over various periods of time. Horse domestication was not a single event, as studies of mitochondrial DNA reveal considerable genetic diversity among early domesticated horses.

Scholar Edwin Pulleyblank has posited that the development of the composite bow was the most significant factor of all in explaining the success of militarized nomads. The composite bow was a laminate constructed from a range of materials, including different types of wood, animal horn, and sinew.

Wood was used to make the core of the bow. A thin layer of animal horn or bone, usually from goats or sheep, was then attached to the inner side, and some type of animal sinew, usually harvested from the legs and back of wild deer, was attached to the outer side. A strong glue made by boiling animal hide was used to bind the layers together. In ideal conditions, when an archer drew back the bow prior to firing, the horn and sinew between them stored far more energy than was available in a similarly sized all-wooden bow.*

Conclusion

The presence of horses and composite bows—and the pastoral nomads' skills with each—led to the appearance of enormous contingents of mounted archers in Inner Eurasia. These armies were almost unbeatable by the forces of sedentary states until many of these states adopted similar technologies and strategy.

However, it was not just the horse and composite bow that explains the success of groups like the Mongols and their equally formidable predecessors. These great cavalry contingents were also incredibly well disciplined and could survive off the land. They were superbly tailored for mobility and speed because they did not need to wait for supply trains to catch up with them. They were brilliant archers and were also superbly skilled with swords, axes, daggers, and maces. Additionally, they were incredibly well led.

THE ORIGINS OF EURASIAN STEPPE NOMADISM

LECTURE 2 TRANSCRIPT

Flowing through the heart of the modern nation of Mongolia is the beautiful Orkhon River, part of the extensive Selenge River system that empties eventually into Lake Baikal in Siberia. The central valley of the Orkhon has been a sacred space for all of the militarized nomadic confederations that constructed their vast empires of the steppe, including, of course, the Mongols.

I have stood on the hillside above the central Orkhon and seen in my imagination thousands of yurts—or *gers*, as they are called in Mongolia—erected across the vast plain, with hordes of Mongol cavalry moving backwards and forwards, practicing their drills, just waiting for a great khan like Chinggis or Ogedai or Mongke to climb up that same hill, raise his bow in the air, and give the signal to launch the next campaign of conquest. It is an extraordinary place of power, and the 800 years that have passed between the appearance of the Mongols on the world stage and today just seem to dissolve in the crystal-clear Mongolian air.

The Mongols, like all their predecessors who made the Orkhon Valley home, were a product of the dynamic lifeway of pastoralism, which had first emerged many thousands of years before they burst their way onto the world stage. To help us understand just what a revolution this new lifeway was, let's begin this lecture by thinking about it from a big history perspective.

Humans have been on planet earth for maybe 250,000 years, and for 95 percent of that time, our ancestors survived by foraging and hunting, living off plants and animals provided naturally by the environment, and developing a range of tools and skills to exploit them.

This all started to change at the end of the last Ice Age, around 11,000 years ago, when some human communities transitioned from foraging to farming, a process we might call the Agricultural Revolution. This transition was made possible because of the warming of the earth that followed the end of the Ice Age and the availability of new species of animals and plants that could now be domesticated. But the adoption of agriculture was not a universal phenomenon. Even as sedentary farming communities appeared in places like the Fertile Crescent and along river valleys in south and east Asia, in many other parts of the world, humans continued to live as nomadic foragers.

Eventually, a third option emerged, that of pastoralism, which is essentially nomadic livestock herding. Archaeological evidence reveals that some 7,000 years ago, scattered communities of humans living in the grasslands of Eurasia had learned to exploit their domesticated animals in more efficient and sustainable ways, rather than just killing them for their meat and hides.

This was a result of what archaeologist Andrew Sherratt called the "secondary products revolution." That is, sometime in the 4th millennium BCE, these communities figured out how to use the secondary products of animals while they were alive, such as their wool, their milk, their blood, their traction power to haul carts and plows, and their mobility as a means of rapid transportation, particularly through the development of horse riding. It was through experimentation with these secondary products of animals that this new lifeway of pastoralism gradually became viable.

Now, most of the animal species pastoralists came to depend on—sheep, goats, and cattle, for example—had all been domesticated thousands of years earlier during the transition to agriculture. But it seems to have taken humans a long time to learn how to utilize the secondary products of these same species and also to add some new and incredibly useful domesticates— such as the camel and, in particular, the horse—in order to sustain a viable lifeway. What this really means is that some communities learned how to use their animals to turn grass into energy. Humans can't eat grass, of course, but we can certainly make great use of grass-grazing animals. So pastoralism appeared as a sort of hybrid lifeway that lies somewhere between foraging and farming.

All this is interesting to historians, of course, but what is crucial to the appearance of powerful and highly mobile militarized pastoralists like the Mongols is that the lifeway of pastoralism is at least seminomadic, and in many cases fully nomadic. Pastoralists did practice farming when the environment was favorable to this, but it was their mobility that explains their impact on world history.

Efficient pastoralists were now able to take their food, clothing, tools, and dwelling materials with them as they migrated across the landscape, which meant they could move into and eventually colonize the vast steppe and desert regions of Africa and Eurasia. These were regions had been previously unavailable to humans, but now pastoralists could thrive in them and use their mobility to move backwards and forwards between the border regions of the great agrarian civilizations that began to emerge in the 3rd millennium BCE.

The pastoralists themselves rarely built cities or constructed what we would traditionally identify as states or civilizations, but their mobility meant that the great civilizations of Afro-Eurasia became linked together into great systems of exchange for the first time. Because of their capacity to link these sedentary communities together, pastoralists became crucial to the sharing of technologies and ideas between sedentary civilizations, like those of the Chinese or Romans, and thus exerted a powerful influence on the way history unfolded within that vast world zone for thousands of years.

Although we can more or less guess at the process whereby some human communities transitioned to pastoralism, there is much we still don't know about this, including where the lifeway might first have emerged. Archaeologists have identified certain sites in parts of Ukraine and southern Russia that seem to provide early evidence of an increasing dependence on mobile domesticated animals like the horse, including the site of Dereivka on the Dnieper River in Ukraine.

Because an unusually large number of horse bones and horse-riding materials have been discovered there, some archaeologists think that the residents of Dereivka must have kept unusually large herds of domesticated horses. But others argue that the residents of Dereivka were simply subsistence farmers who supplemented their lifeway through foraging and hunting and that there is no evidence of any systematic horse domestication to be found.

Regardless of precisely where pastoralism first appeared, there can be no doubt that the vast grasslands of the Eurasian steppe were fundamental to the sustainability of this lifeway. Limited agriculture is possible in some places in the steppe, but it is far more conducive to grazing large numbers of animals, which allowed the pastoralists to tap into an otherwise unusable environment and energy source.

The Eurasian steppe is essentially a massive expanse of grassland that stretches 5,000 miles from eastern Europe through central Asia to Manchuria. It is bounded in the north by Siberian taiga (a region of swampy coniferous forest) and in the south by large mountain ranges associated with the Greater Himalaya. The sheer size of the steppe explains why some of the empires constructed by militarized pastoralists were so huge.

The formidable cavalry of the Mongol Empire, for example, was able to range freely from one end of Eurasia almost to the other, because wherever they went, there was pastureland for their horses.

But the steppe does not consist only of grassland; at various places, it is interrupted by mountain ranges, or by rivers like the Orkhon, or by deserts and other geographical features. Few of these features ever proved to be significant barriers to mobile pastoralists, however, and indeed many of them became places of great significance to some of the most militarized confederations.

Certain river valleys became particularly important, notably that of the Orkhon River in Mongolia, which, as I noted, was the sacred heart of virtually all of the great Empires of the Steppe, including the Mongols. The Orkhon Valley was regarded as the site that conferred imperial power, because whoever controlled the valley was believed to have been appointed by the steppe ancestor spirits and by the great sky god Tengri to rule.

Evidence of just how important the Orkhon has been for steppe confederations, and indeed for later religious leaders, can be seen in the fact that many of the most iconic monuments in nomadic and Mongolian Buddhist history are located there. It is in the Orkhon Valley that the great inscription stele and funerary monuments of early Turkic rulers Bilge Kaghan and Kul Tegin were erected; where the Uyghur capital of Khar Balgas was built; where the first Mongol capital of Karakorum was located; where Erdene Zuu, the first Buddhist monastery established in Mongolia, was built using stones taken from Karakorum; and even where the Tövkhön Khiid monastery, established by the legendary 17th-century Buddhist teacher and artist Zanabazar, was constructed in the hills above the valley. As I noted, it is an extraordinary place of power!

Along with river valleys like the Orkhon, the steppe is also interrupted by mountain ranges, including several of the tallest on earth. But rather than impede the progress of pastoralist cavalry, they more often served as places of refuge from pursuing armies. Some mountain ranges were also regarded as sacred to the gods, as the mighty peak Khan Tengri in the Tian Shan mountains so splendidly illustrates. Tengri was the sky god, and this impressive ice-covered peak thrusts itself into the blue sky in a way that is both forbidding and inspiring.

The environment of the modern nation of Mongolia, the heartland not just of the mighty Mongol Empire but of the five great nomadic empires that preceded them, is a quintessential example of the importance of the steppe to the construction of these vast empires.

Mongolia is a landlocked country, of course, dominated by vast rolling plateaus of grassland, along with some important mountains, lakes, and rivers. The land slopes from the high Altai Mountains in the west and north to much lower elevation steppe in the east and south. Its climate is cold and dry, with an average of almost 260 cloudless days per year. Less than 1 percent of the land is arable, perhaps 10 percent is forest, and almost all the rest is pastureland, which explains why pastoralism was a far more viable lifeway here than farming.

Even the Gobi in the extreme south of Mongolia is a type of pastureland. Although the word *Gobi* has become synonymous for many folks with harsh, arid desert, it is in fact a Mongol word to describe a region with insufficient vegetation to support marmots but enough to support camels. So the Mongols (and the Mongolian people today) clearly distinguish Gobi from actual desert. But the Gobi rangelands are incredibly fragile, and any overgrazing will quickly turn it into true desert, where not even the hardy Bactrian camel can survive.

The environment of the Mongolian steppe, the pastureland, the deserts, the mountains, and rivers like the Orkhon determined how pastoralists had to live in order to survive. So as not to overgraze the steppe, pastoralist families lived by themselves or in small clusters of relatives, along with their flocks and herds. They also practiced transhumance pastoralism by rotating their pastures with the seasons.

You still see all of this in Mongolia today: huge areas of grassland occupied by just a few family clusters living in *ger* camps, with thousands of animals grazing all around them. A *ger*—remember, the Mongol name for a yurt—is a portable dwelling that can be set up or packed away quickly. These are round, tent-like shelters traditionally constructed of wooden lattice walls covered by sheets of felt. They are still widely used all over Mongolia today.

Much of the work of moving animals is still done today by boys and young men on horses, who continue to demonstrate the extraordinary riding skills of their Mongol ancestors, although these days you are also likely to see herding done on the back of a motorbike, often with the whole family onboard!

If you are in Mongolia in the late spring, you will also see huge numbers of goats and sheep being sent up to the high alpine pastures for the first time to begin the summer grazing season. The sight of thousands of animals slowly streaming up from the river valley pastures to higher grasslands in the mountains above is quite extraordinary, as of course is the sound of their baaing and bleating in the otherwise silent early morning air.

Since it was the exploitation of the secondary products of these animals that made the lifeway of pastoralism possible, it is hardly surprising that the pastoralist diet consisted mostly of dairy products. These include various types of cow, goat, and sheep cheese, yogurt, and meat. Even their alcohol comes in the form of a powerful fermented mare's milk called kumiss. Along with their food, other animal secondary products that were utilized were hair and wool and horns, and of course leather.

Some of the meat in a pastoralist diet does come from their domesticated animals, but much of it also comes from hunting, and this was particularly true during the Mongol era. But the slaughtering of the family's animals for meat was handled very carefully, very sustainably. Obviously, the very survival of the family depended upon maintaining their herds and flocks. Plus, the size and health of their animals was how the nomads measured their wealth.

But despite the efficiency of pastoral nomads in utilizing the secondary products of their animals to live, and live well, there were some needs that could not be met by their herds and flocks. Because of this, the nomads were never completely self-sufficient, which meant they simply had to interact with contiguous sedentary societies from the beginning.

This interaction might come in the form of trading, or if that didn't work, by raiding. All over Eurasia, archaeological evidence reveals the emergence of a type of symbiotic relationship between pastoralists and neighboring sedentary farming societies. Pastoralists had valuable goods to trade, of course—their animal products and often some of their actual animals themselves, particularly horses. What they wanted in return were textiles like silk, grains, and other foodstuffs not available on the steppe, various metal weapons and tools, and some other luxury items that were produced by artisans in sedentary societies, although many nomadic confederations also possessed superb artisans.

Despite this periodic interaction with sedentary farming communities, pastoralists needed to live in small, sustainable household communities on the steppe, and this obviously influenced the types of social structures that emerged. Everyone had an important role to play in ensuring the survival of the community—men, women, and children—so the type of social structure that emerged was much more egalitarian than that which evolved in sedentary societies.

The transition to farming that many communities made during the Neolithic era gradually changed women's role from equal partners in foraging societies to childrearers and household managers in agricultural communities. This left men freer to take on public roles such as rulers, warriors, or religious leaders. Eventually, this meant that some form of patriarchy was enshrined in virtually every single secular and religious law code produced by agrarian civilizations.

The pastoralists had no such gender-defining "luxury"—every member of the family was vital to the family's survival, so women and women's work were valued as being equal to that of men. Throughout this course, we will meet several extraordinary women who attained very high status in the Mongol world, beginning with Chinggis Khan's own wife, the formidable Borte.

Wherever pastoralism first appeared, perhaps at Dereivka or some other site in western Eurasia, by the time the first cities and states were emerging in Mesopotamia, Egypt, the Indus Valley, and China, pastoralists were on the move. So as not to overgraze the steppe, pastoralists needed to become increasingly nomadic and graze their herds seasonally over larger ecological regions.

Often this resulted in large-scale migrations as multiple groups of pastoralists moved together across the steppe. We actually have pretty good archaeological evidence of these migrations in the form of burial mounds that Soviet archaeologists named kurgans. These are scattered across the Eurasian steppe, and they provide compelling evidence of the relentless movement of pastoralist communities from west to east, through Siberia and central Asia, into Mongolia, and on to the borderlands of China.

The reasons for these large-scale migrations are not always clear, but probably some combination of climate change, overgrazing problems, and population pressure best explains why large numbers of pastoralists literally packed up and traveled long distances across the steppe looking for greener pastures.

Archaeologists give names to some of these migrating pastoralist cultures often based on the modern name of the place where evidence for the arrival of these groups was first discovered. One of the earliest of these is the Yamnaya pastoralist culture, which dates from the late 4th millennium BCE. They were dispersed across the Caucasus region north of the Black and Caspian Seas. Yamnaya artifacts include horse-riding equipment and wheeled vehicles that were probably used to facilitate these migrations across the steppe. But weapons have also been discovered—daggers, maces, axes—that had been obtained from early sedentary societies, probably through trade.

Further east, the oldest pastoralist culture so far known to have emerged in Siberia is that of the Afanasevo, named after the site of Afanaseva Gora excavated by Soviet archaeologists in 1920. Occupying an extensive region of southern Siberia up to the Altai Mountains in western Mongolia, the Afanasevo date to roughly 3300 to 2500 BCE. Many of the artifacts unearthed at Afanasevo sites bear a striking resemblance to Yamnaya and other pit-grave cultures, suggesting they represent an eastern extension of these earlier pastoralist cultures. Some Afanasevo groups may have subsequently migrated further east and south again, towards the borderlands of ancient China.

A later steppe-bronze culture that emerged as a result of this ongoing migration of pastoralists from west to east is the Andronovo, who flourished in western Siberia and the steppe to the south between roughly 2000 and 900 BCE. They are so named after the Russian village of Andronovo, where Soviet archaeologists first began to unearth the culture in the 1920s.

Some Andronovo were almost purely nomadic, but others built fortified villages with subterranean houses. Some of these sedentary communities were surprisingly large, up to 100 homes. But whether sedentary or nomadic, the Andronovo bred cattle, sheep, and goats, and used horses both for riding and for their traction power. There is also archaeological evidence of the use of the chariot by Andronovo and associated Sintashta elites.

However, as devastating a weapon as the chariot proved to be in places like Mesopotamia, Egypt, India, and parts of China, it was not destined to play any sort of significant role in the construction of the great empires of the steppe, such as the Mongol Empire. The chariot was just too impractical for steppe warfare conducted over mixed terrain, and it was soon abandoned by militarized nomads in favor of the much more mobile horse-riding archer warriors, who became skilled with bows and arrows, and indeed with a wide range of weapons.

So let's turn now, in the last part of this lecture, to the transformation of some of these migrating pastoralist nomadic tribes into awesome militarized confederations, with the skills and the weapons, the mobility and endurance, and the inspired leadership that allowed them to challenge and, more often than not, defeat the armies of even the most powerful agrarian civilizations of ancient Eurasia.

We have seen that the lifeway of pastoralism itself first appears in the archaeological record in the 4th millennium BCE. And we have also followed the migrations of various pastoralist cultures eastwards across the steppe in the millennia that followed. But archaeological evidence suggests that it was not until quite late in the history of the pastoralists—so probably sometime in the early 1st millennium BCE—that formidable armies of mounted archers first appear.

We also have excellent literary evidence of the activities of some of the most powerful of these early militarized groups, such as ancient Greek historian Herodotus's account of the Scythians, or the Saka, and ancient Chinese historian Sima Qian's account of the activities of the Xiongnu, the Wusun, and the Yuezhi. Each of these groups would use their military prowess to establish what can only be described as Empires of the Steppe.

Of course, these were not empires in a traditional sense—they looked nothing like the Han Chinese or Roman Empires in administration and infrastructure development—but the success and often longevity of these steppe empires showed that well-led pastoralist confederations could prosper in large, organic structures that essentially took control of Inner Eurasia. The Mongols constructed the most famous of these steppe empires, but they had many successful precursors to look to for inspiration.

Several factors help explain the success of these steppe empires, but fundamental to all of them were the supreme horse-riding skills of the cavalry and their effective use of the composite bow and arrows. We have no time here to explore the evolution and early history of the horse, but suffice it to say by the 5th millennium BCE, large numbers of wild horses were flourishing in various regions of Inner Eurasia.

Eventually, human communities living at places like Dereivka learned to domesticate some of these horses, and the process of domestication then spread outwards from some focal point, and certainly spread eastwards as a result of the pastoral nomadic migrations that we have just explored. Actually, horse domestication was not a single process it seems, but occurred in multiple places at various times, based on the study of mitochondrial DNA, which shows considerable diversity amongst early domesticated horses.

Can we think of any animal that has had a more important influence on human history than the horse? Even today, we remember just what an energy revolution the domestication of the horse was by measuring the strength of our engines in horsepower! Every group that constructed a steppe empire was deeply aware of just how important the horse was to their success. Each of the militarized confederations held their horses in the highest regard and looked after them both physically and even spiritually. For example, the Mongols would scatter mare's milk on the ground before setting out on their campaigns, and sometimes the horses of great khans and other military commanders were sacrificed to help carry them to heaven. Every boy who joined the Mongol army would have learned this maxim: "A Mongol without his horse is like a bird without its wings."

A crucial technological development that allowed skilled horse-riding pastoralists to gain an even more significant military advantage over their opponents was the development of a very powerful weapon in the form of the composite bow. Canadian scholar Edwin Pulleyblank, one of the most important historians in this field, believed that the development of the composite bow was the most significant factor of all in explaining the success of militarized nomads.

The composite bow was, as its name suggests, a laminate constructed from a range of materials including different types of wood, animal horn, and sinew. Wood was used to make the core of the bow. A thin layer of animal horn or bone, usually from goats or sheep, was then attached to the inner side, and some type of animal sinew, usually harvested from the legs and backs of wild deer, was attached to the outer side. A strong glue made by boiling animal hide, and this was used to bind the layers together.

In ideal conditions, when an archer drew back the bow prior to firing, the horn and sinew between them stored far more energy than was available in a similarly sized all-wooden bow. I say ideal conditions because the bow worked best in a dry environment. Too much rain or humidity and the glue would begin to lose its binding power. So this type of bow would not have been of much use to Romans fighting in Scotland or Han Chinese soldiers in Vietnam, for example, but in the dry and generally sunny Eurasian steppe, the composite bow gave the pastoralist mounted archers a huge advantage.

We can't be really certain about when and where the composite bow was first developed, both because it was invented by early pastoral nomads who left no written records, of course, and because the materials from which it was constructed are organic and thus left little in the form of archaeological evidence.

The culture associated with the Andronovo I mentioned earlier, the Sintashta culture that also adopted the chariot, may have been involved in the innovation of this powerful new weapon. Some arrowheads have been discovered by archaeologists at sites associated with the Sintashta, such as in chariot burials at Krivoe Lake in the Ural Mountains in Russia, dating from between 2100 and 1700 BCE. But the bows that fired these arrows have not survived.

So it was the domestication of the horse and the subsequent development of superb horse-riding skills by migrating pastoral nomads, coupled with the innovation of the composite bow and the acquisition of superb skills with bow and arrow by the same horse-riding cavalry, that led directly to the appearance of enormous contingents of mounted archers in Inner Eurasia.

These armies were almost unbeatable by the forces of sedentary states—until, that is, many of these states adopted similar technologies and strategies. As we will see next time, the only way the Han Empire of ancient China was able to take on the awesome power of the Xiongnu was by adopting a massive horse-breeding scheme, turning their infantry into cavalry, adopting the composite bow, and even copying the tactics that were being employed against them so successfully by the nomads.

It was not just the horse and composite bow that explains the success of groups like the Mongols and their equally formidable predecessors. As we will explore in this course, these great cavalry contingents were also incredibly well disciplined. They could survive off the land and so were superbly tailored for mobility and speed because they did not need to wait for supply trains to catch up with them. They were brilliant archers, of course—whether firing forwards, sideways, or backwards—but were also superbly skilled with swords, axes, daggers, even maces.

Finally, they were incredibly well led. The commanders of all the successful steppe armies carried out very carefully planned campaigns that used reconnaissance to collect accurate intelligence about the strength and deployment of the forces arrayed against them. And we cannot deny that nomadic armies were also incredibly skilled at using terror and fear to control conquered peoples and to send brutal messages to others of what would happen to your city if you dared to stand against them, as the Mongols so supremely demonstrated.

For many of their contemporaries, the Mongols were like nothing they had ever seen before. But for people who had lived in the general vicinity of Mongolia and other contiguous regions, the Mongols were just another in a long line of powerful mounted armies that had been devastating the region for millennia.

Next time, we'll consider the predecessors to the Mongols, who each carved out a vast empire of the steppes and left their own dramatic imprint on world history in the process.

NOMADIC PREDECESSORS OF THE MONGOLS

This lecture examines the Mongols' regional predecessors. A series of early steppe empires created effective templates for the construction and maintenance of huge tribal confederations and also for supremely efficient military organization—templates that would later be used so brilliantly by the Mongols.

The Xiongnu

The Xiongnu made their appearance on the stage of world history when they began raiding into Chinese territory late in the 3rd century BCE. This brought them into contact with the formidable military of the newly established Chinese Qin dynasty, which had just defeated a series of rival kingdoms to bring an end to the Warring States era and reunify China under their hegemony.

According to the Han Dynasty historian Sima Qian, writing late in the 1st century BCE, the founder of the first Xiongnu confederation was Shanyu Touman.* It was under his brilliant and ruthless son Modu, who brutally killed his father and claimed his title, that the Xiongnu began to realize their awesome power and potential.

---

* Shanyu is a title that means Supreme Ruler.

Under Modu, the Xiongnu became a formidable military force. For example, archaeological evidence shows that Xiongnu mounted archers used stirrups and saddles with pommels. The Mongols would later use similar strategies and technologies to construct their own empire.

Modu's Strategy

Modu's initial strategy was to unify other nomadic tribes. In so doing, he constructed a confederation that eventually stretched from Lake Baikal in the north to the new Chinese Great Wall in the south. It also stretched from the Tian Shan mountains in the west to Manchuria in the east. Modu next turned on the Xiongnu's only real rivals in the region, the equally powerful Yuezhi nomadic confederation, who were headquartered near Dunhuang in western China.

After several decades of war between the two, the Xiongnu defeated the Yuezhi around 166 BCE. This forced the Yuezhi to undertake a 30-year migration to the west, until they settled eventually in the valley of an eastern section of the Oxus River on the border of Afghanistan and Uzbekistan. From there, they went on to establish their own enormous and influential Kushan Empire.

China versus the Xiongnu

Meanwhile, in China in the year 200 BCE, just a handful of years after the Han dynasty had replaced the Qin, the new Han emperor launched a campaign against the Xiongnu. But Xiongnu forces ambushed and trapped Emperor Gao at Baideng for seven days. Gao was forced to submit. A treaty was signed two years later recognizing that all the territories north of the Great Wall belonged to the Xiongnu, while those to the south belonged to the Han.

It was only with the advent of Han Emperor Wudi in 141 BCE that the Chinese decided to take the fight back to the Xiongnu. Wudi adopted Xiongnu military technologies and strategies, and enormous Han cavalry contingents worked relentlessly over the decades that followed to drive the Xiongnu back to the north. They were sometimes successful and sometimes not.

After several victorious campaigns, the Han gained enough breathing room to extend the Great Wall deeper into central Asia. They also established a series of military agricultural garrisons through the modern Gansu and Xinjiang provinces. However, following the reign of Wudi, Chinese strength and will waned, and incessant border warfare between the Chinese and the Xiongnu broke out again, allowing the nomads to reestablish their presence in northern and western China.

Eventually, in the middle of the 1st century CE, a revitalized Later Han dynasty was able to recover these territories and force the Xiongnu back into the steppes north of the Gobi. The Later Han also established a new official position, the Protector General of the Western Regions, who used his mobile cavalry to great effect in confronting the Xiongnu wherever they appeared along the Silk Roads. Eventually, the Xiongnu empire went into serious decline after it split in two.

One way in which the Xiongnu were clearly influential on the Mongols was through their military organization. Sima Qian offers a detailed account on how the Xiongnu organized the political and military administration of their empire. It was probably Modu himself who introduced the structural reforms that created a system capable of controlling a confederation of ethnically diverse tribes spread over enormous distances. The Mongols would adopt and adapt many elements of the Xiongnu political and military administrative structure.

After the Han Dynasty

In 220 CE, the Han dynasty collapsed, and power fell into the hands of warlords. This situation continued for the next three and a half centuries, during which various regional states rose and fell, none strong enough to reunite China.

Regional warlords recruited skilled Xiongnu horsemen into their cavalry and settled many of them in Shaanxi province. But as the political situation in China descended into chaos, civil war broke out and raged into the 4th century. This gave the Xiongnu forces living in China the opportunity they had been waiting for. In 311, Xiongnu cavalry sacked the imperial city of Luoyang. Five years later, they sacked the great ancient imperial city of Chang'an, the capital for so many of China's early dynasties.

Xiongnu cavalry sacking city of Luoyang, c. 311

Rival warlords continued to battle for supremacy. One powerful non-Chinese group were the Xianbei, originally from southern Mongolia and probably related to the Xiongnu. The Tuoba clan of the Xianbei established a stable state, the Northern Wei dynasty, which ruled much of northern China between 386 and 534.

With roughly 2 million Xianbei living in the midst of perhaps 30 million Chinese, it was inevitable that Xianbei elites would become more and more influenced by Chinese cultural traditions. The Xianbei emperor Xiaowendi relocated his capital to the ruined Luoyang, which was now rebuilt as a magnificent Chinese-style city.

The tough Xianbei soldiers guarding the northern frontiers came to detest the Xianbei aristocrats in Luoyang for their soft lives. In 529, Luoyang was sacked by Xianbei cavalry, and 2,000 of their officials were slaughtered.

Turkic Activities

China was eventually united late in the 6th century by the Sui dynasty, whose success paved the way for the powerful Tang dynasty that followed. The Tang had to deal with a formidable militarized nomadic confederation emanating from the Mongolian steppe, this one constructed by Turkic rulers like Bilge Kaghan.

The name Turk appears for the first time in history in Chinese annals discussing a new nomadic people who had created a substantial steppe empire that stretched westward from Mongolia almost as far as the Black Sea. This was the first Turkic khaganate, founded in the year 552. It lasted as a unified steppe empire only until 581, after which a split gradually divided the empire into eastern and western Turkic khaganates.

The founder of the first Turkic khaganate was Bumin Kaghan, who used diplomacy and warfare to take control of the Mongolian steppe. It was after Bumin's death that the confederation split into an eastern half, ruled by Bumin's son Muqan from the Orkhon Valley, and a western half, ruled by a viceroy from a camp in a valley in the Tian Shan mountains.

The western Turkic khaganate had a significant impact on European history. Turkic forces initially expanded westward and gained control of some major central Asian commercial cities such as Samarkand and Panjakent. The successful Sogdian merchants who lived in these towns became Turkic vassals.

The Turks then entered into a long struggle with the Sasanians, who had constructed their own enormous empire that ruled much of Persia and the Middle East. As the Turks campaigned into Sasanian territory, other militarized nomads like the Avars moved further west and entered into Europe, where they interacted with Byzantines, Lombards, and even Frankish kings. This flight of the Avars was seen as treachery by the rulers of the western Turkic empire, so Turkic contingents followed hot on their heels, and they became very active in European affairs for a time.

While these events were unfolding in the west, the eastern Turks were similarly flourishing and expanding throughout the 6th century. However, just as the Sui dynasty emerged in China after three and a half centuries of chaos, the eastern Turkic khaganate self-destructed through civil war.

The Sui dynasty was short-lived, and as it crumbled, Turkic power was reasserted on the steppe. By the time the first emperor of the Tang dynasty came to power, the Turks were strong enough to force him to pay them tribute. The first emperor's son, Taizong, came to the throne in 626. Like his father, he had no option but to pay the Turks an enormous ransom to force them to leave Chinese territory. Taizong swore to revenge this humiliation and established multiple units of mounted archers to match the mobility of the Turks.

Following a disastrous volcanic eruption somewhere on the Mongolian steppe in 626, climate change and brutal winters led to famine. Chinese cavalry used this opportunity to attack Turkic forces, and by 630, the Turkic khaganate had essentially ceased to exist.

After the First Khaganate

For the next 50 years, the Turks were placated by Chinese gifts and marriage alliances, and many of them adopted Chinese cultural customs. Other Turkic leaders resisted, particularly a new ruler called Ashina Qutlugh and his advisor Tonyukyuk. They reunited the confederation of tribes and established the second Turkic khaganate, which controlled the steppe until 745 CE.

The Turks crushed their nomadic rival, and they forced the Tang empress Wu to pay them an enormous treasure. However, when they tried expanding westward in 712, they suffered a heavy defeat at the hands of Muslim forces under Qutayba.

The second Turkic khaganate came back from this defeat under the leadership of an inspired triumvirate: Bilge Kaghan, his brother Kul Tegin, and the aging advisor Tonyukyuk, now in his 70s. This trio kept the tribes united and even offered a peace alliance with the Tang emperor Xuanzong. This he foolishly rejected, and he was subsequently forced to pay an enormous tribute to the Turks in 721.

The three leaders all died between 725 and 733. As Uyghurs gradually took control of the steppe, several of the Turkic tribes migrated out of Mongolia to settle on the fringes of the Abbasid caliphate, where they gradually converted to Islam.

The Conversion

The conversion of these Turkic clans, which included the Seljuqs and the ancestors of the Ottomans, was of great historical significance. As the Turks continued their migrations, they carried their new faith with them, helping to expand Islam throughout western Eurasia.

By the second half of the 10th century, large numbers of Seljuqs were being employed as mercenaries by the Abbasids and had settled within the borders of the Abbasid caliphate.

The Seljuqs became increasingly powerful until eventually the Seljuq leader Tughril Beg was proclaimed sultan by the Abbasid caliph. By 1055, he had gained control of Baghdad. For the next two centuries, Seljuqs dominated the region, reducing the role of the Abbasid caliphs to that of figurehead.

In 1071, the Seljuqs inflicted a devastating defeat on the Byzantines at the Battle of Manzikert, which opened up much of the Byzantine Empire to Turkish occupation. However, early in the 13th century, the Seljuq Empire began to crumble.

The migration of the Turks into western Eurasia had a profound impact on subsequent world history. Islam spread rapidly under the Seljuqs. By 1453, when the Ottomans conquered Constantinople, Anatolia was a Turkish and Islamic realm, which it has remained ever since.

A separate wave of Turkish migration also dramatically influenced the history of India. In the 11th century, the Ghaznavid Turks under their ruler Mahmud of Ghazna launched a series of raids into India. They eventually consolidated their hold on the region until the Turkish sultanate of Delhi controlled much of northern India. Because Mahmud and his successors actively (and violently) promoted Islam at the expense of Buddhism and Hinduism, another result of these migrations was the establishment of a significant Muslim presence in northwestern India.

Battle of Manzikert

Events in Mongolia

Back in Mongolia, a new Turkic regime had emerged under the Uyghurs, who spoke a Turkic dialect and used a runic script. However, instead of raiding China and forcing tribute as their predecessors had done, they skillfully exploited China through trade on their terms.

Ignoring the advice of Tonyukyuk, the Uyghur khans built two walled cities in north-central Mongolia: Ordu Baliq and Bay Baliq. Eventually, Sogdian advisers overreached themselves in trying to influence Uyghur rulers. When the Tang emperor Daizong died in 779, the chief Sogdian adviser of the Uyghur khan urged the Uyghurs to launch a surprise attack on China. This led to a disastrous split among the Uyghurs and widespread anti-Sogdian sentiment, although the Uyghur regime continued to flourish until the 820s.

A devastating winter on the steppe in 839–840 led to famine and epidemics. Kyrgyz forces took this opportunity to attack and killed the Uyghur khan. The Uyghur tribes dispersed in all directions, but mostly into Gansu and the Tarim Basin, where their descendants live to this day in the modern Chinese province of Xinjiang.

Events in China

In China, the failing Tang dynasty collapsed in 907. That year also marked the rise of the Khitan, who, under the ruler Abaoji, founded the Liao dynasty, which ruled from 907 to 1125. This was the last nomadic steppe empire before that of the Mongols.

For the next two centuries, the Khitan remained the dominant power of the steppe, taking control of former Chinese and Turkic-Uyghur territories. They established five capital cities, one of which was a regional capital near Beijing. They divided the population of their empire into two separate groups, a practice that probably also influenced the Mongols. The nomadic peoples of the empire were governed according to nomadic customs; the sedentary populations by the laws of their states.

In the early 1100s, a new group of militarized nomads appeared on the eastern steppe: the Jurchen, who gradually absorbed the Khitan. The Jurchen used their formidable military skills to eventually defeat the Song dynasty in China. They established their own sedentary Jin dynasty, which would rule the northern half of China until the arrival of the Mongols.

NOMADIC PREDECESSORS OF THE MONGOLS

LECTURE 3 TRANSCRIPT

This is how Bilge Khagan (which means "the wise king"), one of the founders of the Second Turkic Empire, centered on the Mongolian steppe, describes the ascent of the Turks and their creation of a vast steppe empire. This passage is inscribed in Chinese characters and Turkic runes on an enormous stone that was erected in the Orkhon River Valley in the 8th century:

> When the blue sky above and the dark earth below were created, human beings were created between the two. My ancestors Bumin Kaghan and Istami Kaghan rose above the sons of men. Having become their masters, they governed and established the empire and the institutions of the Turkic people. They had many enemies in the four corners of the world, but waging military campaigns, they subjugated and pacified them, making them bow their heads and bend their knees.

Although Chinggis Khan is credited with creating the first Mongol state, one could argue that the real beginning of statehood in the region that has become the modern nation of Mongolia was much earlier, perhaps with the Turkic rulers in the 7th and 8th centuries, or even a thousand years earlier again, in the 3rd century BCE, with the advent of the Xiongnu steppe empire.

The ethnic and linguistic identity of the core Xiongnu remains a matter of debate even today. Some historians argue that they were of Mongolic origin and thus ethnic predecessors to the later Mongols; others argue for a Turkic origin and that the Xiongnu were precursors to the subsequent Turkic and Uyghur empires.

There were certainly many cultural similarities between all the groups that made Mongolia their homeland, including the Xiongnu, the Turks, and the Mongols. These included the use of *gers* for accommodation, superb skills at horse-riding and with the composite bow and arrow, and even common board games and epic songs. Mongolian long song, for example, which is still practiced today, dates back thousands of years. Its origins are discussed in the Chinese annals of the Northern Wei dynasty, written in the 5th century of the Common Era.

We also know that a series of powerful militarized nomadic confederations made Mongolia their administrative and sacred homeland and used the steppe, river valleys, and mountains of that region to construct steppe empires that grew to an enormous size. We cannot be sure whether the groups that controlled these confederations were ethnically related, but we can be sure that they shared many similar military skills and cultural practices that allowed them to compete with and often dominate not only other contiguous nomadic groups but also the great sedentary civilization of China to the south.

This was certainly true of the Mongols, but it was also true of their regional predecessors, and it is these predecessors who are the subject of this lecture. This series of early steppe empires created effective templates for the construction and maintenance of huge tribal confederations, and also for supremely efficient military organization—templates that would later be used so brilliantly by the Mongols.

First to the Xiongnu, who make their appearance on the stage of world history when they began raiding into Chinese territory late in the 3rd century BCE. This brought them into contact with the formidable military of the newly established Chinese Qin Dynasty, which had just defeated a series of rival kingdoms to bring an end to the Warring States era and reunify China under their hegemony.

The Qin had been successful partly because they had adopted nomadic military technologies and strategies, including horse breeding, the wearing of trousers, and the use of mounted archers with stirrups. In this first incident, the Qin army was able to force the Xiongnu back across the Yellow River before pursuing them across the Gobi in a ruthless punitive expedition. It was in direct response to the danger posed by the Xiongnu that the first Qin emperor, Shi Huangdi, ordered a series of older stamped-earth defensive walls to be connected together to create the first Great Wall of China, which stretched for more than a thousand miles along the northern borders of the Qin state.

According to Han Dynasty historian Sima Qian, writing late in the 1st century BCE, the founder of the first Xiongnu confederation was Shanyu Touman. *Shanyu* is a title that means "Supreme Ruler." But it was under his brilliant and ruthless son Modu, who brutally killed his father and claimed his title, that the Xiongnu began to realize their awesome power and potential.

Under Modu, the Xiongnu became a formidable military force indeed, using strategies like feigned retreats, ambushes, constant harassment of weakened enemies, and exceptional discipline to defeat their foes. Sima Qian tells us that in battle, the Xiongnu used composite bows and iron-tipped arrows that could penetrate armor, and also that they were adept with swords and spears.

Archaeological evidence also shows us that Xiongnu mounted archers used stirrups and saddles with pommels. In the 13th century, the Mongols would use all these same strategies and technologies to construct their own empire, borrowing and enhancing techniques first introduced by their distant predecessors 1,400 years earlier. Sima Qian was in no doubt about the dangers posed by Modu and his military: "When Modu came to power … the Xiongnu reached the peak of their strength and size, subjugating all of the other barbarian tribes of the north and turning south to confront China as a rival nation."

Modu's initial strategy was to unify other nomadic tribes. In so doing, he constructed a confederation that eventually stretched from Lake Baikal in the north to the new Chinese Great Wall in the south, and from the Tian Shan mountains in the west to Manchuria in the east. Modu next turned on the Xiongnu's only real rivals in the region, the equally powerful Yuezhi nomadic confederation, who were headquartered near Dunhuang in western China.

After several decades of war between the two, the Xiongnu finally defeated the Yuezhi, probably in the year 166 BCE. This forced the Yuezhi to undertake a 30-year migration to the west, until they settled eventually in the valley of an eastern section of the Oxus River (modern Amu Darya) on the border of Afghanistan and Uzbekistan, from where they went on to establish their own enormous and influential Kushan Empire.

In China, meanwhile, in the year 200 BCE, just a handful of years after the Han Dynasty had replaced the Qin, the new Han emperor launched a campaign against the Xiongnu. But Xiongnu forces ambushed and trapped Emperor Gao at Baideng for seven days, until Gao was forced to submit. A treaty was signed two years later recognizing that all the territories north of the Great Wall belonged to the Xiongnu, while those to the south belonged to the Han.

In order to persuade the Xiongnu to sign this treaty, the Han were obliged to pay an enormous annual tribute to the Xiongnu in the form of silk and treasure, and also to provide Han princesses as consorts to the Xiongnu shanyu. But this "marriage alliance," known to the Chinese as the *heqin* policy, was never particularly successful, and the Xiongnu continued to raid into the fertile farmlands of northern China almost at will. By the middle of the 2nd century BCE, the Xiongnu were effectively in control of much of northern and western China as part of a domain that was something like 1.5 million square miles in area.

It was only with the advent of Han emperor Wudi in 141 BCE—his name means "Martial Emperor"—that the Chinese decided to take the fight back to the Xiongnu. Wudi adopted Xiongnu military technologies and strategies, including instituting a massive horse-breeding program, and enormous Han cavalry contingents now worked relentlessly over the decades that followed to drive the Xiongnu back to the north, sometimes successfully, sometimes not.

After several victorious campaigns, the Han gained enough breathing room to extend the Great Wall deeper into central Asia and also established a series of military agricultural garrisons through modern Gansu and Xinjiang Provinces. But following the reign of Wudi, Chinese strength and will waned, and incessant border warfare between the Chinese and the Xiongnu broke out again, allowing the nomads to reestablish their presence in northern and western China.

Eventually, in the middle of the 1st century of the Common Era, a revitalized Later Han Dynasty was able to recover these territories and force the Xiongnu back into the steppes north of the Gobi. The Later Han also established a new official position, the Protector General of the Western Regions, who used his mobile cavalry to great effect in confronting the Xiongnu whenever they appeared along the Silk Roads.

Eventually, the Xiongnu Empire went into serious decline after it split in two, allowing the Han to further weaken the confederation by using bribes to play one shanyu off against the other. One of these divided groups, the Northern Xiongnu, may have evolved into the Huns that so terrorized Europe during the later periods of the Roman Empire, although that identification remains somewhat tenuous.

In terms of the central argument of this lecture—that early Mongolian-centered steppe empires established a template that was later perfected by the Mongols—one way in which the Xiongnu were clearly influential was through their military organization. Sima Qian offers a detailed account on how the Xiongnu organized the political and military administration of their empire.

It was probably Modu himself who introduced the structural reforms that created a system capable of controlling a confederation of ethnically diverse tribes spread across enormous distances. Power was delegated by the shanyu to 24 Great Leaders who constituted a sort of Council of State. Directly beneath the shanyu were the four most senior members of the council (known as wang, or kings). They were ranked in order of seniority from one to four.

In order to eliminate problems of succession following the death of a shanyu, these four wang were also the recognized successors to the shanyu and the four most senior military commanders. The most senior king was called the Wise King of the Left, responsible for the Xiongnu's important eastern wing along the northern borders of the Han Dynasty. Second in the hierarchy was the Luli King of the Left, who was responsible for the forces behind (or to the north of) the Wise King of the Left, ready to support as necessary. Third was the Wise King of the Right, responsible for the western wing, including regions north of the Gansu. And fourth was the Luli King of the Right, in charge of the forces behind and north of the Wise King of the Right, again ready to lend support as required.

Beneath these four supreme commanders were the remainder of the 24 Great Leaders, each of whom was personally entitled to a military unit known as the Ten Thousand Cavalry. Each Great Leader had the right to appoint his own Lesser King to take charge of his personal staff and administrative matters. These Lesser Kings were often selected from amongst the chiefs of federated tribes that were probably of very different ethnic and linguistic makeup from the core Xiongnu. So this was a highly effective way of keeping together a stable confederation of ethnically and linguistically diverse tribes who had all sworn allegiance to the shanyu.

The Mongols would adopt and adapt many elements of this political and military administrative structure, which facilitated the formation of the first great Xiongnu Empire of the Steppe. In their ability to unite disparate tribes, their political organization, and their military strategy, technology, and prowess, the Xiongnu essentially established the template for the five great steppe empires that followed them.

In 220, the Han Dynasty collapsed, and power fell into the hands of warlords, a common enough story in the history of China. This situation continued for the next three and a half centuries, during which various regional states rose and fell, none strong enough to reunite China. A reasonable comparison can be made between China after the Han and Europe during the so-called decline and fall of the Roman Empire. Both regions entered a sort of dark age of disunity, and both faced continuous threats of invasion by different militarized nomadic groups at more or less the same time.

The invasion of Europe by Hunnic forces in the 4th century upset the balance of power between the Romans and various Germanic tribes that dwelt along the eastern borders of the empire. Many Germans were eventually recruited into the Roman military, and large German communities were settled within the Roman Empire.

Something very similar happened in China: Regional warlords recruited skilled Xiongnu horsemen into their cavalry and settled many of them in Shaanxi Province. But as the political situation in China descended into chaos, civil war broke out and raged into the 4th century. This gave the Xiongnu forces living in China the opportunity they had been waiting for. In 311, Xiongnu cavalry sacked the imperial city of Luoyang, and five years later, they sacked the great ancient imperial city of Chang'an, the capital for so many of China's early dynasties.

Following the arrival of the Huns in Europe decades later, Germanic tribes also eventually overran and occupied much of the western empire. Rome itself was sacked twice: by the Visigoths in 410, and by the Vandals in 455. Germanic states were then established all over western Europe as the western Roman Empire dissolved.

In China at about the same time, rival warlords continued to battle for supremacy. One powerful non-Chinese group were the Xianbei, originally from southern Mongolia and probably related to the Xiongnu. Like their Germanic counterparts in Europe, the Tuoba clan of the Xianbei established a stable state, the Northern Wei Dynasty, which ruled much of northern China for a century and a half between 386 and 534.

With something like 2 million Xianbei living in the midst of perhaps 30 million Chinese, it was inevitable that Xianbei elites would become more and more influenced by Chinese cultural traditions, something that certainly also happened with German elites living in western Europe. Indeed, this would be a problem faced by all subsequent nomadic confederations, including the Mongols: how to maintain core cultural values whilst ruling a state made up of millions of sedentary Persians or Chinese, for example.

Xianbei Emperor Xiaowendi, bowing to the inevitable, relocated his capital to the ruined Luoyang, which was now rebuilt as a magnificent Chinese-style city. He ordered his men to dress like the Han, to speak their language, and to adopt Han surnames. He even encouraged intermarriage between the Xianbei and Han, which contributed to the amalgamation of the various nationalities now living in northern China.

But these reforms were looked upon with disgust by the tough Xianbei soldiers guarding the northern frontier. They came to detest the Xianbei aristocrats in Luoyang for their soft, Sinicized lives. In 529, Luoyang was sacked by Xianbei cavalry, and 2,000 of their own "soft" officials were slaughtered!

China was eventually united late in the 6th century by the Sui Dynasty, whose success paved the way for the powerful Tang Dynasty that followed. But like their predecessors the Han, the Tang also had to deal with a formidable militarized nomadic confederation emanating from the Mongolian steppe, this time one constructed by Turkic rulers like Bilge Kaghan, whose inscription we read at the beginning of this lecture.

The name "Turk" actually appears for the first time in history in Chinese annals discussing a new nomadic people who had created a substantial steppe empire that stretched westwards from Mongolia almost as far as the Black Sea. This was the first Turkic Khaganate, founded in the year 552. It lasted as a unified steppe empire only until 581, after which a split gradually divided the empire into the eastern and western khaganates.

The founder of the First Khaganate was Bumin Kaghan, one of the khans named in the inscription, who used diplomacy and warfare to take control of the Mongolian steppe. It was after Bumin's death that the confederation split into an eastern half, ruled by Bumin's son Muqan from the Orkhon Valley, and a western half, ruled by a viceroy from a camp in a valley in the Tian Shan mountains.

This western khaganate had a significant impact on European history. Turkic forces initially expanded westwards and gained control of some major central Asian commercial cities, such as Samarkand and Panjakent. The successful Sogdian merchants who lived in these towns became Turkic vassals.

The Turks then entered into a long struggle with the Sasanians, who had constructed their own enormous empire that ruled much of Persia and the Middle East. As the Turks campaigned into Sasanian territory, other militarized nomads like the Avars (who had also originally come from Mongolia and spoke a Mongolian dialect) moved further west again and entered into Europe, where they interacted with Byzantines, Lombards, and even with Frankish kings. This flight of the Avars was seen as treachery by the rulers of the western Turkic Empire, so Turkic contingents followed hot on their heels and themselves became very active in European affairs for a time.

While these events these were unfolding in the west, the eastern Turks were similarly flourishing and expanding throughout the 6th century. But just as the Sui Dynasty emerged in China after three and a half centuries of chaos, the eastern Turkic khaganate self-destructed through civil war. Sui Emperor Wendi was very effective at playing the Turks off against each other.

But the Sui Dynasty was short-lived, and as it crumbled, Turkic power was reasserted on the steppe. By the time the first emperor of the Tang Dynasty came to power, the Turks were strong enough to force him to pay them tribute. The first emperor's son Taizong came to the throne in 626, and like his father had no option but to pay the Turks an enormous ransom to force them to leave Chinese territory. But Taizong swore to revenge this humiliation and established multiple units of mounted archers to match the mobility of the Turks.

Following a disastrous volcanic eruption somewhere on the Mongolian steppe in the year 626, climate change and brutal winters led to famine. Chinese cavalry used this opportunity to attack Turkic forces, and by 630, this Turkic khaganate had essentially ceased to exist. For the next 50 years, the Turks were placated by Chinese gifts and marriage alliances, and many of them adopted Chinese cultural customs. Other Turkic leaders resisted, however, particularly a new ruler called Ashina Qutlugh and his advisor Tonyukyuk. They reunited the confederation of tribes and established the Second Turkic Khaganate, which controlled the steppe until 745 CE.

The Turks crushed their nomadic rivals, the Khitan and the Kyrgyz, and forced Tang empress Wu (the only woman ever to rule China, by the way) to pay them an enormous treasure. But when they tried expanding westwards in 712, they suffered a heavy defeat at the hands of Muslim forces under Qutayba ibn Muslim.

But the Second Khaganate came back from this defeat under the leadership of an inspired triumvirate: Bilge Kaghan, who put up the inscription; his brother Kul Tegin; and the aging advisor Tonyukyuk, now in his 70s. This trio kept the tribes united and even offered a peace alliance with Tang emperor Xuanzong. This he foolishly rejected and was subsequently forced to pay an enormous tribute to the Turks in 721.

Tonyukyuk advised Bilge not to adopt elements of Chinese culture, nor to build Daoist and Buddhist monasteries, nor fortified cities. If I can quote Tonyukyuk: "If we build fortresses to live in them and change our old habits," he famously said, "then one day we will be beaten and we will be annexed by the Chinese."

This was the dilemma faced by all successful nomadic empires, and one that the Mongols would also have to deal with 500 years later. Tonyukyuk argued that the strength of nomadic cavalry came from the pastoral steppe lifeway of the soldiers, but cities, which would confine the relatively small number of troops to a few places, were booby traps from which they would never escape. He also saw Buddhism and other organized religions as too pacifist and thus opposed to nomadic existence; plus, they took young men out of the military and into monasteries.

The three leaders all died between 725 and 733, and as Uyghurs gradually took control of the steppe, several of the Turkic tribes migrated out of Mongolia to settle on the fringes of the Abbasid Caliphate, where they gradually converted to Islam. The conversions of these Turkic clans, which included the Seljuqs and the ancestors of the Ottomans, was of great historical significance, because as the Turks continued their migrations, they carried their new faith with them, helping to expand Islam throughout much of western Eurasia. By the second half of the 10th century, large numbers of Seljuqs were being employed as mercenaries by the Abbasids and had settled within the borders of the Abbasid Caliphate.

The Seljuqs became increasingly powerful, until eventually the Seljuq leader Tughril Beg was proclaimed sultan by the Abbasid caliph. By 1055, he had gained control of Baghdad, and for the next two centuries, Seljuqs dominated the region, reducing the role of the Abbasid caliphs to that of figureheads. Tughril Beg's successor, Alp Arslan, led the Seljuqs on invasions of Georgia, Armenia, Syria, Palestine, and Anatolia. Large numbers of Turkish peoples then migrated into Anatolia (the heartland of the Byzantine Empire), leading to conflict with the Byzantine emperor.

In 1071, the Seljuqs inflicted a devastating defeat on the Byzantines at the Battle of Manzikert, which opened up much of the Byzantine Empire to Turkish occupation. But early in the 13th century, the Seljuq Empire began to crumble. Much of it would later be overrun by the Mongols and incorporated into their empire.

The migration of the Turks into western Eurasia had a profound impact on subsequent world history. Islam spread rapidly under the Seljuqs, and by 1453, when the Ottomans conquered Constantinople, Anatolia was a Turkish and Islamic realm, which it has remained ever since. The Ottomans' superb military organization allowed them to not only become masters of the former Seljuq and Byzantine realms, but also to go on and found a world state, the Ottoman Empire, that eventually controlled an enormous region stretching from Vienna to the Indian Ocean, and from North Africa to the Caucasus Mountains.

A separate wave of Turkish migration also dramatically influenced the history of India. In the 11th century, the Ghaznavid Turks, under their ruler Mahmud of Ghazna, launched a series of raids into India. They eventually consolidated their hold on the region until the Turkish sultanate of Delhi controlled much of northern India. Because Mahmud and his successors actively (and violently) promoted Islam at the expense of Buddhism and Hinduism, another result of these migrations was the establishment of a large Muslim presence in northwestern India.

Back in Mongolia, meanwhile, a new Turkic empire had emerged under Uyghurs, who spoke a Turkic dialect and used a runic script. However, instead of raiding China and forcing tribute as their predecessors had done, they skillfully exploited China through trade on their terms. They pursued these policies so effectively that for a time, the Tang state was little more than a Uyghur protectorate, paying vast quantities of silk to the Uyghurs.

But ignoring the advice of Tonyukuk, the Uyghur khans actually built two walled cities in north central Mongolia—Ordu Baliq and Bay Baliq. I have visited the ruins of Ordu Baliq (which means "City of the Royal Camp") near the western bank of the Orkhon River. The city functioned as a residence for the ruler, but also as a trade center and weapons storage center. It had high walls, various quarters, and open spaces for erecting *gers*. Traces of irrigation have been discovered by archaeologists, indicating that agriculture was also practiced there.

The focal point of the city was a rectangular palace with impressive mudbrick walls that are still 20 feet high today. In one corner of the palace was a 36-meter-high platform on which the golden *ger* of the khagan was erected. The tent was described by an Islamic traveler, one Tamin ibn Bahr, in 821: "From a distance of 16 miles before he arrived in the town, he caught sight of the tent made of gold belonging to the khan. It stands on the flat top of his castle and can hold 100 men."

Eventually, Sogdian advisers overreached themselves in trying to influence Uyghur rulers. When Tang emperor Daizong died in 779, the chief Sogdian advisor of the Uyghur khan urged the Uyghurs to launch a surprise attack on China. This led to a disastrous split amongst the Uyghurs and widespread anti-Sogdian sentiment, although the Uyghur empire continued to flourish until the 820s.

A devastating winter on the steppe in 839–40 led to famine and epidemics. Kyrgyz forces took this opportunity to attack and killed the Uyghur khan; plus, they burned the city of Ordu Baliq. The Uyghur tribes dispersed in all directions, but mostly south into Gansu and the Tarim Basin, where their descendants live to this day in the modern Chinese province of Xinjiang.

In China, the failing Tang Dynasty collapsed in 907, a year that also marks the rise of the Khitan, who, under ruler Abaoji, founded the Liao Dynasty, which ruled from 907 to 1125, the last nomadic steppe empire before that of the Mongols. The Khitan were probably of Xianbei descent, the same Xianbei who took control of northern China back in the 4th century only to have the tough Xianbei soldiers stationed along the northern frontier turn on and eventually slaughter their own "soft" Sinicized officials.

For the next two centuries, the Khitan remained the dominant power of the steppe, taking control of former Chinese and Turkic-Uyghur territories. They established five capital cities, one of which was a regional capital near modern Beijing. They divided the population of their empire into two separate groups, a practice that probably also influenced the Mongols. The nomadic peoples of the empire were governed according to nomadic customs, the sedentary populations by the laws of their states.

Abaoji was afraid that using Chinese administrators to run the state would blur the Khitan's own ethnic identity, so a conscious effort was made to retain tribal foods, clothing, customs, and names. Clearly, Abaoji had learned the lesson of the fate of the Xianbei elites. As the Mongols would later do, the Khitan also created their own writing system.

In Korea, meanwhile, the expansion of the new Koryo state to the north eventually brought Koryo forces into conflict with the Khitan. In the winter of 1010, a Khitan army of 400,000 troops crossed the frozen Yalu River and drove south for the Koryo capital (near modern Pyongyang), which they sacked and pillaged. With their supply lines stretched thin, the Khitan then fought a bloody retreat back to the Yalu, at the cost of perhaps 40,000 men.

In the early 1100s, a new group of militarized nomads appeared on the eastern steppe, the Jurchen, who gradually absorbed the Khitan. The Jurchen used their formidable military skills to eventually defeat the Song Dynasty in China and established their own sedentary Jin Dynasty, which would rule the northern half of China until the arrival of the Mongols.

This was the geopolitical context for the appearance of the Mongols less than a century later—a divided China with a lengthy history of interacting with the series of powerful steppe empires that had formed and reformed along the northern and western borders. For the Chinese and the Jurchen, the Mongols were probably regarded as just another militarized nomadic group, the latest in a long line they had dealt with over the centuries. But as the Chinese and the rest of Eurasia were to learn, the Mongols under Chinggis Khan were something else again.

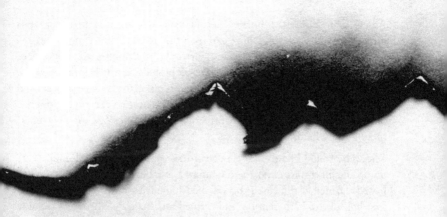

THE RISE OF
CHINGGIS KHAN

This lecture's goal is to unfold the story of the rise of Chinggis Khan—originally known as Temujin—from exiled child to supreme ruler. It draws on the most important source of information available about the early life of Temujin: *The Secret History of the Mongols*, an anonymous work that was written for the Mongol royal family sometime after Chinggis Khan's death in 1227.

The Beginning

The Secret History of the Mongols opens with a discussion of the semi-mythical genealogy of Temujin's family: "At the beginning there was a blue-grey wolf, born with his destiny ordained by Heaven Above. His wife was a fallow doe." The text describes Temujin's father as a member of the Mongol nobility and a prominent military leader who formed an alliance between a number of Mongol clans that swore allegiance to him. But when Temüjin was about 10 years old, rivals killed his father by poisoning to make sure the alliance would dissolve.

As eminent Mongol scholar Peter Jackson has argued, however, it is difficult to know how much we can trust this account of Temujin's father's circumstances. Still, Jackson and virtually all Mongol scholars agree that the *The Secret History of the Mongols* provides a much more accurate description of the sort of bitter blood feuds and clan rivalries that existed between all the tribes of the Mongolian steppe in the years before the rise of the Mongol empire and also of the role the dynasties of China played in fueling those feuds.

The web of blood feuds and clan rivalries began well before Temujin was born. The Jin empire of northern China was established by Jurchen nomads. It was alarmed at the emergence of the Mongols as a unified power in the first half of the 12th century and formed an alliance with the rival Tatar nomads against the Mongols.

Faced with this powerful new alliance, the Mongols tried to make peace with the Tatars by forging a marriage alliance. But the Tatars captured Mongol leader Ambaghai and sent him to the Jin, who brutally executed him. This temporarily weakened the Mongols and allowed the Tatars to become the dominant power of the steppe.

Temujin's Parents and Early Life

The Mongols were not destroyed and fought many battles with the Tatars. Although the Tatars tended to win most of these, one leader of the Mongol clans did enjoy some success. This was Yesugei of the Borjigin clan, the father of Temujin. Temujin's mother, Hoelun, came from the lower status but still noble Durlukin clan.

She had been betrothed to a leader of the rival Merkit tribe, but Yesugei kidnapped her after apparently falling in love at first sight. Yesugei married her and made Hoelun his primary wife. Together they had five children spaced two years apart, with Temujin the eldest. However, Yesugei also had two children with his secondary wife, so Temujin was the second oldest son. There is a legendary story that when Temujin was born, he was clutching a large blood clot in one of his tiny hands, which was immediately interpreted as a portent of greatness.

The story that unfolds in *The Secret History of the Mongols* picks up when Temujin is about nine years old. His parents had decided it was time to find a suitable bride for their son. Marriages were such an important part of clan relationships that it often took years for negotiations between families to be conducted.

Yesugei had already determined that Temujin's bride must come from a certain clan, for strategic diplomatic reasons. Fate intervened while Yesugei and his son were on their way to secure the marriage. En route, they met with a leader of another tribe, Dei Sechen of the Onggirad, a clan renowned for the beauty of their women. Dei Sechen imparted to his guests a recent dream he had had of a white falcon flying toward him, with the sun and moon in his talons, which Yesugei interpreted as another sign that his son was destined for greatness.

Dei Sechen then offered his daughter Borte to become Temujin's wife. Yesugei accepted the offer and then departed the camp, leaving Temujin behind in the care of Dei Sechen. This was to be the last time Temujin ever saw his father.

On the way home, Yesugei stayed for a night in a camp of Tatars, who poisoned Yesegui's food. The poison hit Yesugei during his ride home the following day. By the time the news had reached Temujin and he had ridden hard back to his father, Yesugei was dead and the feud with the Tatars was far more bitter than ever.

After Abandonment

The more immediate problem for Temujin, his mother Hoelun, and the rest of his siblings was that the Borjigin clan was immediately seen as being lower in status compared to other tribes that were in the ascendancy. This was particularly true of the Tayichi'ud clan. As a result, Hoelun and her family were deserted by their supporters.

This led to years of hardship on the steppe. The family was reduced to a subsistence lifeway. It was sometime during these years of hardscrabble existence that a feud broke out between Temujin and his older half-brother Bekhter, the son of Yesegui's secondary wife. The situation deteriorated until Temujin killed his older brother. Hoelun was outraged, but the deed was done.

Sometime later, Temujin was captured by the Tayichi'ud in a raid. Instead of killing him, they decided to humiliate him by locking him into a cangue, a wooden device similar to a European stock or pillory. Temujin remained in captivity for months, perhaps years, and was passed around from ger to ger each night so that no one family had to bear the burden of feeding him. One such family, that of a poor herdsman, took pity on him and released him from the cangue each evening.

Changing Fortunes

While locked in the cangue in another ger, Temujin took advantage of a night of revelry in camp to escape. Temujin returned to the helpful family of the herdsman, who removed the cangue, kept him hidden, and gave him food and a horse, which he used to return to his family.

Temujin's fortunes continued to improve. He gained several followers, including a man named Bo'orchu, who would become a lifelong friend. He also finally married Borte, who would be highly influential on his life.

A more immediate benefit of the marriage was that Temujin gained possession of a highly valuable black sable cloak presented as a wedding gift, which he decided to use in an attempt to win the support of a powerful protector. Temujin now traveled to the camp of the Kereit clan in and met with the Kereit leader Toghril Khan.

Chinggis Khan and Börte Khatun at the Genghis Khan Statue Complex in Mongolia

Temujin asked Toghril to accept him as one of his formal followers, a position known as a *nokor*. Toghril agreed, thus securing for himself the loyalty of Temujin and his followers, not to mention the gift of the valuable cloak. Temujin had forged an alliance with the Kereit clan and also gained for himself a powerful protector. As Peter Jackson points out, the friendship and military cooperation between the two were of fundamental importance in Temujin's subsequent rise to power.

Grudges Continue

The Merkits eventually decided to seek revenge for Temujin's father's abduction of Hoelun many years earlier. One night, they attacked Temujin's camp without warning. Temujin and his brothers escaped, but his wife, Borte, was captured.

Temujin's protector Toghril agreed to help him rescue his wife from the Merkits, but it was not until several months later that they were in a position to march. As the troops were being assembled, Temujin met up with a boyhood friend named Jamuqa, who was now Toghril's war chief. *

After about a year, a successful attack was launched against the Merkits, and Borte was rescued. She was heavily pregnant. Toghril urged Temujin to unite his camp with that of Jamuqa and study the arts of warfare. While Temujin stayed with Jamuqa and studied warfare, Borte gave birth to a baby boy. Although it was unlikely the boy was Temujin's, given the amount of time that had passed between Borte's abduction and rescue, Temujin accepted the boy as his son and named him Jochi.

Temujin's Leadership Expands

As Temujin mastered the art of war with Jamuqa, his charismatic style of leadership gained him many more followers, including a number who left Jamuqa's camp for that of Temujin. Among them was a young man named Subedai, who went on to become perhaps the greatest general the Mongols ever produced.

The trickle became a flood, and Jamuqa was virtually abandoned by his followers. Even some of the most elite members of the Mongol aristocracy came over to Temujin, enhancing his legitimacy in the wider Mongol realm. Inevitably, tensions between Jamuqa and Temujin intensified, and skirmishes often broke out between their followers.

It was in one such skirmish that Jamuqa's brother was killed by a group of Temujin's supporters, which Jamuqa viewed as an act of war. In the battle that followed, Temujin's forces were defeated, which left Temujin isolated again and in a dangerous position on the steppe.

Temujin Leaves, then Rises

We know little about what happened to Temujin in the 10 years following his defeat by Jamuqa; it is as though he dropped off the map of Mongol affairs. It is a reasonable assumption that he moved south and entered the borderlands of the Jin dynasty in northern China. One later source suggests that Temujin became a slave during his decade with the Jin.

Back on the Mongolian steppe, Jamuqa was becoming increasingly tyrannical. Even Toghril was forced to flee to escape the rage of Jamuqa. In the year 1195, Temujin returned, only to find that he already had a large group of supporters from all strata of Mongol society and from many different clans. Temujin had also apparently amassed considerable wealth during his decade in China, and he used this partly to sponsor a large gathering of the clans, a

Jamuqa, Genghis Khan Statue Complex

quiriltai, in 1196. Unfortunately, this ended in a drunken brawl.

A few years later, Temujin joined forces with the powerful Toghril, who had also returned to the steppe, to launch a campaign against the Tatars, the former allies of the Jin dynasty. The Jin also sent forces to join Temujin and Toghril. The Tatars were soundly defeated by this combined army.

But when Temujin returned to camp after the battle, he found that the Jurkin, who had been insulted by their treatment at the *quiriltai*, had attacked and sacked his camp. Temujin promptly attacked the Jurkin camp in turn and massacred the elites of the clan, while accepting the commoners into his own camp.

Temujin's status was now so high that tensions between Toghril and himself increased. Although clashes occasionally broke out between their followers, the two maintained their alliance. Other Mongol elites also became increasingly wary of Temujin, particularly because he did not follow the accepted social rules and promoted commoners like Subedai to positions of high rank and authority. The disaffected Mongols convened their own *quriltai* in 1201 and elected Jamuqa as Great Khan.

This made war between Temujin and Jamuqa inevitable. The combined forces of Toghril and Temujin crushed those of Jamuqa in a battle on the eastern Mongolian steppe, and Jamuqa fled. He was captured by Toghril, who granted him clemency.

Temujin also pursued and defeated the Tayichi'ud, who had supported Jamuqa. He accepted submission from another clan, that of Onggirad. Temujin continued to show his leadership genius by accepting into his ranks any of the followers and soldiers of these now defeated and largely dissolved clans, further bolstering both his prestige and power.

His status was enhanced even further in 1202 when he destroyed the Tatars and executed all of their male elites, although not the children. This meant that only three major powers now remained in Mongolia: the Naiman in the west, the Kereits under Toghril in the center, and Temujin and his combined forces in the east.

Eventually, swayed by his advisers, including Jamuqa, Toghril decided to turn on Temujin, despite the close relationship between them. The two armies met in 1203, and the Mongol army was badly defeated by the Kereits led by Jamuqa.

Becoming Chinggis Khan

Temujin simply regathered his forces, rested them for a few days, even gained support from groups that defected from the Kereits. He attacked Jamuqa and the Kereits while they were still celebrating their victory.

Mongol success was nearly complete, although Jamuqa, Toghril, and a few other elites escaped. Temujin accepted oaths of allegiance from the Kereits and formed further alliances through intermarriage between Mongol and Kereit elites.

With Temujin now in complete control of eastern and central Mongolia, the Naiman realized they had to act immediately if they were to have any chance of stopping his rise. The Naiman formed a coalition that included Jamuqa. When Temujin heard of their plans, he launched a daring and unexpected raid against them in the early summer of 1204, confronting the surprised Naiman in the foothills of the Khangai Mountains in far western Mongolia. His forces crushed the Naiman.

During the two years that followed, Temujin consolidated his position, and he somewhat reluctantly gave Jamuqa an honorable death. Years of struggle culminated at the *quriltai* of 1206, when Temujin was proclaimed Chinggis Khan. The Great Khan had united all the tribes of the Mongolian steppe and assembled an extraordinary military force.

THE RISE OF CHINGGIS KHAN

This is how *The Secret History of the Mongols* describes the oath sworn to Mongol leader Temujin by three of his followers on the day he was proclaimed Chinggis Khan:

Altan, Quchar and Sacha Beki, all of them having agreed among themselves, said to Temujin "We shall make you khan. When you, Temujin, become khan, we as vanguard shall speed after many foes for you. Fine-looking maidens and ladies of rank, palatial tents, and geldings with fine croups we shall bring. When in a hunt, for you we shall drive the beasts up the steep banks until their thighs press together. In the days of war, if we disobey your commands, deprive us of all our goods and belongings, and our noble wives, and cast our black heads on the ground! In the days of peace, if we violate your counsel, cut us off from our retainers and possessions, and our wives, and cast us out into the wilderness!"

> Thus they pledged their word and in this way they swore the oath of loyalty and made Temujin khan, naming him Chinggis Khan.

This was an extraordinary achievement for Temujin, the son of a minor Mongol chief who had been born on the eastern Mongolian steppe probably in the year 1162. He was named Temujin, which means Man of Iron, and he was forced to prove his strength and mettle many times during his early career. When his father was killed by enemies, Temujin spent years in exile on the steppe, gathering followers and using tribal war and diplomacy to patch together a new Mongol confederacy. His efforts were crowned in 1206 when, at the age of 44, he was recognized by the Mongol confederation as Chinggis Khan, a title that can mean Strong or Universal Ruler, a title that proclaims the aspirations to world power held by the new ruler of the Mongols.

With his position secure, Chinggis Khan would turn the Mongol tribes into one of the most powerful military forces ever seen and use them to create the largest contiguous empire in world history. As well as constructing his enormous empire, Chinggis Khan would also essentially create the state of Mongolia, complete with a system of laws and taxation and a sophisticated administrative structure. He would name his new state Yeke Mongol Ulus, or Great Mongol State.

Despite these extraordinary achievements, Chinggis Khan left no monuments to himself, no castles, no inscriptions, and even his tomb remains a secret. So travelers in Mongolia today might find it difficult to find historical echoes of the man who rose to become, as many Mongolian T-shirts proudly proclaim, the Man of the Millennium.

Our aim in this lecture is to use what evidence we do have to try and unfold the story of the rise of Chinggis Khan from exiled child to supreme ruler of the Yeke Mongol Ulus. The most important source of information we have about the early life of Temujin is *The Secret History of the Mongols*, an anonymous work that was written for the Mongol royal family sometime after Chinggis Khan's death in 1227.

The anonymous author wrote the text in Mongolian script, and as such, it is also the earliest written work in the Mongolian language. However, all of the earliest surviving versions of *The Secret History* we have today are transcriptions in Chinese. These transcriptions were made during the Ming Dynasty late in the 14th century. It was the Ming who successfully drove the Mongols out of China and restored native rule to the country, as we shall see.

There are three key questions associated with the production of *The Secret History*: the identity of the author, why it was composed, and when and where was it first publicly presented and read.

The author must surely have been either a member of Chinggis Khan's family or someone with intimate knowledge of the family and all that had gone on within it during the Great Khan's lifetime. One candidate is Sigi Qutuqu, who lived from roughly 1180 to 1260. Sigi was adopted by Chinggis Khan's mother as a young man and became a trusted adviser to the family and particularly to Chinggis Khan himself. In 1206, the Great Khan appointed him to the position of grand judge and entrusted him with keeping population and legal data.

However, scholar Igor de Rachewiltz, the best-known translator of *The Secret History* into English, has argued that Khan Ogedai himself, Chinggis Khan's immediate successor, might perhaps have been the author, or at least have been deeply involved in directing the compilation of the text. Professor de Rachewiltz's suggestion is tied up with the question of why *The Secret History* was composed in the first place, and what were the circumstances under which it was first presented to the Mongol elites.

The text itself tells us that "the writing was completed at the time when the Great Assembly convened and when, in the Year of the Rat, in the month of Roebuck, the Palaces were established at Doloan Boldaq." This seems exceptionally precise, but the problem is to try and determine which Year of the Rat the text is referring to. The only probable dates are 1228 or 1240, and of the two, the most likely is 1228, when a Great Assembly was scheduled to elect a successor to Chinggis Khan, who had died the year before. There was considerable tension around this assembly because there were rival claimants to the crown, and so the assembly did not finally resolve these political differences and meet until August of the following year, 1229.

Chinggis Khan had made known his preference that his third son, Ogedai, should be his successor. But it was Chinggis's fourth and youngest son, Tolui, who by Mongol tradition had assumed temporary leadership of the realm following his father's death. And there was also considerable support for the candidacy of Chinggis's oldest surviving son, Chagatai. So when the Great Assembly, the yeke quriltai, did finally convene in August 1229, we know from various sources that there was considerable disagreement and internal strife, which delayed any vote on the successor until mid-September.

With all this in mind, it is possible that *The Secret History* was completed just before this assembly convened, and it may have had its first oral presentation to the assembled Mongol elites at this quriltai. The argument supporting this assertion, which is by no means shared by all Mongol scholars, is that the presentation would have strengthened the conservative element's claim that Chinggis Khan's wishes should be respected and that Ogedai should be proclaimed successor.

One could further argue that the one-year delay in convening the assembly might have been arranged by supporters of Ogedai to allow for the compilation of *The Secret History*, which would have achieved two purposes: to unfold the extraordinary story of Chinggis Khan's rise to power for younger members of the assembly who might not be so familiar with it, and to emphasize to all dignitaries assembled the importance of maintaining Mongol traditions.

In the end, Ogedai was proclaimed Great Khan, and, as we shall see, he proved a very effective ruler indeed for the 12 years he spent in that role before his death. But it is intriguing to think of the politicking that must have gone on in the months following the death of Chinggis Khan and the role that *The Secret History* may have played in securing the throne for Ogedai.

Whether or not the first oral presentation occurred at the Great Assembly, that was not the end of the story of *The Secret History*. During the 34-year reign of Mongol emperor Qubilai Khan, founder of the Yuan Dynasty in China, the original text of *The Secret History* was significantly edited and changed. A Department of Mongol History was established as part of the College of Literature in China. By 1290, scholars in the academy had assembled all known drafts of the text, which was then revised and translated into Chinese, a task that was finished by 1303. The Chinese scholars did their work well, because specialists cannot detect any particular Chinese bias in these later revisions.

Later, Chinese Ming Dynasty scholars decided to use *The Secret History* to create a dictionary of Mongolian and Chinese words and characters. It was during this period that a decision was apparently made to divide the hitherto seamless and continuous text into 12 chapters of roughly equal length, presumably to aid students in their education. It is this version, along with two others, that somehow survived the centuries to become the basis for *The Secret History* we have today.

Arbitrary or not, the 12 chapters are helpful in making sense of the material contained in the text. The first two chapters discuss Temujin's childhood and adolescence. The next four describe the incredibly complex, almost torturous relationship between Temujin and various other Turkic-Mongolic tribes on the Mongolian steppe, including the Tatars, Kereits, and Naiman, and other powerful steppe leaders such as Jamuqa, the sometimes ally, sometimes foe of Temujin. This section culminates with Temujin being elected Chinggis Khan. Later chapters describe the early campaigns of Chinggis Khan against the Uyghurs, the Jin Dynasty in China, and the Khwarazm-Shah in central Asia, and also the subsequent campaigns of expansion led by Ogedai following Chinggis's death.

The Secret History opens with a discussion of the semi-mythical genealogy of Temujin's family: "At the beginning there was a blue-grey wolf, born with his destiny ordained by Heaven Above. His wife was a fallow doe." The text describes Temujin's father as a member of the Mongol nobility and a prominent military leader who formed an alliance between a number of

Mongol clans that swore allegiance to him. But when Temujin was about 10 years old, rivals killed his father by poisoning to make sure the alliance would dissolve.

As eminent Mongol scholar Peter Jackson has argued, however, it is difficult to know how much we can trust this account of Temujin's father's circumstances. Jackson points to the existence of a report written by a Chinese Song Dynasty envoy in 1221 which suggests that his father was not of Mongol nobility at all but of rather humble stock.

Furthermore, where *The Secret History* uses imperial titles like Qaghan to describe earlier ancestors of Temujin, such as his grandfather, this was done purely for political purposes to promote the legitimacy of Chinggis Khan's newly founded dynasty. In fact, pre-Mongol clan alliances were always temporary, and there was no Mongol empire of any sort, let alone an all-powerful imperial ruler like a Qaghan, before Chinggis Khan constructed one in the early 13th century.

However, Jackson and virtually all Mongol scholars agree that *The Secret History* provides a much more accurate description of the sort of bitter blood feuds and clan rivalries that existed between all the tribes of the Mongolian steppe in the years before the rise of the Mongol Empire and also of the role the dynasties of China played in fueling those feuds.

It is this story we turn to for the rest of this lecture, a story that recounts the rise to power of Chinggis Khan based partly on his extraordinary military prowess but also on his ability to navigate the complexities of these shifting alliances and clan rivalries. Indeed, as another eminent Mongol historian, Tim May, puts it: "The rise of Chinggis Khan is something of a marvel, as there was no particular reason Temujin ... should have become the greatest conqueror in history as well as a lawgiver and the founder of the nation." But that, of course, is exactly what Temujin did.

The web of blood feuds and clan rivalries began well before Temujin was born. The Jin Empire of northern China, established by Jurchen nomads, alarmed at the emergence of the Mongols as a unified power in the first half of the 12th century, formed an alliance with the rival Tatar nomads against the Mongols. This had been standard operating procedure by Chinese dynasties since the Han Dynasty, more than a thousand years earlier, had tried to form an alliance with the Yuezhi against the Xiongnu.

Faced with this powerful new alliance, the Mongols tried to make peace with the Tatars by forging a marriage alliance. But the Tatars captured Mongol leader Ambaghai and sent him to the Jin, who brutally executed him. This temporarily weakened the Mongols and allowed the Tatars to become the dominant power of the steppe. But the Mongols were not destroyed and fought many battles with the Tatars. Although the Tatars tended to win most of these, one leader of the Mongol clans did enjoy some success. This was Yesugei of the Borjigin clan, the father of Temujin.

Temujin's mother, Ho'elun, came from the lower-status but still noble Durlukin clan. She had been betrothed to a leader of the rival Merkit tribe, but Yesugei kidnapped her after apparently falling in love at first sight. Yesugei married her and made Ho'elun his primary wife. Together they had five children spaced two years apart, with Temujin the eldest. However, Yesugei also had two children with his secondary wife, so technically, Temujin was the second-oldest son. There is a legendary story that when Temujin was born, he was clutching a large blood clot in one of his tiny hands, which was immediately interpreted as a portent of greatness.

We know nothing more about almost the first decade of the life of Temujin. The story that unfolds in *The Secret History* picks up when Temujin is about nine years old. His parents had decided it was time to find a suitable bride for their son. Marriages were such an important part of clan relationships that it often took years for negotiations between families to be conducted. So, although no actual marriage could take place until the betrothed had reached adolescence, starting to search when they were still children made a lot of sense.

Yesugei had already determined that Temujin's bride must come from a certain clan for strategic diplomatic reasons. But fate intervened while Yesugei and his son were on their way to secure the marriage. En route, they met with a leader of another tribe, Dei Sechen of the Onggirad, a clan renowned for the beauty of their women. Dei Sechen imparted to his guests a recent dream he had had of a white falcon flying towards him, with the sun and moon in his talons, which Yesugei interpreted as another sign that his son was destined for greatness.

Dei Sechen then offered his daughter Borte, a striking girl a few months older than Temujin, to become Temujin's wife. The name Borte can be translated as "woman with fire in her eyes," and this relationship was to have enormous consequences for world history. As historian Anne Broadbridge has demonstrated, Borte would quickly become the most important woman in Temujin's life, and ultimately a woman who made "unparalleled contributions to his political career and the establishment of the empire."

Yesugei accepted the offer and then departed the camp, leaving Temujin behind in the care of Dei Sechen. This was to be the last time Temujin ever saw his father. On the way home, Yesugei stayed for a night in a camp of Tatars who, recognizing this opportunity to get rid of a troublesome opponent, broke all the rules of nomad protocol and poisoned Yesugei's food. The poison was slow acting, because it only hit Yesugei during his ride home the following day. By the time the news had reached Temujin and he had ridden hard back to his father, Yesugei was dead and the feud with the Tatars was far more bitter than ever.

But the more immediate problem for Temujin, his mother Ho'elun, and the rest of his siblings was that with the death of Yesugei, the Borjigid clan was immediately seen as being lower in status compared to other tribes that were in the ascendancy. This was particularly true of the Tayichi'ud clan. As a result, Ho'elun and her family were deserted by their supporters, who simply packed up their *gers* and physically moved off from the camp of Ho'elun, presumably towards the camps of the Tayichi'ud.

This led to years of hardship on the steppe. The family was reduced to a subsistence lifeway. It was sometime during these years of hardscrabble existence that a feud broke out between Temujin and his older half-brother Bekhter, the son of Yesugei's secondary wife. The situation deteriorated until Temujin killed his older brother. Ho'elun was outraged and said the boys should have been fighting the Tayichi'ud instead of each other, but the deed was done. According to *The Secret History*, news of Temujin's actions spread widely, which, as Tim May points out, "makes one wonder just how ostracized Temujin's family really was."

Sometime later, Temujin was captured by the Tayichi'ud in a raid. Instead of killing him, they decided to humiliate him by locking him into a cangue, a wooden device that locked his head and hands into holes, similar to a European stock or pillory. Temujin remained in captivity for months, perhaps years, and was passed around from *ger* to *ger* each night so that no one family had to bear the burden of feeding him. One such family, that of a poor herdsman, took pity on him and released him from the cangue each evening.

While locked in the cangue in another *ger*, Temujin took advantage of a night of revelry in camp to escape. He first used the heavy wooden stock as a weapon to knock his captors about, then jumped into a stream where the wood kept his head above water. He floated far away, and although the Tayichi'ud searched for him, they could not find him. Temujin returned to the helpful family of the herdsman, who removed the cangue, kept him hidden, and gave him food and a horse, which he used to return to his family.

Temujin's fortunes continued to improve. He gained several followers, including a man named Bo'orchu, who would become a lifelong friend, and he also finally married Borte. Anne Broadbridge argues that Borte's influence on the fortunes of Temujin "began immediately upon their marriage, and continued uninterrupted until the moment in 1226 when he chose one of her sons to succeed him."

A more immediate benefit of the marriage was that Temujin gained possession of a highly valuable black sable cloak presented as a wedding gift, which he decided to use in an attempt to win the support of a powerful protector. Temujin now traveled to the camp of the Kereit clan in the Orkhon River Valley and met with the Kereit ruler Toghril Khan. Temujin reminded Toghril that he had once been the *anda*, a sort of blood brother of Temujin's father, Yesugei, and that Yesugei had saved Toghril on several occasions. Temujin asked Toghril to accept him as one of his formal followers, a position known as a *nokor*. Toghril agreed, thus securing for himself the loyalty of Temujin and his followers, not to mention the gift of the valuable cloak.

But this was a win for Temujin too; he had forged an alliance with the Kereit clan and also gained for himself a powerful protector. As Peter Jackson points out, the friendship and military cooperation between the two were of fundamental importance in Temujin's subsequent rise to power.

Despite now having the protection of the powerful Toghril of the Kereits, other tribes still bore a grudge against Temujin for various past slights he and his family had inflicted upon them. One such tribe was the Merkits, who decided to seek revenge for Temujin's father's abduction of Ho'elun many years earlier. One night, they attacked Temujin's camp without warning. Temujin and his brothers escaped, but his wife, Borte, was captured.

Temujin's protector Toghril agreed to help him rescue his wife from the Merkits, but it was not until several months later that they were in a position to march. As the troops were being assembled, Temujin met up with a boyhood friend named Jamuqa, who was now Toghril's war chief. Actually, Temujin and Jamuqa were more than friends; they had been *andas*, or blood brothers, to each other, but had lost contact over the years.

After about a year, a successful attack was launched against the Merkit, and Borte was rescued, although she was heavily pregnant. Toghril urged Temujin to unite his camp with that of Jamuqa and study the arts of warfare, which, because of the early death of his father, was ironically a part of his education that Temujin had missed out on.

While Temujin stayed with Jamuqa and studied warfare, Borte gave birth to a baby boy. Although it was unlikely the boy was Temujin's, given the amount of time that had passed between Borte's abduction and rescue, Temujin accepted the boy as his son and named him Jochi, which means "guest," perhaps a reference to the fact he was born in the camp of Jamuqa, or to his unknown pedigree. The question of exactly who Jochi's father was would haunt Temujin for the rest of his life, although he always treated Jochi as his son.

As Temujin mastered the art of war with Jamuqa, his charismatic style of leadership gained him many more followers, including a number who left Jamuqa's camp for that of Temujin. Among these new followers, drawn from both Mongol nobility and commoners, was a young man named Subedei, who as we will see went on to become perhaps the greatest general the Mongols ever produced.

The trickle became a flood, and Jamuqa was virtually abandoned by his followers. Even some of the most elite members of the Mongol aristocracy came over to Temujin, enhancing his legitimacy in the wider Mongol realm. Inevitably, tensions between Jamuqa and Temujin intensified, and skirmishes often broke out between their followers. It was in one such skirmish that Jamuqa's brother was killed by a group of Temujin's supporters, which Jamuqa viewed as an act of war. In the battle that followed, Temujin's forces were defeated by the more experienced military commander Jamuqa, which left Temujin isolated again and in a dangerous position on the steppe.

We know little about what happened to Temujin in the 10 years following his defeat by Jamuqa; it is as if he dropped off the map of Mongol affairs. It is a reasonable assumption that he moved south and entered the borderlands of the Jin Dynasty in northern China. One later source suggests that Temujin actually became a slave during his decade with the Jin.

Back on the Mongolian steppe, Jamuqa was becoming increasingly tyrannical. Even Toghril was forced to flee to escape the rage of Jamuqa. Various stories describe the gruesome way he killed those who had left his camp to join Temujin—boiling them alive, decapitating them, dragging their heads tied to the tail of his horse through the dirt, and so on. All this served to make Jamuqa even more unpopular and increased the numbers of Mongols who preferred to attach their camps to that of Temujin, should he ever return.

After 10 years, in the year 1195, Temujin did indeed return, only to find that he already had a large group of supporters from all strata of Mongol society and from many different clans. Temujin had also apparently amassed considerable wealth during his decade in China, and he used this partly to sponsor a large gathering of the clans, a quriltai, in 1196. Unfortunately, the quriltai ended in a drunken brawl, with one clan—that of the Jurkin— deeply insulted by the treatment meted out to them by Temujin.

A few years later, Temujin joined forces with the powerful Toghril, who had also returned to the steppe, to launch a campaign against the Tatars, the former allies of the Jin Dynasty. But the Jin had become increasingly concerned about the power of the Tatars, and actually sent their forces to join Temujin and Toghril. The Tatars were soundly defeated by this combined army.

But when Temujin returned to camp after the battle, he found that the Jurkin, who had been insulted by their treatment at the quriltai, had attacked and sacked his camp. Temujin promptly attacked the Jurkin camp in turn and massacred the elites of the clan, while accepting the commoners into his own camp. So in the space of a couple of days, he had destroyed two rival clans, the Tatars and the Jurkin.

Temujin's status was now so high that tensions between Toghril and himself increased. Although clashes occasionally broke out between their followers, the two maintained their alliance. Other Mongol elites also became increasingly wary of Temujin, particularly because he did not follow the accepted social rules and promoted commoners like Subedei to positions of high rank and authority. The disaffected Mongols convened their own quriltai in 1201 and elected Jamuqa as Great Khan. This made war between Temujin and Jamuqa inevitable. The combined forces of Toghril and Temujin crushed those of Jamuqa in a battle on the eastern Mongolian steppe, and Jamuqa fled. He was captured by Toghril, who granted him clemency.

Temujin, meanwhile, despite being seriously wounded in the battle, pursued and defeated the Tayichi'ud, who had supported Jamuqa. He also accepted submission from another clan, that of the Onggirad. Temujin continued to show his leadership genius by accepting into his ranks any of the followers and soldiers of these now defeated and largely dissolved clans, further bolstering both his prestige and his power.

His status was enhanced even further in 1202, when he destroyed the Tatars and executed all of their male elites, although not the children. This meant that only three major powers now remained in Mongolia—the Naiman in the west, the Kereits under Toghril in the center, and Temujin and his combined forces in the east.

Eventually, swayed by his advisers, including Jamuqa, Toghril decided to turn on Temujin, despite the close relationship between them. The two armies met at the Battle of Qalaqalit Sands in 1203, where the Mongol army was badly defeated by the Kereits led by Jamuqa. But Temujin simply regathered his forces, rested them for a few days, even gained support from groups that defected from the Kereits, and attacked Jamuqa and the Kereits while they were still celebrating their victory. Mongol success was near complete, although Jamuqa, Toghril, and a few other elites escaped. Temujin accepted oaths of allegiance from the Kereits and formed further alliances through intermarriage between Mongol and Kereit elites.

With Temujin now in complete control of eastern and central Mongolia, the Naiman realized they had to act immediately if they were to have any chance of stopping his rise to even greater power. The Naiman formed a coalition that included Jamuqa. When Temujin heard of their plans, he launched a daring and unexpected raid against them in the early summer of 1204, confronting the surprised Naiman in the foothills of the Khangai Mountains in western Mongolia. Using his highly disciplined troops and new tactics honed from years of warfare on the steppe, Temujin's Mongol forces crushed the Naiman.

During the two years that followed, Temujin consolidated his position and somewhat reluctantly gave his *anda* Jamuqa an honorable death. Years of struggle culminated at the quriltai of 1206, when Temujin was proclaimed Chinggis Khan. The Great Khan had united all the tribes of the Mongolian steppe and assembled an extraordinary military force. His next priority was to consolidate his rule through a complete reorganization of Mongol society.

But Chinggis Khan also knew that his new state had been forged through near constant warfare, and the only way to keep his forces united was to take them out of Mongolia on campaigns of conquest. It was the only logical course of action to follow. Waging war on enemies surrounding Mongolia would not only enhance the security of the new Mongol state but also keep his soldiers happy by allowing them to do what they did best: fight and collect booty. And so the new Mongol state was about to become the Mongol Empire.

CHINGGIS KHAN'S
EARLY CONQUESTS

B y 1206, Chinggis Khan was the supreme leader of the Mongols, having been proclaimed so at the great *quriltai* that same year. This lecture focuses on Chinggis Khan's first campaigns of conquest as leader of the Mongol world.

The Situation in 1206

As far as Chinggis Khan was concerned, the most pressing geopolitical problem facing him in 1206 was how to deal with China. But China itself had been dealing with its own political challenges over the previous 300 years. By 1206, China was divided into three states: the Song dynasty in the south, the Jin dynasty in the north, and the Xi Xia state in the northwest. Both the Song and Jin Dynasties ruled vast populations of sedentary, mostly agricultural Han and other ethnic Chinese peoples. The rulers of Xi Xia were Tanguts, originally from the Tibetan plateau, and they ruled a more mixed though still enormous population that included both farming and pastoral nomadic peoples.

One of the leading rebels who had opposed Temujin was the Kereit ruler Senggum. After the Mongol defeat of the Kereit in 1203, Senggum had sought protection from the rulers of Xi Xia. From the moment Temujin was declared Chinggis Khan, he had dispatched Mongol forces on raids into Xi Xia, looking for Senggum and gathering intelligence.

These initial Mongols forays did not succeed in capturing Senggum, but his own behavior was lawless enough that the Tangut soon evicted him from their territory. Senggum fled south and was killed in the Tarim Basin by Turkic forces pillaging northwards from Afghanistan. It is not certain whether Chinggis Khan was aware of Senggum's death, because Xi Xia would continue to be of great military interest in the early years of his rule.

Another consideration for Chinggis Khan was the existence of dangerous groups to the north of the Mongolian plateau, living in the forests of southern Siberia. Although they consisted of various peoples and lifeways, they were known collectively as the Hoi-yin Irgen, or the Forest People.

Westward, beyond the Xi Xia, lay the realm of another Chinese substate, that of the Qara Khitai, which also had long standing friendly ties with the Naiman. Beyond the Qara Khitai lay the vast Dar al-Islam, the realm of Islam. During the 12th century, power in the Islamic world had been assumed by the Seljuq Turks. But after the death of Seljuq sultan Sanjar in 1157, a new Turkish family had emerged to claim power: that of the Khwarazm-Shah. When Temujin claimed the title Chinggis Khan in 1206, the ruler of the Khwarazm-Shah was Ala ad-Din Muhammad II.

As Chinggis Khan surveyed potential targets for military campaigns, the Khwarazm-Shah would have seemed very formidable opponents. Farther west still, beyond the realm of the Khwarazm-Shah, the Abbasid Caliphate continued its weakened and nominal rule of the Dar al-Islam, with a particular focus on the modern region of Iraq.

Selecting Targets

It is highly likely that Chinggis Khan and his advisers decided early on that their principal focus had to be the Jin dynasty in China. Ever since the Xiongnu, the Chinese state had been the focus for nomadic raiding and conquest. Each of the empires of the steppe had come to the same conclusion: the Chinese would do all they could to meddle in and hopefully destroy the nomads.

Before he could launch full-scale assaults against the Jin, there was tidying up to do closer to home. In 1207, troops were dispatched to deal with the Hoy-yin Irgen to the north. The Mongols forced the submission of the remnants of many of the tribes that had originally opposed them before fleeing north, including the Oirat and Kyrgyz.

That same year, a separate campaign was launched westward, also on a search-and-destroy mission against the remnants of disaffected tribes such as the Naiman and Merkit. After crossing the Altai Mountains, the Mongols forced the rebels into battle at the Irtysh River, defeating if not destroying their enemies. Naiman refugees led by Guchulug fled south, seeking refuge among the Uyghurs, who rejected and expelled them.

Some months later, the Naiman found refuge with the Qara Khitai. The ruler of the Qara Khitai accepted Guchulug as his suzerain and married one of his daughters off to the Naiman leader, hoping that an alliance with the Naiman would improve the fortunes of the Qara Khitai.

After their defeat at the Irtysh River, Merkit refugees had bypassed the Qara Khitai and headed west. They eventually settled with other Turkic nomadic tribes on steppe lands north of the Aral Sea in modern Kazakhstan. Although aware of the potential dangers these various disaffected refugees posed, Chinggis Khan decided that the victory over them at the Irtysh River was enough for now.

The Xi Xia

Eventually in Xi Xia, a new, more aggressive ruler named Li Anquan came to the throne. This might have been partly responsible for the decision to launch a large-scale Mongol invasion of Xi Xia in 1209, led by Chinggis Khan personally.

The armies of Xi Xia had no answer to the extraordinary discipline of Mongol troops, nor to the military genius of Chinggis Khan. The Mongols further astonished their rivals with their creativity in attacking the near-impregnable city of Zhongxing. Chinggis Khan ordered his men to build a huge dyke that redirected the Yellow River's waters against the city's stamped-earth walls. The waters undermined parts of the walls and poured into the city, flooding many houses and drowning thousands.

The plan ultimately backfired, however. The pressure from the swollen river on the dyke wall constructed by the Mongols eventually destroyed the dyke, and both the city and the Mongol camp were flooded. Still, after this display of military creativity and persistence, the Tanguts decided it was in their best interests to make peace with the Mongols. Li Anquan and Chinggis Khan agreed to a treaty, and the Tangut ruler presented one of his daughters to Chinggis Khan as a wife. The Tanguts also agreed to provide troops for the Mongol army, and to pay a substantial tribute including camels and falcons. The peace agreement held for several years.

The Jin Dynasty

Chinggis Khan was now finally free to focus on his main goal: the destruction of the powerful Jin dynasty in China. Chinggis led the first campaign into China in 1211, but the Jin would not be finally defeated until 23 years later in 1234, seven years after the death of the Great Khan.

In preparation for the campaign, he first sent one of his generals, Toquchar, to safeguard the western passes into Mongolia and China, thus reducing any danger still posed by the Qara Khitai and Naiman refugees. He also appointed his youngest brother, Temuge Otchigin, as regent to look after affairs in Mongolia during his absence. With these measures in place, the invasion of the Jin dynasty could begin.

The first campaign began with a three-pronged attack on Jin domains just outside of the heartland, in western and north central China. One goal was to bring firmly to heel various tribes that dwelt in the region. Chinggis Khan succeeded in bringing them into the Mongol fold, giving him control of the regions between Mongolia and Manchuria.

The Mongol military also struck at Manchuria itself, the original home of the Jurchen militarized nomads that had constructed the Jin dynasty. The Jin sent some armies against them, but the Mongols crushed them in the field and confiscated a large amount of territory, including the region where the imperial horse herds grazed. This allowed the Mongols to capture large numbers of Jin horses and take them back to Mongolia when Chinggis Khan withdrew his forces in February 1212.

In the fall of 1212, the attack was renewed with greater strength, and with what appear to have been longer-term goals to annex and permanently occupy Jin territory. Two powerful armies marched southward, both equipped with siege weapons. One army was led by Chinggis Khan, the other by his youngest son, Tolui.

As the Mongols marched into Jin China, their allies, the Tanguts, invaded from Xi Xia in the west. Famine broke out among the peasantry of northern China, exacerbated by the military operations which now extended into 1213. An insurrection against the Jin erupted in the east, led by Khitans.

With these crises unfolding, the brand new Jin emperor Xuanzong, who only came to the throne that same year of 1213, sent envoys to the Mongols asking for peace and offering valuable goods if they broke off the campaign. The Mongols rejected the offer, much to the Jin court's surprise. Instead, they marched on the Jin capital city of Zhongdu.

Attacking Zhongdu

The immensity of the city initially awed Chinggis Khan, who left it blockaded and then proceeded to devastate the surrounding territory using three separate Mongol armies. Although they had brought siege equipment with them, they had previously not wasted any time on protracted sieges.

The capital city of Zhongdu was a different matter, though. As panic set in among the citizens, the Mongols continued to attack the city. The Jin sent armies from elsewhere to drive the Mongols away, but the Mongols destroyed them in the field.

In April 1214, the Jin court sought peace again. The emperor offered to make regular tribute payments of horses, gold, and silk to the Mongols, and to give Chinggis Khan one of the daughters of Xuanzong's predecessor to become his wife. Chinggis Khan agreed and withdrew his forces. Howeever, almost immediately, the Jin emperor abandoned his northern capital of Zhongdu and fled to the southern capital of Kaifeng.

News of this reached Chinggis Khan before he had even returned to Mongolia. Seeing this as a breach of the treaty, and perhaps an effort by the Jin emperor to raise fresh troops against him, a furious Chinggis Khan immediately marched back to Zhongdu and renewed the siege.

The Mongols descended on the city from several directions at once, using their sophisticated siege equipment operated by skilled Chinese engineers who had deserted from the Jin.

Famine set in among the besieged inhabitants of Zhongdu, who, so the sources inform us, reverted to cannibalism. In 1215, the city surrendered. Mongol soldiers rampaged through the city for weeks.

The fall of Zhongdu, although a devastating blow to the Jin, did not mean the end of their dynasty. Shut up in the heavily fortified city of Kaifeng in the south, Emperor Xuanzong refused to submit to Chinggis Khan. The Mongols then divided their forces and struck on many fronts at once.

Other Campaigns

With other Mongol armies ravaging the west, and Muqali conducting a superb campaign in the east, Chinggis Khan was forced to abruptly return to Mongolia in 1216 to deal with a rebellion that had broken out among the Hoi-yin Irgen forest peoples in the north.

Additionally, as the war in China continued, Chinggis Khan was increasingly distracted by events to the west. Ever since 1208, Mongol forces had been actively pursuing remnants of the Naiman and Merkit tribes, which had continued to flee to the west. In pursuit of these rebel leaders, Mongol forces led by General Subedai eventually found themselves far from home on the Kipchak steppes, but they were nonetheless successful in defeating Merkit forces and their protectors in battle.

As Subedei was on the march back to Mongolia, however, serendipitous events were about to occur that would have unexpected long-term consequences. Muhammad II, sultan of the Khwarazmian empire, happened to be in the area when he stumbled upon the battlefield of the recent contest between Subedai and the Merkit. Intrigued, Muhammad gave chase to the Mongols and attacked.

Muhammad's army was much larger, but the Mongols completely outmaneuvered and outfought them. At the end of the day, both sides retired to their camps. But when Muhammad awoke in the morning, the Mongols had gone. He did not pursue them because, according to a Persian chronicler, the battle of the previous day had quite unnerved him.

Muslims and Mongols fighting

As a result of these campaigns in the western regions, various other tribal groups, including the Uyghurs and Qarluqs, now offered their submission to Chinggis Khan. By 1218, the Mongol empire extended all the way west to the banks of the Syr Darya in Uzbekistan.

Chinggis Khan appears to have been ambivalent at this stage. One source suggests that Chinggis wrote to Shah Muhammad II, expressing hopes that there would be peace and profitable trade relations between the two empires.

In 1218, a caravan of 450 Muslim merchants traveling from within the Mongol empire and under Mongol protection arrived at the Khwarazm frontier town of Otrar. The governor of Otrar was suspicious and assumed the merchants to be spies. With the tacit permission of Shah Muhammad, he massacred the entire caravan, and governor and shah then divided the loot between them.

One merchant escaped and sent word back to Chinggis Khan, who was enraged but first tried diplomacy, sending a small group of envoys to the shah and asking for financial restitution. He also asked for the governor of Otrar to be sent to him.

Shah Muhammad refused these requests. He killed one diplomat and singed the beards of the others before sending them back to Chinggis Khan, a serious insult. There could be no possible response from Chinggis Khan now other than a declaration of war.

CHINGGIS KHAN'S EARLY CONQUESTS

LECTURE 5 TRANSCRIPT

By 1206, Chinggis Khan was the supreme leader of the Mongols, having been proclaimed so at the great quriltai that same year. His most pressing concern was to reorganize the Mongol tribes into a new state-like confederation that would end the sort of bitter clan rivalries and blood feuds that had so blighted Mongol history for centuries.

This reorganization—which through enlightened innovations in government, social relations, taxation, and laws essentially created the Yeke Mongol Ulus, the Great State of Mongolia—will be the subject of our next lecture. But in this lecture, we are focused on warfare and on Chinggis Khan's first campaigns of conquest as leader of the Mongol world.

Once these administrative reforms were underway, Chinggis Khan was faced with an equally pressing problem of what to do next with the formidable military force he had created. As noted Mongol specialist David Morgan sees the problem, "Unless something decisive was done with the newly formed military machine, it would soon devolve into quarrelling factions again, and Mongolia would revert to its former state."

Professor Morgan makes a persuasive argument, then, that whatever ambitions for world conquest Chinggis Khan may have possessed, one obvious explanation for the beginning of the Mongol campaigns was the necessity of using the army externally to keep it and the new Mongol state from fragmenting into division and chaos, as it had done so often in the past.

So, after taking a year or so to tie up loose ends in Mongolia, Chinggis Khan began to think about the most effective way of using his powerful new military force, which he must surely have realized would be virtually unbeatable in the field. The only question was where to take his army first. But before we follow the Mongol forces on their first campaigns outside of Mongolia, let's pause for a moment and consider the geopolitical situation in inner Eurasia at the beginning of the great khan's reign.

As we have seen, all the steppe nomadic empires had formed with their epicenter in Mongolia, and attempts by various Chinese dynasties to neutralize the threat these empires posed had been the most important relationship for both sides for about 1,500 years.

For the Han Dynasty in the centuries either side of the BCE/CE divide, the challenge had been to deal with the potent threat posed by the Xiongnu, using both tribute and warfare. For the Tang Dynasty between the 7th and 10th centuries, the problem had been how to navigate increasingly complex diplomatic and military relationships with the Turks and Uyghurs to their north and west.

And as we have also seen, even during the rise to power of Temujin, the Jin Dynasty in northern China had done its best to sow division on the steppe by allying first with the Tatars against the other tribes and then with the Mongols against the Tatars. This meant that as far as Chinggis Khan was concerned, the most pressing geopolitical problem facing him in 1206 was how to deal with China.

But China itself had been dealing with its own political challenges over the previous 300 years. Following the collapse of the Tang Dynasty in 907 CE, the Chinese state had fragmented into two short-lived though tumultuous periods known as the Five Dynasties and Ten Kingdoms eras.

In the north, dynasties had followed each other in quick succession, none lasting longer than 16 years. Irrigation systems fell apart, floods devastated the countryside, and famine was widespread. Hundreds of thousands of refugees had fled to southern China, where, although the political situation was more stable, warfare between warlords was also endemic.

This chaotic half-century was ended by the Northern Song Dynasty, which was proclaimed in 960 CE, and which by 978 had reimposed imperial rule over most of China. The Song Dynasty is actually divided into two periods: the Northern Song, which dates from 960 to 1126 and which ruled from the capital city of Kaifeng in northern China, and the Southern Song, which ruled between 1127 and 1279 from their southern capital in the modern city of Hangzhou.

The reason for this division is that the Northern Song struggled to construct a stable, efficient state, such as the Han and Tang had done before them. Not particularly strong militarily, the Northern Song had faced continual threats from various nomadic confederations on the northern steppe. One such group was the Khitan, which the Song placated with huge payments of silver and silk, putting an enormous strain on the Song economy.

But a far more potent threat came from the Jurchen, who defeated the Khitan and then began raiding into northern China. In 1123, they launched a full-scale invasion of China, capturing the Song capital of Kaifeng and establishing the Jin Dynasty. The Song emperor and his court fled southwards, and by 1141, an uneasy border had been established across the middle of the plains between the Yellow and Yangtze Rivers. This had remained the situation through into the early 13th century. It had been the Jin Dynasty in the north that had been so involved in nomadic politics through the period of the rise to power of Chinggis Khan.

By 1206, China was divided actually into three states: the Song Dynasty in the south, the Jin Dynasty in the north, and the Xi Xia state in the northwest. Both the Song and Jin Dynasties ruled vast populations of sedentary, mostly agricultural Han and other ethnic Chinese peoples. But the rulers of Xi Xia were Tanguts, originally from the Tibetan plateau, and they ruled a far more mixed, though still enormous, population that included both farming and pastoral nomadic peoples. The rulers of Xi Xia had also grown wealthy through their control of trade along ancient Silk Roads routes which passed through their territory.

One of the leading rebels who had opposed Temujin was the Kereit ruler Senggum. After the Mongol defeat of the Kereit in 1203, Senggum had sought protection from the rulers of Xi Xia. From the moment Temujin was declared Chinggis Khan, he had dispatched Mongol forces on raids into Xi Xia, looking for Senggum and gathering intelligence. This was in keeping with policies that had been followed over the previous decades of struggle in the steppe: hunt down and destroy rebel leaders and then integrate their peoples and military into his own confederation.

These initial Mongol forays did not succeed in capturing Senggum, but his own behavior was lawless enough that the Tangut soon evicted him from their territory. Senggum fled south and was killed in the Tarim Basin by Turkic forces pillaging northwards from Afghanistan. It is not certain whether Chinggis Khan was aware of Senggum's death, because Xi Xia would continue to be of great military interest in the early years of his rule.

Another consideration for Chinggis Khan in this geopolitical survey of inner Eurasia on the brink of the Mongol conquests was the existence of dangerous groups to the north of the Mongolian plateau, living in the forests of southern Siberia. Although they consisted of various peoples and lifeways, they were known collectively as the Hoi-yin Irgen, which means the "Forest People."

Chinggis Khan held a grudge against them because one of their groups, the Oirat, had supported Jamuqa against Temujin and had then formed an alliance with the Naiman, who had also opposed Temujin. Another reason the Hoi-yin Irgen would have been on Chinggis Khan's radar is because remnants of one of the more powerful tribes he had defeated during his rise to power, the Merkit, had escaped into regions contiguous to the Forest Peoples. For all these reasons, campaigns against the Hoi-yin Irgen would have also figured high in Chinggis Khan's prioritizing about where to send his armies first.

Westwards, beyond the Xi Xia, lay the realm of another Chinese substate, that of the Qara Khitai, which also had long-standing friendly ties with the Naiman. And beyond the Qara Khitai lay the vast Dar al-Islam, the realm of Islam. During the 12th century, power in the Islamic world, then nominally ruled by the Abbasid Caliphate from its capital of Baghdad, had been assumed by the Seljuq Turks. But after the death of Seljuq sultan Sanjar in 1157, a new Turkish family had emerged to claim power—that of the Khwarazm-Shah.

Khwarazm was located in the fertile lowlands along the Oxus River, the modern Amu Darya, all the way north to where it enters the Aral Sea, and its shahs had emerged from a provincial governor who had been placed in the region by the Seljuqs in the 11th century. When Temujin claimed the title Chinggis Khan in 1206, the ruler of the Khwarazm-Shah was one Ala ad-Din Muhammad II. By 1210, Muhammad had taken control of large regions of modern Uzbekistan and was ruling from his capital at Samarkand. Five years later, Muhammad had also conquered much of Afghanistan from rulers known as the Ghurid sultans.

As Chinggis Khan continued his survey of potential inner Eurasian targets for military campaigns, the Khwarazm-Shah would have seemed very formidable opponents indeed, although we now know with the benefit of hindsight that the Khwarazmian Empire was already facing all sorts of internal problems.

Further west again, beyond the realm of the Khwarazm-Shah, the Abbasid Caliphate continued its weakened and nominal rule of the Dar al-Islam, with a particular focus on the modern region of Iraq. The Mongols were in fact destined to kill the last Abbasid caliph in 1258, but this was well into the future and well beyond the bounds of Chinggis Khan's more immediate strategic thinking.

Beyond the Abbasids lay states that the Mongols had probably never even heard of—crusader states in Syria and Egypt, Seljuq Turks in Anatolia, Byzantines in western Anatolia and the Balkans, early Russian states on the steppes north of the Black and Caspian Seas, and a range of kingdoms in eastern, central, and western Europe. None of these political structures would have had any serious knowledge of the Mongols nor could have imagined the destruction and utter devastation they would eventually unleash upon this myriad of states and their peoples.

It is highly likely that Chinggis Khan and his advisers would have decided early on that their principal focus had to be the Jin Dynasty in China. Ever since the Xiongnu, the Chinese state had been the focus for nomadic raiding and conquest. Each of the empires of the steppe had come to the same conclusion: The Chinese would do all they could to meddle in and hopefully destroy the nomads. As David Morgan concludes, China "would do whatever it could to destroy Chinggis Khan's power, if he did not strike first."

But before he could launch full-scale assaults against the Jin, there was a little tidying up to do closer to home. In 1207, troops were dispatched to deal with the Hoy-yin Irgen, the Forest Peoples to the north. The Mongols forced the submission of the remnants of many of the tribes that had originally opposed them before fleeing north, including the Oirat and Kyrgyz.

That same year, a separate campaign was launched westwards, also on a search-and-destroy mission against the remnants of disaffected tribes such as the Naiman and the Merkit. After crossing the Altai Mountains, the Mongols forced the rebels into battle at the Irtysh River, defeating, if not destroying, their enemies. Naiman refugees led by Guchulug fled south, seeking refuge amongst the Uyghurs, who rejected and expelled them.

Some months later, the Naiman found refuge with the Qara Khitai. The ruler of the Qara Khitai accepted Guchulug as his suzerain and married one of his daughters off to the Naiman leader, hoping that an alliance with the Naiman would improve the fortunes of the Qara Khitai.

After their defeat at the Irtysh River and the death in battle of their leader, Toqtoa Khan, Merkit refugees had bypassed the Qara Khitai and headed much further west. They eventually settled with other Turkic nomadic tribes on steppe lands north of the Aral Sea in modern Kazakhstan. Although aware of the potential dangers these various disaffected refugees posed, Chinggis Khan decided that the victory over them at the Irtysh River was enough for now. He had much bigger fish to fry!

As noted earlier, the former Kereit ruler Senggum had found refuge with the Xi Xia, and from the moment Temujin was declared Chinggis Khan, he had dispatched Mongol forces on raids into Xi Xia, looking for Senggum. The Tangut rulers of Xi Xia made one failed attempt to defeat Mongol forces in the field, but thereafter retired to their fortified cities to pursue a defensive policy. A new, more aggressive ruler named Li Anquan then came to the throne, and this might have been partly responsible for the decision to launch a large-scale Mongol invasion of Xi Xia in 1209, led by Chinggis Khan personally.

The armies of Xi Xia had no answer to the extraordinary discipline of Mongol troops, nor to the military genius of Chinggis Khan. Although the Xi Xia forces also mostly consisted of skilled mounted archers, they were easily swept away by the Mongols. The Mongols further astonished their rivals by their creativity in attacking the near-impregnable city of Zhongxing.

Although the Mongols would later become masters of the art of siege warfare, that was in the future. In this case, Mongol forces initially made little headway against the defenses of the city. But then Chinggis Khan noticed early in 1215 that winter rains in the mountains had swollen the notoriously flood-prone Huang He (or Yellow River) to dangerous proportions, putting pressure on the irrigation canals and dykes around Zhongxing. He ordered his men to build a huge dyke that redirected the Yellow River's waters against the city's stamped-earth walls. The waters undermined parts of the walls and poured into the city, flooding many houses and drowning thousands.

The plan ultimately backfired, however. The pressure from the swollen river on the dyke wall constructed by the Mongols eventually destroyed the dyke itself, and both the city and the Mongol camp were flooded. But after this display of military creativity and persistence, the Tanguts decided it was in their best interest to make peace with the Mongols. Li Anquan and Chinggis Khan agreed to a treaty, and the Tangut ruler presented one of his daughters to Chinggis Khan as a wife.

Chinggis gained more than a wife out of this arrangement. The Tanguts also agreed to provide troops for the Mongol army and to pay a substantial tribute including camels and falcons. The peace agreement held for several years, and Chinggis Khan was now finally free to focus on his main goal: the destruction of the powerful Jin Dynasty in China. In the end, this would prove a hard-won victory. Chinggis led the first campaign into China in 1211, but the Jin would not be finally defeated until 23 years later, in 1234, seven years after the death of the Great Khan.

In preparation for the campaign, which Chinggis Khan realized from the beginning would be long, arduous, and potentially dangerous for his new Mongol confederation, he first sent one of his generals, Toquchar, to safeguard the western passes into Mongolia and China, thus reducing any danger still posed by the Qara Khitai and Naiman refugees. He also appointed his youngest brother, Temuge Otchigin, as regent to look after affairs in Mongolia during his absence. With these measures in place, the invasion of the Jin Dynasty could begin.

Chinggis was well aware of one significant weakness in Mongol military capacity that could be a serious impediment on a campaign such as this, where major cities would have to be subdued. The Mongols had proven that they were supreme in the field and could sweep aside any army sent against them, whether by nomadic or sedentary powers. But as his experience at Zhongxing had already shown him, besieging formidable, well-defended cities was another problem entirely.

With this in mind, it is doubtful that the Mongols were focused on conquest and permanent occupation of China, at least in this early campaign. After all, some historians estimate that the Jin could put something close to half a million men in the field to defend their state, whereas the Mongols may have had only around 65,000 men in the cavalry contingent that left Mongolia. But to counter this, the Mongols were aware that the Jin themselves were an occupying force and that many Chinese, including those serving in the Jin military, may have had little love for their Jurchen overlords.

The first campaign began with a three-pronged attack on Jin domains just outside of the heartland, in western and north-central China. One goal was to bring firmly to heel various juyin tribes that dwelt in the region as potential challengers to the Mongols. By military strength and also eventually by marriage alliance, Chinggis Khan succeeded in bringing the juyin into the Mongol fold, giving him control of the regions between Mongolia and Manchuria.

The third prong of the Mongol military struck at Manchuria itself, the original homeland of the Jurchen militarized nomads that had constructed the Jin Dynasty. The Jin sent some armies against them, but the Mongols crushed them in the field and confiscated a large amount of territory, including the region where the imperial horse herds grazed. This allowed the Mongols to capture large numbers of Jin horses and take them back to Mongolia when Chinggis Khan withdrew his forces in February 1212. The Mongols had amassed considerable booty through plunder, particularly these highly valuable horses, and the Jin were now very much on the back foot.

In the fall of 1212, the attack was renewed with greater strength and with what appear to have been longer-term goals to annex and permanently occupy Jin territory. Two powerful armies marched southwards, both equipped with siege weapons that could be assembled as necessary, transported by Bactrian camel caravans. One army was led by Chinggis Khan, the other by his youngest son, Tolui.

As the Mongols marched into Jin China, their allies the Tanguts invaded from Xi Xia in the west. Famine broke out amongst the peasantry of northern China, exacerbated by the military operations which now extended into 1213. And an insurrection against the Jin erupted in the east, led by Khitans.

With these crises unfolding, the brand new Jin emperor Xuanzong, who only came to the throne that same year of 1213, sent envoys to the Mongols asking for peace and offering valuable booty if they broke off the campaign. The Mongols rejected the offer, much to the Jin court's surprise. Instead, they marched on the Jin capital city of Zhongdu, which they may have already had under surveillance since the previous campaign.

The immensity of the city initially awed Chinggis Khan, who left it blockaded and then proceeded to devastate the surrounding territory using three separate Mongol armies. Although they had brought siege equipment with them, they had previously not wasted any time on protracted sieges, but simply moved on, leaving the wary defenders of the cities fully aware that the Mongols could return at any moment. The capital city of Zhongdu was a different matter, though. As some sort of panic set in amongst the citizens, the Mongols continued to attack the city. The Jin sent armies from elsewhere to drive the Mongols away, but the Mongols destroyed them in the field.

In April 1214, the Jin court sought peace again. The emperor offered to make regular tribute payments of horses, gold, and silk to the Mongols, and to give Chinggis Khan one of the daughters of Xuanzong's predecessor to become his wife if he agreed to sign a peace treaty. Chinggis Khan did agree and withdrew his forces. But almost immediately, the Jin emperor abandoned his northern capital of Zhongdu and fled to the southern capital of Kaifeng.

News of this reached Chinggis Khan before he had even returned to Mongolia. Seeing this as a breach of the treaty, and perhaps an effort by the Jin emperor to raise fresh troops against him, a furious Chinggis Khan immediately marched back to Zhongdu and renewed the siege. The Mongols descended on the city from several directions at once, using their sophisticated siege equipment operated by skilled Chinese engineers who had deserted from the Jin.

Famine set in amongst the besieged inhabitants of Zhongdu, who, so the sources inform us, reverted to cannibalism. The terrified citizens realized that there was no escaping the noose that the Mongols had tied around their necks, and in 1215, the city surrendered. Mongol soldiers rampaged through the city for weeks, plundering, raping, and killing. One source wrote that 60,000 virgins leapt to their death from the walls of the city rather than risk being raped by Mongols. Tim May, a leading Mongol specialist at the University of North Georgia, is doubtless correct in suggesting that "this was probably propaganda, perhaps encouraged by the Mongols."

The fall of Zhongdu, although a devastating blow to the Jin, did not mean the end of their dynasty. Shut up in the heavily fortified city of Kaifeng in the south, Emperor Xuanzong refused to submit to Chinggis Khan. The Mongols then divided their forces and struck on many fronts at once. One force, under Chinggis Khan's brother Qasar and General Muqali, invaded Manchuria and the Liaodong Peninsula, intent upon establishing permanent Mongol rule there.

With other Mongol armies ravaging the west and Muqali conducting a superb campaign in the east, Chinggis Khan was forced to abruptly return to Mongolia in 1216 to deal with a rebellion that had broken out amongst the Hoi-yin Irgen Forest Peoples in the north. The circumstances behind this rebellion are complex, but Chinggis Khan, enraged by what he saw as disloyal behavior among certain rebels, dispatched a Mongol army under General Boroqul. But Boroqul was attacked and killed by the rebels in 1217.

Two new armies were now sent—one led by General Dorbei, the other by Chinggis Khan's eldest son, Jochi—and these effectively crushed the rebellion. The rebels were dealt with harshly, particularly after the killing of Boroqul, a respected general and associate of Chinggis Khan.

As the war in China continued, ably led by General Muqali, Chinggis Khan was increasingly distracted by events to the west. Ever since 1208, Mongol forces had been actively pursuing remnants of the Naiman and Merkit tribes, which had continued to flee further west. In pursuit of these rebel leaders, Mongol forces led by General Subedei eventually found themselves far from home on the Kipchak steppes, but were nonetheless successful in defeating Merkit forces and their protectors in battle.

As Subedei was on the march back to Mongolia, however, serendipitous events were about to occur that would have unexpected long-term consequences and that would lead eventually to the Mongol invasion of vast regions of central and western Eurasia. It just so happened that Muhammad II, sultan of the Khwarazmian Empire, happened to be in the area, leading his own completely unrelated military campaign, when he stumbled upon the battlefield of the recent contest between Subedei and the Merkit. Intrigued, Muhammad gave chase to the Mongols and attacked.

Muhammad's army was much larger, but the Mongols completely outmaneuvered and outfought them. At the end of the day, both sides retired to their camps. But when Muhammad awoke in the morning, the Mongols had gone. He did not pursue them because, according to a Persian chronicler, the battle of the previous day had quite unnerved him.

As a result of these campaigns in the western regions, various other tribal groups, including the Uyghurs and Qarluqs, now offered their submission to Chinggis Khan. The Mongols also incorporated the formerly powerful Qara Khitai state into their empire. Through these various endeavors, and for the expenditure of relatively little military capital, by 1218, the Mongol Empire extended all the way west to the banks of the Syr Darya in Uzbekistan, contiguous with the empire of the Khwarazm-Shah.

Chinggis Khan appears to have been ambivalent about the Khwarazm-Shah at this stage. One source suggests that Chinggis wrote to Shah Muhammad II expressing hopes that there would be peace and profitable trade relations between the two empires. The Mongols were also apparently happy to write off the unfortunate clash between Khwarazmian forces and the army of Subedei. So it is difficult to know how relations between the two states would have evolved had Muhammad not taken matters into his own hands, making war inevitable between himself and Chinggis Khan.

In 1218, as a prelude to the possibility of establishing trade relations between the Mongols and the Khwarazm Chinggis Khan had proposed in his letter to Muhammad, he sent a caravan of 450 Muslim merchants traveling from within the Mongol Empire and under Mongol protection to the Khwarazm frontier town of Otrar on the Syr Darya. The governor of Otrar was suspicious and assumed the merchants to be spies. With the tacit permission of Shah Muhammad, he massacred the entire caravan, and governor and shah then divided the loot between them.

One merchant escaped, however, and sent word back to Chinggis Khan, who was enraged. But with the war in China somewhat bogged down and with other potential security threats to deal with closer to home, he was reluctant to get involved in a full-scale war with such a distant foe. So he first tried diplomacy, sending a small group of envoys to the shah and asking for financial restitution. Many of Chinggis's own family had probably invested in the caravan. He also asked for the governor of Otrar to be sent back to him.

Shah Muhammad not only refused these requests, but killed one diplomat and singed the beards of the others before sending them back to Chinggis Khan, a serious insult. There could be no possible response from Chinggis Khan now other than a declaration of war. It is difficult to know whether the Mongols would eventually have expanded into the vast Khwarazmian Empire at some stage in the future, but one source, Yelu Chucai, who actually accompanied Chinggis Khan on this new campaign, stated unequivocally that the massacre at Otrar was the sole reason for this new war in the west.

Tim May suggests that if this is true, it is a "far cry from attempting to conquer the world." And David Morgan notes that whatever the ultimate motivation of the Mongols might have been in expanding westwards, "the Khwarazmshah took the matter out of Chinggis Khan's hands and made war inevitable." Morgan is also clear on the consequences of the war that was about to break out: "[This] was probably the greatest calamity ever to befall the people of the eastern Islamic world."

The course of this brutal war will be followed in a future lecture, which will describe the utter devastation the Mongols inflicted on the peoples and lands of central Asia, including the shocking sacking of the great Silk Roads cities of Bukhara and Samarkand. Just after the conclusion of this war, Chinggis Khan would die from wounds received in a hunt. But as a result of the campaigns he led in central Asia in the final decade of his life, the world would never be the same again.

MONGOL INSTITUTIONS
UNDER CHINGGIS KHAN

This lecture discusses a few of the administrative and social innovations put in place by Chinggis Khan and his immediate successors. These transformed a bitterly divided, clan-based culture into a relatively harmonious, unified state. The innovations were the reorganization of Mongol society, taxation reforms, and the creation of a new law code: the Great Yasa.

The Reorganization of Mongol Society

When Temujin was declared Chinggis Khan in 1206, he realized that the Mongol way of life was one that had traditionally been dominated by blood feuds and bitter fragmentation along tribal lines. Determined to retain the unity that he had forged, he knew he would have to act quickly to ensure that that unity would not be as ephemeral as it had thus far always proven to be.

His answer to keeping his army unified was to almost immediately take it out of Mongolia and launch military campaigns in various directions, starting with an assault on the Jin dynasty in China to the south.

In his quest to forge a unified state, Chinggis Khan achieved nothing less than a social revolution among the Mongols. Part of the social revolution Chinggis Khan ignited was to reorganize the Mongol peoples themselves by using the same system he had created for his army.

Like the military, Mongol society was now reorganized into a series of *minqan*, essentially a group of 1,000 families. Mongol elites, including those who had supported Temujin during his years of struggle on the steppe, were assigned to be leaders of various *minqan*, and some of his closest followers were put in charge of more than one *minqan*. (The plural of *minqan* is *minqad*.)

These *minqad* were subdivided into 10 units of 100, which were subdivided again into 10 units of 10. Having both the military and Mongol society organized in this same decimal fashion made administration simpler, and it also meant that a *minqan* of 1,000 households was essentially supporting a *minqan* of 1,000 troops through the taxes the households paid and through the provision of young men to join the army.

Another aspect of Chinggis Khan's reorganization of the state was the introduction in 1206 of a new military unit that also served an important social function. This was the *keshik*, a military unit of 10,000 men made up of the sons of his military officers and commanders. The *keshik* served as a training school for potential new officers and government officials. Its duties were constantly extended, however, and eventually the *keshik* effectively functioned as Chinggis Khan's household staff.

Taxation Reforms

This lecture now turns to Chinggis Khan's taxation reforms. For 2,000 years before the advent of the Mongols, various militarized steppe nomadic societies across Eurasia had gained income and treasure through plundering the resources of nearby sedentary societies. Once the Mongols came to power, a more stable form of revenue was created through the introduction of a two-part taxation system. The two components were *alba*, which means "tribute," and *qubchur*, which was a type of special levy.

The *alba* was a form of tribute paid in goods and services to the ruling elite. In terms of social organization, it was also a mechanism whereby Mongol pastoralist families could demonstrate their loyalty to their leaders.

The *qubchur* was a levy that had traditionally only been applied in extraordinary times, when there was a specific need for resources. The *qubchur* was usually a one percent levy applied to the flocks and herds of all pastoralists, and it was also payable by individual Mongol soldiers. As the empire expanded further, however, the *qubchur* levy system evolved into something quite different from its original purpose. Following successful military campaigns, Mongol commanders would levy goods and services from recently conquered peoples.

This new hybrid form of taxation became known as the *alba qubchuri*, which included elements of both the old *alba* regular tribute and the *qubchur* extraordinary levy. The rate of the *alba qubchuri* differed if it was being applied to nomadic or sedentary subjects; the latter were always taxed at a higher rate than the nomads.

The system evolved again during the reign of Ogedai, the successor to Chinggis Khan, because of the influence of new non-Mongol administrators. One of these officials, Yelu Chucai, convinced Ogedai of the merits of conducting a census on the sedentary population of northern China in order to offer the khan a forecast of potential taxation revenue.

Yelu Chucai did this between 1235 and 1236, and then used the data he had collected to make the case that regular taxation would provide a much more stable source of income to the Mongols than plundering. His arguments were persuasive, and a taxation system based on the household was introduced.

As the Mongols continued to expand their empire, first under Chinggis Khan and then under his successors, the huge territories now under their control were eventually divided into a series of military and administrative units. In addition, to facilitate the regular collection of taxes, the empire was also divided into a series of regional fiscal units.

Laws

This lecture closes with a look at the laws introduced by Chinggis Khan. The original code, known as the Great Yasa, was revised at the *quiriltai* of 1218 and again at subsequent gatherings. The functions of the Great Yasa have been outlined by Frank McLynn, into some of its component parts, beginning with his "systematization of the traditional taboos of the steppes."

There undoubtedly existed numerous traditional steppe taboos and laws within all pastoral nomadic societies, particularly among the more militarized confederations, and writing these down would have made a great deal of sense.

Livestock animals had to be killed in a particular way, for example, generally with the restrained animal on its back while the butcher did his work cutting open the chest. In this way, all the blood would be retained inside the animal. The pastoral nomadic lifeway demanded that no part of the precious animals be wasted.

The most valuable animal of all, the horse, was protected by a slew of prohibitions. Striking a horse in anger was taboo, as was wounding the animal or, worst of all, stealing someone else's horse. These laws to protect the horse extended to include the implements one used to control the animal. Mongol soldiers were forbidden from leaning on their horsewhips and even from touching the whip with an arrow, thus defiling it.

Other taboos demonstrated the general reverence steppe nomads felt for other forms of life trying to eke out their existence in the harsh environment of the steppe. Young birds should never be caught, for example. Fire and water were also protected.

Another component of the Great Yasa is the guidance it provides for proper military conduct. It contains many quasi-proscriptive provisions concerned with military matters: how to mobilize the army efficiently, how to conduct successful campaigns, and what sort of relations needed to be established with conquered foreign states. If any officer failed in his duty or disobeyed his superiors, particularly the khan, the only penalty was death.

Soldiers faced the death penalty if they pillaged before having been given permission to do so by their commander. Failure to pick up the weapon of a fallen comrade would also result in death.

The Great Yasa also apparently contained explicit laws about the order of succession following the death of Chinggis Khan, part of his attempts to think about potential future problems in administering the empire. Although he was happy to promote military soldiers and commanders based on their merit, any successor to the position of Great Khan would have to be a direct descendant of Chinggis Khan himself.

MONGOL INSTITUTIONS UNDER CHINGGIS KHAN

LECTURE 6 TRANSCRIPT

This is how Ata-Malik Juvaini, one of the most important Persian sources on the early years of the Mongol Empire and a contemporary of many of the events he comments upon, describes the transformation of the pastoral nomadic tribes of the Mongolian Steppe following the rise of Chinggis Khan:

> Before the appearance of Chinggis Khan, they had no ruler or chief. Each tribe or two tribes lived separately, and there was constant fighting and hostility between them. Some of them regarded robbery and violence, immorality and debauchery as deeds of manliness and excellence. … Their clothing was of the skins of dogs and mice, and their food was the flesh of those animals and other dead things.

> And they continued in this indigence, privation and misfortune until the banner of Chinggis Khan's fortune was raised and they issued forth from the straits of hardship to the amplitude of well-being, from a prison into a garden, from the desert of poverty into a palace of delight and from abiding torments into reposeful pleasances.

Now, determining precisely what Juvaini's purpose was in writing this passage, or indeed in creating his entire work, the splendidly titled *History of the World Conqueror*, is not always easy. Juvaini, who was born in Eastern Persia in 1226, came from a family of experienced government administrators. His grandfather had served as Minister for Finance under Shah Muhammad Jalal al-Din of the Khwarazmian Empire, and his father occupied the same important role under Mongol khan Ogedai, the successor to Chinggis Khan.

Juvaini followed them both into public office, serving as a senior administrator for various Mongol khans, and even visiting the Mongol capital of Karakorum on two occasions. His history of the Mongols actually starts in 1252 during one of his visits to Karakorum, and it ends in 1260, some two decades before his death. Juvaini was present when Khan Hulegu sacked the great Abbasid Caliphate capital of Baghdad in 1258, so in every way, Juvaini was an eyewitness to many of the great and terrible things the Mongols did in creating their empire. Because of his proximity to many of the events he describes, he is an important and generally reliable source on the rise of the Mongols, but his point of view is not always easy to pin down.

On the one hand, he never shrinks from describing the brutality of the Mongols, nor the destruction they unleashed, which one of his contemporaries, Ibn al-Athir, described as the greatest calamity ever to befall mankind. But Juvaini himself, employed by the Mongol khans in a high-status administrative position, could hardly have openly repeated this sort of condemnation. In several places, Juvaini actually blames Islamic rulers, such as the Khwarazm-Shah Muhammad, as much as the Mongols, for the devastation that was unleashed upon their kingdoms, suggesting that this was the fulfilment of the will of Allah.

In other places, such as the passage with which we opened this lecture, Juvaini offers what we can only interpret as genuine high praise for the Mongol leadership. In particular, as Juvaini's most important translator into English, J. A. Boyle, points out, "he had a genuine admiration for the military genius of Chinggis Khan, of whom Alexander himself, he says, would have been content to be a pupil."

But as we have just heard, it is not only the military genius of the Mongol leaders that Juvaini extols; he also praises their social virtues. In particular, he praises the spirit of harmony that prevailed amongst the Mongols, along with their social informality and their religious tolerance. When we think of the spirit of decided disharmony that clearly prevailed between the Turkic-Mongolic tribes on the steppe before the rise of Chinggis Khan, we must acknowledge that the great khan's genius clearly extended well beyond the realm of just the military.

And that is the subject of this lecture: to discuss a few of the administrative and social innovations put in place by Chinggis Khan and his immediate successors in order to transform a bitterly divided steppe clan-based culture into a relatively harmonious, unified state. His ability to achieve this was as much responsible for subsequent Mongol success as the military effectiveness of the army.

In this lecture, we'll explore three innovations introduced by Chinggis Khan to unify and modernize the Mongol state he had created: his reorganization of Mongol society, his taxation reforms, and the creation of a new law code, the so-called Great Yasa.

To his social reorganization first. When Temujin was declared Chinggis Khan at the quriltai of 1206, he realized that as his own life experiences had exemplified, the Mongol way of life was one that had traditionally been dominated by blood feuds and bitter fragmentation along tribal lines. Determined to retain the unity that he had forged, he knew he would have to act quickly to ensure that that unity would not be as ephemeral as it had thus far always proven to be. His answer to keeping his army unified was to almost immediately take it out of Mongolia and launch military campaigns in various directions, starting with an assault on the Jin Dynasty in China to the south.

In his quest to forge a unified state, Chinggis Khan achieved nothing less than a social revolution amongst the Mongols in order to retain the fragile unity he had created through his personal strategic and diplomatic skills. Part of the social revolution Chinggis Khan ignited was to reorganize the Mongol peoples themselves—the civilians, if you like—by using the same system he had created for his army.

Like the military, Mongol society was now reorganized into a series of *minqan*, essentially a group of 1,000 families. Mongol elites, including those who had supported Temujin during his years of struggle on the steppe, were assigned to be leaders of various *minqan*, and some of his closest followers were put in charge of more than one *minqan*.

Also like the army, these *minqad*, which is the plural of *minqan*, were subdivided into 10 units of 100, which were subdivided again into 10 units of 10. Having both the military and Mongol society organized in this same decimal fashion not only made administration simpler, but it also meant that a *minqan* of 1,000 households was essentially supporting a *minqan* of 1,000 troops through the taxes the households paid and through the provision of young men to join the army.

Of course, Chinggis Khan had to take special care of the members of his own family, and he did this by granting them territories to control and by giving many of them a *minqan* to lead. But he also assigned trusted military commanders to help supervise these *minqad*, and their role was to advise and in effect supervise the members of Chinggis Khan's family. This was a system that had been used many times in the past by Chinese emperors as a way of ensuring that family members would not conspire against the ruler nor become too autonomous in the territories and households they controlled.

Chinggis Khan's military officers were generally hard-nosed professional soldiers who had risen through the ranks because of their skills and tenacity, which meant that their position was based not on social rank but on the esteem and respect the great khan held for each of them. This meant that Chinggis Khan could trust these men to do their jobs, both in battle and in advising his relations in the administration of their *minqad*, because these men owed absolute loyalty to the great khan, who had been responsible for them achieving their rank.

Chinggis Khan's own family was assigned extraordinary status in the new Mongol social world, a situation that would have long-term historical implications. With few traditional aristocratic families having survived the various military campaigns during Temujin's rise to power, his own family was now designated the *altan urugh*, or the Golden Kin, the Golden Family. They were further recognized as the *chagan yasun*, which means the white-boned elite, in contrast to the surviving remnants of the old Mongol aristocracy who were the *qara yasun*, the black-boned elite, who were very definitely subordinate to the Golden Family.

Another clever way Chinggis Khan attempted to erase the old tribal affiliations, so prone to splintering, was to populate most of each *minqad* with those households that had supported him during his rise to power. Once an enemy tribe like the Naiman or Merkit had been defeated in battle, they were then diffused and distributed amongst many pre-existing *minqad*. In addition, moving from one *minqan* to another was strictly forbidden. By these various methods, Chinggis Khan did everything he could to ensure that former enemies could never again form a unified block of resistance.

Another aspect of Chinggis Khan's reorganization of the state was the introduction in 1206 of a new military unit that also served an important social function. This was the *keshik*, or bodyguard, a military unit of 10,000 men made up of the sons of his military commanders and officers.

We will have more to say about military implications of this later in the course, but we should note here that the *keshik* served as a training school for potential new officers, but also for new government officials. Its duties were constantly extended, however, and eventually the *keshik* effectively functioned as Chinggis Khan's household staff, tasked with all sorts of duties to ensure the smooth functioning of the state and empire.

And of course, comprising as it did the sons of his military commanders, it helped ensure the loyalty of those commanders to the supreme commander, Chinggis Khan himself.

Taken together, these measures constituted a brilliant piece of social engineering. As Tim May puts it, "In doing this, Chinggis Khan created a single tribe or nation, the Yeke Mongol Ulus or Great Mongol State. No longer were they Kereit, Tatars or any other identity, but Mongols."

Let's turn now from Chinggis Khan's social reorganization, the effectiveness of which is widely acknowledged by medieval sources and modern scholars alike, to his taxation and law reforms. There is far less agreement amongst scholars over the effectiveness of these reforms, and indeed whether these taxation and legal innovations even deserve to be called "systems."

David Morgan, for example, in assessing Mongol taxation, asks: "Can what the Mongols did in this sphere be dignified with the name of system?" Thomas Allsen, on the other hand, is equally explicit in writing that one of Chinggis Khan's successors, Mongke Khan, "created a new system of Mongol-Inspired tribute to which all adults were subject." Tim May also argues that the Mongols eventually established "a formal taxation system," although not so much under the first khan, Chinggis.

Some 2,000 years before the advent of the Mongols, various militarized steppe nomadic societies all across Eurasia had gained their income and treasure through plundering the resources of nearby sedentary societies. Once the Mongols came to power, a more stable form of revenue was created through the introduction of a two-part taxation system, if I can use that word. The two components were *alba*, which means "tribute," and *qubchur*, which was a type of special levy.

The *alba* was a form of tribute paid in goods and services to the ruling elite. So in terms of social organization, it was also a mechanism whereby Mongol pastoralist families could demonstrate their loyalty to their leaders. The *qubchur* was a levy that had been traditionally only applied in extraordinary times, when there was a specific need for resources. The *qubchur* was usually a 1 percent levy applied to the flocks and herds of all pastoralists, and it was also payable by individual Mongol soldiers.

The Secret History of the Mongols describes one such *qubchur* levied by Chinggis Khan himself on his subjects to support a leader of the Keraits who had arrived impoverished at Chinggis Khan's camp. As Mongol rule progressed, the *qubchur* became formalized, and families were expected to tithe 10 percent of their possessions to the state.

As the empire expanded further, however, the *qubchur* levy system evolved into something quite different from its original purpose. Following successful military campaigns, Mongol commanders would levy goods and services from recently conquered peoples, and this new hybrid form of taxation became known as the *alba qubchuri*, which included elements of both the old *alba* regular tribute and the *qubchar* extraordinary levy. The rate of the *alba qubchuri* differed if it was being applied to nomadic or sedentary subjects; the latter were always taxed at a higher rate than the nomads.

But this was not the end of the development of Mongol taxation. The system evolved again during the reign of Ogedai, the successor to Chinggis Khan, because of the influence of non-Mongol administrators. One of these officials, Yelu Chucai, convinced Ogedai of the merits of conducting a census on the sedentary population of northern China in order to offer the khan a forecast of potential taxation revenue. Yelu Chucai did this between 1235 and 1236 and then used the data he had collected to make the case that regular taxation would provide a much more stable source of income to the Mongols than plundering. His arguments were persuasive, and a taxation system based on the household was introduced in keeping with millennia of taxation of households by previous Chinese dynastic administrations.

A version of this system was also introduced in central Asia by Muslim administrator Mahmud Yalavach, although with a significant variation. Yalavach used the old term for an extraordinary levy, the *qubchur*, but converted this into a poll tax levied on adult males that had to be paid in cash. Some historians wonder if this was influenced by the Islamic form of taxation that had been in place in the region for centuries, the *jizya*.

Another possible influence on these taxation innovations might have come from the Uyghurs, now well incorporated into the Mongol Empire. Thomas Allsen has argued that a version of the *qubchar* based on a cash poll tax had been used by the Uyghurs in the administration of their empire several centuries earlier, and that the Mongols might have adopted this from their imperial steppe predecessors. Whatever its precedents, as central Asian/ Persian models of administration became more widely used across the vast Mongol Empire, a similar cash poll tax on individuals was also introduced in China after 1236.

As the Mongols continued to expand their empire, first under Chinggis Khan and then under his successors, the huge territories now under their control were eventually divided into a series of military and administrative units. In addition, to facilitate the regular collection of taxes, the empire was also divided into a series of regional fiscal units.

By the reign of Guyuk Khan in the 1240s, there were three such fiscal districts: northern China, Turkestan in central Asia, and Khurasan-Mazandaran in Persia. Various pastoral nomadic peoples had their homes in each of these three regions, but the taxation revenue the Mongols collected from these fiscal districts was mostly levied from the sedentary farming and artisan populations. By 1257, large swathes of territory formerly controlled by the princes of Kievan Rus had also been incorporated into the Mongol empire, and these were added as an additional fiscal administrative unit.

In the 1250s, the taxation "system" evolved again. It now consisted partly of taxes levied at the local level and additional "extraordinary" levies enacted a couple of times each year, often two or three years in advance. Mongke Khan attempted to modify this system by replacing these extraordinary levies with a system of tribute payable to the Mongols by all adults living within the empire.

Farmers were also subject to an additional agricultural tax (from which the nomads were exempt), and there were also duties levied on all commercial transactions, but more on this in just a moment. By these various measures, and particularly by having only representatives of the Mongol government collect the taxes, Mongke hoped to further consolidate power within the Mongol imperial elite and diminish the power of local elites and administrators.

Like most militarized nomadic steppe empires, the Mongols strongly encouraged commerce within their empire and put in place a system whereby merchants were afforded official accreditation and thus Mongol protection.

Ever cognizant of the profits to be made from successful commerce, the Mongols also granted merchants exemption from regular *qubchur* or *alba* taxation. But in return for this support and safeguarding of commercial activity, the Mongols did levy a special tax on all commercial transactions.

This tax was known as the *tamgha* and was generally levied at the rate of 5 percent on each transaction. It was mostly charged to the sale of goods but also apparently to some services, as one source mentions that it was levied on prostitution. Some scholars wonder whether the Mongols' support of business and trade was in some way a reflection of their inability to adjust to sedentary rural or city life. Whether they remained mostly nomadic or semi-sedentary, the Mongols would always appreciate the importance, and financial value to them, of trade within the empire and within the regions beyond.

It wasn't just merchants who enjoyed immunity from regular taxation, however; many religious organizations and spiritual leaders were also granted maximum exemptions. As further evidence of the Mongols well-deserved reputation for religious tolerance, these exemptions were extended to religious and spiritual leaders from virtually all faiths: Buddhism, shamanism, Islam, Nestorian, Christianity, and so on. We will have more to say about this in a future lecture.

The motive for the raft of taxes introduced by Chinggis Khan and his successors was obviously to produce income for the Mongols, pure and simple. As David Morgan puts it, "the purpose of the taxes imposed on the conquered populations was quite simply the maximum conceivable degree of exploitation." Once much of the Islamic world had fallen to the Mongols, the burden of taxation that fell on the people dwelling in the realm was heavier even than it had been under the Khwarazm-Shah.

As we have just seen, experienced administrators like Yelu Chucai in China and Mahmud Yalavach in central Asia were able to convince their Mongol overlords of the value of a steady revenue income as opposed to debilitating *qubchur*-like extraordinary levies. But the bottom line is that the Mongol approach to taxation was essentially the same as that of most conquerors in world history: to enrich themselves. The way of achieving this end certainly changed over time, but as Morgan puts it, "enrichment remained the most important concern of the Mongol elites."

Finally, let's turn to the laws introduced by Chinggis Khan following the quriltai of 1206, which has traditionally been regarded as one of his greatest achievements. The original code, known as the Great Yasa, was subsequently revised at the quriltai of 1218 and again at subsequent gatherings. It is difficult to precisely sum up the many purposes and concerns of the Great Yasa, but this is how historian Frank McLynn thoughtfully does so:

> It was partly a "King's Regulations" guide to military conduct, partly the systematization of the traditional taboos of the steppes, partly a collection of the various ideas, jottings and aperçus of the great khan himself, and partly an attempt to think through some of the problems the empire might face in the future.

As with Mongol taxation, there is disagreement between scholars concerning the Yasa. Because no definitive written version of the code exists, some scholars wonder whether it ever did exist in written form at all, or whether Chinggis Khan simply promoted the idea that it existed so that he could issue decrees and rulings at will and justify them by saying it was all in the code. This would be particularly useful in a society that was essentially illiterate, for no one would ever be able to check whether what the khan said was in the code actually was in the code.

Yet the important 14th-century Islamic traveler Ibn Batutta, arguably the greatest traveler of the premodern world, wrote that the Yasa did indeed exist as a written, systematic document, and that it was written in the Uyghur script. Juvaini also devotes part of his *History of the World Conqueror* to the Yasa, although intriguingly, another major Persian source on the Mongols, Rashid al-Din, makes no mention of it.

Let's break the list of functions of the Yasa, as outlined by McLynn, into some of its component parts, beginning with his "systemitization of the traditional taboos of the steppes." There undoubtedly existed numerous traditional steppe taboos and laws within all pastoral nomadic societies, particularly amongst the more militarized confederations, and writing these down in the Yasa would have made a great deal of sense.

Livestock animals had to be killed in a particular way, for example, generally with the restrained animal on his back while the butcher did his work cutting open the chest. In this way, all the blood would be retained inside the animal. The pastoral nomadic lifeway demanded that no part of the precious animals be wasted.

The most valuable animal of all, the horse, was protected by a slew of prohibitions. Striking a horse in anger was taboo, as was wounding the animal or, worst of all, stealing someone else's horse. These laws to protect the horse extended to include the implements you used to control the animal. So Mongol soldiers were forbidden from leaning on their horsewhips and even from touching the whip with an arrow, thus defiling it.

Other taboos demonstrated the general reverence steppe nomads felt for other forms of life trying to eke out their existence in the harsh environment of the steppe. Young birds should never be caught, for example. Fire and water were also protected. A fire should never be "beheaded" by touching it with a knife; one should never wash in a running stream in spring or summer, to keep the water clean. Nor should one ever urinate into water, or spill liquid on the ground. There were also strict taboos against spitting food on the ground, which was seen as a very serious breach of steppe etiquette, punishable by death. And it was strictly forbidden to tread on the threshold of a khan's tent, which was sacred.

If Chinggis Khan did actually arrange to have all these taboos written down and incorporated into the Great Yasa, the effect would have been, like the impact of his social reforms, to achieve even greater unity amongst the disparate peoples that now found themselves part of the new Mongol state, unified behind one ruler and by a common set of laws.

Another component of the Yasa is the guidance it provides for proper military conduct. The organization and tactics of the Mongol military will be the subject of another lecture, but here we can note that the Yasa does indeed contain many quasi-proscriptive provisions concerned with military matters: how to mobilize the army efficiently, how to conduct successful campaigns, and what sort of relations needed to be established with conquered foreign states.

If any officer failed in his duty or disobeyed his superiors, particularly the khan, the only penalty was death. In order to ensure the khan's officers could never conspire against him, the leaders of the *minqad* could communicate directly only with the khan, not with each other. And if *minqad* leaders committed some sort of offence, they had to prostrate themselves before the often-low-class messenger Chinggis Khan would inevitably send to recall them to further their humiliation. All military commanders also had to attend a meeting with Chinggis Khan once a year so that he could assess their continued ability to lead.

To help ensure that military service remained highly attractive to the young men of the steppe, the Yasa discouraged eligible men from pursuing any sort of alternative by declaring that should they choose not to enlist in the military, they would have to do harsh and unpaid work for the state instead. Soldiers reporting for duty after the call for mobilization had to be fully prepared to march with equipment and horses in peak condition or risk being fined. And if a soldier failed to report for duty, his wife might be appointed in his place.

According to the Yasa, soldiers faced the death penalty if they pillaged before having been given permission to do so by their commander. Failure to pick up the weapon of a fallen comrade would also result in death. And if many Mongols fell in a particular battle, the survivors might also be put to death as punishment for failure. As Frank McLynn points out, the harsh attitude Chinggis Khan exhibited towards his soldiers was meant to inculcate the same attitude as the Spartans: Come back from a battle either victorious and carrying your shield, or dead and carried on it.

The Great Yasa also apparently contained explicit laws about the order of succession following the death of Chinggis Khan—part of his attempts to think about potential future problems in administering the empire. Although he was happy to promote military soldiers and commanders based on their merit, any successor to the position of great khan would have to be a direct descendant of Chinggis Khan himself. The Chingissids would thus be the only clan ever to rule the empire, and centuries after the empire had disappeared, Chingissid descendants would still be claiming and receiving special status all across inner Eurasia.

By these various methods, then—a social revolution and the introduction of various innovations in taxation and law, as loose as they might seem to some modern understandings—Chinggis Khan was able to achieve the very thing Juvaini praised him for in the passage that opened this lecture. Once Chinggis Khan's banner was raised, the Mongols "issued forth from the straits of hardship to the amplitude of well-being, from a prison into a garden, from the desert of poverty into a palace of delight and from abiding torments into reposeful pleasances."

Let's also leave the final thoughts in this lecture to Juvaini. We last left Chinggis Khan and his army poised to begin an invasion of the vast realms of the Khwarazm-Shah Muhammad II, who through his various actions (including murdering the khan's merchants and envoys) had so insulted Chinggis Khan that the only possible response could be war.

This is the portrait Juvaini paints of the Mongol army on the eve of the invasion—an army honed by warfare and unified by the various laws and procedures Chinggis Khan had put in place to bring them to the peak of their effectiveness: "They were archers who by the shooting of an arrow would bring down a hawk from the hollow of the ether, and on dark nights with the thrust of a spear-head would cast out a fish from the bottom of the sea; who thought the day of battle the marriage night, and considered the pricks of lances the kisses of fair maidens."

These were the troops about to descend on central Asia and the great cities of Samarkand, Bukhara, Merv, and Nishapur, which frankly never stood a chance against them. In the year 1218, the invasion began, and that invasion will be the subject of our next lecture.

CHINGGIS KHAN'S KHWARAZMIAN CAMPAIGN

In the early 1220s, central Asia saw a campaign of dreadful but brilliant warfare unleashed by Chinggis Khan. That campaign, which was waged against the ruler of the Khwarazmian empire, Shah Muhammad, is the subject of this lecture. If any single campaign is responsible for history bestowing on the Mongols their reputation for brutality and terrorism, it is this.

Background and the Beginning

Chinggis Khan and his army came to the brink of an invasion of central Asia after Muhammad grievously insulted the Mongols. The shah allowed the governor of the city of Otrar to massacre a trade delegation that Chinggis Khan had dispatched in 1218. Chinggis, although enraged, decided to seek financial restitution from the governor and shah rather than attacking another huge empire. The governor not only refused this attempt at diplomacy but further exacerbated the situation by killing the khan's envoy and singeing the beards of his guards before sending them back to Chinggis Khan.

This was an insult that could not be overlooked. The only possible response now was war. Leaving his general Muqali and a contingent of troops to continue the campaigns against the Jin dynasty in China, Chinggis Khan marched 2,000 miles westward, reinforced by troops provided by his Uyghur and Qarluq allies. He was determined to attack and destroy the Khwarazmian Empire and its shah.

The first strategic target for the Mongols was the town of Otrar, where the governor had massacred Chinggis Khan's caravan of merchants. Otrar's fortification had been reinforced, and the governor now had up to 60,000 troops at his disposal. After camping in front of the town, Chinggis Khan divided his forces, dispatching his generals and their troops to various locations. He personally headed into the desert, ultimately toward the great commercial city of Bukhara, leaving his sons Ogedai and Chagatai in charge of the assault on Otrar.

The town was so well fortified that this turned into a siege of several months' duration, but eventually the outer town fell and was looted and devastated by Mongol soldiers. The Mongols departed with the governor in chains. When the armies reunited, Chinggis Khan executed him with ironic brutality. Because of the governor's greed in murdering the merchant caravan and seizing its assets, the Mongols poured molten silver into his ears and throat, and he died an agonizing death.

Tolui

The Siege of Bukhara

The larger campaign then proceeded with successful assaults by different Mongol armies and generals on other towns and small cities. Shah Muhammad, desperate to know the whereabouts of these dangerous forces, was frustrated by the lack of intelligence.

In February 1220, Chinggis Khan, with his youngest son Tolui and his army, suddenly and shockingly reappeared hundreds of miles from where Muhammad had last known him to be, right in front of the walls of Bukhara. Chinggis Khan had crossed the harsh and arid Kyzlkum Desert.

Bukhara was one of the largest cities in the Islamic world, perhaps 36 square miles in area and surrounded by a high wall, with an impressive and heavily fortified inner citadel. Bukhara's defenses had been bolstered with thousands of new troops, information Chinggis Khan was able to gain from spies dwelling in the poorer parts of the city.

The Mongol siege of Bukhara lasted for 12 days. It was so relentless and its outcome so clearly inevitable that the defensive forces commander lost his nerve and tried to escape with 20,000 troops on the 12th night. The army was pursued and massacred on the banks of the Amu Darya. The citizens of Bukhara promptly surrendered to the Mongols, although a small garrison of defenders in the citadel held out for another 11 days before they were captured and killed around February 15, 1220. The walls of Bukhara were levelled, and all the inhabitants were driven out of the city.

The Siege of Samarkand

Word of the capture and destruction of Bukhara spread throughout the Khwarazmian Empire, including to the residents of the great city of Samarkand. Samarkand was the obvious next target for Chinggis Khan. It was another splendid city that had grown wealthy from centuries of trade and successful irrigation agriculture. In the 1220s, it was home to perhaps 100,000 people.

The walls of the city were tremendous and thought to be impregnable. To increase its defensive capabilities, the shah had stationed 60,000 Turkic troops and 50,000 Tajiks inside those massive walls. The shah himself had also fled to Samarkand to escape the Mongol armies.

The army of Chinggis and Tolui was now reinforced by that of Ogedai and Chagatai, following their victory in the siege of Otrar. The Mongols also placed dummies and propped up unmanned shields in the fields to make their forces look even more numerous.

The Mongol assault began on the third day, as wave after wave of the captured residents of Bukhara were sent charging against the defenses as fodder. When many of these men broke and fled away from the defenders on the walls, the commanders in the city wrongly imagined it was the Mongols that had broken. As the shah's forces came charging triumphantly out of the city, they fell right into the Mongol ambush and were slaughtered by the tens of thousands by the real Mongol soldiers.

The Mongols now poured into the suburbs while the remaining defenders retreated to the heavily fortified inner city. Shah Muhammad, psychologically broken, escaped in the night with 30,000 horsemen and fled into the heartland of Khurasan. Chinggis Khan immediately dispatched the formidable military leaders Jebe and Subedai and their troops to pursue him.

A delegation of citizens now came out of Samarkand to offer their surrender to Chinggis Khan. Five days later, the garrison inside the fortified inner city asked for terms of surrender. Chinggis promised he would spare them, but once they had surrendered, they were slaughtered. The great city was completely secured a day later. By the end of March 1220, Samarkand belonged to the Mongols. The usual aftermath followed. Useful artisans were sent back to Mongolia, others were recruited to be human shields at the next assault, and various treasuries were confiscated. Chinggis Khan then gave his men permission to rape, plunder, and kill at their discretion.

The Campaign Resumes

In May, the campaign was resumed. City after city was now destined to endure Chinggis Khan's wrath. Termez, an ancient and sacred Buddhist city on the Amu Darya, experienced this first; after the city fell, each Mongol soldier was given a quota of men and women to kill, and the residents were struck down without mercy.

Next was Balkh to the south, another legendary commercial city of the ancient Silk Roads. The city authorities and elders, hoping to spare the fate of Samarkand and Termez, came out to surrender, offering the Mongols all sorts of tribute and treasure. Chinggis Khan did not trust this promise of submission, however; he knew that the shah's son Jalal al-Din was active in the region. He decided that none should be allowed to live.

Chinggis had been right to worry about al-Din. Word now reached him that the Khwarazmian general had just defeated a badly outnumbered Mongol contingent commanded by Shigi Qutuqu. Al-Din then escaped south over the Hindu Kush. Enraged, Chinggis Khan pursued him through modern Afghanistan, in as merciless a mood as could be imagined. At the fall of the town of Bamiyan, he ordered that every living creature in the city be killed.

Meanwhile, as this terrible pursuit of Jalal al-Din continued, another Mongol contingent led by Tolui and Chinggis's son-in-law Toghutshar was dispatched to attack perhaps the greatest of the Silk Roads cities of central Asia: Merv. After unsuccessful efforts to repel the Mongols, the commander of the forces inside the city quickly came to the decision that the only hope of survival lay in surrendering.

The Mongols rode in through the gates and ordered all the inhabitants to leave the city, a process that took several days. They separated the men from the women and took a few hundred useful artisans and the most beautiful women. Then, Tolui gave the order that everyone else was to be killed.

Historians estimate that somewhere between 700,000 and 1 million people probably died in the massacre at Merv, one of the most brutal sackings of a city in the history of the world. Merv was just one of many cities destroyed by Tolui during his campaign in the region known as Khurasan.

The Siege of Nishapur

After the conquest of Merv, Tolui's army headed east toward Nishapur in modern Iran. As they rode, they encountered groups of refugees fleeing from the devastation of Merv, which the Mongols cut down and killed.

Shah Muhammad had fled to Nishapur from Balkh. Once there, surrounded by bad omens, he warned the people to flee the city before the Mongols arrived. When the inhabitants mostly ignored his warning, the shah used the excuse of a hunting trip to escape the city, joined by a few others.

The Mongol advanced guard soon arrived at the gates, and the governor, uncertain what to do, gave them food. Then, an army of 10,000 Mongols led by Toghutshar arrived. These were the vanguard of Tolui's forces. As Toghutshar tried to enter the gates of Nishapur, defenders fired arrows down upon the Mongols, one of which dealt Toghutshar a mortal wound.

At this, the Mongols withdrew and spent some time destroying smaller towns in the vicinity of Nishapur. Winter intervened and the Mongols withdrew, leaving the dispirited residents of Nishapur to survive on limited supplies of food.

In the spring of 1221, Tolui was back, this time with all the siege equipment necessary to take the city. At dawn on April 7, 1221, the siege commenced. As the days progressed, the Mongols gradually filled the moat and scaled the walls on ladders. Thousands of Mongols were eventually in the streets, laying waste and killing at will. After the campaign ended, Tolui and his forces marched back across the Amu Darya, leaving Khurasan in ruins.

The Pursuits End

Meanwhile, the relentless pursuits of the shah and his son continued, with Chinggis Khan's army chasing Jalal al-Din in southern Afghanistan. The army of Jebe and Subedai pursued Shah Muhammad, who was fleeing all over his former empire in panic. Eventually, the shah fled northwest to the shores of the Caspian Sea with Jebe and Subedai in pursuit. At times, they split their forces in two to sack cities along the way.

The shah decided to seek refuge on a small island in the Caspian Sea itself. The Mongols, never comfortable at sea, nonetheless launched an amphibious assault on the island, but by the time they arrived the shah had fled to another. Sometime in January 1221, he died a miserable death— possibly of dysentery, pleurisy, or pneumonia—and he was buried on the island, wrapped in a torn white shirt for a shroud.

Jalal al-Din was still at large. He continued to flee southward into the Indus Valley of modern Pakistan. Chinggis Khan and his forces finally caught their intrepid foe on the banks of the Indus River. Refusing to be captured, Jalal al-Din spurred his horse to the edge of a cliff. Both horse and master fell into the Indus River, escaping his pursuers by swimming across to the other side.

He was joined by other elements of the Khwarazmian army, and they rode south through thick forests and then out onto the great plains of northern India. At Chinggis's command, Mongol commander Dorbei Doqshin pursued their quarry into these same Indian plains. But after sacking a few towns, they lost the scent of Jalal al-Din and returned to rejoin the main Mongol army in Afghanistan. After this, the Khwarazmian campaign was essentially over. The bulk of the Mongol army now regrouped and rode back to Mongolia.

The future of the regions devastated in these campaigns was incredibly bleak. Hundreds of thousands of these people were now dead, and the formerly lush and fertile agricultural lands were ruined.

CHINGGIS KHAN'S KHWARAZMIAN CAMPAIGN

I have been fortunate enough in my life to visit on several occasions two of the most fabled cities in the long history of the Silk Roads, Bukhara and Samarkand, both located in the modern nation of Uzbekistan. These are thriving cities today, with large populations of successful Uzbeks going about their business in modern suburbs and the superbly preserved historical centers. Both cities have histories dating back thousands of years, and they have endured and prospered under the rule of many a foreign conqueror, including Persians, Macedonians, Parthians, Sasanians, Arabs, Samanids, Russians, and so many others. Yet both these cities undoubtedly faced their darkest hours when Chinggis Khan and the devastating Mongol war machine suddenly appeared below their walls in 1220 and then proceeded to utterly destroy them.

Samarkand can trace its history back a long way, perhaps to as early as 700 BCE, when it was founded as a Sogdian commercial settlement. Bukhara is probably a couple of centuries younger, founded sometime around 500 BCE, also by Sogdians, although traces of human settlement in the Bukharan oasis have been found dating back to the 3rd millennium BCE. So these cities have long records of durability and survival, of destruction and rebirth, of triumphant renewal despite the ravages of conquerors, and both did indeed rebuild following the Mongol devastation.

I have also walked the walls of Merv, one of the greatest cities of ancient Eurasia, located in the modern nation of Turkmenistan. Merv's history is perhaps even more extraordinary than that of Samarkand or Bukhara. Merv is incredibly old, dating back to the 3rd millennium BCE. It was founded in the Murghab delta, a lush oasis in the heart of the Kara-Kum Desert, a superbly strategic location for migrants, farmers, and merchants on the Silk Roads.

Merv also flourished under a range of foreign conquerors: the Persian king Cyrus; Alexander and the Macedonians; the powerful kings of the Parthian and Kushan Empires; Sasanian king Ardashir I; Qutayba ibn Muslim, the general who led the conquest of central Asia for the Arabs; Seljuk rulers like Alp Arsalan and Sultan Sanjar—the list goes on and on.

By the mid-12th century, Merv was one of the largest cities in the world, with a population of 200,000 people in the city alone, and many, many more in the surrounding region. As Ata-Malik Juvaini describes it:

> Merv was the residence of Sultan Sanjar and the rendezvous of great and small. In extent of territory it excelled among the lands of Khorasan, and the bird of peace and serenity flew over its confines. The number of its chief men rivalled the drops of April rain, and its earth contended with the heavens.

But in February 1221, Chinggis Khan's youngest son, Tolui, turned up, leading a skilled and battle-hardened Mongol army. By the time they had finished, the city was utterly devastated, its irrigation infrastructure destroyed, and somewhere between 700,000 and 1 million people were dead. So many were killed that, as Juvaini describes it, "by nightfall ... the plain was soaked with the blood of the mighty."

Subsequent rulers of the region made sporadic attempts to rebuild parts of the once-great city, but to little avail. Today the city is just a collection of mounds of earth, the remains of palaces and citadels and walls. The devastation heaped upon Merv by the Mongols was so overwhelming that the city never recovered.

In all these cities of central Asia, those that recovered and those that did not, the Mongol legacy is still palpable today, the living memory of a single campaign of dreadful but brilliant warfare unleashed on the region by Chinggis Khan in the early 1220s. This campaign, waged against the ruler of the Khwarazmian Empire, Shah Muhammad, and his cities and people, is the subject of this lecture. If any single campaign is responsible for history bestowing on the Mongols their reputation for brutality and terrorism, it is this.

We last left Chinggis Khan and his army on the brink of an invasion of central Asia after Muhammad had so grievously insulted the Mongols by allowing the governor of the city of Otrar to massacre a trade delegation that Chinggis Khan had dispatched in 1218. Chinggis, although enraged, decided to seek financial restitution from the governor and shah rather than attacking another huge empire. The governor not only refused this attempt at diplomacy but further exacerbated the situation by killing the khan's envoy and singeing the beards of his guards before sending them back to Chinggis Khan.

This was an insult that could not be overlooked. The only possible response now was war. Leaving his general Muqali and a contingent of troops to continue the campaigns against the Jin Dynasty in China, Chinggis Khan marched 2,000 miles westwards, reinforced by troops provided by his Uyghur and Qarluq allies, determined to attack and destroy the Khwarazmian Empire and its shah.

Muhammad, who you might remember had had a previous encounter with a unit of superb Mongol cavalry, was immediately unnerved. He raised fresh troops and decided on a strategy of defending the cities of the empire and avoiding any sort of confrontation with the Mongols on open ground. His gallant and militarily gifted son Jalal al-Din opposed the strategy, but Muhammad probably had no real alternative than to increase the fortifications of his cities and wait, as Tim May puts it, "for the hammer to fall."

The first strategic target for the Mongols was the town of Otrar, where the governor had massacred Chinggis Khan's caravan of merchants. Otrar's fortification had been reinforced, and according to Juvaini, the governor now had up to 60,000 troops at his disposal. After camping in front of the town, Chinggis Khan divided his forces, dispatching his generals and their troops to various locations. He personally headed into the desert, ultimately towards the great commercial city of Bukhara, leaving his sons Ogedai and Chagatai in charge of the assault on Otrar.

The town was so well fortified that this turned into a siege of several months' duration, but eventually the outer town fell and was looted and devastated by Mongol soldiers. The governor took refuge in the citadel with 20,000 troops and resisted for another month, but with most of his men dead, he was eventually captured. The citadel and its walls were leveled; a large number of useful individuals, including artisans, were recruited; and the Mongols departed with the governor still in chains.

When the armies reunited, Chinggis Khan executed him with ironic brutality. Because of the governor's greed in murdering the merchant caravan and seizing its assets, the Mongols poured molten silver into his ears and throat, and he died an agonizing death.

The larger campaign then proceeded with successful assaults by different Mongol armies and generals on other towns and small cities. Shah Muhammad, desperate to know the whereabouts of these dangerous forces, was frustrated by the lack of intelligence. Jochi led his forces along the River

Jaxartes (the modern Syr Darya), heading to the commercial city of Urgench and the Khwarazmian heartland. Ogedai and Chagatai headed for the same strategic targets but by a different route. And Chinggis Khan and his forces simply disappeared completely from Muhammad's radar.

The Mongols were now in the fabled land of Transoxiana, essentially the region east of the Oxus River (the modern Amu Darya) and west of the ancient Jaxartes River (the modern Syr Darya). As Juvaini describes it, "Transoxiana comprises many countries, regions, districts and townships, but the kernel and cream thereof are Bukhara and Samarkand." Chinggis Khan had decided to personally lead the assault on these two great cities, fabled since the first great Silk Roads era had first connected much of Eurasia 1,300 years earlier.

As we have already noted, in February 1220, to Shah Muhammad's utter dismay, Chinggis Khan, with his youngest son Tolui and his army, suddenly and shockingly reappeared hundreds of miles from where the shah had last known him to be, right in front of the walls of Bukhara. As further testament to Chinggis Khan's strategic brilliance and the stamina of his cavalry, he had crossed the harsh and arid Kizil Kum Desert, which I can assure you from personal experience is no place to take an army.

Frank McLynn argues that this march through the desert to outflank the shah's forces was one of the most extraordinary exploits in the long annals of military history; it was brilliant, innovative, creative, and is further evidence that Chinggis Khan was a "strategist of genius."

Juvaini offers a graphic description of the reaction of the citizens of Bukhara as they looked out from their city walls next morning, which we related in our very first lecture: "When the inhabitants ... beheld the surrounding countryside choked with horsemen and the air black as night with the dust of cavalry, fright and panic overcame them, and fear and dread prevailed."

Bukhara was one of the largest cities in the Islamic world, perhaps 36 square miles in area and surrounded by a very high wall, with an impressive and heavily fortified inner citadel. The city was a mixture of ramshackle suburbs and wooden dwellings, of beautiful mosques, sumptuous residences and gardens, great centers of learning, and was undoubtedly very wealthy. Bukhara's defenses had been bolstered with thousands of new troops, information Chinggis Khan was able to gain from spies dwelling in the poorer parts of the city.

The Mongol siege of Bukhara lasted for 12 days and was so relentless and inevitable that the nerve of the commander of the defensive forces cracked, and he tried to escape with 20,000 troops on the 12th night. The army was pursued and massacred on the banks of the Amu Darya. The citizens of Bukhara promptly surrendered to the Mongols, although a small garrison of defenders in the inner citadel held out for another 11 days before they were captured and killed, probably on February 15th, 1220.

According to Juvaini, the walls of Bukhara were leveled, and all the inhabitants were driven out of the city, after maximum booty had been extracted from the wealthy. The Mongols then sent a contingent of talented artisans back to Mongolia and pressed into service a great number of young men who would function as arrow fodder for the next assault on Samarkand. Compared to the fate of other cities Chinggis Khan would take on this Khwarazmian campaign, Bukhara actually got off pretty lightly, although as the Mongols were departing, a great fire broke out in the ramshackle wooden suburbs of the city, causing tremendous destruction to those areas that had survived the original assault.

Word of the capture and destruction of Bukhara spread throughout the Khwarazmian Empire, including to the residents of the great city of Samarkand, the obvious next target for Chinggis Khan. Samarkand was another splendid city which had grown wealthy from centuries of trade and successful irrigation agriculture, and it was home to perhaps 100,000 people in the 1220s. The walls of the city were tremendous and thought to be impregnable. To increase its defensive capabilities, Juvaini informs us that the shah had stationed 60,000 Turkic troops and 50,000 Tajik troops inside those massive walls. The shah himself had also fled to Samarkand to escape the Mongol armies but now must have felt the noose tightening around him.

The army of Chinggis and Tolui was now reinforced by that of Ogedai and Chagatai, following their victory in the siege of Otrar. The Mongols also placed dummies and propped up unmanned shields in the fields to make their forces look even more numerous. The shah sent armies to attack the Mongols in the field, but one fled and the other was destroyed.

After a leisurely inspection of the defenses, the Mongol assault began on the third day, as wave after wave of "arrow fodder," the poor captured residents of Bukhara, were sent charging against the defenses. When many of these men broke and fled away from the defenders on the walls, the commanders in the city wrongly imagined it was the Mongols that had broken. But as the shah's forces came charging triumphantly out of the city, they fell right into the Mongol ambush and were slaughtered by the tens of thousands by the real Mongol soldiers.

The Mongols now poured into the suburbs while the remaining defenders retreated to the heavily fortified inner city. Shah Muhammad, psychologically broken, escaped in the night with 30,000 horsemen and fled back across the Amu Darya into the heartland of Khurasan. Chinggis Khan immediately dispatched the formidable Jebe and Subedei and their troops to pursue him, a pursuit that would prove so relentless that the shah never had a moment to rest.

A delegation of citizens now came out of Samarkand to offer their surrender to Chinggis Khan, and five days later, the garrison inside the fortified inner city also asked for terms of surrender. Chinggis promised he would spare them, but once they had surrendered, they were slaughtered. The great city was completely secured a day later when a thousand defenders who had retreated to the citadel were finally overcome, and by the end of March 1220, Samarkand belonged to the Mongols.

The usual aftermath followed. Useful artisans were sent back to Mongolia, others were recruited to be human shields at the next assault, and various treasuries were confiscated. Chinggis Khan then gave his men permission to rape, plunder, and kill at their discretion. So devastating was their work that perhaps 75 percent of the population of Samarkand was killed. After this, he and his army retired for two months R and R in the Hisar Mountains, which Chinggis thought was necessary following almost a year now of continuous campaigning by the troops.

In May, the campaign was resumed, a campaign that author W. B. Bartlett argues was to leave "the blackest stain of all on his reputation." City after city was now destined to feel the wrath of Khan. Termez, an ancient and sacred Buddhist city on the Amu Darya, experienced this first. After the city fell, each Mongol soldier was given a quota of men and women to kill, and the residents were struck down without mercy. One woman begged for mercy by saying she would give her captors a large pearl that she had swallowed. Immediately, her belly was slit open, and several pearls were discovered. Juvaini notes that "on this account Chinggis Khan commanded that they should rip open the bellies of all the slain," looking for swallowed treasure.

South next to Balkh, another legendary commercial city of the ancient Silk Roads. The city authorities and elders, hoping to spare the fate of Samarkand and Termez, came out to surrender, offering the Mongols all sorts of tribute and treasure. But Chinggis Khan, who knew that the Shah's son Jalal al-Din was active in this region, and not trusting this promise of submission, decided that none should be allowed to live. Juvaini describes the dreadful scene that followed: "Therefore Chinggis Khan commanded that the population of Balkh, small and great, few and many, both men and women, should be driven out onto the plain and divided up according to the usual custom into hundreds and thousands to be put to the sword; and that not a trace should be left of fresh or dry."

The only beneficiaries of the slaughter, according to Juvaini, were the lions, wolves, and vultures of the region. Nearly 50 years later, Marco Polo would pass through the city of Balkh, and he commented that "it used to be much greater and more splendid; but the Tatars"—which is what he called the Mongols—"have sacked and ravaged it. For I can tell you that there used to be many fine palaces and mansions of marble which are still to be seen, but shattered now and in ruins. Such was the legacy of Chinggis Khan in all the formerly great cities of central Asia that he attacked and destroyed.

Chinggis had been right to worry about Jalal al-Din, because word now reached him that the Khwarazmian general had just defeated a badly outnumbered Mongol contingent commanded by Sigi Qutuqu—the possible author of *The Secret History*, you might remember—before escaping south over the Hindu Kush. Enraged, Chinggis Khan pursued him through modern Afghanistan, in as merciless a mood as could be imagined. At the fall of the town of Bamiyan, where the great carved Buddhas later destroyed by the Taliban were located, he ordered that every living creature in the city be killed.

Meanwhile, as this terrible pursuit of Jalal al-Din continued, another Mongol contingent led by Tolui and Chinggis's son-in-law Toghutshar was dispatched to attack perhaps the greatest of the Silk Roads cities of central Asia, Merv. Merv, called Marv i-Shahjahan in Arabic, the Queen of the World, such reflects its size, beauty, and strategic significance. As noted at the start of this lecture, Merv was one of the most populous cities in the world when the Mongols arrived, with 200,000 people living inside the city and hundreds of thousands more in the surrounding region.

Tolui realized that taking the formidable city of Merv would not be easy, and he spent several days carefully studying the walls, looking for any sign of a weakness. I can assure you that even today, the remnants of those walls are still incredibly impressive. But the defenders of the city adopted a strategy that was doomed to fail. They sallied forth in small contingents to try and carry out guerilla-style raids on the Mongols, but of course, they were easily repulsed and destroyed. The commander of the forces inside the city quickly came to the decision that the only hope of survival lay in surrendering.

The Mongols rode in through the gates and ordered all the inhabitants to leave the city, a process that took several days. The Mongols then separated the men from the women, detached a few hundred useful artisans and the most beautiful of the women, and then Tolui gave the order that everyone else was to be killed. Every soldier was given a quota of 400 citizens to massacre. The city was then destroyed, its great walls torn down, and the largest mosque set on fire. Those residents who had been hiding in the city were forced out and also massacred. As I noted earlier, historians estimate that somewhere between 700,000 and 1 million people probably died in the massacre at Merv, one of the most brutal sackings of a city in the entire history of the world.

Merv was just one of many cities destroyed by Tolui during his campaign in the region known as Khurasan. Those cities that attempted to keep out the Mongols were ruthlessly crushed, their irrigation infrastructure destroyed, and their entire populations massacred. Those who did submit were required to destroy their walls and thus leave themselves defenseless. This was not a campaign of conquest but one of destruction, particularly of any strongpoints within the region or of populations that might be stirred into action again by the shah or his son Jalal al-Din.

After the conquest of Merv, Tolui's army headed east towards Nishapur in modern Iran. As they rode, they encountered groups of refugees fleeing from the devastation of Merv, which the Mongols cut down and killed with their swords and their spears. As Bartlett notes, "what is most striking about this campaign is the savagery of it, pitiless even by Mongol standards." Shah Muhammad had actually fled to Nishapur from Balkh, and once there, surrounded by bad omens, he warned the population of the city to flee before the Mongol storm descended. When the inhabitants mostly decided to ignore his warning, the shah used the excuse of a hunting trip to escape the city, joined by a few others.

The Mongol advance guard soon arrived at the gates, and the governor, uncertain what to do, gave them food. Then an army of 10,000 Mongols led by Toghutshar, a kinsman of Chinggis Khan, arrived. These were the vanguard of Tolui's battle hardened forces. As Toghutshar tried to enter the gates of Nishapur, however, defenders fired arrows down upon the Mongols, one of which dealt Toghutshar a mortal wound. At this, the Mongols withdrew and spent some time destroying smaller towns in the vicinity of Nishapur and massacring their entire populations as a sort of dire warning of what was now inevitably in store for Nishapur. Then winter intervened, and the Mongols withdrew, leaving the dispirited residents of Nishapur to survive on limited supplies of food.

In the spring of 1221, Tolui was back, this time with all the siege equipment necessary to take the city. Huge mangonels were employed, ready to fire heavy rocks against the walls and the buildings of the city. The death of Chinggis Khan's kinsman Toghutshar meant there was no possibility of mercy. At dawn on April 7th, 1221, the siege commenced, and as the days progressed, the Mongols gradually filled the moat and scaled the walls on ladders, entering the city in small groups, then larger contingents, until finally thousands of Mongols were in the streets, laying waste and killing at will.

The mayhem that followed is difficult to describe. All the residents were killed, their bodies piled into great separate hills of men, women, and children. Toghutshar's widow presided over the appalling rituals that accompanied the slaughter, and even the domestic animals that were found in the city—that is, the pets of the former residents—were killed. Then the city buildings and walls were destroyed and the city ploughed into the ground as though it had never existed. As Bartlett concludes, "The scale of the slaughter in this and the other cities taken had never been seen before, and perhaps, in its stark totality, has never been seen since."

After the campaign was over, Tolui and his forces marched back across the Amu Darya, leaving Khurasan in ruins. Juvaini sums up the unprecedented destruction thus: "With one stroke a world which billowed with fertility was laid desolate, and the regions thereof became a desert, and the greater part of the living dead, and their skin and bones crumbling dust; and the mighty were humbled and immersed in the calamities of perdition."

Meanwhile, the relentless pursuits of the shah and his son continued, with Chinggis Khan's army hot on the heels of Jalal al-Din in southern Afghanistan, and the armies of Jebe and Subedei pursuing Shah Muhammad, who was fleeing all over his former empire in panic. As we have seen, Muhammad had fled south to Balkh, then southwest to Nishapur, which he reached in April 1220, before escaping again before the arrival of Tolui. The shah then fled northwest to the shores of the Caspian Sea, with Jebe and Subedei sometimes splitting their forces in two to sack cities as they pursued the shah, hot on his heels.

With the noose closing around his neck, and almost deserted by his troops, Shah Muhammad decided to seek refuge on a small island in the Caspian Sea itself, as Mongol arrows came crashing into his boat. The Mongols, never comfortable at sea, nonetheless launched an amphibious assault on the island, but by the time they arrived, the shah had fled to another. By all accounts, the shah was now out of his mind with despair and anxiety, and also gravely ill. Sometime in January 1221, he died a miserable death, possibly of dysentery or pleurisy or pneumonia, and was buried on the island, wrapped in a torn white shirt for a shroud.

So perished the once-great shah of the Khwarazmian Empire, who had incurred the wrath of Chinggis Khan, for which he, his kingdom, and his people had paid a terrible price. The Khwarazmian Empire was no more, but the empire of Chinggis Khan now stretched from the seas of China to the Caspian, from the Siberian steppe to southern Afghanistan.

Remember, this was a campaign that Chinggis Khan had tried to avoid when he offered the shah the opportunity to pay restitution for the merchants and envoys that had been robbed and murdered by the governor of Otrar with the tacit support of the shah. But once it was clear that the only way forward was war, the destruction of the shah's empire was carried out with brilliant planning and appallingly ruthless execution.

But the campaign was not quite over, as Jalal al-Din was still at large. He continued to flee southwards, across the Hindu Kush and into the Indus Valley of modern Pakistan. Chinggis Khan and his forces finally caught their intrepid foe on the banks of the Indus River. Refusing to be captured, Jalal al-Din spurred his horse to the edge of a cliff, and both horse and master fell into the Indus River, escaping his pursuers by swimming across to the other side.

He was joined by other elements of the Khwarazmian army, and they rode south through thick forests and then out onto the great plains of northern India. At Chinggis's command, Mongol commander Dorbei Doqshin pursued his quarry into these same Indian plains. But after sacking a few towns, they lost the scent of Jalal al-Din and returned to rejoin the main Mongol army in Afghanistan.

The heat and humidity of India debilitated their horses and their bows, and thus proved a sort of environmental limit to Mongol expansion, which otherwise had thus far known no limits whatsoever. One can only wonder what sort of reception Dorbei received after returning to Chinggis Khan to inform him that the quarry had escaped.

After this, the Khwarazmian campaign was essentially over. The bulk of the Mongol army now regrouped and rode back to Mongolia. Some Mongol forces remained in the key heartland regions of the empire in case Jalal al-Din should return and attempt to reoccupy them. The regions occupied were also the wealthy and commercial heart of the former empire, and the Mongols had every intention of exploiting these commercial opportunities in the future. But the regions that had been utterly devastated were now simply abandoned following this, as Tim May puts it, "masterpiece of Mongol warfare at all levels."

The future of the regions devastated in these campaigns was incredibly bleak. These formerly lush and fertile agricultural lands, watered through ancient and elaborate irrigations systems, were now ruined. So many cities that had once thronged with people engaged in all manner of commerce and life were now no more than smoldering wrecks. And hundreds of thousands of these people were now dead, ending their days in great mountains of skulls and bones on the now desolate plains of Khwarazmia.

A Muslim author and contemporary to these events, Ibn al-Athir, wrote that the devastation caused by the Mongol Khwarazmian campaign were so unprecedented that "it may well be that the world from now until its end … will not experience the like again." Al-Athir concluded: "Alas! I would have preferred my mother never to have given birth to me, or to have died without witnessing all these evils. If one day you are told that the earth has never known such calamity since God created Adam, do not hesitate to believe it, for such is the strict truth."

As difficult as this is to believe, fate might have saved parts of the former Khwarazmian Empire from even greater destruction. Chinggis Khan's decision to withdraw from the region and march back north of the Amu Darya was partly based on news he received about a revolt amongst the Xi Xia, closer to Mongolia. The campaign that Chinggis Khan would now inevitably unleash against the Tangut elites of Xi Xia was destined to be the last campaign Chinggis Khan—the World Conqueror, as Juvaini names him—would ever lead.

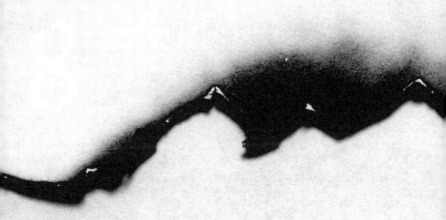

THE DEATH OF CHINGGIS KHAN

T his lecture considers the death of Chinggis Khan from a hunting accident in 1227. Then, it turns to the legacy of Chinggis Khan, including his many extraordinary achievements and his reputation for brutality.

The Hunting Accident

Chinggis Khan's death occurred as he was attempting to redress a past grievance he had with the king of the Tangut state of Xi Xia in northwestern China. The king of Xi Xia had accepted client status from Chinggis Khan many years earlier, and as part of this arrangement had provided troops for the Mongol army. Chinggis Khan had demanded that more be sent to join his Khwarazmian campaign, but apparently the king had refused. This is the standard story used to explain the cause of the war against Xi Xia.

In reality, the Tangut king was good to his word and had been supplying whole armies of young men to fight for the Mongols against the Jin in China. The grudge Chinggis Khan had against the Tangut king was of a different nature. It seems that when the great Mongol general Muqali, who had been leading the fight against the Jin for many years, died suddenly in 1223, the Tangut king went behind the Mongols' back and made peace with the Jin emperor to bring his men home.

Chinggis Khan was incensed when he heard this, but he first attempted to resolve the situation diplomatically. Foolishly, the Tangut elites and royal family hesitated until Chinggis lost his patience and declared war against the state of Xi Xia and its rulers. However, the Mongol soldiers had been away from home for eight years on the Khwarazmian campaign, so they needed rest before launching another war.

In March 1226, the Mongols invaded Xi Xia and advanced rapidly into the region. Chinggis Khan was in overall command of an army perhaps 70,000 strong, and he appointed his sons Tolui and Ogedai, along with brilliant general Subedai, to be his deputy commanders.

Before setting out on the campaign against Xi Xia, he had organized a great hunt that took place on the frigid Mongolian steppe in January 1226. During this particular hunt, Chinggis Khan sustained serious injuries.

Planning for the Future

As the campaign continued, Chinggis Khan's condition deteriorated, and he was forced to remain in his bed in a weak and sickened state. Conscious that his days might be numbered, he convened a *quriltai*. In planning for the future of the vast regions he had conquered, he decided the only viable option was to divide the empire into four distinct territories. He informed the *quriltai* that these were to be ruled by his surviving sons—Chagatai, Ogedai, and Tolui—and his grandson Batu. He also allotted to each ruler some 4,000 families as feudal followers.

Chinggis Khan declared Ogedai to be his chosen successor because he was the most balanced in skills and abilities, and he was the leader with the greatest chance of keeping the previously fractious Mongol tribes united through his astute political skills.

By the end of July 1227, Chinggis Khan was gravely ill. He spoke to his sons again and made sure they understood the new arrangements for imperial administration. He also told his advisors that he wanted a new Mongol capital city called Karakorum to be built in the heartland of the Mongol empire.

Chinggis Khan died sometime in August 1227 at roughly the age of 65. As for the campaign against the Tanguts, Chinggis Khan's final orders were followed to the letter. The city of Zhongxing and much of its population were destroyed, and the Tangut royal family was eliminated. Most of the rest of the population was left unharmed, and they were fully integrated into the Mongol state.

The burial of Chinggis Khan is shrouded in mystery. Frank McLynn argues that the most probable scenario is that in the heat of August, with the Tangut campaign to be concluded and no possibility of embalming the body, he was buried near to where he died, somewhere in the Ordos loop of northern China.

Conclusion

This lecture closes with a look at Chinggis Khan's impact on the world, beginning with the terrifying wars he waged against the Jin dynasty in Northern China and the Khwarazmian Empire in central Asia. Historian David Morgan, after acknowledging that some historians have attempted to revise the seriousness of this impact, is unequivocal in arguing that the Mongol conquests were "a disaster on a grand and unparalleled scale."

Additionally, in central Asia in the 13th century, Chinggis Khan and his force systematically tried to raze the farmlands of the region and the irrigation systems that sustained them.

Mongol devastation was not universal in scale. Rather, it was much worse in some places than others. For instance, the Persian region of Khurasan and the lands known as Transoxiana undoubtedly fared the worst. However, many other parts of the former Khwarazmian empire were barely touched at all.

A different way of assessing the impact of Chinggis Khan is to consider his genetic legacy. This biological legacy first came to light in a 2003 paper that used genetic science to help understand historical processes. The paper came to the extraordinary conclusion that millions of men living in Eurasia today were direct descendants of Chinggis Khan.

Since 2003, other genetic studies have pushed back a little against this hypothesis. Still, sources suggest that Chinggis Khan may have sired hundreds if not thousands of children. His genetic imprint must have been distributed widely throughout Eurasia.

Being able to claim descent from Chinggis Khan carried enormous prestige in both the Mongol and post-Mongol eras in inner Eurasia. Many people claimed some sort of direct descent from Chinggis Khan's family lineage as a way of enhancing their prestige and claims to power.

Some of the most important dynasties in Eurasian history are demonstrably descended from the Chinggisids. This includes the dynasties that were established by Chinggis Khan's descendants in the khanates that emerged in the fragmentation of the empire following his death in 1227. Some examples are the Yuan dynasty in China, established by Chinggis's grandson Qubilai Khan; the Ilkhanids of Persia; and the Jochids of the Golden Horde in Russia.

THE DEATH OF CHINGGIS KHAN

If you have been fortunate enough to visit Ulaanbaatar, the high-energy capital of the modern nation of Mongolia, you might have looked up from a city street or out of a window and noticed an enormous image of Chinggis Khan looking back at you from a hillside above the city. I had this experience a few years ago after a very late-night flight into Chinggis Khaan International Airport and a 2:00 am check-in to my hotel. Somewhat bleary-eyed, I pulled open the curtains of my room next morning, and there was Chinggis Khan staring at me from a distance across the bustling city streets.

The image, made of white stones laid out on the green slopes of a mountain above the city, is enormous—some 455 feet high. It was erected as part of a series of celebrations that took place in Mongolia in 2006 to mark the 800th anniversary of the great quriltai of 1206 at which Temujin was elected Chinggis Khan.

Nor is this the only larger-than-life representation of the great khan you will find in or about Ulaanbaatar. In the imposing main square at the heart of the city, Sukhbaatar Square, sits a large and imposing bronze statue of Chinggis Khan, flanked by two of his most famous successors, son Ogedai and grandson Qubilai, all three of them seated in front of the Government Palace. Bronze statues of two famous Mongol generals, Boruchu and Muqali, also stand guard as if protecting the trio. This impressive collection of statues and a marble colonnade to house them was also completed in time for the 800th anniversary of the quriltai.

But perhaps the most jaw-dropping representation of all is a 130-feet-tall statue of Chinggis Khan on horseback, located in the Tuul River Valley 34 miles outside of the capital. The statue looks towards the great khan's birthplace in the eastern Mongolian steppe. I have had the experience of climbing up inside the chest and neck of the enormous horse before stepping out on its head and enjoying the panoramic view. This statue was erected in 2008 as yet another reminder of the tremendous importance of Chinggis Khan as a symbol of greatness and unity in the modern nation of Mongolia.

We should note that in their understandable affirmation of Chinggis Khan as the founder of the modern state of Mongolia, Mongolians do tend to gloss over his reputation as a brutal conqueror and instead promote him as the man of the millennium, a visionary, a great statesman, a creator of just laws and fair taxation, and a champion of religious tolerance. And one could certainly argue he was all of those things. We also need to remember that he lived eight centuries ago, and his actions were more or less in keeping with those of all the other militarized steppe nomadic leaders who had preceded him.

In a story filed for the Associated Press in 2006 about the 800th anniversary celebrations, journalist Charles Hutzler reports on a press conference held by Tsend Munkh-Orgil, a member of Mongolia's parliament. Munkh-Orgil's comments seem entirely relevant as we try and tease out the legacy of the great khan. The minister argued that Chinggis Khan could help forge "the national unity and national consensus" that he believed had been missing in the country since the emergence of capitalism and democracy 15 years earlier. Munkh-Orgil, who has a law degree from Harvard, concluded that "Our ancestor 800 years ago not only brought war and destruction, but he also brought liberation and freedom. As to the methods, it was the thirteenth century. What could we say?"

In this lecture, we consider the legacy of Chinggis Khan, his many extraordinary achievements, his reputation for brutality, and his legacy in the world of the 21st century. But before we can do this, we must first bring the story of his life to a close, including his death from, of all things, a hunting accident in 1227 as he was attempting to redress a past grievance he had with the king of the Tangut state of Xi Xia in northwestern China.

The king of Xi Xia had many years earlier accepted client status from Chinggis Khan and the Mongols, and as part of this arrangement had provided troops for the Mongol army. Despite the fact that a significant number of troops from the kingdom were already fighting for the Mongols in Jin China, Chinggis Khan had demanded that more be sent to join his Khwarazmian campaign, but apparently the king had refused. Or at least this is the standard story used to explain the cause of the war against the Xi Xia.

Actually, the Tangut king, good to his word, had been supplying whole armies of young men to fight for the Mongols against the Jin in China, and there is no real evidence of any refusal by the king to provide further troops for the Khwarazmian campaign. The grudge Chinggis Khan had against the Tangut king was of a different nature. It seems that when the great Mongol general Muqali, who had been leading the fight against the Jin for many years, died suddenly in 1223, the Tangut king went behind the Mongols' back and made peace with the Jin emperor in order to bring his men home.

Chinggis Khan was incensed when he heard this, but he first attempted to resolve the situation diplomatically. Foolishly, the Tangut elites and royal family prevaricated for too long, until Chinggis lost his patience and declared war against the state of Xi Xia and its rulers. Despite his impatience to punish the Tangut elites, before starting the campaign, Chinggis first took his troops all the way back from the Amu Darya in central Asia to the Tuul River in central Mongolia for a rest. The Mongol soldiers had been away from home for eight years on the Khwarazmian campaign, so some sort of R and R was definitely required before launching another war.

As Tim May points out, that Chinggis could leave Mongolia for eight years then return with his authority and power undiminished is a "testament to the foundations of his rule and the governing institutions that he had established in his rise to power." There had been no revolt against his leadership, nor any attempt by the various tribes to fragment again, despite the fact that the ruler of Mongolia had been thousands of miles away from his country for almost a decade. Such was the authority of Chinggis Khan.

In March 1226, the Mongols invaded Xi Xia and advanced rapidly into the region. Chinggis was in overall command of an army perhaps 70,000 strong, and he appointed his sons Tolui and Ogedai, along with brilliant general Subedei, to be his deputy commanders. As he had done so effectively on so many occasions, Chinggis immediately divided his forces and sent them against different targets. Chinggis himself marched directly for the capital of Xi Xia, Zhongxing. Realizing the trouble they were in, the Tangut made a desperate effort to restart peace talks, but to no avail. Chinggis Khan was so set upon punishing the Tangut that nothing could save them now, not even his own death.

Before setting out on the campaign against Xi Xia, Chinggis had organized a great hunt that took place on the frigid Mongolian steppe in January 1226. Now, we will discuss these hunts in detail in a later lecture, but they were a passion of all Mongols and also served as a superb training ground for the building of endurance and the sharpening of military skills before a campaign. But during this particular hunt, Chinggis Khan sustained serious injuries. This is how the incident is described in *The Secret History of the Mongols*:

In the winter Chinggis Khan, riding his steed Josotu Boro, on the way hunted the many wild asses of Arbuqa. When the wild asses passed close by them Josotu Boro took fright. Chinggis Khan fell off the horse and, his body being in great pain, he halted at Co'orqat. He spent the night there and the following morning … his body [was] hot with fever.

Chinggis had several years earlier sustained significant injuries on a wild boar hunt during the Khwarazmian campaign, but he had recovered from those. This time, the internal injuries were clearly much more severe, although they in no way seem to have impaired his strategic thinking in conducting the Xi Xia campaign.

As the campaign continued, Chinggis's condition deteriorated, and he was forced to remain in his bed in a weak and sickened state. The Tangut, who knew nothing about this accident, continued to sue for peace, and Chinggis's sons and commanders urged him to accept so that he could return to Mongolia. But the great Khan was resolute and demanded from his officers and sons that even if he died, the war against the Tangut should be sustained until, to quote from *The Secret History* again, they were "maimed and tamed."

Conscious that his days might be numbered, however, even in the midst of the campaign, Chinggis convened a gathering, or quriltai. In planning for the future of the vast regions he had conquered, Chinggis decided the only viable option was to divide the empire into four distinct territories. He informed the quriltai that these were to be ruled by his surviving sons—Chagatai, Ogedai, and Tolui—and his grandson Batu, son of his eldest son Jochi, who had died a couple of years earlier. He also allotted to each ruler some 4,000 families as feudal followers, which he figured would be enough to support the leaders in terms of taxation and the provision of young men for their armies but insufficient for them to establish independent khanates, although he must have realized that was a very real possibility.

In deciding who to nominate to be his successor as overall great khan, Chinggis would have taken into consideration the personalities and qualities of his three sons. Chagatai was stern and ruthless and had been relentless in his condemnation of Chinggis's oldest son Jochi, whose paternal parentage had always been in question. Tolui was a superb military commander who had spearheaded many of the Mongols' most brilliant victories. And Ogedai, although a heavy drinker, was a shrewd and clever politician. There was no perfect choice, but in the end, Chinggis declared Ogedai to be his chosen successor, simply because he was the most balanced of the three in skills and abilities and the leader with the greatest chance of keeping the previously fractious Mongol tribes united through his astute political skills.

By the end of July 1227, Chinggis Khan was gravely ill. He spoke to his sons again and made sure they understood the new arrangements for imperial administration. He also told his advisors that he wanted a new Mongol capital city called Karakorum to be built in the heartland of the Mongol Empire, the central Orkhon River Valley, which had also been sacred to most of the great nomadic confederations that had preceded the Mongols. His final words to his sons are reported to have been: "Life is short. I could not conquer all the world. You will have to do it!"

Chinggis Khan died sometime in August 1227, at the age of 65 or thereabouts, or as *The Secret History* puts it, "in the Year of the Pig he ascended into heaven." The exact date is uncertain, but the 16th, 18th, 25th, or 27th of August have all been offered as plausible. As with other rulers of such extraordinary historical impact, various legends about how the great khan had actually died began to circulate almost immediately.

Some claimed he was struck by lightning. Marco Polo later reported that he died from an arrow wound in the knee that became infected. Poisoning was proposed by other sources, or even that the Tangut royal family had cast a fatal spell on Chinggis. But somehow, his death in a simple nomadic *ger* from some internal illness following a bad hunting fall seems appropriate. As Jack Weatherford notes, this "illustrated how successful he had been in preserving the traditional way of life of his people."

As for the campaign against the Tanguts, Chinggis Khan's final orders were followed to the letter. The city of Zhongxing and much of its population were destroyed and the Tangut royal family eliminated. Most of the rest of the population was left unharmed, and now, with the elimination of the king and his family, they were fully integrated into the Mongol state. Officials were appointed to administer the former kingdom of Xi Xia, which was now regarded in every way as simply another region within the state of Mongolia.

Just as with the cause of his death, the burial of Chinggis Khan is also shrouded in mystery. There are various legends, of course. One suggests he was buried under a lone tree that he took a fancy to somewhere in the Liupan Mountains. Another that Mongol elites tried to take his body back to be buried on Burkhan Khaldun mountain in Mongolia but got bogged down in a storm and had to bury the body somewhere nearby. Frank McLynn argues that the most probable scenario is that in the heat of August, with the Tangut campaign to be concluded and no possibility of embalming the body, Chinggis was buried near to where he died, somewhere in the Ordos loop of northern China.

One persistent legend suggests that the Mongols were so intent on keeping the Great Khan's burial site a secret that the 50 Mongols involved in his burial were all killed by a special assassination squad, and that this squad was in turn killed soon afterwards by another group of assassins. The possibility that this might have occurred is strengthened by the documented certainty that this practice was followed in the death of later khans, as we shall see.

There is one other account of the burial of Chinggis Khan that has persisted to this day, particularly in Mongolia itself. This is that he was indeed transported back to the Mongolian heartland and buried in a secret grave somewhere on the steppe with no tombstone or any other marker. As Jack Weatherford, who supports this theory, puts it: "At burial Chinggis Khan disappeared silently back into the vast landscape of Mongolia from whence he came." After this, Mongol soldiers sealed off an area of several hundred square miles around the tomb in an area called the Ikh Khorig, or the Great Taboo, and prevented anyone from entering for the next century.

The Ikh Khorig might even have remained off-limits during the Soviet era in the 20th century. Certainly, we know that the Soviet government in Mongolia did designate a region of the steppe as a highly restricted area, perhaps to make sure that the burial site of Chinggis Khan would not become a symbol of nationalism for anticommunist rebels. But given that the Soviets carried out military drills in this restricted area, it might just have been declared off-limit for another more pragmatic reason. All we can say for sure is that the burial site of Chinggis Khan remains a complete mystery to this very day, but the fact that this Khan Khentii Protected Area is still kept off-limits by the Mongolian government today only adds to the intrigue.

As we turn next in this lecture to a consideration of the legacy of Chinggis Khan, it might be worth keeping Mongolian politician Munkh-Orgil's words in mind: "Our ancestor 800 years ago not only brought war and destruction, but he also brought liberation and freedom. As to the methods, it was the thirteenth century. What could we say?" So we need to try and offer a balanced and historically appropriate assessment of the great khan's legacy, considering both the negatives and the positives of his impact on the world.

Let's start with the negatives by looking at the impact of the terrifying wars Chinggis Khan waged against the Jin Dynasty in northern China and the Khwarazmian Empire in central Asia, on the people and infrastructure of large swathes of Eurasia. Historian David Morgan, after acknowledging that some historians have attempted to revise the seriousness of this impact, is unequivocal in arguing that the Mongol conquests were "a disaster on a grand and unparalleled scale."

But they could perhaps have been even worse. There is an often repeated although possibly apocryphal story that the Mongols at one stage had decided to eradicate in some genocidal way the entire population of the Jin Dynasty in China and turn their farmlands and villages into grazing pasture for their horses. They were only dissuaded from following through on this plan by a Khitan adviser who pointed out the amount of taxation revenue they would earn by not murdering the entire population of northern China.

In his subsequent campaign to the west, Chinggis Khan has also been accused by numerous historians of attempting something like genocide on the populations of central Asia and Persia. Collectively, the Persian and Arabic sources that are most contemporary to the actual events they describe paint a bleak and horrifying picture. One source, Sayfi Harawi, says that the sack of the Persian city of Herat alone came at the cost of 1.6 million dead, and that more than 1.7 million died in the taking of Nishapur. There is no way of verifying the accuracy of these figures, of course, although they are surely exaggerated, and Minhaj al-Siraj Juzjani even more so when he puts the death toll at Herat at 2.4 million people.

But David Morgan argues persuasively that even if these figures are exaggerated, they are evidence of the traumatized state of mind of the chroniclers who observed firsthand the scale of Mongol destruction of so many of these great cities of the ancient Islamic world. As Morgan puts it, "The shock induced by the scale of the catastrophe had no precedent: hence these enormous figures. This must imply that the death and destruction which produced that shock had no precedent either."

It is not only the authors closest to the events that seem so traumatized; numerous chroniclers and commentators over the decades that followed had much the same response. Certainly, the Persian historians Juvaini and Rashid al-Din convey a similar horror, as do various European and Islamic travelers who passed through these regions in the decades that followed, including Marco Polo, Ibn Battuta, John of Plano Carpini, and William of Rubruck. More about each of these important observers in future lectures.

Some modern scholars such as Bernard Lewis have suggested that we need to consider the scale of Mongol death and destruction in the context of the global wars of the 20th century and perhaps judge them less harshly. Lewis argues that the destruction and death caused by Adolph Hitler and the Nazis in the Second World War was on an enormously grander scale that that caused by Chinggis Khan and the Mongols in the 13th century. He also suggests that given that Europe recovered so quickly from the war, perhaps the people and city-states of inner Eurasia also recovered more quickly from the Mongols than their contemporary chroniclers suggest.

However, one big difference between the destruction caused by the Second World War in Europe and that caused by the Mongols in central Asia is that by the end of the war in 1945, although many cities and buildings had been damaged, the agricultural capacity of Europe was largely unaffected. In central Asia in the 13th century, on the other hand, Chinggis Khan and his force systematically tried to utterly destroy the farmlands of the region and, worst of all, the irrigation systems that sustained them.

Even today, agriculture in modern countries such as Iran, Turkmenistan, and Uzbekistan is utterly dependent on irrigation infrastructure, including canals and the important underground qanat water storage system. *Qanat* is actually a Persian word that describes underground water channels that store and distribute water in arid environments. Qanats are connected to aquifers, oases, or streams swollen by melting snow in the spring, and they use a system of underground storage facilities and channels to distribute this water into the fields.

We know that many of these were systematically destroyed during the Khwarazmian campaign, and even those that survived could no longer be maintained because so many farmers in the region were dead, so they fell into disuse, and the settlements, towns, and cities they had once supplied with water became unsustainable. Some of the worst of this destruction, particularly in the regions between the Tigris and Euphrates Rivers in modern Iraq, occurred after the death of Chinggis Khan during Hulegu's subsequent invasion of the region in the 1250s. But Hulegu was surely just continuing the destruction that had commenced during Chinggis's campaign in the 1220s.

What we can say, I think, is that Mongol death and devastation was not universal in scale but rather much worse in some places than in others. The Persian region of Khurasan, home to the cities of Herat and Nishapur, and the lands known as Transoxiana since ancient times, which included cities like Samarkand, Bukhara, and Merv, undoubtedly fared the worst. But many other parts of the former Khwarazmian Empire were barely touched at all.

This impression is borne out by reports from Marco Polo and Ibn Battuta, who regularly noted that some cities had not recovered from the Mongols, but others were already flourishing again. Subsequent Mongol support of trade along the ancient Silk Roads routes would undoubtedly have helped strategically located cities like Samarkand and Bukhara recover more quickly.

Another very different way of assessing the physical impact of Chinggis Khan on the people of inner Eurasia is to consider his genetic legacy. This biological legacy first came to light in a 2003 paper that used genetic science to help understand historical processes in a way that has now become incredibly useful for all scholars of the ancient world. The paper came to the extraordinary conclusion that millions of men living in Eurasia today were direct descendants of Chinggis Khan.

This conclusion was based on studies of Y chromosomes, which seemed to indicate that all these men were descended from a single individual who lived approximately 750 to 1,000 years ago. Y chromosomes can only be passed on from father to son, so the Y record provides a clear record of patrilineage. The study suggested that roughly 8 percent of men living in a wide region of inner Eurasia stretching from Uzbekistan to China, which represented about 0.5 percent of all the men alive in the world in 2003, or some 16 million men in total, carried a Y chromosome that had come directly from Chinggis Khan.

Since 2003, other genetic studies have pushed back a little against this hypothesis. One paper published in 2010 noted that "although such a connection is by no means impossible, we currently have no way of assessing how much confidence to place in such a connection. ... Claims of connections ... between specific uniparental lineages and historical figures or historical migrations of peoples are merely speculative."

On the other hand, all the sources suggest that Chinggis Khan was very sexually active and may have sired hundreds if not thousands of children, so his genetic imprint must have been distributed widely throughout Eurasia. This is a quote widely attributed to Chinggis: "The greatest joy for a man is to defeat his enemies, to drive them before him, to take from them all they possess, to see those they love in tears, to ride their horses, and to hold their wives and daughters in his arms." Actually, this passage sounds like a motto that all the Mongols probably shared, which suggests that the genetic impact of the Mongols as a whole was undoubtedly enormous.

Being able to claim descent from Chinggis Khan carried enormous prestige in both the Mongol and post-Mongol eras in inner Eurasia. Everyone from individuals up to entire dynasties would claim, sometimes accurately but sometimes fraudulently, some sort of direct descent from Chinggis Khan's family lineage as a way of enhancing their own prestige and claims to power.

Some of the most important dynasties in Eurasian history are demonstrably descended from the Chinggisids. This includes obviously the dynasties that were established by Chinggis's descendants in the khanates that emerged in the fragmentation of empire following the great khan's death in 1227. These include the Yuan Dynasty in China, established by Chinggis's grandson Qubilai Khan, the Ilkhanids of Persia, and the Jochids of the Golden Horde in Russia, whose name is derived from that of Chinggis's oldest son, Jochi.

Other important post-Mongol dynasties that can be traced back to the Chinggisids include the Shaybanids and the Astrakhanids, both of which played important roles in the post-Mongol history of central Asia. Any individual prince that could demonstrate direct lineage from the Chinggisids was able to claim significant respect in the Mongol, Tatar, and Turkic worlds. As we will see, late 14th-century conqueror Timur would also claim descent from the Chinggisids through his mother's lineage, and even Babur and Humayun, the founders of the Mughal Empire in India in 1526, 300 years after Chinggis Khan's death, used their status as Chinggisids to justify their claims to power.

In closing, then, what can we say finally about the historical legacy of Chinggis Khan? Frank McLynn concludes his lengthy and superb biography of the khan by comparing Chinggis to his exact European contemporary, Francis of Assisi, who died one year before Chinggis. McLynn argues that in this sort of comparison, Chinggis must be judged "a moral pygmy." But McLynn also acknowledges the irony that it was Franciscan missionaries and emissaries who were destined to be the first Europeans to make contact with the Mongols and bring back to Europe, to quote McLynn again, "an amazing story that will endure as long as mankind itself: the career of Genghis Khan!"

Jack Weatherspoon, author of *Genghis Khan and the Making of the Modern World*, wonders at the kind of image Chinggis Khan imagined he was leaving to the world. He notes that in a conversation Chinggis was purported to have had with an imam, a conversation recorded by Persian author Juzjani, Chinggis Khan offered the rather boastful claim that "A mighty name will remain behind me in the world." Boastful or not, the name Chinggis Khan has undoubtedly remained mighty, respected, and feared over the eight centuries that have followed his death.

The death of Chinggis Khan was not the end of the Mongol impact on the world, of course—far from it! Remember the final words he is recorded as having said to his sons just before he died? "Life is short. I could not conquer all the world. You will have to do it!" Let's leave the final word on the legacy of Chinggis Khan to an author better known for his chronicling of the decline and fall of the Roman Empire, 18th-century British historian Edward Gibbon: Chinggis Khan "died in the fullness of years and glory, with his last breath, exhorting and instructing his sons to achieve the conquest of the Chinese Empire." And this is exactly what his successor Ogedai set out to do.

OGEDAI KHAN'S WESTERN CAMPAIGNS

C hinggis Khan's third son, Ogedai, was elected great khan at the *quriltai* held in 1229. The new khan distributed a large quantity of the massive amount of loot Chinggis Khan had accumulated over decades of plundering to many of those assembled at the *quriltai*, including commoners and soldiers. Then it was down to the business of governing a vast world state.

Early Governance

Ogedai decreed that all of the laws and pronouncements of Chinggis Khan remained in place. He then pardoned any criminals who had committed their crimes before he had come to the throne, but he warned that any new crimes committed against the proscriptions of the Great Yasa law code would be severely punished.

The first military priority had to be the reignition of the war against the Jin dynasty in China. The outstanding Mongol general Muqali had singlehandedly maintained the pressure on the Jin, even as the bulk of the army had spent eight years far to the west on the Khwarazmian campaign.

Muqali had died in 1223, however, and the conflict had bogged down with no headway on either side. The decision was made to renew this war with a vengeance, in a campaign to be led by Tolui and Ogedai.*

It was also decided that at the same time General Subedai would lead a Mongol force thousands of miles to the west as far as the Volga River in modern Russia to secure territories that Jochi had conquered during the Khwarazmian campaign. In addition, a smaller force was sent north into the Siberian steppe to secure tribute from the nomads dwelling there.

While these campaigns were in their early stages, word reached the Mongol high command that Jalal al-Din, the son of the late Khwarazmian shah who had escaped from Chinggis Khan by spurring his horse into the Indus River, had returned and was actively trying to reconstitute part of his father's empire in Persia. A fourth campaign was launched back across the Amu Darya, led by Chormaqan Noyan and his second-in-command, Dayir. Their job was to catch and kill Jalal al-Din and also permanently occupy Afghanistan, which had been conquered by Chinggis but never secured.

Attacking the Jin

In Northern China, Tolui's military brilliance against the Jin was immediately on full display, but in the year 1232, Tolui suddenly died in somewhat mysterious circumstances. Rumors emerged that Ogedai had had him killed, although no motive for this has ever been determined. Despite his younger brother's death, Ogedai was determined to keep up the pressure on the Jin, and so he recalled Subedai from the Volga River to take charge of the campaign.

Ogedai Khan, Mongolia

In China, Subedai did his job brilliantly and quickly. Within one campaign season the Jin were reduced to controlling only a small region around the city of Kaifeng. Then Subedai simply turned his horse around and rode 3,500 miles back again to the western front. The following year, 1234, the Jin capital of Kaifeng fell, and the Jin dynasty ceased to exist soon afterward.

The Song dynasty, which had been controlling southern China, had agreed to supply the Mongols with some food during the final stages of the campaign. Ogedai initially agreed to the alliance, but when the Song moved to occupy former Jin territory, a furious Ogedai ordered the beginning of military operations against the Song. This would prove to be a lengthy campaign.

Ogedai now turned to affairs of state and the consolidation to the empire, even as military operations continued in all directions. One of the first tasks he focused on was the construction of the Mongol capital of Karakorum.

Chormaqan Noyan's Campaign

Even as the new capital began to rise in the Orkhon Valley, thousands of miles to the west, the Mongol army led by Chormaqan Noyan was relentlessly pursuing Jalal al-Din. Jalal al-Din moved into northern Iran, then north into the Caucasus.

The Mongol strike force caught up with Jalal al-Din and the remnants of the Khwarazmian army as he was making merry in a camp in the Caucasus. The Khwarazmians fought hard and Jalal al-Din escaped again, but he was soon captured and killed by unknown forces deeper in the mountains, perhaps by Kurdish peasants.

Chormaqan's campaign was by no means finished with the death of Jalal-al-Din. In 1233, he occupied a lush plain located in the modern nation of Azerbaijan, using this as a base to gradually expand the size of his domain over the next two years. His position was soon strong enough to launch an invasion of Armenia and Georgia, two states that had been weakened by raids from Jalal-al-Din before his death. The rulers of Armenia and Georgia decided not to confront the Mongols in the field, and instead tried to defend themselves in mountain fortresses. These were picked off one by one by Chormaqan and his troops.

As these campaigns were going on in the north, other forces associated with Chormaqan's larger campaign successfully occupied Afghanistan and then began raiding into northern and southern Iraq. The Mongols had no plans to occupy the region at this stage, simply to raid and pillage.

A New Target

With all this military activity happening on several fronts at once, Ogedai decided to convene another *quriltai* in 1234 near his new capital of Karakorum, to discuss with his elite advisers and commanders where the Mongol forces should be concentrated next.

Subedai proposed to the *quriltai* that it was time for a fresh target, a massive campaign far to the west to Russia and Europe. This was a region most Mongols were only dimly aware of, but Subedai argued that enormous wealth was probably there for the taking.

Jochi Khan, Mongolia

Ogedai apparently found Subedai's arguments persuasive. A massive campaign to the west was launched in 1236 at the orders of Ogedai Khan. One explicit goal of this campaign was to take control of a region large enough for the descendants and followers of Jochi to occupy and settle. Jochi's descendants required a domain commensurate with the prestige of Jochi, the eldest son of Chinggis Khan.

An additional goal was to try and defeat the seminomadic Kipchak Turks who occupied the steppes north of the Caspian Sea. As part of this task, the Mongols also wanted to force the king of the nomadic Bulgars, who also dwelt on the steppe, to submit to the Mongols. He had previously refused to do so when it was demanded by Subedai during the Khwarazmian war in the 1220s.

The Mongol force that marched toward Russia and Europe was likely 150,000 strong. The leadership included a glittering array of the Mongol elites: Ogedai's son Qadan, Chagatai's son Baidar, and Tolui's eldest son, Mongke. The son of Jochi was nominal leader of the campaign, but his was really a figurehead position. General Subedai was actually in command of this massive invasion force.

The Westward Campaign

Following the military strategy established from the beginning of Mongol expansion by Chinggis Khan, the army immediately divided into two once it crossed the Volga River. One force led by Mongke marched against the Kipchaks. Many Kipchaks fled west, but many others stood and fought until they were defeated. Another army marched north, under the leadership of Batu and other sons of Jochi, to bring the Bulgars and other Siberian steppe tribes to heel.

With the first aim of the campaign successfully completed, by the end of 1237 the Mongols were ready to launch operations against the various city states and principalities of Rus, the western regions of modern Russia. The notoriously divided princes of Rus struggled to form any sort of unified response. Although it was now deep winter, the Mongols had no hesitation in attacking the Rus strongholds.

Mongol forces besieged the city of Riazan first, and they captured it just before Christmas 1237. Then, they divided their forces again. One set off to engage the army of the nominal ruler of all the princedoms of Rus, Grand Prince Vladimir, defeating him in battle on the banks of the Sit River. Other Mongol contingents used brilliant siege skills to capture city after city. In the end, the princes of the northern Rus city-states, which had so far escaped the carnage in the south, had no option other than to surrender, which most had done by the spring of 1238.

Siege of Riazan

The Mongols then rested for the summer and fall of 1238 before launching a new campaign against the remaining southern principalities of Rus in the winter of 1238. Throughout the remainder of that year and the next, cities continued to fall one by one. By the autumn of 1240, the Mongols stood before the walls of the important and prosperous city of Kiev, the capital of modern-day Ukraine.

The siege of Kiev was led by Chinggis Khan's grandsons Mongke, eldest son of Tolui, and Batu, eldest son of Jochi. The city fell on December 6, 1240, and the Mongols looted it and burned it to the ground. Other cities of Rus quickly submitted, which largely brought the Russian phase of the campaign to an end.

Qadan, Berke, and Mongke

As Batu and Subedai mopped up the remaining southern cities, another Mongol army led by Qadan, Berke and Mongke headed south to the steppe regions north of the Black and Caspian Seas. Their goal was to bring rebel Kipchak and other steppe nomadic peoples dwelling there to heel. Some leaders submitted, and Berke was able to turn the region into part of his personal *ordu*, or camp.

The Mongols now looked westward again, with Europe firmly in their sights. As the Mongols rested prior to the invasion, Hungarian king Bela IV built new fortifications, strengthened existing fortresses in the Carpathian Mountains, and also formed a strategic alliance with the Cumans. The Hungarian king also welcomed thousands of Kipchak refugees into his realm as potential mercenaries against the Mongols, although the unruly Kipchaks ultimately did more harm than good. When a Mongol envoy demanded of Bela IV that he return the Kipchaks, the king refused. This meant war with the Hungarians and their allies was now inevitable.

The campaign opened on a huge front in 1241. One force, perhaps 20,000 strong under the command of Chagatai's son Baidar and Ogedai's son Qadan, launched an assault against Poland in the north, while the main force of 50,000 warriors under the command of Batu and Subedai headed directly for Hungary. The Mongols were also careful to leave an occupying force on the Black Sea steppe to consolidate their conquest of that region.

Mongol Invasion of Poland

Baidar and Qadan immediately devastated eastern Poland, while the rulers of western Poland hastily assembled an army. Knights under the command of Henry II came from Silesia. Teutonic knights also came from Prussia, and knights under the command of Vaclav I, Henry's brother-in-law, set out from Bohemia as reinforcements. The well-informed Mongols knew that Vaclav was coming, and so they forced battle with the 30,000 Silesian and Prussian knights and conscripts at Legnica (modern Liegnitz) on April 9, 1241.

The Mongols, who had thus far hidden their real numbers from the Europeans, had chosen a perfect open field as the place of battle. They used feigned retreats to exhaust the Europeans in their heavy armor before cutting them down with siege equipment and superb archery. Something close to 25,000 of Henry's force of 30,000 were killed, and Henry's head was cut off and paraded outside the walls of the city of Liegnitz.

The Mongols also pressed into service a large number of German gold miners that Henry had conscripted and sent them a huge distance back across Eurasia to work in mines in the mountains of modern Kyrgyzstan.

When Vaclav I, who was on his way to join the allies at Legnica, heard about the defeat, he and his Bohemian knights turned around and began to head home. The Mongol commanders Baidar and Qadar immediately gave chase, forcing Vaclav away from Hungary, where the main Mongol force was poised to attack.

The blow came later in April 1241 at the Battle of Mohi, beside the swollen Sajo River. The Hungarian forces were destroyed, although Bela and few nobles escaped. The Mongols arrived at Buda and Pest the next day and sacked both cities.

There was now seemingly nothing to prevent an attack on the Holy Roman Empire and the destruction of Western Europe itself. The worst fears of the Europeans seemed to be realized when Mongol scouting parties suddenly appeared near Vienna near the end of 1241.

However, at the beginning of 1242, they simply packed up their camps and disappeared back into the eastern steppe from whence they had come. Word had reached Batu and Subedai that Great Khan Ogedai had died on December 11, 1241.

OGEDAI KHAN'S WESTERN CAMPAIGNS
LECTURE 9 TRANSCRIPT

Chinggis Khan's third son, Ogedai, was elected great khan at the quriltai held in 1229. Although there was some tension surrounding the choice—with the followers of Chinggis's second son, Chagatai, and his youngest son, the brilliant military commander Tolui, both feeling that their leaders had a better claim to the throne—in the end, there was no choice but to elect Chinggis's chosen heir. Ogedai initially made a show of declining the position, arguing that his brothers were indeed more worthy, but the assembled Mongol elites and commoners convinced him by making the following argument, as reported by Juvaini:

> This task Chinggis Khan has confided to thee of all his sons and brethren and has entrusted to thy counsel the binding and loosing, the tying and untying thereof. How then may we suffer any change or alteration of his words or allow any transformation or violation thereof. Today, which according to the astrologers is a fortunate day and a fortunate and auspicious time, thou must, with the aid of God [and this would have been Tengri, the sky god] be established upon the throne of universal sovereignty and adorn the world with justice and beneficence.

Now, Juvaini is certainly prone to hyperbole, but the argument presented to Ogedai was probably very much along these lines. However Tolui and Chagatai felt personally about the choice of Ogedai, they certainly played their parts well when it came time to install their brother upon the throne. After all the assembled elites had removed their hats and belts as a sign of obeisance towards the new khan, Chagatai gripped Ogedai's right arm, Tolui grabbed his left, and together with the uncle of all three men, Chinggis Khan's brother Temuge Otchigen, who grabbed Ogedai by the belt, the three men literally placed him upon the throne. Then the assembled nobility came forward one by one and pledged their loyalty to Ogedai.

Immediately after this, a massive transfer of military resources took place as Ogedai also became supreme military commander of the Yeke Mongol Ulus. Let me quote from *The Secret History*, the clearest source on this transfer: "The nightguards, the quiverbearers and the eight thousand dayguards who had been protecting the precious life of their father Chinggis Khan, and the personal slaves and the ten thousand guards who had been in close attendance on the person of his father the Khan, were all handed over by elder brother Chagatai and Tolui to Ogedai Khan."

After all the official and ceremonial components of the accession were done, the party began. The new khan distributed a large quantity of the massive amount of loot Chinggis had accumulated over decades of plundering to many of those assembled at the quriltai, including commoners and soldiers. Sacrifices were also made in Chinggis's honor. These included prized Mongol horses donated by the top military commanders for Chinggis to ride in the afterlife. And also, less festively, 40 of the most beautiful Mongol women, daughters and wives of the elite military commanders, were also sacrificed to attend to his every need.

Then it was down to the business of governing a vast world state. Ogedai decreed that all of the laws and pronouncements of Chinggis Khan remain in place. He then pardoned any criminals who had committed their crimes before he had come to the throne but warned that any new crimes committed against the proscriptions of the Great Yasa law code would be severely punished. Only then did Ogedai and the Mongol elites turn their attention to one of the last statements Chinggis had made to his sons: "Life is short. I could not conquer all the world. You will have to do it!"

This exhortation by Chinggis Khan was now viewed as something much more than a mere encouragement to keep up the good work. The rise and extraordinary military victories of Chinggis Khan were regarded with awe by the Mongols, who were frankly astonished at their success. They genuinely saw this as a historic chapter in the history of their people and as something that could only have been decreed by the gods, and by the great sky god Tengri in particular. As Tim May puts it, "it was as if Tenggri (heaven) had decreed the earth to the Mongols." This belief now evolved into a fully worked up spiritual ideology, similar in some ways to the Chinese concept of the Mandate of Heaven. The gods had decreed that the Mongols should conquer the whole earth, and that is exactly what they would continue to do under the new khan Ogedai.

The first military priority had to be the reignition of the war against the Jin Dynasty in China. Outstanding Mongol general Muqali had single-handedly maintained the pressure on the Jin, even as the bulk of the army had spent five years far to the west on the Khwarazmian campaign. Muqali had died in 1223, however, and the conflict had bogged down with no headway on either side. The decision was made to renew this war with a vengeance in a campaign to be led by Tolui and Ogedai himself, although Ogedai was always conscious that his younger brother was the superior strategist and would call all the military shots.

As further evidence of the Mongols' ability to fight on several fronts at once, it was also decided that at the same time, General Subedai would lead a Mongol force thousands of miles to the west as far as the Volga River in modern Russia to secure territories that Jochi had conquered during the Khwarazmian campaign. In addition, a smaller force was sent north into the Siberian steppe to secure tribute from the nomads dwelling there.

While these campaigns were in their early stages, word reached the Mongol high command that Jalal al-Din, the son of the late Khwarazmian Shah, who had escaped from Chinggis Khan by spurring his horse into the Indus River, had returned and was actively trying to reconstitute part of his father's empire in Persia. So a fourth campaign was launched back across the Amu Darya led by Chormaqan Noyan and his second-in-command, Dayir. Their job was to catch and kill Jalal al-Din and also permanently occupy Afghanistan, which had been conquered by Chinggis but never secured.

In northern China, Tolui's military brilliance against the Jin was immediately on full display, but then, in the year 1232, only the second year of the campaign, Tolui suddenly died in somewhat mysterious circumstances. Rumors emerged that Ogedai had had him killed, although no motive for this has even been determined. Despite his younger brother's death, Ogedai was determined to keep up the pressure on the Jin, and so he recalled Subedai from the Volga River to take charge of the campaign. Just think about that for a moment: From the Volga to northern China is a distance of some 3,500 miles. But that was nothing to the Mongols!

In China, Subedai did his job brilliantly and quickly. Within one campaign season, the Jin were reduced to controlling only a small region around the city of Kaifeng. Then Subedai simply turned his horse around and rode 3,500 miles back again to the western front—extraordinary! The following year, 1234, the Jin capital of Kaifeng fell, and the Jin Empire ceased to exist soon afterwards.

The Song Dynasty, which had been controlling southern China after the north had been overrun by the Jurchen more than a century earlier, had agreed to supply the Mongols with some food during the final stages of the campaign in the hope that once the Mongols had destroyed the Jin, the Song would be able to reclaim some of their former territories. Ogedai initially agreed to the alliance, but when the Song did move to occupy former Jin territory, a furious Ogedai ordered the beginning of military operations against the Song. This would prove to be a lengthy campaign indeed, and ultimately, it would be up to Tolui's son Qubilai Khan to lead the campaigns that finally destroyed the Song nearly 40 years later. We will hear much more about Qubilai Khan in future lectures.

The Jin campaign was the last military operation Ogedai would ever personally participate in. He realized that the Mongols were replete with brilliant field commanders and that his father had chosen him for different skills. And so Ogedai now turned to affairs of state and the consolidation of the empire, even as military operations continued in all directions. One of the first tasks he focused on was the construction of the Mongol capital of Karakorum, and that is a subject we will return to in the very next lecture.

Even as the new capital began to rise in the Orkhon Valley, thousands of miles to the west, the Mongol army led by Chormaqan Noyan was relentlessly pursuing Jalal al-Din. Local rulers in various parts of central Asia had attempted to deal with Jalal, including the ruler of the Sultanate of Delhi, who evicted him from his territories, and the ruler of Urgench on the Amu Darya, who tried to defeat him in the field.

Jalal al-Din moved further west into northern Iran, then north into the Caucasus, all the while pursued by the army of Chormaqan Noyan. As the Mongols had campaigned through northern Iran, they had besieged and captured a few cities, but regional rulers quickly realized the power of the Mongol army and voluntarily submitted. The only holdout was the city of Isfahan, which Jalal al-Din declared to be his new capital, but then he had to immediately flee from the city into the mountains when news of the approach of the Mongol army reached him.

A Mongol strike force caught up with Jalal al-Din and the remnants of the Khwarazmian army as he was making merry in a camp in the Caucasus. The Khwarazmians fought hard, and Jalal al-Din escaped again, but he was soon captured and killed by unknown forces deeper in the mountains, perhaps by Kurdish peasants who have a long history of military prowess. The remnants of the Khwarazmian force raced back to the security of Isfahan, but only succeeded in putting their heads in the noose as the Mongols ambushed and slew most of them. The remnants escaped further west, heading towards Egypt.

Chormaqan's campaign was by no means finished with the death of Jalal-al-Din. In 1233, he occupied a lush plain located in the modern nation of Azerbaijan, using this as a base to gradually expand the size of his domain over the next two years. His position was soon strong enough to launch an invasion of Armenia and Georgia, two states that had been weakened by raids from Jalal-al-Din before his death. The rulers of Armenia and Georgia decided not to confront the Mongols in the field and instead tried to defend themselves in mountain fortresses. But these were picked off one by one by Chormaqan and his troops.

The bravery of several of these princes in defending their mountain states impressed the Mongols, and once they had submitted, they were treated fairly, so long as they paid their taxes to the Mongols and provided troops when requested. But the Georgian queen Rusudan refused to submit and fled further west to a heavily fortified stronghold. She was left isolated there by the Mongols until her grudging submission a few years later.

As these campaigns were going on in the north, other forces associated with Chormaqan's larger campaign successfully occupied Afghanistan and then began raiding into northern and southern Iraq. But the Mongols had no plans to occupy the region at this stage—simply to raid and pillage.

With all this military activity happening on several fronts at once, Ogedai decided to convene another quriltai in 1234 near his new capital of Karakorum to discuss with his elite advisers and commanders where the Mongol forces should be concentrated next. Jack Weatherford paints a dramatic picture of this gathering, with various commanders arguing for campaigns into India, or an expansion of the raids in Iraq, or perhaps onto Syria, or for an intensification of the offensive against the Song in Southern China. But as Weatherford describes the situation:

One man ... had a different proposal. Subedai, fresh from his victory over the Jurchen, had been the greatest general in Chinggis Khan's army. ... He was now 60 years old, probably blind in one eye, and according to some reports so fat that he could no longer ride a horse, and had to be hauled around in an iron chariot. Despite these limitations, his mind was sharp and vigorous.

Subedai proposed to the quriltai that it was time for a fresh target, a massive campaign far to the west to Russia and Europe. This was a region most Mongols were only dimly aware of, but Subedai argued that enormous wealth was probably there for the taking. And Subedai was speaking from experience as one of the few commanders that had some personal history in the region, both during the Khwarazmian war in the early 1220s, and again in 1229 following Ogedai's accession.

In 1223, Subedai and Jebe had confronted a substantial Russian army on the Kalka River and destroyed it. Thereafter, the commanders had turned east and headed back into Khwarazmia to continue the war against the shah. Following this brief period of devastation and then retreat, the peoples of Armenia, Georgia, and Russia had been utterly mystified as to who the Mongols were and where they had come from. As one chronicle of the Russian city of Novgorod put it, "the Tatars turned back from the Dnieper River and we know not whence they came, nor where they hid themselves again; only God knows whence he fetched them against us for our sins." But now the Mongols were coming back.

Despite some evidence suggesting there was tension between the two men, Ogedai apparently found Subedai's arguments persuasive. And so a massive campaign to the west was launched in 1236 at the orders of Ogedai Khan. One explicit goal of this campaign was to take control of a region large enough for the descendants and followers of Jochi to occupy and settle. Jochi's descendants required a domain commensurate with the prestige of their illustrious founder, the eldest son of Chinggis Khan.

An additional goal was to try and defeat the semi-nomadic Kipchak Turks who occupied the steppes north of the Caspian Sea, and as part of this task, the Mongols also wanted to force the king of the nomadic Bulgars, who also dwelt on the steppe, to submit to the Mongols. He had previously refused to do so when it was demanded by Subedai during the Khwarazmian war in the 1220s.

As Subedai had noted, Mongol armies certainly had some previous experience in the region the new campaign was now targeting. During the Khwarazmian war of the 1220s, Subedai and Jebe had rampaged through Armenia and Georgia and fought with the formidable Kipchaks at the Battle of the Kalka River in 1223. And immediately following the accession of Ogedai in 1229, Subedai had recommenced operations along the Volga River before Ogedai had recalled him to China to take command of the war against the Jin. Mongol forces had remained in the region and pushed on as far as the Ural River, but it appears with no real plan of operation.

This campaign was to have significant ramifications for both Russia and Europe, and indeed the conquest of Russia and the incursions into Europe are often described as the key purpose of the campaign. Certainly, Weatherford's dramatic interpretation of Subedai's arguments at the quriltai support this. And David Morgan is certainly correct in claiming that "the main achievements of the reign [of Ogedai] were the invasion of Russia and eastern Europe." But Tim May is also probably correct in pointing out that "these actions were ancillary to the Mongols' goals."

And yet, despite May's arguments and the apparently limited aims of the campaign—to bring the Kipchaks under control and create a realm for the followers of Jochi—the western invasion of 1236 had all the hallmarks of a campaign of imperial expansion. One could make a larger argument here that Chinggis Khan brilliantly conquered enormous regions of Eurasia, but it was Khan Ogedai who actually created the Mongol Empire.

The Mongol force that marched towards Russia and Europe was probably 150,000 strong. The leadership included a glittering "who's who" of the Mongol elites: Ogedai's son Qadan, Chagatai's son Baidar, and Tolui's eldest son, Mongke. The son of Jochi was nominal leader of the campaign, but his was really a figurehead position; it was General Subedai who was actually in command of this massive invasion force.

Following the military strategy established from the beginning of Mongol expansion by Chinggis Khan, once the army crossed the Volga River, it immediately divided into two. One force led by Mongke marched against the Kipchaks. Many Kipchaks fled west, but many others stood and fought until they were defeated, their khans killed, and their warriors incorporated into the Mongol army. Another army marched north under the leadership of Batu and other sons of Jochi to bring the Bulgars and other Siberian steppe tribes to heel.

With the first aim of the campaign successfully completed, by the end of 1237, the Mongols were ready to launch operations against the various city-states and principalities of Rus, the western regions of modern Russia. The notoriously divided princes of Rus struggled to form any sort of unified response. Although it was now deep winter, the Mongols had no hesitation in attacking the Rus strongholds. Indeed, as Tim May so accurately puts it, "the Mongols did not fear the Russian winter—they welcomed it. The frozen rivers served as highways and not obstacles." Remember, Mongol soldiers had learned the art of war in the massive hunts they carried out on the steppe in the middle of winter. The princes of Rus had no idea what was about to come at them across the frozen plains of Russia.

Mongol forces besieged the city of Riazan first and used their sophisticated siege craft and engineers to capture it just before Christmas 1237. Then they divided their forces again. One set off to engage the army of the nominal ruler of all the princedoms of Rus, Grand Prince Vladimir, defeating him in battle on the banks of the Sit River. Other Mongol contingents used brilliant siege-craft skills to capture city after city. The ever-inventive Mongols even converted some of their siege engines into a type of field artillery, using them to hurl huge rocks to smash through their opponents like bowling balls.

The overall strategy was no less brilliant and was based on the huge *nerge* hunts, in which an area hundreds of miles square was encircled by Mongol soldiers who then marched inwards in an ever-tightening circle. The forces of the kingdom of Rus now found themselves trapped like animals waiting for the slaughter. In the end, the princes of the northern Rus city-states, which had so far escaped the carnage in the south, had no option other than to surrender, which most had done by the spring of 1238.

The Mongols then rested for the summer and fall of 1238 in the lush grasslands of the steppe surrounding the River Don before launching a new campaign against the remaining southern principalities of Rus in the winter of 1238. Throughout the remainder of that year and the next, cities continued to fall one by one, and by the autumn of 1240, the Mongols stood before the walls of the most important and prosperous city in all of Greater Rus, Kiev, the capital of the modern nation of Ukraine. As Jack Weatherford reminds us, even in the 13th century, Kiev was not only the capital of Rus, it was also "the largest and most important political and religious center in the Slavic world."

The siege of Kiev was led by Chinggis Khan's grandsons Mongke, the eldest son of Tolui, and Batu, the eldest son of Jochi. As the Mongols surrounded the walls, they apparently made a tremendous noise, so loud that the residents of the city could not hear each other speak. Despite its formidable fortifications, the Mongols breached the walls with ease and swarmed into the city streets. The terrified residents sought refuge in the many churches of Kiev in hopes of divine salvation. One church was so packed inside that the doors were locked. In desperation, those locked outside climbed up the walls and onto the roof, which then promptly collapsed, crushing everyone inside. Other churches were set ablaze by the Mongols, and everyone inside was burnt to death.

The city fell on the 6th of December 1240, and the Mongols looted it and burnt it to the ground. Later travelers noted that the roads from the city were still strewn with the bones of the former citizens of Kiev who had tried to flee the conflagration. Other cities of Rus quickly submitted, which more or less brought the Russian phase of the campaign to an end.

As Batu and Subedai mopped up the remaining southern cities, another Mongol army led by Qadan, Berke, and Mongke headed south to the steppe regions north of the Black and Caspian Seas to try and bring rebel Kipchak and other steppe nomadic peoples dwelling there to heel. Some leaders submitted, and Berke was able to turn the region into part of his personal ordu, or camp.

The Mongols now looked westwards again, with Europe firmly in their sights. But where the Rus states had not undertaken any real preparations when news of the Mongol invasion had reached them, the powerful Hungarian state, which dominated large regions of central Europe, had not sat passively by and waited for the hammer to fall. As the Mongols rested prior to the invasion, Hungarian King Bela IV built new fortifications, strengthened existing fortresses in the Carpathian mountains, and also formed a strategic alliance with the Cumans.

The Hungarian king also welcomed thousands of Kipchak refugees into his realm as potential mercenaries against the Mongols, although the unruly Kipchaks ultimately did more harm than good. When a Mongol envoy demanded of Bela IV that he return the Kipchaks, the king refused, which meant war with the Hungarians and their allies was now inevitable and, in the eyes of the Mongols who believed the Kipchaks were their property, justified.

The campaign opened on a huge front in 1241. One force, perhaps 20,000 strong, under the command of Chagatai's son Baidar and Ogedai's son Qadan, launched an assault against Poland in the north, while the main force of 50,000 warriors under the command of Batu and Subedai headed directly for Hungary. The Mongols were also careful to leave an occupying force on the Black Sea steppe to consolidate their conquest of that region.

Baidar and Qadan immediately devastated eastern Poland, while the rulers of western Poland hastily assembled an army. Knights under the command of Henry II the Pious came from Silesia. Teutonic knights also came from Prussia, and knights under the command of Vaclav I, Henry's brother-in-law, set out from Bohemia as reinforcements. But the ever-well-informed Mongols knew that Vaclav was coming and so forced battle with the 30,000 Silesian and Prussian knights and conscripts at Legnica on the 9th of April 1241.

The Mongols, who had thus far hidden their real numbers from the Europeans, had chosen a perfect open field as the place of battle. Once again, their tactics were brilliant, using feigned retreats to exhaust the Europeans in their heavy armor before cutting them down with siege equipment and superb archery. Something close to 25,000 of Henry's force of 30,000 were killed, and Henry's head was cut off and paraded outside the walls of the city of Legnica.

The Mongols also pressed into service a large number of German gold miners that Henry had conscripted and sent them a huge distance back across Eurasia to work in mines in the mountains of modern Kyrgyzstan. When Vaclav I, who was on his way to join the allies at Legnica, heard about the defeat, he and his Bohemian knights turned around and began to head home. Mongol commanders Baider and Qadar immediately gave chase, forcing Vaclav away from Hungary, where the main Mongol force was now poised to attack.

The blow came later in April 1241 at the Battle of Mohi, beside the swollen Sajo River, a site specifically chosen by Subedai because of the advantages it offered for the Mongol art of battle. But because the river was so wide and formidable, the first clash actually occurred on the only bridge across it. Using their siege weapons as artillery, the Mongols captured the bridge and drove the Hungarians away. Hungarian forces then hastily formed a formidable defensive circle of wagons and heavy iron chains that was more or less impervious to Mongol arrows.

The Mongols did not engage the fortified position, but surrounded it and bombarded it with all manner of flammable bombs, including substances like naphtha and flaming oil. But the shrewd Subedai also carefully left a gap in the Mongol encirclement, and the Hungarians played right into his hands by trying to escape through this and flee towards the safety of the nearby twin cities of Buda and Pest. But of course, they had simply put themselves into a fatal trap. The Mongols attacked the fleeing Hungarian forces from behind and destroyed them, although Bela and a few nobles escaped.

Thomas of Spolato, a religious authority living in the modern city of Split in Croatia and a contemporary to these events, described the dreadful flight to Buda and Pest like this: "The dead fell to the right and to the left; like leaves in winter the slain bodies of these miserable men were strewn along the whole route; blood flowed like torrents of rain."

The Mongols arrived at Buda and Pest the next day and sacked both cities. Qadan was recalled from Poland to hunt down the fugitive King Bela, although he did eventually escape by fleeing to an island in the Adriatic Sea. In the aftermath, Hungary was tamed and pillaged by Subedai and Batu, although Bulgaria submitted and became a client state of the Mongols. Jack Weatherford, drawing on contemporary accounts, argues that "European knighthood never recovered from the blow of losing 100,000 soldiers in Poland and Hungary, what the Europeans mourned as the flower of their knighthood and aristocracy."

There was now seemingly nothing to prevent an attack on the Holy Roman Empire and the destruction of western Europe itself. Even the heavens seemed to portend disaster when an eclipse occurred on Sunday, October 16th, widely interpreted as a sign of impending doom. European rulers and clergy, who had no idea where these "cannibals from hell" had come from, concocted all sorts of quasi-religious theories about the Mongols. But a scapegoat was needed, and, as usual, this conveniently became the Jews, who were attacked and murdered by angry Christian mobs in cities all across western Europe.

The worst fears of the Europeans seemed to be realized when Mongol scouting parties suddenly appeared near Vienna near the end of 1241. But astonishingly, this was to be as close to western Europe as the Mongols would ever come, because at the beginning of 1242, they simply packed up their camps and disappeared back into the eastern steppe from whence they had come.

Word had reached Batu and Subedai that Great Khan Ogedai had died on December 11th, 1241. And Chagatai had died soon afterwards, so the four sons of Chinggis Khan were all gone. It would take his grandsons and their cousins a decade to sort out the succession tensions between them, and in that decade, the world would be temporarily safe from further Mongol devastation.

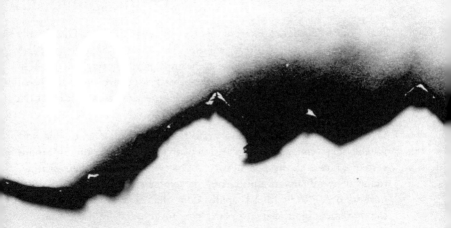

MONGOL QUEENS AND
THE CONTEST FOR THE EMPIRE

The death of Ogedai Khan on December 11, 1241 saved western Europe from seemingly inevitable Mongol devastation. His death meant that a new *quriltai* had to be convened to decide on the crucial matter of a successor. Most of the Mongol male elites had been campaigning in Russia and Europe for the past several years, but there was no alternative now other than to break off all military campaigns and return to Mongolia for this critically important gathering.

As most of the Mongols continued on the long trek back to Mongolia, they could hardly have guessed that for the next 10 years, virtually all Mongol military expansion would essentially grind to a halt. The eventual effect of this would be the division of the Mongol empire into a series of khanates, each controlled by descendants of the sons of Chinggis Khan.

Ogedai's Impact

Replacing Ogedai was never going to be easy. Despite the chronic alcoholism that probably killed him, he had turned out to be a very effective successor to Chinggis Khan.

It was under Ogedai's leadership that the Jin dynasty in China had finally been destroyed and the offensive against the southern Song dynasty had begun. It was also under Ogedai that the great imperial campaign had been dispatched to the west, inspired by the new spiritual ideology that Ogedai had promoted: the idea that Tengri (or heaven itself) had decreed that the Mongols should conquer the world.

Ogedai had also proven to be a very effective administrator. One of his most notable achievements was the creation of an empire-wide communications system known as the *jam* network. Once in place, the network had tremendous military, administrative, and commercial advantages. It allowed military orders to be spread rapidly along the network, and it facilitated the movement of official envoys carrying royal orders from the capital to the provinces.

Another of his accomplishments was the construction of the first Mongol capital of Karakorum. None of the Mongol khans ever actually lived in their capital, but they visited from time to time for ceremonial affairs of state. Ogedai and his successors preferred to live in their mobile ger camps somewhere outside of the walls of the city.

After Ogedai

Even before his death in 1241, Ogedai Khan was often too drunk to conduct affairs of state, so he had given his most capable wife Toregene administrative power, even though she was not his senior wife.* After Ogedai's death, Toregene became regent, ruling initially with the support of a Chinggisid prince. Toregene was keen to push her son Guyuk forward as a potential new khan, and the first step in this campaign was to convene a *quriltai*. When calls to convene the *quriltai* arrived, Batu stalled for several years. In the end, the *quriltai* was not convened until 1246, five years after the death of Ogedai.

When the *quriltai* was finally convened, it was boycotted by Batu, although he did send two sons as representatives. This was a massive gathering attended by Mongol and other elites from all across the empire.

Toregene was remarkably successful in the world of Mongol politics. As historian Anne Broadbridge puts it, "she overcame a weak political position" and other factors to position Guyuk well. As Guyuk was preparing to take up that throne, a coup of sorts was attempted by Chinggis Khan's younger brother Temuge Otchigin, but this was thwarted through the arrival of Ogedai's youngest son and his forces. After taking power, Guyuk ordered an inquiry to the affair, headed by Mongke, the eldest son of Tolui. Temuge was found guilty and executed.

For the first several months of his reign, Guyuk's mother held on to the strings of power, but following her death, he moved to reverse some of the worst of her administrative policies. He invited several of Ogedai's bureaucrats who had survived her regency back into government. Guyuk's reforms were also supported by Mongke, demonstrating a degree of collegiality between the descendants of the sons of Chinggis Khan.

Guyuk also moved to tighten up the *jam* communications network by restricting the official Mongol passports given to travelers to only those with legitimate business. Toregene had freely distributed these passports as a way of gaining more support and income.

Oghul Qaimish and Sorkaktani

Guyuk died suddenly in 1248, bringing the empire to a standstill. Another Mongol queen took control of the empire: Guyuk's primary wife, Oghul Qaimish. The sources on the regency of Oghul Qaimish are ambiguous, but some suggest that it was her neglect of imperial administration that ultimately brought an end to the primacy of the house of Ogedai.

At this point, another exceptional woman became quite relevant: Chinggis Khan's daughter-in-law Sorkaktani. At about the age of 26, Sorkaktani had become one of the wives of Chinggis Khan's youngest son, Tolui, when Tolui was 12 or 13 years old. As Mongol expansion continued through the decades that followed, Sorkaktani acquired considerable status in the Mongol world, particularly as she gave birth to four remarkable sons.

Sorkaktani took one of her sons with her as she traveled to her new home at Zhengding, in present-day Hebei province some 160 miles south of Beijing. This son was destined to be remembered as one of the greatest Mongol khans of all, Qubilai Khan, future emperor of the Yuan dynasty in China. As overlords of their new domain, mother and son worked hard to repair the damage caused by war and to build up a successful farming estate system that contributed regular taxation income. Sorkaktani also launched several successful commercial ventures.

Once Sorkaktani heard of the death of Guyuk, she sent tribute and condolences to his widow Oghul Qaimish. Meanwhile, Batu sent word throughout the realm that all Mongol princes should meet with him at a place called Ala Qamaq to choose a new khan. This was clearly a breach of protocol: Instead of waiting for the regent to declare a *quriltai*, Batu went above her and called for the gathering anyway, although he did propose that she stay on as regent in the meantime.

The location—which was in Siberia, 2,000 miles away from the traditional *quriltai* location in central Mongolia—was too remote, and many princes did not attend. The plans to elect a new khan continued anyway, and Batu, now supported by Sorkaktani, decided to champion the merits of Sorkaktani's oldest son, Mongke. Oghul Qaimish refused to attend, although she did send two of her sons as representatives. Two of Ogedai's sons also attended.

Queen Sorkaktani with Tului

Mongke in Command

In the end, Mongke received the majority of votes, although the princes asked the sons of Guyuk to continue to rule until yet another *quriltai* officially confirming Mongke could be held. Oghul Qaimish and her sons plotted to ambush Mongke, but they never carried out the plan. Oghul Qaimish continued to rule in name, but she was marginalized.

Her two sons now left their mother and set up their own independent courts, thus bringing the administration to a crashing halt and creating disorder throughout the empire. Another pretender to the throne, Shiremun, the grandson of Ogedai, refused to accept the decision that Mongke would be crowned khan. Forming an alliance with other embittered Chinggisid princes, he hatched a dastardly plot to ambush and kill Mongke and his supporters.

According to John Man, a falconer uncovered and reported the plot. At first, Mongke did not believe the falconer's story, so he insisted that the princes at the head of this army be brought to him for interrogation. As Mongke realized they were guilty, one prince committed suicide while the other was executed. This was the start of what historians have dubbed the Toluid revolution. With the explicit support of Batu, Mongke now began a systematic purge of his rivals across the empire, with the principal targets being Ogodeid and Chagatayid princes and other elites.

Hit squads were dispatched throughout the empire carrying lists of those to be detained and executed in the great purge of late 1251 and early 1252. In the end, perhaps 300 of the most elite members of the Mongol royalty were executed. During the purge, Sorkaktani died at the age of 72.

After the purge, Mongke was secure on the throne of the empire. The clans of Ogedai and Chagatai were decimated, while the clans of Jochi and particularly Tolui were the beneficiaries. Sorkoktani's careful, diplomatic cultivation of Batu and the Jochids had helped pave the way for Mongke's success. Batu clearly liked and trusted her, and this relationship ensured Jochid support in the Toluid revolution. In return for his support, Batu was granted virtual autonomy over his now vast holdings in the steppes of Russia.

Mongke moved to symbolically legitimize his claim to power. He introduced a cult-like worship of Chinggis Khan in 1252, complete with elaborate ceremonies. His father, Tolui, who had been buried in the same mysterious grave as Chinggis Khan, was posthumously promoted to the status of a khan and was also venerated like a god. The reputation of Sorkaktani was now seen as beyond reproach, while Toregene and Oghul Qaimish were publicly denigrated.

Now the Mongol world waited to see what sort of khan Mongke would become. They would not be disappointed. During his eight-year reign, Mongke would prove to be a very efficient administrator, and Mongol military expansion was also about to be reignited in all directions across Eurasia.

MONGOL QUEENS AND THE CONTEST FOR THE EMPIRE

LECTURE 10 TRANSCRIPT

The death of Khan Ogedai on December 11th, 1241, saved western Europe from seemingly inevitable Mongol devastation. His death meant that a new quriltai had to be convened to decide on the crucial matter of a successor. Most of the Mongol male elites had been campaigning in Russia and Europe for the past several years, but there was no alternative now other than to break off all military campaigns and return to Mongolia for this critically important gathering.

During the early months of 1242, the Mongols reassembled their troops and began the march from Europe back through Russia. Somewhat disappointed with the loot they had amassed from the European campaigns, Mongol leaders made arrangements en route with Venetian and Genoese merchants who had established colonies on the coast of the Black Sea.

Although the Mongols had little to show in the way of treasure from their victories in Europe, they had captured a large number of prisoners. The Mongols now exchanged many of these European captives with the merchants in return for substantial quantities of commercial goods. The Venetians and Genoese then sold the young captives as slaves in markets all around the Mediterranean.

The Italian merchants sold many of these slaves to a sultan in Egypt who recruited most of the young men into his slave army, which already contained many Kipchaks who had escaped the Mongol campaigns against them a few years earlier. Ironically, it would be this same slave Mameluke army that would ultimately stop the Mongols in their tracks about 20 years later and gain the reputation as one of the few armies that ever defeated the Mongols in the field.

But that was well in the future. As most of the Mongols continued on the long trek back to Mongolia, they could hardly have guessed that for the next 10 years, virtually all Mongol military expansion would essentially grind to a halt as the elites of the Mongol world found themselves almost gridlocked in an intense jockeying for power. The eventual effect of this would be the division of the Mongol Empire into a series of khanates, each controlled by descendants of the sons of Chinggis Khan. Only when this succession issue was resolved would imperial expansion be renewed.

It is this decade-long hiatus that is the subject of this lecture, which considers the roles played by male princes and female queens in determining the future of the empire. But before turning to that decade of intrigue and division, we must first offer an assessment of the achievements of Ogedai Khan. The impact of his 12 years on the throne would also have been on the minds of the Mongols as they marched back across the immense Eurasian steppe.

Replacing Ogedai was never going to be easy, because despite the chronic alcoholism that probably killed him, he had turned out to be a very effective successor to Chinggis Khan indeed. It was under Ogedai's leadership that the Jin Dynasty in China had finally been destroyed and the offensive against the southern Song Dynasty begun. It was also under Ogedai that the great imperial campaign had been dispatched to the west, inspired by the new spiritual ideology that Ogedai had promoted—the idea that Tengri (or heaven itself) had decreed that the Mongols should conquer the world.

Fired up by this ideology, Mongol armies had hunted down Jalal al-Din then conquered Afghanistan, Persia, Iraq, the Caucasus, Georgia, and Armenia, the tough Kipchaks of the Eurasian steppe, the city-states and princedoms of Rus, including the great city of Kiev, before finally destroying something like 100,000 German, Hungarian, and Polish knights on the battlefield, the cream of European knighthood.

But creating a huge empire through conquest is just the first step; it then had to be administered, and here again Ogedai had proven a very effective administrator. Two of his achievements in particular need to be noted: the creation of an empire-wide communications system and the construction of the first Mongol capital of Karakorum. As David Morgan points out, "it would hardly have been possible to rule an empire the size of the Mongols effectively without an adequate system of communications." Chinggis Khan had introduced a sort of ad hoc system called the *Jam*, but this seems to have been confined to communications only within Mongolia. Both *The Secret History* and Rashid al-Din note that a genuine empire-wide system was created by Ogedai.

Once in place, the *Jam* network had tremendous military, administrative, and commercial advantages. It allowed military orders to be spread rapidly along the network, and it facilitated the movement of official envoys carrying royal orders from the capital to the provinces. It also evolved into a commercial network that, as with previous iterations of the Silk Roads, facilitated the movement of goods and services vast distances across Eurasia.

The Secret History notes that the system in place before Ogedai came to the throne had imposed enormous burdens on regions through which imperial envoys had passed because they needed to be fed and housed by local people. So in 1234, Ogedai instituted a new network, initially just within the territories he controlled personally, but later to also include the regions controlled by his brothers Chagatai and Tolui, plus those now under the control of Jochi's son Batu.

Army units in various parts of the empire were charged with the responsibility of maintaining the *Jam*, although it was local people who were expected to provide the horses and supplies. A series of post stations were constructed one day's journey from each other, roughly 25 or 30 miles apart, although sometimes more in the remotest regions of the empire. Each station was stocked with provisions for authorized travelers, but they had to demonstrate their legitimacy by producing proper documentation in the form of an official tablet called a *gerege*, or a *paiza*, made of wood, silver, or gold and decorated with various heraldic symbols depending upon the status of the traveler.

For most envoys, the rate of travel was roughly 25 to 30 miles in a day, but when news had to really move quickly—say, orders from a khan in Mongolia to commanders thousands of miles away in the field—it could move incredibly quickly. Both Marco Polo and Rashid al-Din report that express couriers could travel 200 miles or more in a single day. These Pony Express riders used bells or horns that hung from their belts to signal their imminent arrival at the next post station so that they could collect supplies and leap onto another horse virtually without stopping.

The introduction of this extraordinary *Jam* system, which the Mongols may have based on preexisting networks that they dramatically expanded and intensified, not only greatly helped in the administration of their vast empire but also brought east and west Eurasia together in a way that had not been seen since the collapse of the old Silk Roads. This is certainly a theme we will return to towards the end of the course: the role of the Mongols in reunifying Eurasia and helping in the transmission of technologies and ideas from China to the West—technologies like gunpowder, paper, and printing that would profoundly impact the future.

Ogedai's other great achievement in the administration of his empire was the construction of the first Mongol capital at Karakorum. Ogedai chose a site in the Orkhon Valley that had also been used by the Mongols' Xiongnu, Turkic, and Uyghur predecessors as the sacred heartland of their steppe empires. Some of the criteria Ogedai probably considered in choosing the site were similar to the considerations that had traditionally gone into choosing a good campsite.

Jack Weatherford enumerates these criteria: "It was on an open steppe with good wind to keep the mosquitoes down, with ample water far enough away that it would not be polluted by the people living in the city, and with mountains nearby as a winter sanctuary for the herds. In all regards the site of Karakorum … was perfect!"

Work commenced in 1235 with the construction of a palace, using skilled laborers and artisans the Mongols had acquired from the Jin Dynasty and also from the city-states of the former Khwarazmian Empire. Ogedai may also have utilized the traditional Mongol system of measurement by shooting arrows in different directions to outline the dimensions.

The first wing was built with dimensions based on where the first arrow had fallen, then a second wing was constructed as far as an arrow fired in the other direction had fallen. And when these two wings were completed, a large pavilion was erected between them. When the palace complex was finished, it was 2,500 meters square, with green painted walls, underfloor heating, and a Chinese-style roof covered in green and red tiles. Then a wall was built around the palace, and it is from the material used to build this wall that the city acquired the name of Karakorum, which means "black stones."

I have visited the former site of Karakorum, and I can assure you that apart from some artifacts collected in a superb small museum there, nothing of the palace or the city that grew up around it survives today. However, many of these same black stones and other materials were later used to construct the huge and impressive Erdene Zuu Buddhist monastery complex that was built on the site of the former city. But, of course, we do have numerous eyewitness accounts of the city at various stages of completion, including the extension of the complex that continued under the reign of Mongke Khan decades later.

The earliest account comes from Ata-Malik Juvaini, who first visited the city in 1252. Of the palace, he writes: "Inside it was a throne having three flights of steps, one for the Khan alone, another for his ladies, and a third for the cupbearers and table-deckers, and on the right and left, houses for his brothers and sons ... the walls [of which] were painted with pictures."

Even at its peak under Mongke, the city was never large, housing perhaps 10,000 people at most. A European traveler to the city, William of Rubruck, who visited in 1254, two years after Juvaini, famously dismissed the city as being no bigger than the Parisienne suburb of St. Denis. But he also described it as a culturally and religiously tolerant place.

None of the Mongol khans ever actually lived in their capital, but rather they visited from time to time for ceremonial affairs of state. Ogedai and his successors preferred to live in their mobile *ger* camps somewhere outside of the walls of the city. But many other administrators and merchants did live in Karakorum, people who had been brought from far away to help administer the empire, or who had traveled across the Mongol realm to conduct business there. So in every way, Karakorum functioned as a genuine capital—at least for a few decades—home to the bureaucrats, ambassadors, and merchants of the empire who required 900 cartloads of food and other supplies each day, according to some sources.

Because there were so many foreign merchants established in Karakorum, several markets were developed, and religious buildings were constructed to meet their spiritual needs, including Buddhist and Daoist temples, mosques, and even a Christian church. Ogedai's eventual successor, Mongke, continued to develop the city and beautify the city, even employing a French sculptor and silversmith captured in the campaign in Hungary, one Guillaume Boucher of Paris, to construct a magnificent fountain.

Contemporaries describe the fountain as being shaped like a huge silver tree. Mare's milk flowed from the mouth of a silver lion, while wine, fermented mare's milk, mead, and other alcoholic beverages flowed from four silver snake heads. On order, a servant would blow a pipe that extended from an angel on top of the tree as a signal that servants should begin pumping out the drinks.

Let's turn in the second part of this lecture to the 10-year hiatus in imperial expansion that followed the death of Ogedai in December 1241. Even before his death, the khan was often too drunk to conduct affairs of state, so he had given his most capable wife, Toregene, administrative power, even though she was not his senior wife.

This was not unusual. As Mongol men were far away fighting wars for years at a time, Mongol women from all strata of society assumed control of affairs at home. In keeping with all pastoral nomadic societies, the Mongols did not have the luxury of developing patriarchal structures that designated women as being of lesser status. There are numerous examples of elite Mongol women taking the reins of power, as events following Ogedai's death amply demonstrate. As Jack Weatherford points out, for the next several years, Toregene "and a small group of other women controlled the largest empire in world history."

After Ogedai's death, Toregene became regent, ruling initially with the support of a Chinggisid prince. Toregene was keen to push her son Guyuk forward as a potential new khan, and the first step in this campaign was to convene a quriltai. But this was complicated by the attitude of Batu, son of Chinggis Khan's eldest son, Jochi. Although Jochi's suspect parentage made Batu ineligible for the role of khan, this in no way diminished his status in the Mongol world. As other Mongol elites made their way back to Mongolia for the gathering, Batu pointedly chose to remain in the former Kipchak steppes of southern Russia to consolidate the realm he had created for himself there.

Ogedai's son Guyuk had set out on the great western campaign as a senior officer, but General Subedai had been forced to dismiss him from the campaign after Guyuk insulted Batu over his parentage. Sent back to Ogedai for punishment, Guyuk was stripped of his rank and ordered to China to fight in the front lines of the Song campaign. But Ogedai had died before the order was carried out, and now Guyuk, with the support of his mother, waspromoting himself as a strong candidate for his father's throne.

So when calls to convene the quriltai arrived, Batu, realizing that Guyuk's mother Toregene was now regent and favorably disposed towards her son's candidature, refused to return to Mongolia. Batu stalled for several years, and in the end, the quriltai was not convened until 1246, five years after the death of Ogedai.

Toregene, who was probably not unhappy with the delay, used the time well, cementing alliances with other princes and promoting the merits of Guyuk. But in her administration of the empire, the Persian commentators, who were probably aghast at the very idea of a woman ruling an empire, imply that Toregene focused on short-term enrichment rather than long-term sustainability, particularly in her manipulation of the taxation system. In order to do this, she dismissed some of Ogedai's best administrators, including the advisor Yelu Chucai, the bureaucrat who had first demonstrated to the Mongols the value of a stable and reasonable system of taxation.

Other administrators, fearing for their lives under Toregene, fled to the court of another of Ogedai's sons, Korten, who refused to return them to his mother. Another Persian administrator, Masud Beg, fled all the way west to the steppe camp of Batu. In the absence of these bureaucrats, Toregene was able to use her authority to manipulate the tax system in her favor, amassing the wealth needed to finance the candidacy of Guyuk, to essentially buy the supreme throne of the Mongol realm.

When the quriltai was finally convened in 1246, it was boycotted by Batu, although he did send two sons as representatives. This was a massive gathering attended by Mongol and other elites from all across the empire. The visitor who probably traveled furthest was the 65-year-old friar John of Plano Carpini, a former disciple of Francis of Assisi who had been commissioned as an envoy by Pope Innocent IV in Rome. Guyuk's mother Toregene had been a Christian, and the khan himself was favorably disposed to Christianity, so he was apparently pleased with the attendance of the papal envoy.

In fact, there were so many representatives of different faiths attending that the sources comment on the many debates that occurred at the quriltai between eloquent representatives of all the religions that now flourished in the vast multicultural empire. The gauntlet was thrown down to these religious worthies to try to convert Guyuk Khan to one or other of their faiths, but no one succeeded in doing so. Carpini was nonetheless impressed with Guyuk's intelligence, even noting in a letter to the pope that whatever Guyuk's personal faith and convictions, this would not interfere with his efficient management of the Mongol Empire.

Of course, many of the 3,000–4,000 worthies gathered at the quriltai were fully aware that Ogedai had once sentenced Guyuk to the Song front as a punishment, but in the end, Toregene's campaign was successful, and Guyuk was elected third khan of the Mongol Empire.

Despite the negative attitude displayed by the Persian sources towards Toregene, we must acknowledge that she was remarkably successful in the world of Mongol politics. As historian Anne Broadbridge puts it, "she overcame a weak political position, consolidated significant authority, and openly thwarted her husband's will in order to place their son Guyuk on a throne he could not have held without her backing."

As Guyuk was preparing to take up that throne, a coup of sorts was attempted by Chinggis Khan's younger brother Temuge Otchigin, but this was thwarted through the arrival of Ogedai's youngest son and his forces. After taking power, Guyuk ordered an inquiry into the affair, headed by Mongke, the eldest son of Tolui. Temuge was found guilty and executed.

For the first several months of his reign, Guyuk's mother held on to the strings of power, but following her death, he moved to reverse some of the worst of her administrative policies, inviting several of Ogedai's bureaucrats who had survived her regency back into government. Guyuk's reforms were also supported by Mongke, demonstrating a degree of collegiality between the descendants of the sons of Chinggis Khan.

Guyuk also moved to tighten up the *Jam* communications network by restricting the official Mongol passports given to travelers to only those with legitimate business. Toregene had freely distributed these passports as a way of gaining more support and income, and this had strained the resources available in the post stations and regions through which they traveled. Old passports were now declared void and new ones issued, but only to officials who could demonstrate their right and need to possess one. Guyuk also ordered an empire-wide census as the basis for a restructuring of the taxation system.

Some smaller-scale military campaigns did continue during Guyuk's rule. One Mongol force under the leadership of Eljigedei was sent to the Middle East to confront a group known as the Nizari Ismailis, more popularly known as the Assassins, who had killed a Mongol military commander in the region. A low-key campaign was also maintained against the Song

Dynasty in China, under the leadership on the venerable Subedai. Guyuk even started making plans to return to Europe with a large Mongol army, although this might have been a cover for Guyuk's real intention to attack and destroy Batu, who still opposed his khanship.

We will never know what might have happened with that campaign, because Guyuk died suddenly in 1248, bringing the empire to a standstill. This time, it was another Mongol queen, Guyuk's primary wife, Oghul Qaimish, who took control of the empire. The sources on the regency of Oghul Qaimish are ambiguous, but some suggest that it was her neglect of imperial administration that ultimately brought an end to the primacy of the house of Ogedai.

It is at this point in the story that we need to introduce yet another exceptional woman, Chinggis Khan's daughter-in-law Sorkaktani, who John Man describes as "the most remarkable woman of her age." At about the age of 26, Sorkaktani had become one of the wives of Chinggis Khan's youngest son, Tolui, when Tolui was only 12 or 13 years old. As Mongol expansion continued through the decades that followed, Sorkaktani acquired considerable status in the Mongol world, particularly as she gave birth to four remarkable sons. This gave her the status to petition Ogedai to give her an estate in northern China after the conquest of the Jin Empire. Because Ogedai respected her status and advice, he agreed, which helped her acquire even more wealth and status.

Sorkaktani took one of her sons with her as she traveled to her new home at Zhengding, in present-day Hebei Province, some 160 miles south of Beijing. This son was destined to be remembered as one of the greatest Mongol khans of all, Qubilai Khan, future emperor of the Yuan Dynasty in China. As overlords of their new domain, mother and son worked hard to repair the damage caused by war and to build up a successful farming estate system that contributed regular taxation income. Sorkaktani also launched several successful commercial ventures, according to Rashid al-Din.

Once Sorkaktani heard of the death of Guyuk, she sent tribute and condolences to his widow Oghul Qaimish. Meanwhile, Batu sent word throughout the realm that all Mongol princes should meet with him at a place called Ala Qamaq to choose a new khan. This was clearly a breach of protocol; instead of waiting for the regent to declare a quriltai, Batu went above her and called for the gathering anyway, although he did propose that she stay on as regent in the meantime. But the location—somewhere in Siberia near Lake Issyk-Kul, 2,000 miles away from the traditional quriltai location in central Mongolia—was just too remote, and many princes did not attend.

The plans to elect a new khan continued anyway, and Batu, now supported by Sorkaktani, decided to champion the merits of Sorkaktani's oldest son, Mongke. Mongke was a superb military commander, they argued, and had a measure of dignity and gravitas that Ogedai had recognized, according to Rashid al-Din. But because so many Mongol princes had not attended this quriltai, a second, more centrally located one had to be convened to legitimately elect Mongke.

This time, it was regent Oghul Qaimish who refused to attend, although she did send two of her sons as representatives. Perhaps realizing that political power was potentially about to shift to another of the families created by the sons of Chinggis Khan, two of Ogedai's sons also attended. They were also possibly sick of the lack of leadership being shown by their mother Oghul Qaimish. In the end, despite all the political tension surrounding these successive quriltai, Mongke received the majority of votes, although the princes asked the sons of Guyuk to continue to rule until yet another quriltai officially confirming Mongke could be held.

Oghul Qaimish and her sons, who had only stayed at the quriltai for two days, were furious when they heard the news and plotted to ambush Mongke, although they never carried out the plan. Oghul Qaimish continued to rule in name, but she was marginalized by the other Chinggisids. According to Juvaini, when she did try to act as regent, she ignored the advice of her administrators and interacted mostly with merchants and with shamans.

Oghul Qaimish's two sons now left their mother and set up their own independent courts, thus bringing the administration to a crashing halt and creating disorder throughout the empire. Another pretender to the throne, Shiremun, the grandson of Ogedai, refused to accept the decision that Mongke would be crowned khan, and forming an alliance with other embittered Chinggisid princes, he hatched a dastardly plot to ambush and kill Mongke and his supporters following the third quriltai. John Man dramatically describes how this plot was uncovered:

A falconer loses a favorite female camel. He sets out to find it, riding for two or three days here and there. He comes across an army. He notices a wagon full of weapons. He strikes up a conversation and discovers a plot to attack Mongke while everyone is feasting. Finding his camel he gallops back and barges in on the new emperor with the news.

At first, Mongke did not believe the falconer's story, so he insisted that the princes at the head of this army be brought to him for interrogation. As Mongke realized they were guilty, one prince committed suicide while the other was executed. This was just the beginning of what historians have dubbed the Toluid Revolution. With the explicit support of Batu, Mongke now began a systematic purge of his rivals across the empire, with the principal targets being Ogodeid and Chagatayid princes and other elites. Even members of the *altan urugh*, the Golden Family, were no longer exempted from death.

Hit squads were dispatched throughout the empire, carrying lists of those to be detained and executed in what became the great purge of late 1251 and early 1252. Nor were women spared. Regent Oghul Qaimish was charged by Mongke with being a witch and was wrapped in felt before being thrown into the Kerulen River to drown. Another queen, the wife of a grandson of Chagatai, was kicked to death in the presence of her husband. In the end, perhaps 300 of the most elite members of the Mongol royalty were executed. In the midst of the purge, Mongke's mother, Sorkaktani, died at the age of 72. She was buried in a Christian church in Gansu Province in northwestern China.

Now Mongke was secure on the throne of the empire. The clans of Ogedai and Chagatai were decimated, their status greatly reduced, while the clans of Jochi, and particularly Tolui, were the beneficiaries. It is clear in retrospect that Sorkoktani's careful, diplomatic cultivation of Batu and the Jochids helped pave the way for Mongke's success. Batu clearly liked and trusted her, and this relationship ensured Jochid support in the Toluid Revolution. In return for his support, Batu was granted virtual autonomy over the now vast holdings in the steppes of Russia, a region what would become the *ulus* of the Golden Horde.

With the purges complete, Mongke now moved to symbolically legitimize his claim to power. He introduced a cult-like worship of Chinggis Khan in 1252, complete with elaborate ceremonies. His father, Tolui, who had been buried in the same mysterious grave as Chinggis Khan, was posthumously promoted to the status of a khan and was also venerated like a god. The reputation of Sorkaktani was now seen as beyond reproach, while Toregene and Oghul Qaimish were publicly denigrated.

Now the Mongol world waited to see what sort of a khan Mongke would become. They would not be disappointed. During his eight-year reign, Mongke would prove to be a very efficient administrator indeed. And Mongol military expansion was also about to be reignited in all directions across Eurasia: back into southern China, of course, but also into Tibet, Korea, Japan, Vietnam, Burma, and most dramatically of all, the Middle East, where the great capital of the Islamic world, Baghdad, awaited its fate.

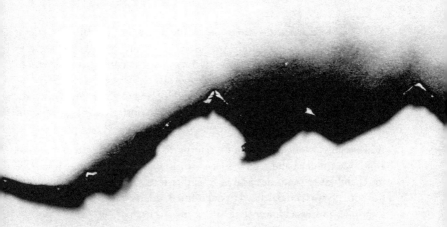

DIVIDING THE EMPIRE:
A TALE OF FOUR BROTHERS

In 1251, Mongke Khan turned to the administration of his realm. The central authority established over the empire by Chinggis and Ogedai had unraveled, and power now lay in the hands of various regional entities, including surviving Chinggisid princes.

Mongke's Bureaucrats and Reforms

In his efforts to restore order to the state, Mongke chose his senior bureaucrats well. His right-hand man for the first two years of his reign was named Menggeser. A Christian from the once rival Kereit tribe, Aqaa Bulghai, was appointed second in command, and was then promoted to senior administrator after Menggeser died in 1253.

One of the earliest jobs of Mongol bureaucrats was to conduct an empire-wide census, including in the regions now controlled by Batu. As a way of further centralizing power in the empire and reducing the autonomy of local rulers, Mongke transformed regional administrative structures into secretariats under the control of a central secretariat in Mongolia. Experienced bureaucrats like Mahmud Yalavach were placed in charge of the north China secretariat, for example, while his son Masud Beg took over in Turkestan.

Mongke also turned his attention to the *jam* communications system, which continued to come under considerable pressure by the various entities that used and abused it. Mongke decreed that the entire network was to be centralized and connected, including private networks. All *gerege*, or passports, then in circulation had to be handed over to government officials, and those who applied for new ones had to demonstrate the legitimacy of their need and be registered with the government.

Additionally, Mongke worked on reforming the taxation system, creating a more centralized and regulated system, and also using revenue resources to rehabilitate regions devastated by earlier wars. The *qubchur* tax paid by the nomads was standardized to one animal for every 100 of its species; but if families possessed fewer than 100 animals, they paid no tax.

Mongke did not insist on collecting back taxes that had been unpaid during the previous chaotic decade. But he vigorously enforced the payment of new taxes now that he was on the throne, including by Mongol elites.

Religion

The attitude of Mongol rulers toward the various religions practiced in their empire might best be described as one of religious neutrality. Everyone was free to practice their own religion unless it caused instability within the empire. However, this did not mean that the Mongols treated the adherents of all religions equally. Certain religions received tax exemptions, such as Buddhism, Daoism, Confucianism, Christianity, and Islam. Some did not, including Judaism, Zoroastrianism, and Manichaeism. The difference lay in the political and economic power and status of the hierarchies of these faiths.

Mongke was deeply interested in religion, although he appears to have ascribed to none of the faiths whose leaders regularly sent emissaries to convert him. Often these conversion attempts resembled sporting events as much as earnest religious debates, with teams of eloquent spiritual leaders squaring off in front of Mongke and other Mongol elites.

The debates were often convened as much for political reasons as for spiritual ones. The khans often brought rival groups together to try to end division and conflict between them, particularly if this was threatening the peace and security of the empire.

War

In the second year of his reign, Mongke convened another *quriltai*. This time, there was only one item on the agenda: war. Mongke had already dispatched his brothers to take control of vast regions of the empire. Qubilai went to China, and Hulagu went to Persia and the Middle East. These assignments now transitioned into serious military campaigns, and the brothers now each held the title of ilkhan.

The ideology of the Mongols toward war was that heaven, and particularly the sky god Tengri, had given the Mongols permission to conquer the whole world. It was this mandate that they set out to obey once again in the 1250s.

To carry out the mandate, the commanders of course needed armies, so Mongke ordered that two soldiers out of every 10 would now ride with Hulagu, and the same number would ride with Qubilai. Tim May estimates that by the early 1250s, the Mongol military probably had roughly 1 million nomadic soldiers enrolled, as well as "untold millions" of non-nomadic troops. Although Mongke had now assigned 40 percent of all Mongol military power to his brothers, this still left plenty of soldiers to ride with the khan himself, who was determined to join Qubilai in his campaign against the Song in southern China.

Attacking the Song

The campaign against the powerful Song had been at a stalemate since the reign of Ogedai. The Song had a formidable defensive structure in place along their entire northern border. Determined to circumvent this, Mongke and Qubilai decided to open a second front against the non-Chinese kingdom of Dali, located in the southwest near Tibet. Once conquered, this would allow the Mongols to attack the Song from an entirely new direction.

The campaign against Dali began in 1252, but it took three years of hard fighting before the kingdom fell. Mongke started attacking the Song's northern border with his forces in 1254, and he became anxious for Qubilai to open a second front through Dali. But Qubilai delayed in the lush pastures of Dali, annoying the impatient Mongke. It took four more years of bitter fighting before Mongke finally broke through the Song's formidable northern defenses and was able to march into eastern China.

Meanwhile, Qubilai moved his forces through central China and then turned south toward the Song capital. Mongol forces under General Uriyang Qadai invaded Song territory from the former kingdom of Dali, while yet another general, Taghachar, opened a fourth front and headed northwest.

Despite now having four separate armies arrayed against them, Song defenses remained formidable throughout their empire. However, the Mongol army was now augmented by hundreds of thousands of skilled soldiers from the former Jin dynasty. The Mongol advance was inexorable. As the four armies converged on the Yangtze Valley, Song collapse seemed inevitable.

Hulagu's Campaign

Hulagu's army campaigned in Persia and the Middle East with the explicit goal of forcing remaining groups to formally submit to Mongol rule. This included the formidable Nizari Assassins and the remnants of the fragmented Muslim Abbasid Caliphate.

Nizari Fortress Alamut

Hulagu's vast army moved slowly through central Asia, seeking steppe grasslands for the huge herds of horses that accompanied his army. His general Ket Buqa Noyan began military assaults against Nizari fortresses in Iran, which fell steadily. With his defenses failing and his people dying, Nizari leader Khurshah was granted safe passage through to Hulagu to formally surrender to the Mongols.

One particularly formidable Nizari fortress held out longest against the Mongols: an almost impregnable stronghold called Alamut on top of a mountain. Alamut finally fell in 1256. After this, Khurshah, who had since been sent back to Mongke, was executed.

Hulagu's way was now clear to march on the Abbasid capital of Baghdad. The Abbasid ruler, Al-Musta'sim, appears to have been somewhat oblivious to the danger the Mongols posed. His vizier Ibn al-Alqami, on the other hand, was deeply concerned with Hulagu's advance and tried to open negotiations with the Mongols—negotiations that were thwarted by the attitude of the caliph.

On January 29, 1258, the Mongols commenced a siege by digging a deep ditch all the way around the city, with Georgian sappers at the forefront. With the trench and wooden ramparts in place, the Mongols then unleashed their sophisticated siege engines and catapults, expertly manned by Chinese engineers led by Guo Kan, to begin pounding the inner city's walls.

Meanwhile, the Mongol cavalry advanced down both banks of the Tigris River. The caliph sent a cavalry force of 20,000 men along the west bank to try and slow the attackers, but Mongol engineers broke a couple of dams across the Tigris, flooding the ground behind the Abbasid cavalry and trapping them in a quagmire where they were systematically destroyed. On February 10, the city formally surrendered. Hulagu paused operations for three days before unleashing his forces for a week of looting, raping, and killing.

Hulagu and the Mongol high command used the three-day pause to amass a vast fortune of gold and other treasures from the caliph's treasury and residence. Appalled at the caliph's greed, Hulagu had the caliph brought before him and demanded he eat some of his own treasure. When the caliph refused, Hulagu sentenced him and all his male heirs to death.

The Mongol devastation of Baghdad was appalling. Mosques and palaces were looted, hospitals burned to the ground, and books from the great library torn apart so that soldiers could turn the leather covers into shoes. At least 90,000 people are estimated to have been killed, either within the city or fleeing from it, and some historians think that figure was much higher.

After Baghdad

After the fall of Baghdad, the Mongol army continued to march west. Many regional powers came forward and offered their obeisance to Hulagu to spare their cities. The Syrian city of Aleppo refused to do so, and it fell to Mongol siege engines in five days. The Mongol army then moved on toward Damascus, which opened its gates and surrendered.

At this point, the Mongol forces divided again. Most of the army marched north, but General Ket Buqa and a sizeable force remained in Lebanon for mopping-up operations, while a third Mongol army was stationed in Gaza.

The Mongols appeared to be firmly in control of Syrian, Lebanon and indeed much of the Middle East. However, as Tim May points out, this was to prove ephemeral: The Mongols "secured their position by the end of April and lost it on 3 September 1260 at the Battle of Ayn Jalut."

The Mamluks

To the south of Lebanon and Gaza was Egypt, where various refugees from the Mongol onslaught had gathered. Egypt was now under the control of the Mamluk slave soldiers, many of whom were Europeans who had been sold by the Mongols returning from Europe decades earlier to Venetian and Genoese merchants dwelling along the Black Sea coast. The Mamluks possessed a powerful army. Aware that only a small Mongol force remained as occupiers of the region, when Mongol envoys turned up in Cairo, the Mamluk sultan Qutuz executed them.

Then Qutuz went on the attack. The Mongol forces at Gaza were quickly routed. Mongol general Ket Buqa immediately marched south to confront the Mamluks, and the two forces met at Ayn Jalut, located in the Jezreel Valley in Israel, not far from Nazareth.

The bulk of the Mamluks skillfully executed an ambush. The Mongols fought fiercely and desperately sought an escape. Eventually, Kut Beqa and most of the Mongol army were destroyed, and only a handful escaped.

After Mongke

The Mamluk victory meant a temporary halt to Mongol expansion in the Middle East. Just as news of the loss reached Hulagu, even more alarming news arrived from a different direction. In the midst of the siege of the Song city of Chongqing thousands of miles to the east, Khan Mongke had died, either from infected wounds or some other illness. Now the race was on to claim his throne, which meant, as had been the case with the death of Ogedai, most Mongol military expansion came to a halt.

Mongke's death would be the catalyst for the disintegration of a unified Mongol empire. An important player in the civil war that was about to erupt was Ariq Boke: the younger brother of Mongke, Qubilai, and Hulagu, and the fourth son of the remarkable Sorkaktani. As the youngest son, tradition demanded that Ariq Boke immediately assume the duties of regent. But even as Mongke was being buried, Ariq Boke was convening a *quriltai* without waiting for his two surviving brothers to return to Mongolia.

When Qubilai received his invitation to the *quriltai*, he ignored it, preferring to continue his campaign against the Song, while Hulagu remained in the Middle East. Ariq Boke went ahead with the *quriltai* anyway, and in the absence of both Hulagu and Qubilai, he was confirmed as khan. Upon hearing news of this, Qubilai, who was accompanied on his campaign by many Mongol princes, promptly convened his own *quriltai* where he was declared rival khan. Civil war was now inevitable.

Qubilai immediately marched north toward Mongolia with his seasoned army, leaving some troops behind to maintain the Song front. Ariq Boke soon realized that the Mongol capital of Karakorum was indefensible, particularly after Qubilai cut off its supplies. The war expanded northward and westward onto the steppes. Ariq Boke placed a Chagatayid supporter, Alghu, on the throne of the central Asian *ulus*, but Alghu soon abandoned Ariq Boke and sided with Qubilai. In the end, Ariq Boke had no option other than to surrender to Qubilai, which he did in 1264.

Hulagu, meanwhile, was involved in his own war with the ruler of the Jochid khanate, Berke. Batu, the son of Jochi and grandson of Chinggis Khan, had died in 1255, whereupon his brother Berke had assumed the throne. Berke now sided with Ariq Boke against Hulagu and Qubilai.

Two years after Ariq Boke's surrender to Qubilai, Ariq Boke died, leaving Qubilai the only remaining claimant for the throne. He declared himself khan, but his legitimacy was always in question. Nonetheless, Hulagu, the Chagatayids in central Asia, and the Jochids in the west all give him some measure of recognition, although none went to him to pledge their formal submission.

One prince of the house of Ogedai, Qaidu, refused to recognize Qubilai and established his own independent power base in the Ili Valley, which drains into Lake Balkhash in Siberia. Neither Qaidu nor Qubilai had the resources to defeat the other, and so both vied to form alliances with other Mongol elites.

Mongke's decision to bestow on his two brothers the title of ilkhan and provide each with an enormous personal army effectively sowed the seeds for the disintegration of the Mongol empire that followed his death. Qubilai Khan was in control of China in the east, descendants of Chagatai were in control of central Asia, descendants of Tolui were in control of Persia and the Middle East, and descendants of Jochi were in control of vast regions of Russia.

DIVIDING THE EMPIRE: A TALE OF FOUR BROTHERS

LECTURE 11 TRANSCRIPT

Now in total command of the Mongol Empire after staging the Toluid Revolution and destroying his political rivals, Mongke Khan was able to turn in 1251 to the administration of this vast world state following a decade of neglect. The central authority established over the empire by Chinggis and Ogedai had unraveled, and power now lay in the hands of various regional entities, including surviving Chinggisid princes.

In his efforts to restore order to the state, Mongke chose his senior bureaucrats well. His right-hand man for the first two years of his reign was named Menggesser, who served as a sort of vizier charged with the day-to-day affairs of imperial administration. A Christian from the once-rival Kereit tribe, Aqaa Bulghai, was appointed second in command and was then promoted to senior administrator after Menggesser died in 1253.

Senior bureaucrats such as these required the assistance of scribes skilled in the many languages and scripts used in this vast multi-ethnic empire. Aqaa Bulghai was fortunate to have available two brilliant Muslim scribes, Imad al-Mulk and Fakhr al-Mulk, who between them had mastered the scripts required to write in Mongolian, Uyghur, Persian, Chinese, and several other languages.

One of the earliest jobs of these bureaucrats was to conduct an empire-wide census, including in the regions now controlled by Batu as the Jochid *ulus*. Apparently the Jochids were OK with this, and the census was carried out in good order. As a result, a decision was made to add a fourth fiscal region to the empire to facilitate taxation. In addition to northern China, Turkestan (which included much of central Asia), and Khurasan in Persia, the Rus principalities were added to help regulate the collection of taxes.

As a way of further centralizing power in the empire and reducing the autonomy of local rulers, Mongke transformed regional administrative structures into secretariats under the control of a central secretariat in Mongolia. Experienced bureaucrats like Mahmud Yalavach were placed in charge of the north China secretariat, for example, while his son Masud Beg took over in Turkestan.

Determined to ensure the long-term primacy of the Toluids over the Ogedeids and Chagatayids, Mongke increased the land holdings of his brother Qubilai in China, a now substantial empire that had started when Ogedai had granted land to the brothers' mother Sorkaktani. Mongke then sent his younger brother Hulagu to the Middle East to take control of the Mongols' extensive holdings there. Although Qubilai and Mongke already possessed more or less unlimited power in their domains, Mongke bestowed on his brothers the new title of ilkhan, or subordinate khan, so they would not forget who the supreme commander of the Mongol realm was.

Mongke next turned his attention to the *Jam* communications system, which continued to come under considerable pressure by the various entities that used and abused it. One example of this abuse: Merchants with ties to various Chinggisid princes often traveled along the routes and expected the way stations and local peoples to supply them with food and other needs. And Mongol princes themselves, traveling with large entourages, regularly used the *Jam*, impoverishing the local sedentary and nomadic communities whose task it was to supply food and resources. Many of these princes had also created their own private *Jam* networks, further straining the resources of the people.

Mongke now decreed that the entire network was to be centralized and connected, including the private networks. All *gerege*, or passports, then in circulation had to be handed over to government officials, and those who applied for new ones had to demonstrate the legitimacy of their need and be registered with the government.

Imad and Fakhr al-Mulk were placed in charge of the reissuing, with explicit orders from Mongke that no *gerege* were to be issued to merchants. Those officials and princes who were successful in gaining a reissued *gerege* had restrictions placed on how much strain they could put on the system in terms of the resources they demanded. Envoys could only remain a short amount of time at any *Jam* post, for example, and even those carrying the elite gold *gerege* were limited to a maximum of 14 horses per journey.

Mongke next turned to reforming the taxation system, creating a more centralized and regulated system, and also using revenue resources to rehabilitate regions devastated by earlier wars. The *qubchur* tax paid by the nomads was standardized to one animal for every hundred of its species, but if families possessed fewer than 100 animals, they paid no tax.

Sedentary populations were taxed differently, as they always had been since the introduction of the system by Chinggis Khan. In the Muslim regions, individuals were taxed in coins on a sliding scale depending on their income. But in China, the tax payable was based on household income and could be paid in high-value commodities such as silk or silver, instead of cash. When silver ended up in short supply, paper money was substituted in north China as an acceptable way of paying tax. In the Rus principalities, taxes could be paid with high-value furs, but Mongke always hoped that most taxes throughout the empire would be paid with coins.

As another example of his pragmatic approach to government, Mongke did not insist on collecting back taxes that had been unpaid during the previously chaotic decade. But he vigorously enforced the payment of new taxes now that he was on the throne, including by Mongol elites. Most scholars believe that the empire may have suffered a reduction of revenue income under Mongke, but also that his efficient administration eliminated corruption at many levels and opened up new and more sustainable sources of income for the government.

From the moment Chinggis had introduced the Mongol taxation system three decades earlier, certain groups had always been exempt from taxes, a practice that had been maintained by Ogedai. Mongke also agreed that most religious leaders—and there were many of them in the Mongol world by this time, practicing a multitude of faiths—would remain exempt from taxes. The attitude of Mongol rulers to these various religions practiced in their empire might best be described as one of religious neutrality.

Everyone was free to practice their own religion unless it caused instability within the empire. But this did not mean that the Mongols treated the adherents of all religions equally. We can see this by simply comparing those religions that received tax exemptions—such as Buddhism, Daoism, Confucianism, Christianity, and Islam—with those that did not, including Judaism, Zoroastrianism, and Manichaeism. The difference lay in the political and economic power and status of the hierarchies of these faiths.

Mongke was deeply interested in religion, although he appears to have ascribed to none of these faiths whose leaders regularly sent emissaries to try to convert him. Often these conversion attempts resembled sporting events as much as earnest religious debates, with teams of eloquent spiritual leaders squaring off in front of Mongke and other Mongol elites. At one such event, the Franciscan friar William of Rubruck believed he had not only won the debate but had Mongke very close to converting to Christianity. But in the end, the khan was unconvinced, informing Rubruck that "just as God has given the hand several fingers, so has he given mankind several paths."

The debates were often convened as much for political reasons as for spiritual ones. The khans often brought rival groups together to try to end division and conflict between them, particularly if this was threatening the peace and security of the empire. We know of one such debate between Buddhists and Daoists presided over by Mongke's brother Qubilai in 1258. Conflict between monks of the two faiths was causing disorder in Qubilai's northern Chinese realm; temples had been destroyed, and pitched battles had even broken out in the towns and cities.

The Buddhists were able to prove to Qubilai that many Daoist texts were actually forgeries, and Qubilai was concerned enough that he ordered the forged texts seized and destroyed. He also ordered the Daoists to return any land and other possessions taken from the Buddhists and warned both sides to end the fighting. In the end, all sides won in this debate. The violence stopped, the Buddhists had nominally won, the Daoists had not incurred the wrath of the khan, and the khan himself had not unduly attacked Daoism itself, which was a very popular faith in his realm. So this was a quintessential example of Mongol political and religious pragmatism at its best.

With this brief discussion of Mongke's administrative and religious reforms in mind, let's turn to Mongol military expansion, which after a decade of desultory activity was renewed with a vengeance by the three Toluid brothers who now ruled the empire. In the second year of his reign, Mongke convened another quriltai, and this time, there was only one item on the agenda: war.

Mongke had already dispatched his brothers to take control of vast regions of the empire: Qubilai to China and Hulagu to Persia and the Middle East. With their new titles as ilkhans secure, these assignments now transitioned into serious military campaigns. The ideology of the Mongols towards war and conquest had not changed. Heaven, and in particular the sky god Tengri, had given the Mongols permission to conquer the whole world, and it was this mandate they set out to obey once again in the 1250s.

To carry out the mandate, the commanders of course needed armies, so Mongke ordered that two soldiers out of every 10 would now ride with Hulagu, and the same number would now ride with Qubilai. Tim May estimates that by the early 1250s, the Mongol military probably had something like 1 million nomadic soldiers enrolled, as well as "untold millions" of non-nomadic troops. So, although Mongke had now assigned 40 percent of all Mongol military power to his brothers, this still left plenty of soldiers to ride with the khan himself, who was determined to join Qubilai in his campaign against the Song in southern China. His order also had the effect of reducing the military power available to other Mongol leaders, such as those of the Chagatayids, who were consolidating their own *ulus*, or state, in central Asia.

The campaign against the powerful Song Dynasty in southern China had been at a stalemate since the reign of Ogedai. The Song, who by this stage constituted the most impressive industrial power in the world with the capacity to churn out huge quantities of iron weapons and armor, had a formidable defensive structure in place along their entire northern border. Determined to circumvent this, Mongke and Qubilai decided to open a second front against the non-Chinese kingdom of Dali, located in the southwest near Tibet. Once conquered, this would allow the Mongols to attack the Song from an entirely new direction.

The campaign against Dali began in 1252, but it took three years of hard fighting before the kingdom fell. Mongke, who had started attacking the Song's northern border with his forces in 1254, was now anxious for Qubilai to open a second front through Dali. But Qubilai delayed in the lush pastures of Dali, annoying the impatient Mongke. It took four more years of bitter fighting before Mongke finally broke through the Song's formidable northern defenses and was able to march into eastern China. Meanwhile, Qubilai moved his forces through central China and then turned south towards the Song capital. Mongol forces under General Uriyang Qadai invaded Song territory from the former kingdom of Dali, while yet another general, Taghachar, opened a fourth front and headed to the northwest.

Despite now having four separate armies arrayed against them, Song defenses remained formidable throughout their empire, and the Mongols were frustratingly delayed by virtually impregnable fortresses guarding the important mountain passes. But the Mongol army was now augmented by hundreds of thousands of skilled soldiers from the former Jin Dynasty so that despite the difficulties, the Mongol advance was inexorable. As the four armies converged on the Yangtze Valley, Song collapse seemed inevitable.

Let's leave the campaign in China for a moment and head far to the west to follow the fortunes of Hulagu's army in Persia and the Middle East. One of the explicit aims of this campaign was to force formal submission to the Mongols by groups that had not yet done so. This included the formidable Nizari Assassins and the remnants of the once mighty but now fragmented Muslim Abbasid Caliphate.

Unlike previous Mongol campaigns to the west, such as those against the Khwarazmians in the 1220s and against Russian and eastern European powers in the 1230s and '40s, Hulagu's advance was positively leisurely. As the vast army moved slowly through central Asia, seeking steppe grasslands for the huge herds of horses that accompanied his army, his general Ket Buqa Noyan began military assaults against Nizari fortresses in Iran, which fell steadily. With his defenses failing and his people dying, Nizari leader Khurshah was granted safe passage through to Hulagu to formally surrender to the Mongols.

One particularly formidable Nizari fortress held out longest against the Mongols: an almost impregnable stronghold called Alamut on top of a mountain. But by using the skills of a company of Chinese engineers that Hulagu had brought with him, Alamut finally fell in 1256. After this, Nizari ruler Khurshah, who had since been sent back to Mongke, was executed.

One interesting aside to the fall of Alamut was that Ata-Malik Juvaini, one of our most valuable sources on the Mongols thus far, was actually present during the assault and personally took part in the negotiations between Mongols and Nizari defenders. Juvaini writes that Hulagu himself gave Juvaini permission to examine the famous library at Alamut. He selected several important books, but was apparently happy to see the rest, which he regarded as full of heresy and error, destroyed by fire. More about Juvaini's account of the capture of the fortress of Alamut in our very next lecture.

Hulagu's way was now clear to march on the Abbasid capital of Baghdad. The Abbasid ruler, Caliph Mustasim ibn Mustasim, appears to have been somewhat oblivious to the danger the Mongols posed, which seems incredible after decades of Mongol victories in the region. His vizier, Ibn al-Alqami, on the other hand, was deeply concerned with Hulagu's advance and tried to open negotiations with the Mongols, negotiations that were thwarted by the attitude of the caliph.

Now there was nothing that could prevent the fall of Baghdad, the greatest city of the Islamic realm. As Jack Weatherford reminds us, "for five hundred years the wealth of the Muslim world had poured into the city where the caliph lavished it on palaces, mosques, schools, private gardens and public fountains." Home to Muslims, Christians, and Jews, the huge city sprawled across both banks of the Tigris River, connected by a bridge. The fortified heart of the city was protected by massive walls.

Aware of the formidable defenses of Baghdad, Hulagu reinforced his army by bringing in forces from Baiju's army, which were occupying Georgia and Armenia, along with other allied specialists. The great Tigris and Euphrates Rivers had historically provided additional defenses for the Abbasid capital, but the Mongols moved across these rivers at will through the use of pontoon bridges. By the last week of January 1258, Baghdad was surrounded, with Mongol soldiers already loose in the suburbs while their commanders planned the assault on the inner city.

Like his grandfather before him, Hulagu was adept at using spies to gain information about what was happening inside the inner city. This time it was disaffected Christians who were employed to carry vital information secretly between the city and the Mongol camp. The caliph, now only too aware of the terrible fate awaiting him and his city, also used Christian emissaries to try and offer submission to the Mongols, but it was too late.

Now Hulagu moved methodically to take the city. On January 29th, 1258, the Mongols commenced the siege by digging a deep ditch all the way around the city, with Georgian sappers at the forefront. With the trench and wooden ramparts in place, the Mongols then unleashed their sophisticated siege engines and catapults, expertly manned by Chinese engineers led by Guo Kan, to begin pounding the inner city's walls.

Meanwhile, the Mongol cavalry advanced down both banks of the Tigris River. The caliph sent a cavalry force of 20,000 men along the west bank to try and slow the attackers, but Mongol engineers broke a couple of dams across the Tigris, which flooded the ground behind the Abbasid cavalry, trapping them in a quagmire so that they could be systematically destroyed by Mongol forces.

The bombardment of the city's defenses by huge stones fired by mangonels and catapults was relentless and terrifying. Large numbers of residents tried to flee, some by boat, but they were picked off by skilled Mongol archers on the shore. By February 5th, the city's walls had been breached, and the defenses were crumbling. In desperation, the caliph tried to reopen negotiations but was rebuffed. Three thousand notable residents of the city also tried to negotiate with Hulagu but were slaughtered for their pains. On the 10th of February, the huge Persian Tower collapsed, and the city formally surrendered that same day. Hulagu now paused operations for three days before unleashing his forces on the 13th for a week of looting, raping, and killing.

Hulagu and the Mongol high command used the three-day pause to amass a vast fortune of gold and other treasures from the caliph's treasury and residence. Appalled at the caliph's greed, Hulagu had the caliph brought before him and demanded he eat some of his own treasure. When the caliph refused, Hulagu sentenced him and all his male heirs to death. But because of the caliph's status, he was granted a bloodless death. Rolled up in a carpet, he was either kicked to death by Mongol soldiers or trampled to death by the hooves of their horses.

The Mongol devastation of Baghdad was appalling, but no worse than the assaults on other great cities they had taken. Mosques and palaces were looted, hospitals burned to the ground, and books from the great library torn apart so that soldiers could turn the leather covers into shoes. So many rare and important books were tossed into the Tigris River that chroniclers report it ran black with ink. At least 90,000 people are estimated to have been killed, either within the city or fleeing from it, and some historians think that figure was much higher, in the several hundreds of thousands. Hulagu famously had to move his camp upwind of the city because of the stench of death emanating from it.

But this would not be the end of the city of Baghdad—far from it. In the aftermath, as Hulagu and his army moved on, Ata-Malik Juvaini would be appointed governor of Baghdad, and indeed of all of lower Mesopotamia. The Nestorian Christian patriarch would be offered the caliph's royal palace as his residence, and a cathedral would be built for the followers of his version of Christianity. Indeed, Baghdad rose again surprisingly quickly to become an important center of Mongol administration, transregional trade, and religious affairs.

After the fall of Baghdad, the Mongol army continued to march west. Many regional powers came forward and offered their obeisance to Hulagu in order to spare their cities. The Syrian city of Aleppo refused to do so and fell to Mongol siege engines in five days. The Mongol army then moved on towards Damascus, which opened its gates and surrendered, and so was spared any serious looting or damage.

Now the Mongol forces divided again. Most of the army marched north, but General Ket Buqa and a sizeable force remained in Lebanon for mopping-up operations, while a third Mongol army was stationed in Gaza. Some crusaders in the Kingdom of Jerusalem skirmished with Mongol forces, but quickly retreated after realizing just how formidable this new invading force was. The Mongols appeared to be firmly in control of Syria, Lebanon, and indeed much of the Middle East. But as Tim May points out, this was to prove ephemeral: The Mongols "secured their position by the end of April and lost it on 3 September 1260 at the Battle of Ain Jalut."

To the south of Lebanon and Gaza was Egypt, where various refugees from the Mongol onslaught had gathered. Egypt was now under the control of the Mamluk slave soldiers, many of whom were Europeans who had been sold by the Mongols returning from Europe decades earlier to Venetian and Genoese merchants dwelling along the Black Sea coast. The Mamluks possessed a powerful army, and aware that only a small Mongol force remained as occupiers of the region, when Mongol envoys turned up in Cairo, Mamluk Sultan Qutuz executed them.

Then Qutuz went on the attack. The Mongol forces at Gaza were quickly routed. Mongol General Ket Buqa immediately marched south to confront the Mamluks, and the two forces met at Ain Jalut, located in the Jezreel Valley in Israel, not far from the city of Nazareth. The Mamluks knew the ground well and stationed the bulk of their troops in the highlands above the valley, out of sight of the Mongols. A Mamluk force then attacked the Mongol army in the valley, constantly harassing Ket Buqa's troops with hit-and-run tactics before finally withdrawing into the hills with the Mongol horsemen following hot on their heels.

As the Mongols rode into the hills, the bulk of the Mamluks suddenly emerged from their hiding places in a skillfully executed ambush. The Mongols fought fiercely and desperately sought an escape. But Caliph Qutuz had kept his own private legion in reserve for just such an eventuality, and when he saw the left wing of the Mameluke army about to crumble, he charged into battle with his forces, driving the Mongols back into the melee. In the fierce fighting that followed, Kut Beqa and most of the Mongol army were destroyed, and only a handful escaped.

We will never know what Hulagu would have done to avenge the defeat at Ain Jalut, one of the very few battles Mongol forces ever lost. Certainly, the Mamluk victory meant a temporary halt to Mongol expansion in the Middle East. But just as news of the loss reached Hulagu, even more alarming news arrived from a different direction. In the midst of the siege of the Song city of Chongqing, thousands of miles to the east, Khan Mongke had died, either from infected wounds or some other illness. Now the race was on to claim his throne, which meant, as had been the case with the death of Ogedai, most Mongol military expansion came to a halt.

But the death of Mongke signaled something much more momentous: His death would be the catalyst for the disintegration of a unified Mongol Empire. As Thomas Allsen puts it:

Hulagu's campaign against the Ismailis and the Abbasids were the last joint military ventures of a unified Mongol Empire. Thereafter, the Chinggisid princes increasingly turned their military energies inwards in a confrontation that lasted, with fits and starts, into the fourteenth century.

We need to introduce another player in the civil war that was about to erupt: the younger brother of Mongke, Qubilai and Hulagu, and the fourth son of the remarkable Sorkaktani, Ariq Boke. As the youngest son, tradition demanded that Ariq Boke immediately assume the duties of regent. But even as Mongke was being buried beside Chinggis Khan and Ogedai in the secret grave, Ariq Boke was convening a quriltai without waiting for his two surviving brothers to return to Mongolia.

When Qubilai received his invitation to the quriltai, he ignored it, preferring to continue his campaign against the Song, while Hulagu remained in the Middle East. Ariq Boke went ahead with the quriltai anyway, and in the absence of both Hulagu and Qubilai, he was confirmed as khan. Upon hearing news of this, Qubilai, who was accompanied on his campaign by many Mongol princes, promptly convened his own quriltai where he was declared rival khan. Civil war was now inevitable.

Some scholars argue that Ariq Boke represented the conservative wing of the Mongol elites, focused on the maintenance of a nomadic lifeway on the steppe, whereas Qubilai represented the progressive wing, determined to integrate the Mongols with the sedentary societies they had conquered.

Hulagu eventually sided with Qubilai, but not until two years had passed. However, despite these ideological differences, the war that followed was essentially between two brothers with an intense ambition for absolute power.

Qubilai immediately marched north towards Mongolia with his seasoned army, leaving some troops behind to maintain the Song front. Ariq Boke soon realized that the Mongol capital of Karakorum was indefensible, particularly after Qubilai cut off its supplies. So the war expanded northwards and westwards into the steppes. Ariq Boke placed a Chagatayid supporter, Alghu, on the throne of the central Asian *ulus*, but Alghu soon abandoned Ariq Boke and sided with Qubilai. In the end, Ariq Boke had no option other than to surrender to Qubilai, which he did in 1264.

Hulagu, meanwhile, was involved in his own war with the ruler of the Jochid Khanate, Berke. Batu, the son of Jochi and grandson of Chinggis Khan, had died in 1255, whereupon his brother Berke had assumed the throne. Berke now sided with Ariq Boke against Hulagu and Qubilai. He was particularly resentful of Hulagu, who had occupied parts of the Jochid realm in his western campaign, and so war also broke out between the Jochid and Toluid forces.

Two years after Ariq Boke's surrender to Qubilai, Ariq Boke died, leaving Qubilai the only remaining claimant for the throne. He declared himself khan, but his legitimacy was always in question. Nonetheless, Hulagu, the Chagatayids in central Asia, and the Jochids in the west all give him some measure of recognition, although none went to him to pledge their formal submission.

One prince of the house of Ogedai, Qaidu, refused to recognize Qubilai and established his own independent power base in the Ili Valley, which drains into Lake Balkhash in Siberia. Neither Qaidu nor Qubilai had the resources to defeat the other, and so both vied to form alliances with other Mongol elites. Qaidu controlled the major trade routes through the center of the empire and also the main avenue of communication between Qubilai and Hulagu, so this conflict would have a tremendous influence on the future of the empire, as we will see.

But let's not lose sight of the larger picture here. After a decade of indecision during the interregnum that followed the death of Ogedai, the Mongols had enjoyed a period of effective administration and tremendous military success under the reign of Mongke throughout the 1250s.

But Mongke's decision to bestow on his brothers the title of ilkhan and provide each with an enormous personal army to expand the empire to the east and west effectively sowed the seeds for the disintegration of the Mongol Empire that followed his death.

As Thomas Allsen reminds us, "by the time Qubilai successfully claimed the qaghanate in 1264, the empire had fragmented into four regional and independent qaghanates." Qubilai Khan was in control of China in the east, descendants of Chagatai were in control of central Asia, descendants of Tolui were now in control of Persia and the Middle East, and descendants of Jochi were in control of vast regions of Russia.

It is the fate of these independent khanates that we need to consider in future lectures. But before doing so, we will first take a closer look at the powerful Mongol military that made possible the construction of the largest empire ever seen in world history.

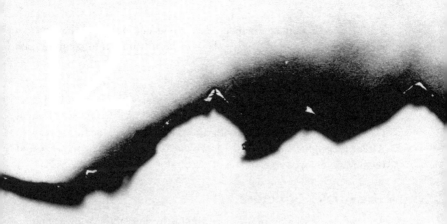

THE STRENGTHS OF MONGOL MILITARY ORGANIZATION

T his lecture is focused on the superb military machine the Mongols had built and maintained from the reign of Chinggis Khan to that of Mongke Khan and beyond. The army was an extension of the very way of life of the steppe. The same skills required for moving herds, covering long distances on horseback over rough ground, and particularly for hunting were the skills required for warfare. *

The *Nerge*

A great annual hunt known as the *nerge* was particularly valuable as a means of military training. The hunt had traditions dating back as long as militarized nomads had been in existence. The *nerge* consisted of a vast ring of mounted hunters that gradually contracted like a noose and trapped the game. The hunts could last anywhere between one and three months, and usually took place early in the bitter Mongolian winter.

The various military contingents involved in the hunt carried out a massive encircling technique over thousands of square miles. Beginning as straight lines, the contingents gradually formed a semicircle as they advanced. As in a military operation, commanders used scouts out in front of the *tumen* to gather intelligence, and drums, flags, or horn trumpets to communicate to nearby contingents.

Once the hunting circle was at its smallest size, the actual killing began, allowing the men to demonstrate their prowess with weapons and their courage in taking on dangerous animals. Some men fought like Roman gladiators, fighting large cats with knife, sword, or even with no weapon. After the slaughter was over, the surviving animals would be released, and the hunters enjoyed several days of celebration and feasting.

The Army's Structure

As is the case with most of the successful institutions of the Mongol empire, the reorganization of the Mongol army can be traced back to the reforms Chinggis Khan instituted following his enthronement at the *quriltai* of 1206. The effectiveness of these reforms can be seen in the near invincibility of the army he created over the decades that followed.

An important early reform was to reintroduce a simple system of military organization based on the decimal system. The smallest unit of the army was a squad of 10 men called an *arban*. Ten *arbans* constituted a company of 100, called a *jaghun*. Ten *jaghuns* made up the equivalent of a regiment of 1,000, known as a *minqan*. Ten *minqad*—the plural of *minqan*—constituted a force of 10,000 mounted warriors called a *tumen*, the equivalent of a modern division. David Morgan argues that, although the *tumen* of 10,000 men became the standard fighting unit, the Mongol soldier probably identified most closely with his *minqan* of 1,000.

At the *quriltai* in 1206, Chinggis Khan assigned one *minqan* to the 95 different commanders, although some commanders received two or even three *minqad* depending on their status and their relationship with Chinggis. Then, following the tradition established by the Xiongnu many centuries earlier, Bo'orchu was appointed commander of the right wing, and Muqali was appointed commander of the left, each in charge of a *tumen* of 10,000 warriors.

The division of forces into left and right divisions had clear geographical meaning; Bo'orchu was essentially in charge of western Mongolia as far as the Altai Mountains, and Muqali was in charge of eastern Mongolia. Chinggis Khan, working with a third general named Naya'a, who also commanded a *tumen*, was in charge of central Mongolia.

Xiongnu People

Chinggis next appointed his adopted younger brother Shigi Qutuqu as chief judge, a position that had both judicial and administrative functions. Another Mongol general, Qubilai, was placed in overall charge of military administration, including logistics and training.

The Impact

Through this series of measures, Chinggis Khan achieved four things in particular. First, he created a superbly organized military structure in which every decimalized unit knew its place and function.

Second, he placed army units under the command of men who had demonstrated their worth and loyalty to the Great Khan, thus reducing the danger of any one commander creating a private army that might challenge him.

Third, he promoted men to the highest positions on the basis of their military acumen and proven skill, not on the status of their birth, although these elite commanders did eventually evolve into a new type of aristocracy known as *qarachu*.

The fourth effect of the reorganization of the army was arguably the most significant: It was actually a reorganization of the entire Turkic-Mongolian social structure of the steppe. Soldiers from the tribes that had most bitterly opposed Temujin—the Tatars, Merkits, Keraits, and Naimans—were now distributed throughout the new military divisions.

This meant that there never was a Naiman *tumen*, for example, nor a Merkit *tumen* that might have turned on their new Mongol overlords. Chinggis Khan created new loyalties for these men: to their commanders, to their *minqan* of 1,000, and to their *tumen* of 10,000. The final genius of this entire system was that, as Morgan notes, beyond these military loyalties, "the Mongol royal house became the ultimate focus of obedience and allegiance."

Chinggis Khan was not finished. At the *quriltai* of 1206, he made another decision to create an additional military unit of 10,000 known as the *keshig*, or bodyguard. The *keshig* was staffed by the sons of the commanders and officers of Chinggis Khan's army. The *keshig* was more than the khan's personal army; it also served as Chinggis Khan's household staff.

Equipping the Soldiers

Chinggis Khan and his successors made sure that all Mongol soldiers were well armed. They were assigned metal helmets with leather neck and ear coverings and armor made of strong and supple leather strips or sometimes of overlapping metal plates. The horses were also protected with armor. This armor was much lighter than that worn by European knights, which is one of the reasons Mongol forces were able to run rings around the heavily armored knights of Hungary and Poland.

Each Mongol soldier carried several composite bows and a good supply of arrows, and the heavy Mongol cavalry also carried a 12-foot lance with a hook on the end to help pull enemy riders off their horses. Officers carried a curved sword, very sharp on one edge. Regular cavalry carried an axe, sword, mace, and a lasso for bringing down enemy horses.

Mongol soldiers were also armed with different types of shields, depending on their role in the attack. A large shield of skin and wood was used for guard duty. A smaller wicker shield was used to protect the front line from arrows. A third, very hard shield made of tortoise shell was used when besieging a city because it offered greater protection from objects hurled down from city walls.

The Mongols carried a long bow and a short bow, depending on the distance arrows needed to be fired, and each soldier carried 60 arrows in two quivers. The two main types of battle arrows were light ones with sharp points, which were useful and accurate over long distances, and heavy arrows with big, wide heads for killing at close quarters. Arrows were tipped with bone or metal heads, and sometimes they were dipped into viper poison.

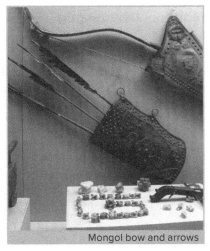
Mongol bow and arrows

The superb composite bow was made of animal horn, sinew, and wood. The long-range bow needed powerful arms to fire it, and Mongol soldiers trained from recruitment at the age of 15 to develop the required muscles and technique. In the proper hands, it was much more effective than the famed English longbow and could fire arrows 300 yards with ease.**

Mongol Intelligence Gathering

Mongol commanders were also distinguished from their contemporaries by the degree to which they gathered valuable intelligence about the enemy before launching any campaigns. This included the strength and disbursement of their military forces, their religion and culture, relationships between various groups within a given city or society, and even the personalities of individual leaders and officers.

Aware that their enemies were also trying to gather intelligence about the Mongols, Chinggis and his successors did all they could to spread disinformation about their own forces. For instance, one tactic was forging documents that were captured by enemy spies. Another was putting Mongol women on spare horses or mounting dummies so that the army would seem much larger to distant observers.

** Chinggis Khan's nephew Yisungge was a spectacular archer who once fired an arrow 550 yards at a contest in 1225.

Mongol Maneuvering

As part of their reconnaissance, each Mongol army would send scouts dozens of miles ahead and on either side of the main force to look for provisions, for good camping spots, and to ensure that no Mongol army would ever be taken by surprise. This, along with the fact that the Mongols sought provisions as they rode and rarely had to wait for a baggage train, allowed Mongol forces to advance at speeds that astonished their opponents.

Inevitably, however, Mongol contingents would have to cross deserts or other terrain that offered little in the way of food, so each soldier carried emergency reserves with him: alcohol in the form of fermented mare's milk called *kumis*, plus dried meat and dried curdled milk, which could be used to make a type of yogurt.

Mongols also become very adept at crossing strongly flowing rivers. In April 1241, for example, Mongol forces crossed the Sajo River in spring flood conditions with 30,000 cavalry during one night before the Battle of Mohi. This was one of the reasons they were so easily able to defeat the Hungarian king Bela IV and lay waste to half of Hungary.

Mongol Attacks

The Mongols became quite skilled at using information and topography to their advantage. Once the topography had been thoroughly studied and an appropriate battle plan devised, a series of silent signals would then be sent to coordinate the attack, with the soldiers keeping their horses and themselves as quiet as possible. The various contingents were regathered and concentrated, and the army was divided up into several divisions. Only when all were in place was the silence broken, with the pounding of drums, the blaring of trumpets, and the yelling of the men.

Now the heavy cavalry rode to the front, forming a formidable barrier of armored men and lances. On signal, they would open their ranks to allow the light cavalry to gallop through at high speed, unleashing a devastating hail of arrows before turning and racing back to the protection of the heavy cavalry.

The heavy cavalry would then launch a frontal charge against the enemy's front line. If the first charge was not successful, charge after charge after charge of heavy cavalry would occur until the enemy's lines were smashed open. At that moment, all units of light and heavy cavalry would attack from a variety of directions in an astonishingly coordinated manner.

If these tactics did not work, the Mongol commanders had other tricks. They would suddenly open gaps in their own lines to encourage ambitious enemies to charge into them, for example. Then, with perfect discipline, the Mongols would snap the gaps closed like the deadly traps they were. False retreats that turned into ambushes were another technique.

The Mongols also became very comfortable in the art of the siege. After the fall of a city or state, Mongol commanders were always very careful to recruit skilled military professionals. For instance, as soon as the Mongols started to attack the Jin dynasty in China, they were quick to recruit Chinese engineers skilled in the manufacture and use of sophisticated siege engines.

THE STRENGTHS OF MONGOL MILITARY ORGANIZATION

LECTURE 12 TRANSCRIPT

As we have seen throughout the course, Persian historian Ata-Malik Juvaini, later appointed governor of Baghdad by Ilkhan Hulagu, was the author of *The History of the World Conqueror* and often wrote about events he had personally participated in. He was an eyewitness, for example, to Hulagu's assault in 1256 on the seemingly impregnable Nizari Assassins fortress in the Alamut region of northwestern Iran. His account is full of hyperbole and pro-Mongol propaganda—after all, Hulagu eventually became his boss—but it nonetheless offers an important contemporary account of the work of the sophisticated Mongol military at its best.

Let me quote some passages from Juvaini by way of introduction to this lecture, which is focused on the superb military machine the Mongols had built and maintained from the reign of Chinggis Khan to that of Mongke Khan and beyond. Juvaini opens his account of the siege of Alamut by describing how Mongol forces surrounded the fortress using the *nerge*, or encirclement technique, they had perfected through years of hunting on the steppe:

And from the direction of Ustundar, which lay on the right, there came Buqa Temur and Koke Ilgei with armies all fire and fury, along steep roads as crooked as the covenant of the wicked. And from Alamut, which lay on the left, came the princes Balaghai and Tutar with a great body of men, all clamoring for vengeance. And behind them came Ket-Buqa Noyan with a host like a mountain of iron. The mountains and valleys billowed with the great masses of men. Thus in one day so many immeasurable armies were joined together to form around said castle … a *nerge*.

We don't need to use our imaginations to wonder how disheartening this encirclement must have been for the defenders of the castle, because Juvaini does this for us:

> And now the inmates of the castle saw how a people numerous as ants had, snake-like, formed seven coils around it. In the daytime, as far as their sight could reach, the people could see nothing but men and standards; and at night, because

of the great quantity of fires, they thought the earth a sky full of stars and a world full of swords and daggers, whereof neither middle nor edge was visible. For excess of grief each of them on the towers and walls mourned in his heart.

Now Hulagu and his commanders prepared for the assault:

With their morning draught the Mongol army struck the harp of war [and] they prepared to do battle with mangonels and stones. And they cut down and trimmed for these mangonels trees which these people had watered for many years past, not realizing what purpose they would serve or what fruit they would ultimately bear. And ... they placed a group of athletes at every *amaj* [roughly a sixth of a mile] to transport the heavy poles and pillars of these mangonels to the top of the hill.

Disheartened though they might be, the Assassins were formidable warriors themselves, and the defenders inside the citadel fought back tenaciously. Juvaini describes them using their mangonels to unleash "a brisk discharge of stones." But the Mongol archers, "flinching neither before stone nor arrow," as Juvaini describes them, unleashed their arrows, which he calls "the shafts of doom" and the "Angels of Death," which were "let fly against those wretches passing like hail through the sieve-like clouds."

On the fourth day of the siege, Juvaini describes the effects of a terrifying ballista, a giant crossbow constructed by Khitan engineers that could hurl flaming javelins 2,500 paces. The impact on the defenders was immediate: "And of the devil-like heretics many soldiers were burned by these meteoric shafts."

Assassin leader Rukh al-Din Khurshah now tried to buy time by sending messengers informing Hulagu that his surrender was imminent. But as Rukh al-Din prevaricated, Hulagu continued his preparations to further assault the castle. Juvaini tells us that "during the coming and going of the messengers suitable sites had been found for the erection of mangonels and the parts had been easily fitted together," clearly an indication of just how practical Mongol siege engines had become. The impact of these mangonels was devastating. Juvaini again:

As for the mangonels that had been erected it was as though their poles had been made of pine trees a hundred years old and with the first stones that sprang up from them the enemy's mangonel was broken and many were crushed under it. And great fear overcame them so that they were utterly distraught. Some who were standing on a tower crept in their fright like mice into a hole or fled like lizards into crannies in the rocks.

This time, Rukh al-Din surrendered for real, arriving at Hulagu's tent and kissing its threshold "in an attitude of shame and contrition." Hulagu treated him well, as he did all those defenders who simultaneously surrendered. But then Juvaini notes: "As the Mongol army entered [the fortress] and began to destroy the buildings, a group of more fanatical defenders that had been in hiding leapt out and began to attack the Mongols." Their defense was stout, but the end was now in sight. Here's how Juvaini describes the endgame:

> For three days and nights they resisted in this manner, but on the fourth day the snake-like warriors and valiant stalwarts of the army scaled that lofty and majestic peak and utterly crushed those serpent-like miscreants and hacked the limbs of those wretches to pieces. And to the other castles in that valley [Hulagu] sent messengers and officers together with orders for their destruction. And the khan turned back, victorious and triumphant.

It's all here, really—everything that made the Mongols such formidable warriors was on full display at Hulagu's siege of the fortress of Alamut: the use of the *nerge* to surround their enemy, incredible archery and sword skills, the athletic ability to scale sheer cliffs and carry heavy equipment and rocks up steep slopes, the use of practical and effective Khitan and Chinese siege engines, Mongol largess if rulers surrendered to them, and brutality to those who did not. Above all, incredible determination and belief in their ability to overcome all odds.

This was the Mongol war machine at its best, all elements working together like a well-oiled machine, from the common soldier to the ilkhan himself. With the exception of Ket-Buqa's defeat at Ain Jalut, the Mongol army generally proved invincible. David Morgan states the obvious when he writes, "without the Mongol army no amount of efficient administration would have kept the Mongol Empire in being. The army must therefore be regarded as the basic and most essential of imperial institutions."

But as Morgan and other scholars note, the army was really just an extension of the very way of life of the steppe, because the same skills required for moving herds, covering long distances on horseback over rough ground, and particularly for hunting were, with very little modification, the skills required for warfare. I can attest personally that even today, Mongol boys and girls learn to ride superbly at a very young age and have remarkably well-developed archery and wrestling skills. As Morgan described it, "the whole of life was a process of military training."

The great annual hunt that we have already discussed on several occasions, the *nerge*, was particularly valuable as a means of military training. The hunt had traditions dating back as long as militarized nomads had been in existence. In an earlier lecture, we discussed how the nomads had to handle the slaughtering of their animals for meat very carefully, because the herds and flocks were essentially the only wealth nomadic families possessed. It was much better to obtain meat through hunting other animals in the wild, and in the Mongol world, this practice had evolved into a massive annual hunt to try to obtain as much meat as possible to sustain entire tribes through the winter.

The hunt was called *nerge* because it consisted of a vast ring of mounted hunters that gradually contracted like a noose and trapped the game. The hunts could last anywhere between one and three months and usually took place early in the bitter Mongolian winter. During Chinggis Khan's lifetime, his oldest son, Jochi, had the responsibility of organizing the hunt. The Great *Yasa*, or law code, had strict protocols for the carrying out of the hunt. For example, any hunter who allowed an animal to escape the ring, whether a tiger or a rabbit, was regarded as having committed a grievous crime, as was anyone who killed an animal before permission had been granted by the khan.

The various military *minqan* and *tumen* contingents involved in the hunt carried out this massive encircling technique over thousands of square miles. Beginning as straight lines, the contingents gradually formed a semi-circle as they advanced. As in a military operation, commanders used scouts out in front of the tumen to gather intelligence, and drums, flags, or horn trumpets to communicate to nearby contingents. As Frank McLynn describes it, "day by day the *minqad* drove animals before them and the semi-circle narrowed until the finishing line was reached. Then part of them wheeled round and eventually closed the ring until the units formed a cordon."

Now, with the hunting circle at its smallest size, the actual killing began, allowing the men to demonstrate their prowess with weapons and their courage in taking on dangerous animals. Some men fought like Roman gladiators, fighting dangerous large cats with knife or sword alone, or even unarmed. After the slaughter was over, the surviving animals would be released, and the hunters enjoyed several days of celebration and feasting.

Edward Gibbon, the esteemed British historian and author of the classic work *The History of the Decline and Fall of the Roman Empire*, had this to say about the effectiveness of the Mongol hunt as preparation for warfare:

> The leaders study, in this practical school, the most important lesson of the military art: the prompt and accurate judgement of ground, of distance, and of time. To employ against a human enemy the same patience and valour, the same skill and discipline, is the only alteration which is required in real war; and the amusements of the chase serve as a prelude to the conquest of an empire.

As with most of the successful institutions of the Mongol Empire, the reorganization of the Mongol army can be traced back to the reforms Chinggis Khan instituted following his enthronement at the quriltai of 1206. The effectiveness of these reforms can be seen in the near invincibility of the army he created over the decades that followed.

An important early reform was to reintroduce a simple system of military organization based on the decimal system, a practice that had been in place on and off since the reign of the Xiongnu 1,500 years earlier. The smallest unit of the army was a squad of 10 men, called an *arban*, essentially a band of brothers. Ten *arbans* constituted a company of a hundred, called a *jaghun*. Ten *jaghuns* made up the equivalent of a regiment of a thousand, a *minqan*. And 10 *minqad*—the plural of *minqan*—constituted a force of 10,000 mounted warriors called a *tumen*, the equivalent of a modern division.

David Morgan argues that although the *tumen* of 10,000 men became the standard fighting unit, the Mongol soldier probably identified most closely with his *minqan* of a thousand. Evidence for this assertion can be found in the persistence into modern times of the name Hazara in central Afghanistan, which describes a particular group of Persian-speaking peoples with distinctly Mongol appearance. Scholars believe the Hazara are descended from a group of Mongol military that were settled in the region, and the word *hazara* is Persian for "one thousand."

At the quriltai in 1206, Chinggis Khan assigned one *minqan*—so one unit of 1,000 fighters—to each of 95 different commanders, although some commanders received two or even three *minqad* depending on their status and their relationship with Chinggis. Then, following the tradition established by the Xiongnu so many centuries earlier, general Bo'orchu was appointed commander of the right wing and Muqali commander of the left, each in charge of a *tumen* of 10,000 warriors.

The division of forces into left and right divisions had clear geographical meaning. Bo'orchu was essentially in charge of western Mongolia as far as the Altai Mountains, and Muqali in charge of eastern Mongolia. Remember, this reorganization was taking place before Mongol campaigns of external conquest had commenced, so it was initially focused on the Mongol steppe itself. Chinggis Khan, working with a third general named Naya'a, who also commanded a *tumen*, was in charge of central Mongolia.

Chinggis next appointed his adopted younger brother Sigi Qutuqu as chief judge of the new Yeke Mongol Ulus, a position that had both judicial and administrative functions. Another Mongol general, Qubilai, was placed in overall charge of military administration, including logistics and training.

Through this series of measures, Chinggis Khan achieved four things in particular. Firstly, he created a superbly organized military structure in which every decimalized unit knew its place and function, each nested inside the other like a matryoshka doll. Second, he placed army units under the command of men who had demonstrated their worth and loyalty to the great khan, thus reducing the danger of any one commander creating a private army that might challenge him.

Thirdly, he promoted men to the highest positions on the basis of their military acumen and their proven skill, not on the status of their birth, although these elite commanders did eventually evolve into a new type of aristocracy known as *qarachu*, or black-boned elites, membership of which did became hereditary.

The fourth effect of the reorganization of the army was arguably the most significant. We have seen how the rise of Temujin to khan was achieved despite the torturous and often bitter clan rivalries and intrigues that had blighted the steppe world for millennia. This reorganization of the army was actually a reorganization of the entire Turkic-Mongolian social structure of the steppe. Soldiers from the tribes that had most bitterly opposed Temujin—the Tatars, the Merkits, the Keraits, and the Naimans—were now distributed throughout the new military divisions.

This meant that there never was a Naiman *tumen*, for example, nor a Merkit *tumen* that might have turned on their new Mongol overlords. Chinggis Khan created new loyalties for these men, to their commanders, and to their *minqan* of a thousand, and to their *tumen* of 10,000. The final genius of this entire system was that, again, as Morgan notes, beyond these military loyalties, "the Mongol royal house became the ultimate focus of obedience and allegiance."

But Chinggis Khan was not finished. At the quriltai of 1206, he made another decision to create an additional military unit of 10,000 known as the *keshig*, or bodyguard. The *keshig* was staffed by the sons of the commanders and officers of Chinggis Khan's army. Men who rose through the ranks did so based on their skill and military acumen, as we have just noted.

The *keshig* was made up of one *minqan* of 1,000 night guards, one *minqan* of 1,000 quiver bearers, and eight *minqan* totaling 8,000 day guards. In *The Secret History of the Mongols*, the duties, structure, and even training of members of the *keshig* is described in detail, showing us how much value Chinggis Khan and the other Mongol elites placed on it.

But the *keshig* was more than the khan's personal army; it also served as Chinggis Khan's household staff. In times of battle, one *minqan* accompanied him at all times, while the remaining 9,000 guarded his camp. In times of peace, some members of the *keshig* tended his flocks and herds; other cooked his food and poured his drinks. This allowed Chinggis to evaluate his men in situations beyond the battlefield, to help determine who might have administrative or intelligence-gathering skills, as well as who was qualified to lead an army. As Tim May sums up: "In short, the *keshig* served as bodyguard and military college, as well as a school for future governors and administrators of the Mongol Empire."

Chinggis Khan and his successors made sure that all Mongol soldiers were very well armed. They were assigned metal helmets with leather neck and ear coverings; armor made of strong and supple leather strips, or sometimes of overlapping metal plates; and the horses were also protected with armor. Mind you, this armor was much lighter than that worn by European knights, which is one of the reasons Mongol forces were literally able to run rings around the heavily armored knights of Hungary and Poland.

Each Mongol soldier carried several composite bows and a good supply of arrows, and the heavy Mongol cavalry also carried a 12-foot lance with a hook on the end to help pull enemy riders off their horses. Officers carried a curved sword, very sharp on one edge. Regular cavalry carried an axe, sword, mace, and also a lasso for bringing down enemy horses.

Mongol soldiers were also armed with different types of shields depending on their role in the attack. A large shield of skin and wood was used for guard duty, a smaller wicker shield was used to protect the front line from arrows, and a third very hard shield made of tortoise shell was used when besieging a city, because it offered greater protection from objects that were hurled down from the city walls.

Over and above, all this equipment and weaponry were the two components that made the Mongols, and indeed all militarized nomads, so invincible—the powerful steppe horse and the composite bow. As McLynn reminds us, "mounted archery is the very definition of nomad warfare." In Chinggis Khan's time, the horses were not shod, and they had the agility of mountain goats. The cavalrymen sat on oiled wooden saddles to facilitate turning rapidly backwards and firing a volley as the horse continued to gallop forwards.

The Mongols carried a long bow and a short bow, depending on the distance arrows needed to be fired, and each soldier carried 60 arrows in two quivers. The two main types of battle arrows were light ones with sharp points, useful and accurate over long distances, and heavy arrows with big, wide heads for killing at close quarters. Arrows were tipped with bone or metal heads, and sometimes they were dipped into viper poison.

In an earlier lecture, we discussed the components of the superb composite bow, made of animal horn, sinew, and wood. The long-range bow needed powerful arms to fire it, and Mongol soldiers trained from recruitment at the age of 15 to develop the required muscles and technique. In the proper hands, it was much more effective than the famed English longbow and could fire arrows 300 yards with ease, although Chinggis Khan's nephew Yisungge was a spectacular archer who once fired an arrow 550 yards at a contest in 1225.

Mongol commanders were also distinguished from their contemporaries by the degree to which they gathered valuable intelligence about the enemy before launching any campaigns. This included not just the strength and disbursement of their military forces, but their religion, their culture, relationships between various groups within that city or society, even the personalities of individual leaders and officers.

Aware that their enemies were also trying to gather intelligence about the Mongols, Chinggis and his successors did all they could to spread disinformation about their own forces. This would range from forging documents that were then "unfortunately" captured by enemy spies, putting Mongol women on spare horses or mounting dummies so that the army would seem much larger to distant observers, and as Juvaini noted in his account of the siege of Alamut, lighting so many fires at night that the enemy "thought the earth a sky full of stars and a world full of swords and daggers, whereof neither middle nor edge was visible."

As part of their reconnaissance, each Mongol army would send scouts dozens of miles ahead and on either side of the main force to look for provisions, for good camping spots, and to ensure that no Mongol army would ever be taken by surprise. This, and the fact that the Mongols sought provisions as they rode and rarely had to wait for any sort of a baggage train, allowed Mongol forces to advance at speeds that astonished their opponents, as we have seen over and over again with Chinggis Khan's war against the Khwarazm-Shah.

However, inevitably, Mongol contingents would have to cross deserts or other terrain that offered little in the way of food, so each soldier carried emergency rations with him: alcohol in the form of fermented mare's milk called kumiss, plus dried meat and dried curdled milk, which could be used to make a sort of yogurt. McLynn sums up all these extraordinary precautions and provisions thus:

> The advance during the strategic phase of a war was thus a marvel of discipline, speed, communications and first-rate staffwork. Warriors could sleep while armed and mounted on their horses and could do so even while the animals grazed. They could ride 65 miles a day ... covering enormous distances without maps; they could link up with another army group with astonishing accuracy and understand all the various signals conveyed by flags, trumpets and lanterns.

> Few armies in the history of the world have come close to equaling the Mongols in preparation, in training, and in strategy. Because of these meticulous preparations, once the

armies reached the actual field of battle, and even though often they were often greatly outnumbered, they were almost invariably successful. The scouts would give the commanders plenty of warning and information about the size and array of the enemy forces ahead and the geography of the land.

We have seen, for example, how effective Mongol forces were at using frozen rivers, which would undoubtedly have been found and checked out by the scouts before the main army arrived. Mongol cavalry used these rivers like interstate highways to provide rapid passage across snow-covered winter landscapes and drive unexpectedly into the heart of large urban settlements built on the banks of these rivers. This was particularly the case with the assaults on the Rus principalities during the reign of Ogedai.

As well as using frozen rivers this way, the Mongols also become very adept at crossing strongly flowing rivers. In April 1241, for example, Mongol forces crossed the eastern European river Sajo in spring flood conditions with 30,000 cavalry during one night before the Battle of Mohi, one of the reasons they were so easily able to defeat the Hungarian king Bela IV and lay waste to half of Hungary.

Other ways in which the Mongols became adept at using information and topography to their advantage was to identify and seize high ground, surprise enemy forces with their backs against a mountain or, even better, their backs against a river so that they could be attacked from three sides.

Once the topography had been thoroughly studied and an appropriate battle plan devised, a series of silent signals would then be sent to coordinate the attack, using flags like semaphores, with the soldiers keeping their horses and themselves as quiet as possible. The various contingents were regathered and concentrated, and the army was divided up into several divisions. Only when all were in place was the silence broken, with the pounding of drums, the blaring of trumpets, and the yelling of the men. You might remember that the siege of Kiev was preceded by a terrifying din so loud that those inside the city could not even converse with each other.

Now the heavy cavalry rode to the front, forming a formidable barrier of armored men and lances. On signal, they would open their ranks to allow the light cavalry to gallop through at high speed, unleashing a devastating hail of arrows, which Juvaini calls the "shafts of doom," before turning and racing back to the protection of the heavy cavalry, turning on their oiled wooden saddles and firing backwards at the enemy as they did so.

The heavy cavalry would then launch a frontal charge against the enemy's front line. If the first charge was successful, so much the better, but if not, charge after charge after charge of heavy cavalry would occur until the enemy's lines were smashed open. At that moment, all units of light and heavy cavalry would attack from a variety of directions in an astonishingly coordinated manner that even had the Mongol units crisscrossing in front of each other and behind each other like some well-practiced marching band.

If these tactics did not work, the Mongol commanders had other tricks up their sleeves, most of them practiced to brilliant effect by their steppe predecessors like the Xiongnu and the Turks for centuries. They would suddenly open gaps in their own lines to encourage ambitious enemies to charge into them, for example, then with perfect discipline snap the gaps closed like the deadly traps they were.

Or they would pretend to retreat, looking suitably demoralized and dejected, perhaps even leaving booty and treasure behind on the battlefield. But as the eager army advanced, they realized too late that they had become victims of a superbly executed ambush. Sometimes these retreats lasted for days, so that, as McLynn puts it, "by the time the trap was sprung the enemy's horses would be exhausted while the Mongol steeds would still be fresh." And once the battle was won, the Mongols were relentless in destroying as many of the enemy as possible, hunting fleeing soldiers and refugees down with a vengeance for days after the battle was won.

Many of these tactics have been ruthlessly practiced by other highly mobile fighters in history, such as, again, the Xiongnu, the Turks, the Huns, or even the Vikings. But uniquely in this esteemed company of warriors, the Mongols also became very comfortable in the art of the siege. After the fall of a city or state, Mongol commanders were always very careful to recruit skilled military professionals into their ranks.

We saw in Juvaini's description of the fall of the fortress at Alamut that Khitan engineers designed and used to great effect a huge ballista that fired giant javelins at the defenders. And as soon as the Mongols started to attack the Jin Dynasty in China, they were very quick to recruit Chinese engineers skilled in the manufacture and use of sophisticated siege engines. Hulagu's huge invasion force into Iraq and Syria included just such a contingent of skilled Chinese siege engineers who could build their machines more or less on the spot using local trees, as Juvaini noted in his account which opened this lecture.

Let's leave the final word on the Mongol military ethos to Jack Weatherford:

> The Mongols did not find honor in fighting; they found honor in winning. They had a single goal in every campaign—total victory. For the Mongol warrior there was no such thing as individual honor in battle if the battle was lost. As Chinggis Khan reportedly said, there is no good in anything until it is finished.

By the beginning of the 1260s, much had been accomplished by the Mongol armies, but nothing had been finished. The Mongol world was plunged into chaos and division following the death of Mongke. Now these incredibly skilled warriors and their commanders would need to turn on each other, as Mongol fought Mongol for control of the fragmenting empire.

QUIZ 1

1. **The term *secondary products revolution* refers to the:**

A. Emergence of new crops as a result of artificial selection by early farmers.

B. Invention of new technologies by early craft workers.

C. Utilization of new products derived from domesticated animals.

D. Expansion of irrigation technologies in response to population increases.

2. **Although the formidable Xiongnu militarized nomadic confederation caused problems for several Chinese dynasties, during which of the following dynasties did the Chinese launch major military campaigns against them?**

A. Zhou.   **B.** Han.   **C.** Shang.   **D.** Tang.

3. **Each of the following was a consequence of the early death of Temujin's father Yesegui except:**

A. Temujin was relatively untrained in the art of steppe warfare.

B. Temujin and his family were quickly designated to a position of lower status.

C. Temujin's feud with the rival Tatars intensified.

D. Temujin was forced to marry Borte to improve the status of his family.

4. **In 1206, the year Temujin was proclaimed Chinggis Khan, China was divided between which of the following three states?**

A. Jin, Song, and Xi Xia.

B. Jin, Song, and Tangut.

C. Song, Tatar, and Qara Khitai.

D. Jin, Song, and Khwarazmia.

5. **The Great Yasa was:**

A. A new tax on merchants introduced by Chinggis Khan.

B. The Mongol law code created by Chinggis Khan.

C. The personal household staff kept by all Mongol khans.

D. The elite status in Mongol society of the Chinggisids.

6. **Jalal al-Din, the son of Shah Mohammad of the Khwarazmians, escaped his Mongol pursuers by:**

A. Jumping into the Indus River with his horse.

B. Finding refuge on an island in the Caspian Sea.

C. Forming an alliance with the Iranian rulers of the city of Nishapur.

D. Disappearing into the swampy forests of the Siberian taiga, where Mongol horses could not go.

7. **According to the *Secret History of the Mongols*, Chinggis Khan's death in August 1227 was a result of:**

A. An arrow wound suffered in his final campaign against the Xi Xia.

B. Hypothermia after being trapped in a winter snowstorm during a hunt.

C. Internal injuries after being thrown from his horse during a hunt.

D. Cholera contracted during the long and exhausting Khwarazmian campaign.

8. **The supreme commander of the massive force Ogedai dispatched westward in 1236 on the Russian and European campaign was:**

A. Ogedai's son Qadan.

B. Jochi's son Batu.

C. Tolui's son Mongke.

D. General Subedai.

9. **All of the following are true in explaining the success of the Mongol *jam* system except:**

A. Although designed originally as a means of speeding the travel of envoys and officials, it evolved into a commercial network.

B. Mongol army units were responsible for maintaining the infrastructure required for the *jam* to operate effectively.

C. Travelers utilizing the system had to produce proper documentation in the form of an official tablet called a *gerege*.

D. The number of horses official envoys could access in a single day's travel was unlimited.

10. **As part of his reform of the taxation system, Mongke Khan did which of the following?**

A. Insisted that all taxes now had to be paid in cash.

B. Eliminated the different types of tax that had been paid by nomadic and sedentary populations within the empire.

C. Increased the price that merchants had to pay to receive the official documentation of the *gerege*.

D. Continued the practice of allowing religious leaders of all faiths to be exempt from taxation.

11. **The Mongol's military organization was based on which of the following?**

A. The decimal system.

B. The election of commanders by the troops.

C. The centrality of the *keshig*.

D. The creation of separate units based on tribal affiliations.

12. **The name Qubilai Khan chose for the new Yuan dynasty in China means:**

A. Foundation of the world.

B. Center of the universe.

C. Strength through unity.

D. Fulfilment of divine prophecy.

Answers:
1: C; 2: B; 3: D; 4: A; 5: B; 6: A; 7: C; 8: D; 9: D; 10: D; 11: A; 12: B

THE MONGOLS IN CHINA

Following the death of Mongke Khan in 1259, civil war broke out among the Mongols, a conflict that involved several of the most illustrious princes of the Chinggisid family and their armies. Ilkhan Hulagu did not return to Mongolia after the death of his older brother, preferring to remain in the domain he had carved out for himself in Persia and the Middle East. He was soon at war with his cousin Berke, grandson of Chinggis Khan's oldest son, Jochi, over control of their respective regional empires.

Farther east, the main conflict was between Qubilai Khan and his younger brother Ariq Boke, the youngest son of Tolui. This ended in 1264, when Ariq Boke surrendered to Qubilai. Qubilai had already declared himself the new great khan of the Mongol empire, a decision that was disputed by various other Chinggisid princes.

In reality, there no longer was a Mongol empire, at least not a unified one. Chinggis's empire had fragmented into four geographically distinct khanates. Qubilai was firmly in control of northern China. Chagatayid and Ogedeid descendants had created their own state in central Asia, Hulagu was ilkhan of Persia and the Middle East, and the descendants of Jochi ruled much of Russia and the steppe. This lecture focuses on the Mongol conquest of the Song dynasty in southern China and the reunification of that vast state for the first time in three centuries as the Mongol-controlled Yuan dynasty.

The Challenge Facing the Mongols

Qubilai Khan was pragmatic. He had unilaterally declared himself khan, a decision many did not support. He decided to demonstrate his right to lead by reigniting the war against the Southern Song dynasty in China, which had more or less ground to a halt.

The Song were the most technologically and industrially advanced state on the planet by the mid-13th century, with tremendous military and logistical resources. Additionally, much of the Song state featured mountainous terrain that slowed the Mongols and rendered their usual fighting tactics much less effective.

Further south, the landscape consisted of enormous regions of rice paddies that were particularly challenging for Mongol horses. The Song had even gone so far as to plant forests of trees in those landscapes that would otherwise have favored Mongol war techniques. The extensive coastline and mighty rivers like the Han and Yangtze also dictated that the Mongols would have to build a navy.

But the Mongols did have one tremendous advantage: intense division of purpose among the Song leadership. Some Song officials and generals had considerable military and civil engineering skills but often put self-interest above that of the state.

Certain Song generals were so disgusted with the incompetence of Song emperors and officials that they turned renegade and joined the Mongols. One in particular, Liu Zheng, convinced Qubilai of the importance of building a navy. The Mongols, who had emerged in a landlocked country and mastered the arts of steppe warfare, duly built a navy and manned it with Korean and Han sailors from the former Jin dynasty.

Xiangyang and Fancheng

Following further advice from Liu Zheng, in 1268 the Mongols decided to focus all of their forces on one point in the Song defenses: the city of Xiangyang and its neighboring city Fancheng. Qubilai Khan placed Aju, the grandson of the great Mongol general Subedai, in charge of the campaign. The new Mongol navy of 500 ships blockaded the Han River so that the cities were unable to receive supplies, but the Song sent a navy of 3,000 ships to destroy them in August 1269.

Counterweight trebuchet

The defenses of the two Song cities were so formidable that the war ground to a halt. The Mongols needed some new weapon or tactic that would break the stalemate. Five years later, this came with the arrival of two brilliant Muslim engineers who had journeyed 3,500 miles from Persia to China. They immediately set about constructing massive counterweight trebuchets.

They fired rock missiles that weighed 220 pounds, hacked out of nearby quarries. The machine was first used against the city of Fancheng to immediate effect. The walls were quickly breached and the city captured. As a warning to the residents of Xiangyang, the Mongol attackers slaughtered 3,000 soldiers and 7,000 residents of Fancheng by cutting their throats, then piled the bodies high up into a hillock visible from Xiangyang.

The huge machines were then dismantled, transported across the Han River, and reassembled in front of the walls of Xiangyang. After one devastating shot, the Mongols were able to convince the leader of the city, Lu Wenhuan, to surrender, which he did on the March 17, 1273.

The Muslim engineers were well rewarded for their work, and they and their sons gained important positions under Qubilai Khan. A military officer named Bayan who had accompanied the engineers from Persia also rose through Mongol ranks. He was married to a niece of Chabi, Qubilai Khan's primary wife. Qubilai was so impressed with Bayan that he placed him in joint command with Aju, charged with the final destruction of the Song, which was in utter dismay and disarray following the fall of Fancheng and Xiangyang.

Later Operations

Bayan and Aju led a force of 100,000 soldiers and a navy of 10,000 ships. On March 19, 1275, Mongol forces defeated a considerably larger Song army and navy led by Jia Sidao. Now the race was on for the capital, and Bayan's formidable reputation as a general was such that many Chinese towns and entire armies surrendered to him as soon as his red banner was sighted.

The endgame was played out as three powerful Mongol armies descended on the huge southern cities of the Song, including the great capital of Lin'an, the modern city of Hangzhou. With the writing on the wall, Empress Dowager Xie surrendered to the Mongols on behalf of her son, the boy emperor, on March 28, 1276. The Mongols spared the city, and most of the Song forces now surrendered.

One group of fanatical loyalists avoided Mongol forces for another three years until they were forced into a final standoff on an island near Macau. The last heir to the Song throne drowned, as did thousands of his loyalists who threw themselves into the sea with weights tied around their legs. At that moment, the Song dynasty officially ceased to exist.

Conclusion

Qubilai Khan was now in control of a massive empire that stretched from the Siberian steppe to the border with Vietnam and from the China Sea to central Asia . This was a larger territorial empire than any Chinese emperor had ever controlled. In 1271, five years before the Song dowager empress surrendered to him, he had already declared himself the emperor of a reunited China.

Qubilai used the ancient political ideology of the Mandate of Heaven to claim that the Song had lost it. Heaven had bestowed it on himself and the Mongols instead. He chose the name of Great Yuan for his new dynasty, a name drawn from one of the five Zhou dynasty classic texts.

Qubilai also decided that he need a new capital city from which to rule his vast empire. Karakoram was too small and too far north, as was the city of Xanadu that he had constructed on the steppe. After considering various options, he settled on Beijing. This was a historically consequential decision: Beijing has remained the capital of China almost continuously from that moment until today. Construction of the new capital began in March 1271, and enough work had been completed by 1274 for Qubilai to conduct his first imperial audience in the palace, which was at the heart of the city.

Ruling a vast and complex agricultural and commercial state like China was a new challenge for the Mongols, and Qubilai was certainly smart enough to listen to his Chinese advisers and adopt many of the norms of Chinese behavior. But it is also fair to say that he never fully trusted local Chinese administrators, and so he and later Yuan emperors tried to maintain political control, social stability, and tax revenue by creating a balance of ethnic power in government and by combining Mongol and Chinese techniques of administration.

One of the early steps Qubilai took to facilitate this was to divide the residents of the Yuan dynasty into four distinct categories or classes, based on their ethnicity. Mongols were on the top, along with other nomadic peoples. Next came a group known as the Semuren, which included all Europeans, Russians, and the many Muslim administrators Qubilai brought from Persia and central Asia. Third on the totem pole were the Hanren, which included ethnic Han Chinese, and also Jurchen, Khitans, and Koreans. At the bottom were the Nanren, southern Chinese people, and other ethnicities dwelling in the south.

MARCO POLO

Much of our knowledge of Yuan government and society comes from the account written by the famous Venetian traveler Marco Polo.

The system was clearly designed to keep the Mongols at the top of the social and political pecking order and also to help them maintain their cultural distinctiveness. To further enhance their superior status, all Mongols living in China enjoyed substantial legal and tax advantages.

Qubilai divided China into 12 new provinces ruled by governors and imperial officials. To guard against the building of local power bases and too much regional autonomy, provincial administrators needed the permission of the imperial supervisors before any major decisions could be made.

Many of these supervisors were Persian because from the moment the Mongols had encountered the Persian officials of the Abbasid Caliphate and other states of central and west Asia, Mongol rulers had been deeply impressed with their skills in government.

THE MONGOLS IN CHINA

LECTURE 13 TRANSCRIPT

Following the death of Mongke Khan in 1259, civil war broke out amongst the Mongols, a scrappy conflict that involved several of the most illustrious princes of the Chinggisid family and their armies. Ilkhan Hulagu did not return to Mongolia after the death of his older brother, preferring to remain in the domain he had carved out for himself in Persia and the Middle East, although he was soon at war with his cousin Berke, grandson of Chinggis Khan's oldest son, Jochi, over control of their respective regional empires.

Further east, the main conflict was between Qubilai Khan and his younger brother Ariq Boke, the youngest son of Tolui. This ended in 1264, when Ariq Boke surrendered to Qubilai. Qubilai had already declared himself the new great khan of the Mongol Empire, a decision that was disputed by various other Chinggisid princes.

In reality, there no longer was a Mongol Empire, at least not a unified one. Chinggis's empire had fragmented into four geographically distinct khanates. Qubilai was firmly in control of northern China, Chagatayid and Ogedeid descendants had created their own state in central Asia, Hulagu was ilkhan of Persia and the Middle East, and the descendants of Jochi ruled much of Russia and the steppe.

So we turn now in the next series of lectures to a consideration of the fortunes of the Mongols in each of these regions, and other regions not yet conquered, beginning in this lecture with the Mongol conquest of the Song Dynasty in southern China and the reunification of that vast state for the first time in three centuries as the Mongol-controlled Yuan Dynasty.

Qubilai Khan was nothing if not pragmatic. He had unilaterally declared himself khan, a decision many did not support, so rather than trying to establish his authority over the entire Yeke Mongol Ulus and risk further civil war, he decided to demonstrate his right to lead by reigniting the war against the southern Song Dynasty in China, which had more or less ground to a halt.

We saw in an earlier lecture that the Song were the most technologically and industrially advanced state on the planet by the mid-13th century, with tremendous military and logistical resources. Their army and large navy may have numbered a million men, although of course their military skills were greatly inferior to the Mongols. But Mongke's death had given the Song a breathing space which they had not wasted, reinforcing their defenses, building a larger military, and generally preparing in every way to resist the inevitable return of the Mongols.

The task facing Qubilai and his forces was formidable, particularly the challenges posed by geography. Much of the Song state featured mountainous terrain that slowed the Mongols and rendered their usual fighting tactics much less effective. Further south, the landscape consisted of enormous regions of rice paddies that were particularly challenging for Mongol horses. The Song had even gone so far as to plant forests of trees in those landscapes that would otherwise have favored Mongol techniques of war. The extensive coastline and mighty rivers like the Han and Yangtze also dictated that the Mongols would have to build their own navy and add naval warfare to their already extensive list of military skills.

But the Mongols did have one tremendous advantage, which soon revealed itself as the campaign was renewed, and this was intense division of purpose amongst the Song leadership. As Tim May puts it, "internal rot doomed the Song as feuds at court undermined imperial objectives and local elites placed local and regional interests against imperial priorities."

Some Song officials and generals had considerable military and civil engineering skills but often put self-interest above that of the state. One such official was Jia Sidao, who the Song emperor had placed in charge of operations against Qubilai Khan in Sichuan. Qubilai's withdrawal from the region to fight the civil war with his brother soon after this appointment was purely coincidental, but it strengthened Jia Sidao's reputation and authority. In the break between campaigns, he strengthened Sichuan's defenses, including those of the major city of Xiangyang. But in other ways, his self-importance and hubris undermined Song efforts to prepare for the Mongols return.

Some Song generals were so disgusted with the incompetence of Song emperors and officials like Jia Sidao that they turned renegade and joined the Mongols. One in particular, Liu Zheng, convinced Qubilai of the importance of building a navy. So the Mongols, who had emerged in a landlocked country and mastered the arts of steppe warfare, duly built a navy, as extraordinary as that sounds, and manned it with Korean and Han sailors from the former Jin Dynasty.

Following further advice from Liu Zheng, in 1268, the Mongols decided to focus all of their forces on one point in the Song defenses, the city of Xiangyang and its neighboring city Fancheng. Qubilai Khan placed Aju, the grandson of the great Mongol general Subedei, in charge of the campaign. The new Mongol navy of 500 ships blockaded the Han River so that the cities were unable to receive supplies, but the Song sent a navy of 3,000 ships to destroy them in August 1269.

Qubilai was absolutely committed to crushing the Song. But despite pouring more men and resources into the campaign and building more boats, the defenses of the two Song cities were so formidable that the war ground to a halt. What the Mongols needed was some new weapon or tactic that would break the stalemate. Five years later, this came with the arrival of two brilliant Muslim engineers who had journeyed 3,500 miles from Persia to China. They immediately set about constructing massive counterweight trebuchets that had never been seen in Song China before, let alone used against their cities.

It is hardly surprising that a technologically advanced state like the Song possessed their own arsenal of trebuchets. These consisted of a frame roughly 12 feet high which supported a pivoting pole up to 36 feet long. John Man estimates that 100 of these Song trebuchets could 'deliver up to 12,000 rocks per hour, hour after hour, day after day." But the Song engineers also fired projectiles of a different kind: gunpowder explosives.

The Chinese had invented gunpowder, of course, and had been experimenting with it for a long time. One of the most lethal projectiles fired by their trebuchets consisted of gunpowder packed into a round bamboo container that was in turn wrapped in broken shards of porcelain—as Man says, "the first known use of shrapnel."

Even worse was the so-called thunder-crash bomb with a huge quantity of gunpowder packed inside metal casing. As it hurtled into enemy camps and cities, it destroyed everything within a radius of about 1,200 square feet. And the Song also need to be credited with the first use of biological weapons in the form of a gunpowder bomb that spread human excrement and poisonous beetles over a wide radius.

It was these formidable Song weapons, along with their huge navy, that had ground the Mongol assault to a halt and dragged the siege of Xiangyang into an epic five-year struggle. But now the two engineers, Ismail al-Din and Ala al-Din, arrived from Mongol-controlled Persia and were building the same type of traction trebuchets that had been used so effectively by Qubilai's brother Hulagu in the siege of Baghdad in 1258.

These trebuchets were the heaviest artillery available in the world in the mid-13th century. Instead of men pulling ropes to "load" the weapon, a box filled with rocks now supplied the "muscle" to pull the pivoting pole back into firing position. This meant that much longer and heavier poles could be used, firing much heavier missiles under considerably greater tension.

The machines were built on site by the brilliant engineers. John Man estimates they weighed 40 tons and were 60 feet high. They fired rock missiles that weighed 220 pounds, hacked out of nearby quarries. The machine was first used against the city of Fancheng to immediate effect. The walls were quickly breached and the city captured. As a warning to the residents of Xiangyang, and in the hope that they would surrender, the Mongol attackers slaughtered 3,000 soldiers and 7,000 residents of Fancheng by cutting their throats, then piled the bodies high up onto a hillock visible from Xiangyang.

The huge machines were then dismantled, transported across the Han River, and reassembled in front of the walls of Xiangyang. Ismail now had his machine fine-tuned, and the first shot he fired hit the city with deadly accuracy. It slammed into a watch tower, and the whole city shook. This one shot was so devastating that the Mongols were able to convince the leader of the city, one Lu Wenhuan, to surrender, which he did on the 17th of March, 1273. The Mongol leadership had promised him there would be no massacre, and they were as good as their word. As a reward for this largess, the Mongol generals also convinced Lu Wenhuan to come over to their side. The Chinese administrator was to prove an invaluable advisor in the remaining years of the war between Qubilai Khan and the Song.

The Muslim engineers were well rewarded for their work, and they and their sons gained important positions under Qubilai Khan. A military officer named Bayan who had accompanied the engineers from Persia also rose through Mongol ranks and was married to a niece of Chabi, Qubilai Khan's primary wife. Qubilai was so impressed with Bayan that he placed him in joint command with Aju, charged with the final destruction of the Song, which was in utter dismay and disarray following the fall of Fancheng and Xiangyang.

Bayan and Aju led a force of 100,000 soldiers and a navy of 10,000 ships. On March 19th, 1275, Mongol forces defeated a considerably larger Song army and navy led by Jia Sidao at the Battle of Dingjia Island. Now the race was on for the capital, and Bayan's formidable reputation as a general was such that many Chinese towns and entire armies surrendered to him as soon as his red banner was sighted.

The endgame was played out as three powerful Mongol armies descended on the huge southern cities of the Song, including the great capital of Lin'an, the modern city of Hangzhou. With the writing on the wall, Empress Dowager Xie surrendered to the Mongols on behalf of her son, the boy emperor, on March 28th, 1276. The Mongols spared the city, and most of the Song forces now surrendered.

But not all. One group of fanatical loyalists avoided Mongol forces for another three years until they were forced into a final standoff at the Battle of Yaishan on an island near Macau. The last heir to the Song throne drowned, as did thousands of his loyalists who threw themselves into the sea with weights tied around their legs. At that moment, the Song Empire officially ceased to exist.

It was Chinggis Khan himself who had led the very first Mongol campaign into China back in 1211, and it had taken the Mongols 23 years to defeat the rulers of northern China, the Jin Dynasty. It took his sons and grandsons another 45 years to finally destroy the great power of southern China, the Song. With the size, population, resources, and technological prowess of China, it is not surprising that Chinese dynasties were rarely defeated by outside forces over the 4,000 years of their existence. But the Mongols proved tenacious and brilliantly inventive enough to bring down the wealthiest and most powerful state on the planet, even though it ultimately took them 68 years to do so.

Qubilai Khan was now in control of a massive empire of his own, stretching from the Siberian steppe to the border with Vietnam, and from the China Sea to central Asia. This was a larger territorial empire than any Chinese emperor had ever controlled. In 1271, five years before the Song dowager empress had surrendered to him, he had already declared himself the emperor of a reunited China. Following the advice of several Chinese ministers, he realized he would have to legitimize his claim by appealing to his new Chinese subjects.

So Qubilai used the ancient political ideology of the Mandate of Heaven to claim that the Song had lost the mandate and that Heaven had bestowed it upon himself and the Mongols instead. He chose the name Da Yuan, Great Yuan, for his new dynasty, a name drawn from one of the five Zhou Dynasty classic texts. In the *I Ching*, or *Book of Changes*, the name Yuan means "the origins of the universe." Qubilai also performed all the standard rites and ceremonies that traditionally occurred with the enthronement of a new emperor, and he dressed in imperial robes and was carried through the streets in a sedan rather than riding through them on a horse.

Qubilai also decided that he needed a new capital city from which to rule his vast empire. Karakoram was too small and too far north, as was the city of Xanadu that he had constructed on the steppe. After considering various options, he settled on Beijing. The city was small and inconsequential and had been devastated by Mongol forces in 1215 during their war against the Jin, but it also had the advantage of being close to Mongolia so that Qubilai could continue to rule and control both his steppe nomadic and Chinese sedentary realms. This was a historically consequential decision, because Beijing has remained the capital of China almost continuously from that moment until today—the capital of the Yuan, Ming, and Qing Dynasties, and of course the People's Republic of China.

He actually chose a new site just north of the old city to construct the capital, which was built around a large lake that had been dug by the northern Song Dynasty three centuries earlier as a playground for elites. The design of the capital was carefully and intentionally based on descriptions in the *Book of Rites*, another of the five classics of Zhou Dynasty literature that had been around for about 2,000 years by that point.

Construction of the new capital began in March 1271, and enough work had been completed by 1274 for Qubilai to conduct his first imperial audience in the palace, which was at the heart of the city. The palace and its gorgeous gardens were surrounded by a wall 30 feet high, its roof was made of multicolored tiles, and its vast central hall, decorated with frescoes depicting animals and other gold and silver decorative motifs, could house up to 6,000 guests. Nothing of Qubilai's palace can be seen in Beijing today.

When the Mongols were finally driven out of China in the 14th century, a vengeful Ming Dynasty had the Forbidden City built right over the top of Qubilai's palace to eradicate all remnants of Mongol rule.

Ruling a vast and complex agricultural and commercial state like China was a new challenge for the Mongols, and Qubilai was certainly smart enough to listen to his Chinese advisers and adopt many of the norms of Chinese behavior. But it is also fair to say that he never fully trusted local Chinese administrators, and so he and later Yuan emperors tried to maintain political control, social stability, and tax revenue by creating a balance of ethnic power in government and by combining Mongol and Chinese techniques of administration.

One of the early steps Qubilai took to facilitate this was to divide the residents of the Yuan Dynasty into four distinct categories, or classes, based on their ethnicity. Mongols were on the top, of course, along with other nomadic peoples. Next came a group known as the Semuren, a group that means "persons of special status" and included all Europeans, Russians, and the many Muslim administrators Qubilai brought from Persia and central Asia. Third on the totem pole were the Hanren, which included ethnic Han Chinese, and also Jurchen, Khitans, and Koreans. At the bottom were the Nanren, southern Chinese, and other ethnicities dwelling in the south.

The system was clearly designed to keep the Mongols at the top of the social and political pecking order and also to help them maintain their cultural distinctiveness and not become Sinicized as so many nomadic conquerors before them had done. To help reinforce this, later Yuan rulers issued a dress code decree in 1314 which dictated that Han officials had to wear Chinese round-collared shirts and folded hats, while Mongols wore their long jackets and soft hats with four edges. Visual evidence of this came to light in a Yuan Dynasty tomb discovered in 2012. The richly decorated walls of the tomb depict different characters, some wearing traditional Chinese clothing, others traditional Mongol clothing.

To further enhance their superior status, all Mongols living in China enjoyed substantial legal and tax advantages. The emperor and court centered their administration on the capital and ruled the provinces through subordinate officials who were supervised by other specially appointed imperial officials, essentially the eyes and ears of the emperor.

Qubilai divided China into 12 new provinces ruled by governors and imperial officials. To guard against the building of local power bases and too much regional autonomy, provincial administrators needed the permission of the imperial supervisors before any major decisions could be made. Many of these supervisors were Persian, because from the moment the Mongols had encountered the Persian officials of the Abbasid Caliphate and other states of central and west Asia, Mongol rulers had been deeply impressed with their skills in government. So Qubilai Khan dismantled the Confucian exam system that had provided China with high quality bureaucrats for some 1,500 years by this point, and instead brought many Persian and other west Asian Muslims to China, where they were given high administrative posts in Yuan Dynasty government.

This policy of excluding Chinese elites from the highest positions of government, the very positions they had dominated for so many centuries as the Confucian bureaucrats, may have had some positive side effects for Chinese philosophy, literature, and visual arts. Some of the skills that candidates were used to demonstrating in the now dismantled Confucian exam system were literary and artistic. With high government posts now closed to them, it is not surprising that many turned to artistic endeavors, and some scholars argue that artists had much greater freedom of self-expression under the Yuan than under any of the traditional Chinese dynasties.

Despite the best efforts of Qubilai and his skilled Persian and central Asian officials, historians have traditionally judged the Yuan administration of China as inefficient. There is evidence in sources like the annals of the Yuan Dynasty that the Mongols tried to root out corruption, and corrupt officials were flogged by the Mongols, in stark contrast to the more civil atmosphere that had characterized the Song court. But despite their efforts to oversee provincial administrators, the provinces were ruled with a considerable degree of independence and self-serving authority.

The only important function of regional officials was to keep the tax revenues and other goods and services flowing to the imperial government, and the Mongols did not really care how this was done. The Yuan Dynasty did introduce some laws, but many of these were ineffectual, and even Han Chinese officials claimed they were too lenient. The argument was that the Mongol government eventually become so lackadaisical that even those Chinese officials employed to work with the Mongols ended up openly criticizing the Yuan government for its decentralization and its inefficiency.

These days, there has been something of a revision of that view, and some historians who study Yuan China have offered a more positive assessment of Yuan government. For example, the *Jam* communication system was extended all over China, utilizing horsemen, or runners where horses were not suitable, which certainly helped bind the provinces together. The Grand Canal of China, expanded in the late 6th century during the reign of Sui emperor Yangdi, was also considerably enlarged and extended under the Mongols, helping facilitate commerce within the country and ensuring faster deliveries of food from the south to the north.

The reign of the first emperor Qubilai was probably the high point of Mongol administration. The most important gift he gave to China was to reunify that vast country under a single dynasty, bringing peace to a state that had been at war for more than a century and allowing the commercial and agricultural infrastructure to heal and flourish. As David Morgan puts it, after centuries of division into separate Liao, Jin, and Song states, Qubilai "gave to China the political unity that it has never since lost."

Much of our knowledge of Yuan government and society comes from the account written by the famous Venetian traveler Marco Polo. Born in or about the year 1254, Polo was a member of a successful family of merchants who operated in the Venetian Republic during the 13th century. In 1271, accompanied by his father and uncle, the 17-year-old Marco set out on an epic journey across Asia, arriving at the court of Qubilai Khan in 1275.

Upon meeting the khan, the Polos presented him with sacred oils from Jerusalem and a letter from the pope. Marco Polo knew several languages and had acquired a great deal of political and geographical knowledge on his travels. According to Marco's own account, these credentials and skills were so impressive that he was employed by Qubilai Khan for the next 17 years as his trusted adviser, which allowed him to observe a great deal about Chinese society and government.

But it is difficult to know precisely what position Marco Polo did acquire in the Yuan court, particularly as there exist conflicting versions of the text that eventually coalesced into *The Travels of Marco Polo*. In some versions, Polo claims he was appointed governor of a province, or governor of a city like Yangzhou. Tim May wonders whether Qubilai might have included Marco in his personal *keshig*, which would have allowed him to interact with the emperor and also travel about as part of Qubilai's household staff, but this is only speculative.

Marco eventually returned to Venice in 1295 after another epic journey, much of it by sea this time. Scholars estimate that he probably traveled a total of 15,000 miles on his twin journeys. Upon returning home, Marco found himself caught up in a bitter war between Genoa and Venice, and he was imprisoned for several years before being released in 1299. It was while he was in prison that he dictated to his cell mate the famous account of his travels and his many years in China.

Marco Polo's detailed descriptions of the sophisticated Chinese court and way of life seemed so absurd to 13th-century Europeans that they were dismissed as a pack of lies. But his accounts of the great canals, granaries, social services, advanced technology, and even regular bathing of the Chinese—all of which were completely unknown in Europe—were so astonishing that his book became a bestseller, and has remained one to this very day.

Polo reported, for example, that China's social welfare system took care of sick, aged, and orphaned children, and that the great emperor had 12,000 personal retainers. But Polo also noted that ethnic animosity was intense in Yuan China. He wrote: "All the Han detested the rule of the Great Khan because he set over them Mongols, or still more frequently Muslims, whom they could not endure for they treated them just as slaves."

Those ethnic Chinese who did work with the Mongols often prospered, but many others had their lands confiscated or were forced into serfdom, often transported far from home. In fact, the Mongols substantially redrew the ethnic map not just of China, but of much of Eurasia, by forcing literally millions of people of different ethnicities to leave their native lands and resettle far away. More about the impact of this towards the end of the course.

Marco Polo was also an eyewitness to the great hunts that Qubilai held, maintaining the tradition of the *nerge* even though he was now emperor of Yuan China. The aim of the hunts was to supply the court with fresh meat, and they were carried out in the countryside over a vast area centered on Beijing. Polo recorded that 14,000 hunters were employed seeking large game for meat, and also for Qubilai's private zoo, which contained a formidable collection of big cats, like cheetahs and tigers, that had been trained to catch and kill larger animals.

The scale and opulence of the spring hunts astonished Marco Polo, but of course, he would not have been aware of the incredibly important role these hunts had played in forging unity and a warrior ethos amongst Mongols and other nomads for centuries. Qubilai traveled in an enormous wooden room, or howdah, decorated with gold filigree on the inside and lion skins hanging on the outside. The room was attached to four enormous elephants that trundled across the landscape, bearing the precious cargo of the emperor and his senior aides.

At the end of each day, Qubilai arrived at a luxurious tent city. Eventually, they reached a camp that would function as hunt headquarters for the next three months, a place teeming with birds and game, and with the plains stretching out in all directions around it. Qubilai's primary wife, Chabi, was there to meet him, along with his three secondary wives, his extended family, and all his senior staff so that the business of court could continue. No wonder Marco Polo was astonished by what he observed, and it is hardly surprising that his European readers found his account beyond belief.

Before we leave Marco Polo, let me remind you that after being released from prison, Marco became a successful and wealthy merchant. But although he sponsored many other successful expeditions into Asia, he himself never left Venice again until his death in 1324.

The fact that Qubilai chose to continue the annual hunt so deeply steeped in Mongol tradition reminds us that although Qubilai was prepared to adopt many of the trappings, rituals, and ceremonies of a traditional Chinese emperor, he always viewed himself as a Mongol khan first and foremost. His wife Chabi was an important adviser in his court, which was very unlike the role of wives in traditional Chinese courts. And of course, the class system he introduced was partly designed to keep Mongols culturally separate from the foreigners and Chinese over whom they now ruled. The Mongol *keshig*, the large body of soldiers and advisers, was also retained as a key military and bureaucratic element of government.

Yet it must be acknowledged that Qubilai was forced to straddle two worlds: that of the nomadic steppe and that of the ancient traditions of Chinese imperial administration forged over millennia. This can be seen in the way he groomed his oldest living son, Jingim, to succeed him. Jingim is the Mongol version of the Chinese name Zhenjin, which means "True Gold." Aware that as future leader Jingim would need to deeply understand the psychology and culture of his Chinese subjects, Qubilai made sure his son received a good Confucian education and was also exposed to Buddhism and Daoism. Gradually, Jingim assumed more administrative and religious responsibilities in the Yuan Court, and in 1273, he was officially named heir apparent by Qubilai.

But the great khan was not finished yet—far from it. Qubilai still had 20 more years to live, and he would use that time like any great Mongol khan would: to obey the wishes of Tengri and continue to expand his already enormous empire. Even before the Song Dynasty had fallen, he had set his sights on other regions like Korea and Vietnam and Burma, and the enigmatic Land of the Rising Sun. One year after naming Jingim his heir apparent, Qubilai launched an invasion of Japan. That invasion, and Qubilai's expansionist activities all over east and southeast Asia, is the subject of our next lecture.

THE MONGOLS IN EAST
AND SOUTHEAST ASIA

C ampaigns into places like Japan, Myanmar, Vietnam, and Indonesia were part of Qubilai Khan's attempts to considerably widen his already enormous Yuan dynasty. One goal was to continue the mandate all Mongols believe had been given to them by heaven itself to conquer the whole world. Another was to allow Qubilai to increase the size of his personal territorial holdings and thus reinforce his claims to be recognized as great khan.

Korea

This lecture begins with Korea, which had actually been conquered by the Mongols decades before Qubilai Khan completed his conquest of China. For a long time, various Korean kingdoms and dynasties had been forced to deal with factions of powerful militarized nomads that occupied steppe regions just to the north of the border between the Korean Peninsula and mainland east Asia.

As early as the 10th century, the founder of the Goryeo dynasty, King Taejo, had extended the northern borders. His successors continued this effort, building formidable garrison forts across the north and pushing Korean-controlled territory toward the Yalu River.

Inevitably, this brought conflict with the Khitan militarized nomads. The Khitan were a formidable foe, and in the winter of 1010, Korean sources describe a Khitan army that drove south for the Goryeo capital at Songdo, which they sacked and pillaged. But with their supply lines stretched thin, the Khitan were eventually forced to fight a bloody retreat back to the Yalu, at the cost of perhaps 40,000 men.

The Goryeo dynasty's other great northern nomadic foe was the Jurchen, who dwelt further east in Manchuria. Fed up with constant harassing attacks from these fierce nomadic peoples, the Goryeo decided to build a huge wall across the northern frontier. The Goryeo wall linked 14 garrison towns in a line that stretched northward from the mouth of the Yalu River, through the mountains, and all the way out to the east coast.

The wall proved initially effective, but eventually the Jurchen began raiding Goryeo again, and their cavalry contingents easily surmounted the wall and defeated the Goryeo armies. This time the Goryeo responded by creating a new military force, which in 1107 drove the Jurchen back to the steppes and then built nine new forts in the northeast to contain them.

Goryeo military forces

China

China was under the control of the powerful Song dynasty, but by 1125, the Jurchen had redirected their expansionary energies to the south. They had succeeded in defeating first the Khitan and then the Song, capturing the Chinese capital at Kaifeng. The Song retreated south, and China was divided between the Jurchen-controlled north and the Song in the south.

Mongol Involvement

The first contact between the Mongols and Goryeo occurred in 1219 when the two formed an alliance to destroy a Khitan army that had crossed the Yalu River. Six years later, in 1225, the Mongols demanded tribute from the Goryeo king, but he refused. To make matters worse, the Mongol envoy was killed returning from Goryeo, and the Mongols used this as a pretext to invade.

In 1231, Ogedai ordered a Mongol army led by General Saritai to cross the Yalu River and drive south, supported by a rebel Goryeo general. Eventually, their capital fell into Mongol hands, and the Goryeo sued for peace. The Mongols demanded an extraordinary amount of tribute. In 1232, Saritai withdrew his main force but left military commanders in charge to ensure the tribute payments were received.

Less than a year later, the Goryeo government decided to relocate all government officials to Ganghwa Island, about 20 miles off the coast. This exploited one of the Mongols' few weaknesses: their fear of the sea. Frustrated, the Mongols instituted a scorched earth policy on the mainland, burning the grain fields and capturing mountain fortresses. In one invasion alone in 1254, the Mongols took back with them 200,000 captives, left countless dead, and reduced huge areas of Korea to ashes.

As the peasants lost their will to resist, the government tried to seek divine assistance by creating a massive woodblock printing of important Buddhist sutras in the form of the *Tripitaka Koreana*. It is renowned as one of the most accurate translations of core Buddhist texts, treatises, and laws ever made, and also for the beauty of the exquisite carving in wood of the Chinese characters in which the text is translated.

Later, the Goryeo king staged a coup against his own government and sought peace with the Mongols. The crown prince traveled to China in 1258 and personally offered his country's submission to Qubilai. Korea became a loyal client tributary state to Qubilai's regime. To maintain their relative autonomy, Korean kings often married Mongol princesses who kept a close watch on the situation at court.

Japan

By 1271, Qubilai Khan had subdued most of China and declared the Yuan dynasty. He then began to consider other regions of east and southeast Asia that might be brought into the fold. He focused on Pagan (modern Myanmar), Vietnam, Indonesia, and most particularly Japan.

The archipelago of Japan was then under the control of the shoguns of the Hōjō clan, and as Qubilai moved toward the final destruction of the Song, the shogun became increasingly concerned that Japan would be next.

He was convinced that Qubilai was determined to recruit the formidable Japanese samurai warriors into his army. Qubilai sent envoys to the shogun demanding submission, but these were ignored. Instead, the Japanese bolstered their defenses, and Qubilai ordered the construction of a navy in southern Korea in preparation for invasion.

A fleet of 3,000 warships and 500 support vessels sailed from Pusan in Korea in the autumn of 1274, manned by thousands of sailors and up to 40,000 Song, Korean, and Mongol troops. After capturing Tsushima and Iki Islands, the force arrived at Hakata Bay on the coast of Kyushu to be met by 6,000 samurai, including Takezaki Suenaga. Mongol archery and the use of trebuchets firing explosive devices forced the samurai back. The town of Hakata, which is modern Fukuoka, was burned, although a Mongol general was seriously wounded in the fighting.

With no more progress to be made against the formidable samurai, the Mongols retreated to their ships to make plans for the next stage of the invasion. But the Japanese sent small fire ships in the night to burn some of the Mongol warships, and then a huge typhoon storm sprang up that devastated the fleet. Many poorly built Song ships were sunk. Others were scattered. Some Korean sources state that 13,000 of the Mongol troops were drowned. The Mongols decided to call off the invasion and return to Korea.

Mongols fighting with Japanese and kamikaze wind

Another Invasion in Japan

When Qubilai sent another envoy to the shogun in 1275 demanding submission, the envoy was not only rebuffed but also decapitated. An incensed Qubilai was determined to invade again. Immediately following the final annihilation of Song loyalists at the Battle of Yaishan in 1279, a new fleet of ships was built and plans were drawn up for a second attempted invasion. But the Japanese had not been idle; they had constructed 12 miles of defensive walls at Hakata Bay.

This time, for an invasion fleet, the Koreans provided 900 ships and 20,000 men, while the Mongols added 20,000 of their warriors. This fleet sailed in 1281 from Korea. At the same time, a second and much larger fleet of 3,500 Song ships manned by 100,000 Chinese troops sailed from Southern China.*

The ships of the Chinese fleet were poorly built, and delays meant it never rendezvoused with the Korean fleet at Iki Island as planned. The Korean fleet waited for a couple of weeks, then pushed on to Hakata Bay and began besieging the walls with trebuchets fired from the ships, while the Japanese again sent fire boats against them. The Chinese fleet meanwhile bypassed Hakata Bay and landed at Imari Bay instead, 30 miles southwest of Hakata. Japanese forces arrived and a two-week battle ensued in the hills around Imari.

Neither army could make any decisive progress against the tenacious Japanese forces, which may have numbered as few as 20,000. The invaders returned to their ships to consider further options. A long stalemate ensued at both Hakata and Imari, and then the Japanese were saved a second time by the intervention of a storm.

A typhoon struck Imari Bay, and in the maelstrom, the thousands of Chinese ships were destroyed. Almost the entire contingent of Chinese troops died. Upon receiving news of the disaster, the Korean fleet left Hakata Bay and returned to Korea. Qubilai half-heartedly planned a third invasion, but this was called off in 1286.

It was superb fighting by the samurai and other Japanese forces, plus poor planning, coordination, and poor-quality Chinese war ships that won the day for the Japanese, but there is no denying the role that the typhoon storms played in destroying both fleets. It was the Japanese themselves who, soon after this second victory, started referring to these storms as *kamikaze*, meaning "divine winds."

The Pagan and Champa Invasions

Qubilai's failure to conquer Japan did not deter him from attempting other invasions in regions contiguous to the Yuan Empire. In 1279, fresh from victory over the last Song loyalists at the Battle of Yaishan, Mongol forces drove further south in an invasion of the kingdom of Pagan, which is modern Burma or Myanmar. The invasion followed a demand from Qubilai that the ruler of Pagan, King Narathihapate, submit to the Yuan dynasty and pay tribute to the Mongols.

The king refused, and so a Muslim Mongol, General Nasir al-Din al-Tusi, led a *tumen* of 10,000 cavalry against the Paganese forces, using the lush grasslands of Yunnan in Southern China as his base. After a period of fighting, King Narathihapate surrendered and agreed to submit to the Mongols and pay them tribute. The Mongols also made sure that some 100,000 households living along the border between Yunnan and Pagan were registered, thus bringing them directly under the control of the Yuan Dynasty.

Farther to the east, Qubilai also became interested in the long, sinuous tropical lands of Vietnam, which by the 13th century was divided into a northern and a southern kingdom. Qubilai Khan turned his attention to Vietnam in 1282.

The southern regions were part of the Champa kingdom, while the northern state was known as Dai Viet. After a short battle, Champa's king had surrendered and agreed to pay tribute. This was much to the Mongols' relief because the humid tropical conditions had played havoc with their composite bows.

Following the fall of the Song, Qubilai decided to send troops back into Vietnam to pursue Song loyalists who had fled there. He also wanted to punish the Champa king, who had refused to travel there himself and make his personal submission to the Yuan court, even though he had sent tribute. The Mongols sent a fleet south down the coast of Vietnam, intent on an invasion of the Champa territory.

In 1282, a small Mongol navy disembarked a sizeable contingent of Mongol troops led by General Sogetu, which quickly gained the upper hand over the Champa forces, including their elephants, and seized the capital and other major cities. The Champa elites fled to the hills, and the locals simply went about their business under new overlords.

The Dai Viet Invasion

Qubilai now turned to the northern kingdom of Dai Viet and demanded that the ruler allow Mongol troops to travel through his territory from Yunnan to Champa. The rulers of Dai Viet refused, and so the Mongols sent an invasion force from the north, as Sogetu and a contingent of his forces marched into Dai Viet from the south.

The forces of Dai Viet engaged the Mongols in open battle and also harassed them mercilessly with guerilla tactics. The Mongols became hopelessly bogged down. In the end, the Mongols withdrew, but Qubilai had achieved his overall goals of expanding his tributary empire and enhancing trade connections.

Conclusion

Despite having vastly expanded the size of the Yuan tributary empire, Qubilai remained intent on making it larger almost to the end of his life. In 1289, the Mongols sent envoys to King Kertanagara of the Indonesian island of Java, demanding his submission. The Javanese king sliced off the noses of the envoys and sent them back to Qubilai.

In response, the Mongols assembled a naval fleet of 1,000 vessels and an invasion force of 20,000 warriors, which they dispatched to Java. When the Mongols landed early in 1293, they found that a rebellion had broken out and the king was dead. The king's son-in-law, Raden Vijaya, agreed to terms, although he later betrayed the Mongols.

This was to be the last foreign campaign ever conducted by Qubilai Khan. By the time of his death on February 18, 1294, he must have been well pleased with the massive empire and wealth he had created.

THE MONGOLS IN EAST AND SOUTHEAST ASIA

LECTURE 14 TRANSCRIPT

By the mid-13th century, Japan was nominally under the control of a supreme military and political commander known as the shogun. But the shogunate was a very decentralized form of government, and provincial lords and their private armies exercised a great deal of autonomous power in local regions. It was in this political context that the samurai began to play a distinctive role in Japanese life.

Like the knights of European military tradition, the samurai first emerged in Japanese society as unscrupulous mercenaries who hired their services out to local warlords. But over time, they adopted a strict code of conduct and ethics. Above all, the samurai were professional warriors, skilled in martial arts, the bow and arrow, and the sword, and like the Mongols, they were also great horsemen.

The samurai subscribed to the philosophy of Bushido, the Way of the Warrior, not only because it emphasized the development of superb military skills but because it was seen as a way of attaining great honor. Bushido demanded that all samurai demonstrate an extraordinary degree of loyalty to each other, to their local lord (known as the daimyo), and ultimately to the powerless but still respected emperor. So in the end, the samurai became, in the main, trustworthy and honest.

The popular image of the samurai suggests that they had no fear of death, that they would enter any battle no matter the odds, because to die in battle would bring honor to one's family and one's daimyo. Although the samurai were skilled in battle formations and joint assaults, they also sought the opportunity to fight alone, one on one, rather than as part of a contingent. An individual samurai, superbly armed and uniformed, would call out his family's name, rank, and accomplishments, seeking an opponent with similar rank to battle. He often severed his opponent's head, which he took back to his base as proof of his victory.

All the skills of the samurai were on display at Hakata Bay on Kyushu Island in the autumn of 1274, when a sizeable Mongol invasion force landed on the beach. In addition to contemporary Japanese source evidence of this clash of elite warriors, we also have striking visual evidence in the form of a series of paintings that were later joined together to form two scrolls, one focused on the 1274 invasion and the other on a second attempt seven years later.

On the 1274 scroll, we see one samurai warrior in particular, Takezaki Suenaga, very much taking the fight to the Mongols, galloping in through the pine forests with his colleagues, all firing their very long bows with considerable accuracy at the advancing Mongols. In another scene, Suenaga stands over his wounded horse, which is spouting blood, while some sort of Mongol gunpowder bomb is exploding nearby. This was the samurai warrior at his best, dashing in to attack the enemy, intent on victory or death, and the honor this would bring to his family and to his lord. Thanks to the courage of Suenaga and his colleagues, not to mention some very fortunate interventions by mother nature, Japan was twice able to fend off dangerous invasion attempts by the Mongols.

These campaigns were part of Qubilai Khan's attempts to considerably widen his already enormous Yuan Empire. He had several purposes in mind in mounting campaigns to Japan, and also to Myanmar, Vietnam, and even Indonesia. One was to continue the mandate all Mongols believe they had been given to them by heaven itself to conquer the whole world; another was to allow Qubilai to increase the size of his personal territorial holdings and thus reinforce his claims to be recognized as sole great khan. More prosaically, the more regions that could be brought into the Mongol tributary empire, the more trade would flourish between these regions and continue to enrich Mongol elites and administrators, particularly the Chinggisid princes like Qubilai who sat at the top of the Mongol social and political world.

But first, to Korea, which had actually been conquered by the Mongols decades before Qubilai Khan had completed his conquest of China. For a long time, various Korean kingdoms and dynasties had been forced to deal with factions of powerful militarized nomads that occupied steppe regions just to the north of the border between the Korean Peninsula and mainland east Asia. As early as the 10th century, the founder of the Goryeo Dynasty, King Taejo, had extended this northern borders deep into territories that had once been controlled by the ancient Goguryeo Kingdom but had since been occupied by nomads.

His successors continued this effort, building formidable garrison forts across the north and pushing Korean controlled territory towards the Yalu River. Inevitably, this brought Goryeo into conflict with the Khitan militarized nomads. The Khitan were a formidable foe, and in the winter of 1010, Korean sources describe a Khitan army of 400,000 troops that smashed through the garrison forts, crossed the frozen Yalu River, and drove south for the Goryeo capital at Songdo, which they sacked and pillaged. But with their supply lines stretched thin, the Khitan were eventually forced to fight a bloody retreat back to the Yalu, at the cost of perhaps 40,000 men.

The Goryeo Dynasty's other great northern nomadic foe was the Jurchen, who dwelt further east in Manchuria. Fed up with constant harassing attacks from these fierce nomadic peoples, the Goryeo decided to build their own "Great Wall" across the northern frontier. Official records inform us that some 300,000 laborers were employed for 11 years between 1033 and 1044 to build the massive rampart, modeled on China's Great Northern Wall. The Goryeo wall linked 14 garrison towns in a line that stretched northwards from the mouth of the Yalu River, through the mountains, and all the way out to the east coast.

The wall proved initially effective. After it was constructed, the Jurchen decided it made more sense to enter into a trade relationship with the Goryeo, supplying horses and furs for Goryeo salt and iron weapons. But under new leadership, the Jurchen began raiding Goryeo again, and their cavalry contingents easily surmounted the wall and defeated the Goryeo armies. This time, the Goryeo responded by creating a new military force, the Extraordinary Military Corps, which in 1107 drove the Jurchen back to the steppes and then built nine new forts in the northeast to contain them.

While all this was going on, China was under the control of the powerful Song Dynasty, but by 1125, the Jurchen had redirected their expansionary energies to the south and had succeeded in defeating first the Khitan, and then the Song, capturing the Chinese capital at Kaifeng. As we have seen on several occasions, the Song retreated south, and China was divided between the Jurchen-controlled north and the southern Song, who ruled all of southern China from a border roughly halfway between the Huang He (or Yellow River) and the Yangtze. This was a situation Chinggis Khan was well aware of when he first led Mongol armies into China in 1211.

Forty years earlier, in 1170, a military revolt had broken out in Goryeo against civilian officials. The cry of soldiers and officers alike became "Death to all who wear the civil official headdress!" After the massacre of many government officials, the military took control of the state, but its attempt to govern through a supreme council quickly broke down, leaving political and social chaos in its wake.

A powerful general put an end to the chaos by establishing a personal dictatorship, but peasant revolts broke out across the country, the worst in 1193, when 7,000 rebels were slaughtered in battle with the military, and again in 1198, when the entire slave population of the capital was in turmoil. It was in the midst of all this chaos, with the foundations of Goryeo society having been shaken to the core, that the Mongols showed up.

The first contact between the Mongols and Goryeo occurred in 1219 when the two formed an alliance to destroy a Khitan army that had crossed the Yalu River to escape the Mongols. Six years later, in 1225, the Mongols demanded tribute from the Goryeo king, but he refused. To make matters worse, the Mongol envoy was killed returning from Goryeo, and the Mongols used this as a pretext to invade.

In 1231, Ogedai ordered a Mongol army led by General Saritai to cross the Yalu River and drive south, supported by a rebel Goryeo general. The Goryeo government mobilized an army and confronted the Mongols near the towns of Anju and Kuju. The Mongols took Anju but were frustrated by a long siege at Kuju, so Saritai bypassed the town and the Goryeo army and marched on the capital at Gaesong, which the Mongols captured. A smaller Mongol force then headed further south but were frustrated by a slave army led by Ji Gwang-su, which fought to the death.

With their capital in Mongol hands, the Goryeo sued for peace. The Mongols demanded an extraordinary amount of tribute: 10,000 otter skins, 20,000 horses, 10,000 bolts of silk, and many children and crafts workers who were enslaved by the Mongols. In 1232, Saritai withdrew his main force but left military commanders in charge to ensure the tribute payments were received.

But less than a year later, the Goryeo government decided to relocate all government officials to Ganghwa Island, about 20 miles off the coast, to exploit one of the Mongols' few weaknesses at that time, their fear of the sea. The move happened quickly, before the Mongols could respond, and the entire court was soon reestablished on the island behind formidable defenses. The common people were told to flee into the countryside and defend themselves as best they could.

For the next several decades, the Mongols could only glare across the strip of sea separating the mainland from the island, where the ruling class continued to govern and enjoy luxurious lives based on the grain tax revenues that were now shipped to the island. Frustrated, the Mongols instituted a scorched earth policy on the mainland, burning the grain fields and capturing mountain fortresses. In one invasion alone in 1254, the Mongols took back with them 200,000 captives, left countless dead, and reduced huge areas of Korea to ashes.

As the peasants lost their will to resist, the government tried to seek divine assistance by creating a massive woodblock printing of important Buddhist sutras in the form of the *Tripitaka Koreana*. The political ideology of the Goryeo state was Confucianism, but Buddhism also thrived within elite circles. Goryeo Buddhism was focused on using the technology of woodblock printing to create vast translations of the Buddhist canon in an attempt to harness spiritual power to protect the state from nomadic invasion.

The first massive carving of the *Tripitaka* had been done in 1087 as a way of seeking the Buddha's assistance against the Khitan threat. This was destroyed during the Mongol invasion, and a new version completed in 1248 was created as a direct response to Mongol occupation. It can still be seen today at the Haeinsa Temple in South Korea.

The *Tripitaka Koreana* is renowned as one of the most accurate translations of core Buddhist texts, treatises, and laws ever made, and also for the beauty of the exquisite carving in wood of the Chinese characters in which the text is translated. The blocks are made of birch wood that was specially treated to prevent decay, then soaked in seawater for three years, then cut, then boiled in salt water, then exposed to the wind for three years, after which they were finally ready to be carved. After each block was carved, it was covered in a poisonous lacquer to keep insects away and was framed with metal to prevent warping.

Ten years after the carving of the *Tripitaka* was completed, the Goryeo king staged a coup against his own government and sought peace with the Mongols. The crown prince traveled to China in 1258 and personally offered his country's submission to Qubilai. Korea became a loyal client tributary state to Qubilai's Yuan Empire. To maintain their relative autonomy, Korean kings often married Mongol princesses who kept a close watch on the situation at court for the khan.

By 1271, Qubilai Khan had subdued most of China and declared the Yuan Dynasty. He then began to consider other regions of east and southeast Asia that might be brought into the fold. He focused on Pagan (modern Myanmar), Vietnam, Indonesia, and most particularly, Japan.

The archipelago of Japan was then under the control of the shoguns of the Hōjō clan, and as Qubilai moved towards the final destruction of the Song, the shogun became increasingly concerned that Japan would be next. He was convinced that Qubilai was determined to recruit the formidable Japanese samurai warriors into his army. Qubilai sent envoys to the shogun demanding submission, but these were ignored. Instead, The Japanese bolstered their defenses, and Qubilai ordered the construction of a navy in southern Korea in preparation for invasion.

A fleet of 3,000 warships and 500 support vessels sailed from Pusan in Korea in the autumn of 1274, manned by thousands of sailors and up to 40,000 Song, Korean, and Mongol troops. After capturing Tsushima and Iki Islands, the force arrived at Hakata Bay on the coast of Kyushu to be met by 6,000 samurai, including Takezaki Suenaga. Mongol archery and the use of trebuchets firing explosive devices forced the samurai back, and the town of Hakata, modern Fukuoka, was burned, although a Mongol general was seriously wounded in the fighting.

With no more progress to be made against the formidable samurai, the Mongols retreated to their ships to make plans for the next stage of the invasion. But the Japanese sent small fire ships in the night to burn some of the Mongol warships, and then a huge typhoon storm sprang up that devastated the fleet. Many poorly built Song ships were sunk, others scattered, and some Korean sources state that 13,000 of the Mongol troops were drowned.

The Mongols decided to call off the invasion and return to Korea. Qubilai was somewhat reassured by the fact that most of the fleet had survived, that the defenses at Hakata Bay had been wrecked, and that the Mongols had made their point to the shogun, who surely now would accept client tributary status. But the Japanese interpreted the storms that had saved them very differently: This had clearly been an intervention by divine winds to save their island from Mongol invasion.

So when Qubilai sent another envoy to the shogun in 1275 demanding submission, the envoy was not only rebuffed but also decapitated. An incensed Qubilai was determined to invade again. Immediately following the final annihilation of Song loyalists at the Battle of Yaishan in 1279, a new fleet of ships was built and plans drawn up for a second attempted invasion. But the Japanese had not been idle; they'd constructed 12 miles of defensive walls at Hakata Bay, built just 50 yards from the beach to make it more difficult for the Mongols to establish a beachhead.

This time, the invasion fleet was absolutely massive. The Koreans provided 900 ships and 20,000 men, while the Mongols added 20,000 of their own warriors. This fleet sailed in 1281 from Korea. At the same time, a second and much larger fleet of 3,500 Song ships manned by 100,000 Chinese troops sailed from southern China. As John Man points out, this was the largest fleet ever assembled in world history to this point, and it would retain that record for anther 700 years until the Allied invasion of Normandy on D-Day, June the 6th, 1944.

Despite its size, the ships of the Chinese fleet were poorly built, and delays meant it never rendezvoused with the Korean fleet at Iki Island as planned. The Korean fleet waited for a couple of weeks, then pushed on to Hakata Bay and began besieging the walls with trebuchets fired from the ships, while the Japanese again sent fire boats against them. The Chinese fleet, meanwhile, bypassed Hakata Bay and landed at Imari Bay instead, 30 miles southwest of Hakata. Japanese forces arrived, and a two-week battle ensued in the hills around Imari.

Neither army could make any decisive progress against the tenacious Japanese forces, which may have numbered as few as 20,000. Both the Korean-Mongol and the Chinese troops returned to their ships to consider further options. The ships in the Chinese fleet at Imari were lashed together to help prevent single ships being singled out by Japanese fire boats. A long stalemate now ensued at both Hakata and Imari, and then the Japanese were saved a second time by the intervention of divine winds.

A typhoon struck Imari Bay, and in the maelstrom, the thousands of Chinese ships were destroyed, and almost the entire contingent of Chinese troops died. Upon receiving news of the disaster, the Korean fleet left Hakata Bay and returned to Korea. Qubilai half-heartedly planned a third invasion, but this was called off in 1286. Japan had been saved from invasion by the intervention of divine winds for a second time in seven years.

Of course, it was superb fighting by the samurai and other Japanese forces, plus poor planning, coordination, and poor-quality Chinese war ships, that won the day for the Japanese, but there is no denying the role that these typhoon storms played in destroying both fleets. It was the Japanese themselves who, soon after this second victory, started referring to these storms as *kamikaze*—Divine Winds—proof that the *kami*, the spirits that run the world, had been on the side of the Japanese.

It was in an attempt to evoke memories of this divine intervention in the 13th century that the Japanese government in the later stages of the Second World War started naming their suicide pilots kamikaze. This would be a new divine wind sent from heaven to drive out the foreign invaders a third time. But that, of course, was not to be.

Qubilai's failure to conquer Japan did not deter him from attempting other invasions in regions contiguous to the Yuan Empire. In 1279, fresh from victory over the last Song loyalists at the Battle of Yaishan, Mongol forces drove further south in an invasion of the Kingdom of Pagan, which is modern Burma or Myanmar. The invasion followed a demand from Qubilai that the ruler of Pagan, King Narathihapate, that he submit to the Yuan Dynasty and pay tribute to the Mongols.

The king refused, and so a Muslim Mongol general, Nasir al-Din al-Tusi, led a *tumen* of 10,000 cavalry against the Paganese forces, using the lush grasslands of Yunnan in southern China as his base. The enemy decided to take the fight to the Mongols and marched north from Pagan into Yunnan in much greater numbers than Nasir al-Din possessed. In the battle that followed, the Paganese used experienced war elephants in their ranks, protected by heavy padded leather armor. The elephants unsettled the Mongol horses and had hides so thick that not even the Mongol heavy bow and arrows could penetrate.

Like all good Mongol generals, Nasir al-Din realized that traditional tactics would not work against this foe, so he quickly adopted new ones. He ordered his men to dismount and fire their arrows from behind trees in the jungle fringing the grassland. From this cover, they continued their fire against the elephants, wounding and distracting them until the elephants broke ranks and retreated back into their own forces to create chaos there.

This changed the tide of battle, and as the Mongols followed hot on the heels of the elephants and charged into the forces of Pagan, King Narathihapate surrendered and agreed to submit to the Mongols and pay them tribute. Nasir withdrew but came back the following year to make sure the king lived up to his agreement. The Mongols also made sure that some 100,000 households living along the border between Yunnan and Pagan were registered, thus bringing them directly under the control of the Yuan Dynasty.

Further to the east, Qubilai also became interested in the long, sinuous tropical lands of Vietnam, which by the 13th century was divided into a northern and a southern kingdom. The people of Vietnam had a long history of interacting with invaders from the north. As early as the 3rd century BCE, the Chinese Qin Dynasty had attempted to incorporate parts of northern Vietnam into their realm but had met spirited resistance.

In 111 BCE, the Han Dynasty of China did succeed in incorporating the Red River Valley of northern Vietnam into its expansive empire, but because there were so many serious cultural differences between the Chinese and the Vietnamese, it proved very difficult to assimilate, or Sinicize, them. Vietnamese elites, on the other hand, realizing there was much they could learn about governance and imperial expansion from the Chinese, cooperated with the Han over the following three centuries.

The common people were less impressed, and several revolts broke out against the Han imperialists. One of the most dangerous of these was led by two women, the Trung Sisters, who in 40 CE rode their elephants into battle at the head of a powerful guerilla army. The rebellion was put down in the end and the women killed. The radically different attitudes of the Chinese and Vietnamese towards women was one of the major cultural differences that worked against Vietnamese assimilation.

The powerful Chinese military ensured that Vietnam remained part of the Chinese tributary empire until 939, when a massive rebellion following the fall of the Tang Dynasty drove Chinese troops and administrators out for good. A series of Vietnamese dynasties then ruled the country, using Chinese administrative and military techniques to control their own people and also expand their state southwards at the expense of the Khmer and Cham peoples. But as the state expanded deeper into the Mekong Valley, intermarriage with local peoples led to the emergence of two ethnically and culturally distinct groups of northern and southern Vietnamese, and also of separate dynasties which took control of north and south Vietnam as independent states.

This was the situation the Mongols encountered in 1282 when Qubilai Khan turned his attention to Vietnam. The southern regions were part of the Champa Kingdom, while the northern state was known as Dai Viet. After an initial incursion, Champa king Tran Thai Tong had surrendered and agreed to pay tribute, much to the Mongols' relief, because the humid tropical conditions were not to their liking at all and had played havoc with their composite bows.

Following the fall of the Song, Qubilai decided to send troops back into Vietnam, both to pursue Song loyalists who had fled there and also to punish the Champa king who, although he had sent tribute to Beijing, had refused to travel there himself and make his personal submission to the Yuan court. Increasingly confident in their naval ability, the Mongols sent a fleet south down the coast of Vietnam, intent upon an invasion of the Champa Kingdom. As well as his stated goals, Qubilai was probably also hoping to take control of the lucrative maritime trade in exotic goods that emanated out of southern Vietnam.

In 1282, a small Mongol navy disembarked a sizeable contingent of Mongol troops led by General Sogetu, which quickly gained the upper hand over the Champa forces, including their elephants, and seized the capital and other major cities. The Champa elites fled to the hills, and the locals simply went about their business under new overlords.

Qubilai now turned to the northern kingdom of Dai Viet and demanded that the ruler allow Mongol troops to travel through his territory from Yunnan to Champa. The ruler of Dai Viet refused, and so the Mongols sent an invasion force from the north, as Sogetu and a contingent of his forces marched into Dai Viet from the south.

As we just noted, the Vietnamese have a long history of resisting much more militarily powerful invaders, often by using guerilla tactics, something they would do again so effectively against French, US, and allied forces in the Vietnamese Wars of the mid-20th century. The forces of Dai Viet engaged the Mongols in open battle and also harassed them mercilessly with guerilla tactics.

The Mongols became hopelessly bogged down. Men and horses became sick with tropical diseases, and the cavalry was virtually useless in the thick tropical rainforest. The Mongols were able to seize control of the cities, but the countryside remained autonomous and refused to assimilate. In the end, the Mongols withdrew, but Qubilai had achieved his overall goals of expanding his tributary empire and enhancing trade connections, because the rulers of both Champa and Dai Viet both agreed to pay tribute to Qubilai, although they refused to travel to the Yuan capital to pay their respects.

Despite having vastly expanded the size of the Yuan tributary empire, Qubilai remained intent on making it larger almost to the end of his life. In 1289, the Mongols sent envoys to King Kertanagara of the Indonesian island of Java demanding his submission. Qubilai also asked that a famous beauty, the Princess of Thumapel, be sent back to become his wife. The Javanese king was concerned that this demand for submission masked an attempt to take control of the lucrative spice trade that had enriched his and others of the Molucca Islands, so he sliced off the noses of the envoys and sent them back to Qubilai.

In response, the Mongols assembled a naval fleet of 1,000 warships and smaller boats and an invasion force of 20,000 warriors and dispatched this to Java. When the Mongols landed early in 1293, they found that a rebellion had broken out and that the king was dead. The king's son-in-law, Raden Vijaya, agreed to terms, although he later betrayed the Mongols and kicked them off the island without the princess. Qubilai's disappointment was somewhat assuaged by the fact that the fleet returned with a great deal of treasure pillaged from the Javanese court.

This was to be the last foreign campaign ever conducted by Qubilai Khan. Although Jack Weatherford is undoubtedly correct when he notes that Qubilai "had failed to adapt the successful Mongol strategies to the sea," by the time of his death on the 18th of February, 1294, the great khan must have been well pleased with the massive empire he had created and with the wealth that successful internal and external commerce was generating. As David Morgan sums up, "in the favorable commercial environment provided by the Mongols, contacts with other parts of the world prospered," and this was just as true whether these "other parts of the world" had formally submitted to the Mongols or not.

We will return to follow the vicissitudes of Mongol rule in Yuan China in a future lecture, but first, we have to travel progressively further to the west and consider the three other great khanates that the once-unified Mongol realm had divided into following the death of Mongke. Despite this division, the shadow of Chinggis Khan still hovered over the Mongol world, because each khanate was under the control of descendants of each of his four sons.

Descendants of Chinggis's youngest son, Tolui, ruled China of course, and also the Ilkhanate that controlled Persia and the Middle East. Descendants of his middle sons Chagatai and Ogedei ruled large regions of central Asia. And the descendants of his oldest son, Jochi, ruled the Russian steppe as the Golden Horde. We'll explore the fortunes of the other three khanates, and of the military clashes that regularly broke out between them, in our next group of lectures.

THE MONGOLS IN CENTRAL ASIA

When Mongke Khan came to power in 1251, he launched what historians have since called the Toluid revolution, essentially an attempt to destroy the power of the successors of Chinggis Khan's second and third sons, Chagatai and Ogedai. Mongke's brothers Qubilai and Hulagu were appointed as ilkhans and took control of the Chinese and Persian parts of the empire, respectively. The powerful descendants of Chinggis's oldest son, Jochi, remained in control of a large part of Russia. This meant that the surviving Chagatayid and Ogedeid princes were left to fight it out for control of central Asia.

Chagatai and Ogedai

Just before his death, Chinggis had made the decision to divide his enormous empire. Second son Chagatai had been given a large region of central Asia east of the Oxus River. Chagatai had decided to base himself at a place called Almaliq in northwest Xinjiang. Chinggis's third son, Ogedai, who had already been selected to succeed him as great khan, was granted a smaller realm. However, as great khan, he ruled from the Mongol capital of Karakorum and was ultimately in charge of the entire empire.

Although Chinggis's conquest of the region had been brutal, recovery had already begun by the time of the Great Khan's death. But sandwiched between continuing Mongol campaigns of conquest to the east and west, the recovery of central Asian cities and pastoral and rural areas was hampered by the huge amount of human and material resources they needed to continuously supply to support Mongol expansion in other parts of the empire.

Following Chinggis's death, Chagatai kept his camp in central Asia and seems to have completely supported Ogedai's elevation as great khan. As Chinggis's oldest surviving son and also a renowned expert in Mongol law and ritual, Chagatai remained highly respected throughout the empire.

After Chagatai's death in 1242, he was succeeded by his grandson Qara Hulagu, who had officially been designated as Chagatai's successor by Chagatai, Ogedai, and Chinggis Khan before their deaths. But when Guyuk eventually succeeded Ogedai as great khan, he deposed Qara Hulagu in 1246 and installed Yesu Mongke in his place. The alcoholic Yesu Mongke was Chagatai's oldest surviving son and also a friend and ally of Guyuk.

When Guyuk died two years later, most Chagatayids and Ogedeids opposed the succession of Mongke, the son of Chinggis's youngest son, Tolui. Mongke not only became khan, but his brothers Hulagu and Qubilai were appointed ilkhans, and the Toluid brothers then did their best to literally wipe out the Chagatayid and Ogedeid clans.

Most of the Ogedeid princes were killed, and Ogedeid troops were then dispersed widely throughout the empire and incorporated into the armies of other Mongol rulers. A few minor Ogedeid princes offered their support to Mongke and were able to retain small though widely dispersed realms.

The Chagatayids fared somewhat better and were allowed to retain their realm, although many princes were executed or exiled. Yesu Mongke was deposed by the new khan Mongke, and his predecessor Qara Hulagu was reinstated. However, fate intervened, and Qara Hulagu died before he could take up the throne.

Orghina and Civil War

Qara Hulagu's widow Orghina was the granddaughter of Chinggis Khan himself. Immediately following the death of her husband, she returned to their capital of Almaliq to await the arrival of her husband's rival, Yesu Mongke, who she promptly had executed. Orghina then ruled as regent of the Chagatayids, ostensibly for her infant son, Mubarak Shah. In reality, she was quite independent,

The death of Mongke in 1259 led to the outbreak of civil war between Qubilai, who declared himself khan and Mongke's successor, and the youngest Toluid brother, Ariq Boke. Qubilai attempted to form an alliance between the two houses by sending Chagatai's great-grandson Abishqa to marry Orghina, but Ariq Boke had Abishqa arrested before he could arrive.

Arik Boke then attempted to take control of central Asia by installing Chagatai's grandson Alghu as ruler of the Chagatayid realm. Alghu also married Orghina, probably against her will. In the end, Alghu proved a poor choice by Ariq Boke. Once in charge, Alghu switched his allegiance to Qubilai—one of the key reasons that Ariq Boke was later forced to surrender to Qubilai. About a year into his marriage to Orghina, sometime in 1266, Alghu died after an illness. Orghina and the Chagatayid commanders then unilaterally appointed her son Mubarak Shah as new khan of the Chagatayid khanate.

Qaidu

As these events were unfolding among the Chagatayid elites, a new figure appeared on the scene, a grandson of Ogedai named Qaidu, who saw the conflict between Qubilai and Ariq Boke as an ideal opportunity to try to restore the fortunes of the Ogedeid *ulus*. Realizing the threat that Qaidu posed, Alghu attacked Qaidu's forces in southern Kazakhstan just prior to his death. But Qaidu formed an alliance with Khan Berke of the Golden Horde and took control of substantial central Asian territory after Alghu's death.

Qaidu's timing seemed ideal because at this moment, an enormous power vacuum opened up in the Mongol world. Ilkhan Hulagu had died in 1265 and Alghu in 1266. Berke, ruler of the Golden Horde, died in 1267.

In China, Qubilai, having successfully concluded the civil war with Ariq Boke, was now totally focused on destroying the Song. Qaidu used this series of opportunities to expand the size of his realm to the east, but he was pushed back by powerful forces allied with Qubilai.

Qubilai, who opposed the decision by Orghina to install Mubarak Shah on the throne, appointed an allied prince named Baraq to take control of central Asia instead. Baraq duly arrived with his army and attacked and defeated Qaidu in battle in 1268. But Qaidu's alliance with the Golden Horde was too strong to overcome; when Qaidu offered to make a deal with Baraq, the latter somewhat reluctantly agreed.

A *quriltai* was convened at Talas in the spring of 1269, where the decision was made to divide central Asia between three rulers: Qaidu, Baraq, and the new khan of the Golden Horde, Mongke Temur. Baraq was not overly happy with the deal and tried to seize an eastern region of the Persian ilkhan's realm, but he was badly defeated in battle by Ilkhan Abaqa near Herat in August of 1271. In the aftermath, Qaidu took control of all the Chagatayid and Ogedeid realms of central Asia.

Qaidu's claim to the throne was hardly uncontested, with various princes challenging him on several occasions. It wasn't until 1282 that any reconciliation was reached between Chagatayid and Ogedeid princes, when Qaidu appointed Du'a, the son of Baraq, as the new Chagatayid khan.

Qaidu's Takeover

Qubilai became increasingly annoyed as Qaidu's successes accumulated in Central Asia, particularly because Qaidu still refused to acknowledge him as khan. In 1275, Qubilai sent an army against Qaidu, under the joint command of Qubilai's son Nomuqan and a senior general named An Tong, along with some lesser Toluid princes. The plan to rein in Qaidu backfired, however, when the princes defected to Qaidu's camp. Qaidu was free to complete his takeover of central Asia without further interference from Qubilai.

Throughout the 1280s and 1290s, Qaidu's forces were strong enough to reclaim parts of western China from the Yuan dynasty and to support rebellions against Qubilai in Tibet and Manchuria. While Qubilai was distracted by the rebellion in Manchuria, Qaidu and Du'a even invaded Mongolia itself and captured the capital of Karakorum, although Yuan forces recaptured the city a few months later.

Qaidu and Du'a were also causing problems for the ilkhans in Persia by invading the eastern region of Khurasan and supporting rebellions against the ilkhans. Additionally, Qaidu and Du'a enlarged their lands to the south by invading a region of Afghanistan known as Ghazna. They then used Ghazna as a base to start raiding into parts of northern India controlled by the Delhi sultanate.

This reached a head in 1300, when a powerful Mongol army under Qutlugh Khwaja defeated the sultan's army and marched directly on Delhi itself. But because Qutlugh Khwaja was fatally wounded in the battle, the Mongols withdrew after seizing an enormous amount of booty.

Qaidu and Du'a next launched military campaigns to the northwest against their former allies the Golden Horde, which was beset with internal succession squabbles. Qaidu, ever the opportunist, saw his chance and tried to elevate his own candidate to the throne, but the new Golden Horde khan Toqto'a started piecing together a coalition of Golden Horde, Yuan, and Ilkhanate forces against the central Asians. Although the coalition never came to fruition, this effectively reduced the threat of Qaidu against the Golden Horde.

After Qaidu

As the 13th century gave way to the 14th, Qaidu was beset by enemies everywhere, forcing him to divide his troops and garrison his various frontiers. He suffered military defeats against Qubilai's successor as emperor of the Yuan dynasty, Temur, who sent a huge Yuan force against Qaidu and Du'a in 1300. A battle took place in 1301 just south of the Altai Mountains, and although Qaidu eventually won the battle, he died soon afterward, allowing the Yuan to spin this as a victory for them.

Following Qaidu's death, Du'a took over control of the Mongol realm in central Asia, which meant that the Chagatayid *ulus* reclaimed its superior status over the Ogedeid *ulus*. In 1304, Du'a also decided to pursue peace with the Yuan rulers in China, which he justified as an attempt to restore unity among the Chinggisid princes. Yuan ruler Temur responded positively to Du'a's peace overtures.

However, within the central Asian realm, conflict continued between the descendants of Chagatai and Ogedai. Du'a died in 1307, and intrigue and violence plagued his successors, one of whom was assassinated.

The fortunes of Mongol-controlled central Asia improved in the 1320s during the reign of Chagatayid ruler Kebek, under whom the economy of the region prospered. The only military operations pursued by Kebek and his successor Eljigidai, who ruled through to 1330, were against the Delhi sultanate, which the Chagatayids raided at will.

A later successor, Tarmashirin, converted to Islam, which caused a new fracture within the Chagatayids between those who supported his religiosity and those who believed he had abandoned the Mongol Yasa law code for the Islamic Sharia code. A rebellion broke out in 1334, leading to Tarmashirin's overthrow.

There followed a succession of rulers, and the eastern and western parts of the central Asian *ulus* drifted apart. The eastern part gradually became known as Moghulistan, where pastoral nomads followed their traditional lifeways and shamanistic religion. The western regions became known as Mawarannahr, and most residents there converted to Islam, while transregional trade continued to flourish in the great commercial cities.

Ongoing tensions and conflict between the two halves of the central Asian khanate opened the door for other powerful figures to appear on the scene. One such regional ruler was Timur, better known in the West as Tamerlane. By 1370, Timur had taken control of most of central Asia and began to construct his own enormous empire.

THE MONGOLS IN CENTRAL ASIA

LECTURE 15 TRANSCRIPT

When Mongke came to power as great khan in 1251, he launched what historians have since called the Toluid Revolution, essentially an attempt to destroy the power of the successors of Chinggis Khan's second and third sons, Chagatai and Ogedai, by almost literally eliminating the remaining princes of those two lineages. Mongke's brothers Qubilai and Hulagu were appointed as ilkhans and took control of the Chinese and Persian parts of the empire, respectively, while the powerful descendants of Chinggis's oldest son, Jochi, remained in control of a large part of Russia. This meant that the surviving Chagatayid and Ogodeid princes were left to fight it out for control of central Asia, including those regions that had been devastated by Chinggis during the Khwarazmian campaign in the 1220s.

Michal Biran, an expert on Mongol rule in central Asia, emphasizes the long-term impact of Chinggis by noting that "much of the region's subsequent political culture, ethnic composition, and concepts of legitimacy and law go back to Chinggis Khan." But Biran also makes the point that, despite a certain degree of recovery in the great Silk Roads cities such as Samarkand and Bukhara, the post-Chinggisid period was far from being central Asia's golden age.

Just before his death, Chinggis had made the decision to divide his enormous empire into four sub-states to be the realms of his sons and their descendants. Second son Chagatai had been given a large region of central Asia east of the Amu Darya, the Oxus River, which roughly equates with the modern nations of Uzbekistan, Tajikistan, Kyrgyzstan, and some parts of Kazakhstan and Xinjiang in China to rule his state. Chagatai had decided to base himself at a place called Almaliq in the lush Ili River Valley in northwest Xinjiang. Chinggis's third son, Ogedai, who had already been selected to succeed him as great khan, was granted a smaller realm that also included parts of Xinjiang and Kazakhstan. But as great khan, he ruled from the Mongol capital of Karakorum and was ultimately in charge of the entire empire.

Both these realms included substantial populations of nomadic and sedentary peoples and had been flourishing through trade in the period preceding Chinggis's campaigns. As Biran puts it, this "highly cosmopolitan and multilingual territory had enjoyed relative stability and prosperity for most of the second half of the twelfth century." But because of the mix of peoples and lifeways, at no point did it become a unified cultural zone such as was the case in Persia and China.

Although Chinggis's conquest of the region had been brutal, recovery had already begun by the time of the great khan's death. But sandwiched between continuing Mongol campaigns of conquest to the east and west, the recovery of central Asian cities and pastoral and rural areas was hampered by the huge amount of human and material resources they needed to continuously supply to support Mongol expansion in other parts of the empire.

Following Chinggis's death, Chagatai kept his camp in central Asia and seems to have completely supported Ogedai's elevation as great khan. As Chinggis's oldest surviving son and also a renowned expert in Mongol law and ritual, Chagatai remained highly respected throughout the empire. He also remained somewhat aloof from the administration of his realm, preferring to allow his subordinate *qaghans* to deal with local affairs. Occasionally this led to tension, particularly between Chagatayid- and Ogedeid-appointed administrators who had been placed in charge of important cities such as Bukhara and Samarkand. Another source of tension lay along the northwestern fringes of Chagatai's state, where there was an ongoing conflict with Batu, son of Jochi and khan of the Golden Horde, and his ally Toregene, Ogedai's wife and later regent, over control of the region of Khurasan.

After Chagatai's death in 1242, he was succeeded by his grandson Qara Hulagu, who had officially been designated as Chagatai's successor by Chagatai himself, and also by Ogedai and Chinggis Khan before their deaths. But when Guyuk eventually succeeded Ogedai as great khan, he deposed Qara Hulagu in 1246 and installed Yesu Mongke in his place. The alcoholic Yesu Mongke was Chagatai's oldest surviving son and also a friend and ally of Guyuk.

When Guyuk died two years later, most Chagatayids and Ogodeids opposed the succession of Mongke, the son of Chinggis's youngest son, Tolui. As we have seen, Mongke not only became khan, but his brothers Hulagu and Qubilai were appointed ilkhans, and the Toluid brothers then did their best to literally wipe out the Chagatayid and Ogodeid clans.

Most of the Ogodeid princes were killed, and their *ulus*, or state, was dissolved. Ogodeid troops were then dispersed widely throughout the empire and incorporated into the armies of other Mongol rulers. A few minor Ogodeid princes offered their support to Mongke and were able to retain small though widely-dispersed realms. The Chagatayids fared somewhat better and were allowed to retain their *ulus*, although many princes were executed or exiled. Yesu Mongke was deposed by the new khan Mongke, and his predecessor Qara Hulagu was reinstated. However, fate intervened, and Qara Hulagu died before he could take up the throne.

Qara Hulagu's widow Orghina was the granddaughter of Chinggis Khan himself. Immediately following the death of her husband, she returned to their capital of Almaliq to await the arrival of her husband's rival, Yesu Mongke, who she promptly had executed. Orghina then ruled as regent of the Chagatayids, ostensibly for her infant son, Mubarak Shah, but in reality, she was quite independent, a situation that must have been approved by Mongke himself. As Chagatayid monarch, Orghina welcomed Ilkhan Hulagu and his senior wife as they passed through her realm on their way to Persia and the Middle East.

According to Juvaini and Rashid al-Din, Orghina appears to have been independently wealthy, both through taxes she imposed on merchants passing through her territory and also perhaps through her own investments in commerce. Certainly she had the resources to treat her guests with lavish banquets and gifts, which, as Anne Broadbridge notes, "demonstrates the role that all imperial women—not just Orghina as regent—played in hospitality."

In another lecture, we saw how the death of Mongke in 1259 led to the outbreak of civil war between Qubilai, who declared himself khan and Mongke's successor, and the youngest Toluid brother, Ariq Boke. In the military and diplomatic struggle that followed, Chagatayid fortunes improved as both competing brothers sought to form alliances with Chagatayid rulers. Qubilai attempted to form an alliance between the two houses by sending Chagatai's great-grandson Abishqa to marry Orghina, but Ariq Boke had Abishqa arrested before he could arrive.

Arik Boke then attempted to take control of central Asia by installing Chagatai's grandson Alghu as ruler of the Chagatayid realm. And because the Golden Horde was now preoccupied with a conflict with Hulagu in northern Persia, Alghu was able to take control of the Chagatid *ulus* and even expand its territory at the expense of the Golden Horde. Alghu also married

Orghina, probably against her will. But as Anne Broadbridge reminds us, even the most powerful women in Mongol society—and Orghina had ruled as queen for a decade by this stage—were still vulnerable to forced marriage.

In the end, Alghu proved a poor choice by Ariq Boke, because once in charge, he switched his allegiance to Qubilai, one of the key reasons that Ariq Boke's war ended and he was forced to surrender to Qubilai. About a year into his marriage to Orghina, sometime in 1266, Alghu died after an illness. Orghina and the Chagatayid commanders then unilaterally appointed her son Mubarak Shah as new khan of the Chagatayid Khanate. Soon after this decision, which was opposed by Qubilai, Orghina simply disappears from the historical record.

As these events were unfolding amongst the Chagatayid elites, a new figure appeared on the scene, a grandson of Ogedai named Qaidu, who saw the conflict between Qubilai and Ariq Boke as an ideal opportunity to try to restore the fortunes of the Ogodeid *ulus*. Realizing the threat that Qaidu posed, just before his death, Alghu had attacked Qaidu's forces in southern Kazakhstan, but Qaidu formed an alliance with Khan Berke of the Golden Horde and took control of a substantial central Asian territory after Alghu's death.

Qaidu seemed to be the right man in the right place at the right time, because at this moment, an enormous power vacuum opened up in the Mongol world. Ilkhan Hulagu had died in 1265, Alghu in 1266, and Berke, ruler of the Golden Horde, died in 1267. In China, Qubilai, having successfully concluded the civil war with Ariq Boke, was now totally focused on destroying the Song. Qaidu used this series of opportunities to expand the size of his realm to the east but was pushed back by powerful forces allied with Qubilai.

As we just noted, in March 1266, Orghina installed her young son Mubarak Shah on the throne. Qubilai, who opposed the decision, appointed an allied prince named Baraq to take control of central Asia instead. Baraq duly arrived with his army and attacked and defeated Qaidu in battle in 1268. But Qaidu's alliance with the Golden Horde was too strong to overcome, and when Qaidu offered to make a deal with Baraq, the latter somewhat reluctantly agreed.

A quriltai was convened at Talas in the spring of 1269, where the decision was made to divide central Asia between three rulers: Qaidu, Baraq, and the new khan of the Golden Horde, Mongke Temur. Baraq was not overly happy with the deal and tried to seize an eastern region of the Persian ilkhan's realm but was badly defeated in battle by Ilkhan Abaqa near Herat in August of 1271. In the aftermath, Abaqu's troops went over to Qaidu, who now took control of all the Chagatayid and Ogedeid realms of central Asia. As Michal Biran notes, the Battle of Herat thus "led to the accession of Qaidu and to the loss of independence of the Chaghadaid *ulus*."

Qaidu's claim to the throne was hardly uncontested, with various princes challenging him on several occasions. Taking advantage of this instability, Abaqu actually invaded Qaidu's realm and launched a devastating attack on Bukhara in 1273. It wasn't until a decade later in 1282 that some sort of reconciliation was reached between Chagatayid and Ogedeid princes, when Qaidu appointed Du'a, the son of Baraq, as the new Chagatayid khan.

Qubilai became increasingly annoyed as Qaidu's successes accumulated in central Asia, particularly since Qaidu still refused to acknowledge him as khan. In 1275, Qubilai sent an army against Qaidu, under the joint command of Qubilai's son Nomuqan and a senior general named An Tong, along with some lesser Toluid princes. The plan to rein in Qaidu backfired, however, when the princes defected to Qaidu's camp. Nomuqan was sent to the Golden Horde, and Qaidu was free to complete his takeover of central Asia without further interference from Qubilai.

Indeed, throughout the 1280s and '90s, Qaidu's forces were strong enough to reclaim parts of western China from the Yuan Dynasty and to support rebellions against Qubilai in Tibet and Manchuria. While Qubilai was distracted by the rebellion in Manchuria, Qaidu and Du'a even invaded Mongolia itself and captured the capital of Karakorum, although Yuan forces recaptured the city a few months later and drove the rebels back into the steppe.

Qaidu and Du'a were also causing problems for the ilkhans in Persia, invading the eastern region of Khurasan and also supporting rebellions against the ilkhans. The ilkhans seem not to have been particularly bothered by these incursions, however, and were so preoccupied with fighting on other fronts against the Mamluks and the Golden Horde that they did not engage the Chagatayid forces in the field.

The vigorous Qaidu and Du'a also enlarged their lands to the south by invading a region of Afghanistan known as Ghazna, then under the control of an autonomous Mongol group called the Qara'unas. They then used Ghazna as a base to start raiding into parts of northern India controlled by the Delhi Sultanate, beginning in the mid-1290s. This reached a head in 1300, when a powerful Mongol army under Qutlugh Khwaja defeated the sultan's army and marched directly on Delhi itself. But because Qutlugh Khawaja was fatally wounded in the battle, the Mongols withdrew after seizing an enormous amount of booty.

Qaidu and Du'a next launched military campaigns to the northwest against their former allies, the Golden Horde. We will have much more to say about the Golden Horde in a future lecture, but they were beset with internal succession squabbles through the last two decades of the 13th century. Qaidu, ever the opportunist, saw his chance and tried to elevate his own candidate to the throne, but the new Golden Horde khan Toqto'a started piecing together a coalition of Golden Horde, Yuan, and ilkhanate forces against the pesky central Asians. Although the coalition never came to fruition, this effectively reduced the threat of Qaidu against the Golden Horde.

In fact, as the 13th century gave way to the 14th, Qaidu was beset by enemies everywhere, forcing him to divide his troops and garrison his various frontiers. He left a sizeable contingent along the northern border with the Golden Horde and then suffered military defeats against Qubilai's successor as emperor of the Yuan Dynasty, Temur, who sent a huge Yuan force against Qaidu and Du'a in 1300. A battle took place in 1301 just south of the Altai Mountains, and although Qaidu eventually won the battle, he died soon afterwards, allowing the Yuan to spin this as a victory for them.

Michal Biran argues that "Qaidu was the real founder of the Mongol state in central Asia," but he was never strong enough to dominate the Chagatayid interests and forces, who were able to maintain their own *ulus* within the greater realm of Qaidu's. This meant that soon after Qaidu's death, the Ogedeid *ulus* he had created simply dissolved.

Indeed, following Qaidu's death, Du'a took over control of the Mongol realm in central Asia, which meant that the Chagatayid *ulus* reclaimed its superior status over the Ogedeid *ulus*. In 1304, Du'a also decided to pursue peace with the Yuan rulers in China, which he justified as an attempt to restore unity amongst the Chinggisid princes. Yuan ruler Temur responded positively to Du'a's peace overtures, thereby, as Biran notes, "creating a global peace in the Mongol world, which included also the settlement of other inter-Mongol conflicts."

However, although a global peace might have been achieved between the Mongol khanates, within the central Asian realm, conflict continued between the descendants of Chagatai and Ogedai. Several skirmishes broke out in Transoxiana, and Ogedeid elements plundered Bukhara and Samarkand on several occasions, while troops regularly left the *ulus* of one or the other Chagatayid or Ogedeid ruler and switched allegiance to the other side or were absorbed into the Yuan military. In other parts of central Asia, troops that had been loyal to Qaidu now abandoned his *ulus* and surrendered to the ilkhans or khans of the Golden Horde, where they were absorbed.

Du'a died in 1307, and intrigue and violence plagued his successors, one of whom was assassinated, giving Qaidu's sons another chance to try to advance Ogedeid power at the expense of the Chagatayids. But those backfired when the Yuan simply annexed most remaining Ogedeid lands and absorbed them into their empire in 1310. Ogedeid fortunes in the west also took a turn for the worse when the ilkhans claimed parts of the central Asian *ulus* for the ilkhanate.

The fortunes of Mongol-controlled central Asia improved in the 1320s during the reign of Chagatayid ruler Kebek, under whom the economy of the region prospered. The only military operations pursued by Kebek and his successor Eljigidai, who ruled through to 1330, were against the Delhi sultanate, which the Chagatayids raided at will. A later successor, Tarmashirin, converted to Islam, which caused a new fracture within the Chagatayids between those who supported his religiosity and those who believed he had abandoned the Mongol Yasa law code for the Islamic Sharia code. A rebellion broke out in 1334, leading to Tarmashirin's overthrow.

There followed a succession of rulers—shamanistic Mongols, the Buddhist Changshi, a later fanatical Muslim, Ali Sultan, who persecuted non-Muslims—and then chaos as different Chagatayid princes competed for the throne. The eastern and western parts of the central Asian *ulus* drifted apart. The eastern part gradually became known as Moghulistan, where pastoral nomads followed their traditional lifeways and their shamanistic religion. The western regions became known as Mawarannahr, and most residents there converted to Islam, while transregional trade continued to flourish in the great commercial cities.

Those dwelling in the western regions regarded themselves as true Chagatayids and began referring to the nomads in the east as Moghuls. But the Moghuls in turn believed they were the true descendants of Chagatai and called the residents of Mawarannahr the Qara'unas, who were no longer even Mongols.

The ongoing tensions and often open conflict between the two halves of the central Asian khanate opened the door for other powerful figures to appear on the scene. One such regional ruler was Timur, better known in the West as Tamerlane. By 1370, Timur had taken control of most of central Asia and began to construct his own enormous empire. We shall certainly return to the extraordinary Timur and the Timurid Empire later in the course.

Now, this complicated tale of constant internecine strife, not just between the descendants of Chagatai and Ogedai but also with the Mongol rulers of China, Persia, and Russia, makes it a wonder that anything was achieved at all in terms of political and economic administration, but somewhat surprisingly, the central Asian khanate actually functioned quite well.

Unlike the situation in China and Persia, the Mongols of central Asia remained nomadic for most of the period we have just been discussing, making their living through their herds and flocks, hunting, and of course taxing both the nomadic and the sedentary populations of their realm.

The rulers adopted many of the same administrative practices that Chinggis Khan himself had introduced in the Mongol world early in the 13th century. Armies were structured according to the same decimal units, and society organized into *tumen* of 10,000 families who supported 10,000 soldiers. *Tumen* leaders were expected to collect taxes. The *keshig* was also retained both as the private elite guard of the ruler and as his household staff.

The sedentary populations were mostly governed by professional administrators with the title of *qaghans*. At the regional and city level, local rulers retained authority and semi-autonomy over their people, including religious leaders called *sadrs* in cities like Bukhara and Kashgar. The death of Qaidu in 1301 meant that the Chagatayid princes had to resume the government of their *ulus*, which they did by appointing administrators such as emirs, essentially the khan's deputies, and viziers.

Documents that were discovered in an ancient trash dump in the Silk Roads city of Turfan in the Tarim Basin of western China give us some insight into the complicated taxation system in place in the khanate. A general tax was applied based on land ownership and commerce. There was also a labor tax that was used to pay for the communications system, and a *qubchur* poll tax. In some parts of the Chagatayid realm, taxes were paid in kind, including with wine, leather, and cotton. In other regions, they were payable in cash.

As we noted earlier, coinage eventually became widespread in central Asia, utilizing ores of gold, silver, and copper extracted from several mines in the region. When Qaidu came to the throne, his *qaghan* Mas'ud Beg introduced high-quality silver coinage that was created at several mints in regions including in the Fergana Valley and Transoxiana. These coins of Qaidu were anonymous in that there was no identification of the ruling khan's name. But Kebek changed that and had coins minted in his own name. Kebek's coinage included the large silver dinar, which was equal to the value of six smaller silver coins called dirhams. These monetary reforms lasted long after he died and were instrumental in facilitating vigorous coinage-based commerce through the region throughout the 14th century. Kebek's silver coins became known as *kebeks*—or in Russia, *kopeika*, from where the name of the Russian coin, the kopeck, originated.

Indeed, despite what seems like endless strife and warfare, because of its central location, commerce continued to thrive in the ancient heartland of the Silk Roads. Working in conjunction with Chagatayid and Ogedeid princes, Muslim and Uyghur merchants maintained vigorous trade networks which connected most of the Mongol Empire together in another vast trans-Eurasian Silk Roads network. Despite warring with other Mongol factions, both Qaidu and Du'a protected the trade routes, which allowed for an extraordinary array of European, Muslim, and Indian merchants and other travelers to make their way from one end of the Mongol Empire to the other, as we shall see in a future lecture.

As well as acting as a conduit for Chinese goods to move to the west and Persian and Middle Eastern goods to move eastwards, central Asia itself also contributed a range of important agricultural and manufactured products to the network. Fruits like apples and melons were now diffused widely throughout Eurasia, as were various furs, herbs, textile products, wine, and of course slaves.

To support all this trade, a commercial infrastructure was maintained by khanate rulers, including lending institutions, good roads, *Jam* stations, and even reserves of animals like horses and camels that could be hired.

For all these reasons, historians can make a valid argument, I think, that the Mongol Empire through the 13th and 14th centuries constituted the third great era of the Silk Roads.

But we must acknowledge that the regular conflicts that plagued the region were also responsible for a major shift in the mechanism of Eurasian transregional trade. While land-based networks still flourished, gradually the bulk of East-West trade shifted to maritime networks. Large communities of Muslim merchants and mariners lived in the great southern cities of China such as Guangzhou, and tens of thousands of Southeast and South Asian sailors and merchants facilitated the movement of Chinese goods across the Indian Ocean to ports in the Persian Gulf, and of Middle Eastern and European goods back of course to China.

This reality actually leads directly to one of the great conundrums facing Mongol historians today. Because of their support of commerce, the Mongols undoubtedly facilitated the movement of important Chinese material and intellectual property to the West, and for this, authors such as Jack Weatherford argue persuasively that the Mongols deserve to be credited with essentially making the modern world. On the other hand, it increasingly looks like the great bulk of these exchanges took place by sea, and partly because of the geography of the Mongol Empire and the Mongols' fear of the sea, these maritime exchanges largely took place outside of Mongol control. This is an important distinction we will return to in the final lecture of the course, when we sum up the impact of the Mongols on subsequent world history.

Let's conclude this lecture with a brief consideration of cultural and religious developments in central Asia under the Mongols. Unlike the ilkhans and the Yuan emperors, the Mongol princes of central Asia remained nomads and ruled their realm from mobile tent headquarters. These tent cities were also home to all manner of intellectuals, such as physicians, poets, astronomers, and other scientists, and also religious and military leaders. So they must have been fascinating cosmopolitan camps indeed.

Taking control of a region that had been largely Turkic-speaking since the waves of Turkic migration had begun in the 6th century meant that inevitably, Turkic terms and even Turkic languages replaced Mongol. Khans Kebek and Tarmashirin both spoke Turkic and used Turkic names on their seals. However, central Asia remained an ethnically and linguistically complex region, as evidenced by the fact that most coins issued by the

Chagatayids had Arabic legends, and many large buildings erected in cities during the period bore inscriptions both in Arabic and Persian, as can still be seen on many religious and public buildings all over central Asia today.

Most of the Chagatayid khans remained tolerant of the various major religions practiced in their realm. For example, Tughluq Temur, who, despite converting to Islam, also regularly sought advice from a Tibetan Buddhist master. Buddhist monasteries were largely exempt from taxation, in keeping with practices throughout the empire. The khans were also favorably disposed towards Christianity, often maintaining correspondence and diplomatic relations with the pope.

However, given the steady expansion of Islam into central Asia, a process that had begun in the 8th century, it was also inevitable that much of the Mongol central Asian khanate would eventually be Islamicized. Contact amongst Mongol soldiers, many of whom had converted to Islam, along with the activity of Sufi missionaries, were the main reasons Islam gradually took hold. But because Chagatai himself had been regarded as one of the great specialists in Mongol ritual and law, there was more resistance amongst Chagatayid elites to conversion than amongst the elites of the ilkhanate further west, as we will see in our next lecture.

Khan Tarmashirin is often credited as the first Mongol khan of central Asia to convert, but there were already numerous emirs, *qaghans*, and other lesser rulers who had converted long before. Certainly most of the subject population of the Chagatayid khanate was already Muslim. Various Muslim scholars flourished in Mongol-controlled central Asia, including in Bukhara, which had a long history of excellent scholarship. Several madrassahs were constructed in the city, including one built by the mother of Mongke Khan and another by Mas'ud Beg.

Bukhara was also a great center for Sufi missionary activity, with the Kubrawi sect particularly prominent. From Bukhara, Kubrawi Sufis eventually traveled to China, Kashmir, India, and Russia, and as Michal Biran reminds us, "were a major agent of cross-cultural contacts in the khanates."

In the next two lectures, we'll turn to the fortunes of the Mongols in Persia and Russia. Before we leave the central Asian khanate, however, let's sum up its role as part of the greater Mongol Empire. Michal Biran, our main guide through this complex part of the story, offers a pragmatic assessment of the problems associated with the region: "Squeezed between stronger and richer

Mongol khanates and plagued by internal strife and political instability enhanced by its two competing *uluses*, the record of the Chagatayid khanate is less illustrious than that of its neighbors."

While this is undoubtedly true, we also need to acknowledge that despite the often-chaotic situation that prevailed within central Asia—with Chagatayid princes fighting Ogedeid princes for control and both groups often in conflict with the Mongol rulers of China, Russia, and Persia—the Mongol realm in central Asia was nonetheless crucial to the success of the entire empire. Its central position meant that most of the major trade and communication routes passed directly through its territory. As Tim May reminds us, "merchants from the west still needed to pass through it to reach China and other destinations, as did missionaries, adventurers and envoys from the other khanates, and vice versa."

And as we will see later in the course, the prestige of Chinggis Khan's second son, Chagatai, continued to resonate in the region long after the Mongol Empire itself had disappeared. The Turkic-Mongol conqueror Timur, or Tamerlane, explicitly referred to himself as ruler of the ongoing Chagatayid *ulus*. Such was the continuing power of the Chinggisids in Eurasia, an association that Timur would use to reinforce his attempts to emulate Chinggis Khan and create his own enormous empire.

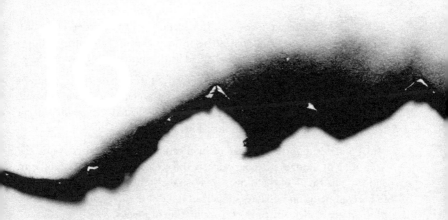

THE MONGOLS IN PERSIA
AND THE MIDDLE EAST

One of the most important primary sources for the story of Mongol rule in Persia is Rashid al-Din, who was born in Hamadan in 1247. Of greatest importance to historians of the Mongol era is the superb work of history he wrote titled the *Compendium of Chronicles*. This lecture uses Rashid al-Din as its guide and turns to the story of Mongol rule in Persia and the Middle East, a region known as the Ilkhanate.

Hulagu's Reign

The first phase of the story of the Ilkhanate concerns the reign of Hulagu, who had been successful with the siege of Baghdad but had tasted defeat at the hands of the Mamluks at the Battle of Ayn Jalut. Soon after this loss, the city of Mosul rebelled against the Mongols, while other regional leaders began forming alliances against them, including the daughter of an old and formidable enemy of the Mongols, none other than Jalal al-Din, son of the Khwarazm-Shah.

With the formerly unified Mongol empire now disintegrating into civil war, Hulagu decided to appoint Persian administrators to run the Ilkhanate very much in the manner that its inhabitants would have been used to.

At the same time, he retained some Mongol political and cultural traditions. Hulagu also bestowed lands within his realm on his sons and other Mongol elites, including both Mongol and allied Turkic military commanders.

Hulagu allowed many regions within the Ilkhanate to remain semiautonomous. In keeping with the Mongol's genuinely tolerant attitude to all religions, Hulagu also sanctioned and protected the worship of all religions that were practiced in the Ilkhanate.*

Hulagu also supported a range of intellectual and cultural pursuits, the beginning of Mongol patronage of arts and sciences that would become an enduring hallmark of the Ilkhanate. Rashid al-Din was later rather caustic in his comments on Hulagu's support of some of these scientific endeavors, particularly of alchemy or the transmutation of metals.

While these various reforms were going on, in 1262, war broke out with the descendants of Jochi over control of the region of modern Azerbaijan in the north, but it was a scrappy conflict with few concrete gains on either side. Before it was concluded, however, Hulagu died from some unknown illness in February 1265.

Abaqa's Reign

Hulagu was succeeded by his son Abaqa, who ruled for the next 17 years and essentially maintained Hulagu's approach to government. Wars with the Jochids continued in the north, and new conflicts broke out with the Mamluks in the west and the Chagatayids in the east.

Along with waging wars simultaneously on several fronts, Abaqa also engaged in diplomatic exchanges with European rulers, including the pope, hoping to forge alliances against the Mamluks. Abaqa also sent emissaries to China acknowledging Qubilai Khan as the legitimate leader of the Mongol realm, and these connections between the Ilkhanate and the Yuan Dynasty resulted in some quite extraordinary cultural exchanges.

The dynamic and capable Abaqa died, probably from alcohol poisoning, on April 1, 1282, which meant a *quriltai* had to be convened to choose a successor. The eventual successor to Abaqa was Teguder, the seventh son of Hulagu, who came to the throne in 1282.

Teguder's Reign

Teguder had converted from Christianity to Islam during his youth, and he preferred to be known by his Muslim name, Ahmad, which angered many Mongols. Court intrigue hampered Ahmad's efforts to govern. Various Muslim advisers conspired with Ahmad and with Arghun, the son of Abaqa, in their jockeying for power. Rashid al-Din informs us that at one stage Ahmad became convinced that a senior administrator, Majd al-Mulk, had to be executed because he had been conspiring with Arghun.

After this, the conflict between Ahmad and Arghun intensified, with followers of each man being captured and often tortured or humiliated by followers of the other. Tensions now turned into open rebellion, and several Mongol military commanders went over to Arghun, concerned that Ahmad was trying to turn the Ilkhanate into an Islamic state. However, as the historian Thomas Allsen points out, despite his conversion, Ahmad remained committed to Mongol norms and rules, and he might have used Islamic formulas and inscriptions in an attempt to broaden his legitimacy among the largely Muslim population of the Ilkhanate.

Regardless of their intentions, these shifts angered many Mongols, including the Yuan emperor Qubilai Khan, who decided to throw his support behind Arghun. Ahmad captured Arghun in a campaign in the Amu Darya valley. He was urged to execute Arghun but hesitated, perhaps unwilling to shed the blood of his nephew. Arghun was liberated by his supporters soon after and then promptly siezed Ahmad's camp. Ahmad and his remaining supporters were captured and executed in 1284.

Arghun and Gaikhatu's Reigns

Ahmad was succeeded by his nephew Arghun. For the seven years of his reign, he pulled back from any attempts to create an Islamic state and also from military expansion. He focused instead on trying to create more effective civil administration. Although Arghun preferred to focus his attention on matters of administration, he was forced into war when a Jochid army invaded the Ilkhanate in March 1288. Arghun proved his military competence by personally leading his army to victory over his enemies.

Arghun died on March 10, 1291, probably from mercury and sulfur poisoning, as he drank medicines prescribed by doctors. Two contenders now vied for the throne: Arghun's brother Gaikhatu and his cousin Baidu. Gaikhatu emerged successful and was elected ilkhan on July 23, 1291.

Gaikhatu then promptly left for Anatolia (modern Turkey), which gave the Mamluks the chance to raid Ilkhanate territories along the Euphrates River valley. The Mamluks withdrew soon after, and the Jochids to the north also agreed to a détente, so Gaikhatu did not face any more serious military conflicts during his reign.

While relations with Mamluks, Chagatayids, and Jochids were strained, the Ilkhanate maintained strong diplomatic relations with the Yuan court in China despite changes in leadership. Just before he died, Arghun had sent a diplomatic mission to Beijing seeking a Chinese wife to further reinforce the Yuan/Ilkhanate alliance. Qubilai Khan sent a Mongolian noblewoman named Kokejin to Arghun, and he also sent Marco Polo and his father and uncle to accompany her on her journey. Most of this journey took place by ship because ongoing conflict within the Chagatayid *ulus* of central Asia made the overland route too dangerous.

Marco Polo provides few details of the long and often harrowing voyage from China, but when the travelers arrived at the Persian Gulf port of Hormuz early in 1294, they found that Arghun was dead and Gaikhatu was on the throne instead. The party received a hospitable welcome nonetheless, and according to Mongol custom, Kokejin was now betrothed to Abuqa's son Ghazan, who was destined to become the greatest of the Ilkhans.

The Polos were well treated by Gaikhatu, who sent them home with tablets of authority issued in the name of the great khan. According to Marco, Kokejin had become so enamored with the Polos that she wept long and hard when they departed. The Polos made it safely back to Venice in 1295 after an absence of 24 years, but sadly, Kokejin died within three years at the age of 22.

Baidu's Rebellion and Ghazan's Taking of Power

As the Polos were arriving back in Venice, support for the rule of Gaikhatu was waning. Baidu rebelled, and on March 24, 1295, Gaikhatu and his supporters were executed. Baidu seized the throne but was almost immediately challenged by Arghun's son Ghazan. Rashid al-Din informs us that because Ghazan converted to Islam just before a decisive battle against Baidu, many of the Muslim soldiers in Baidu's army defected to Ghazan. With these reinforcements, Ghazan was able to defeat Baidu, evict him from the throne, and execute him. Rashid al-Din eventually became the grand vizier of the Ilkhanate under both Ghazan and his successor, Oljeitu.

Mongol historians agree that Ghazan combined the skills of an excellent military leader with those of a skilled administrator. Ghazan's reforms were to prove sweeping and effective, and as a result of Ghazan's rule, the Ilkhanate was effectively transformed into an Islamic empire.

Ghazan's Reforms

Ghazan's reforms were clearly critical to this transformation, but the deeper Islamization of the Mongol state in Persia had undoubtedly begun much earlier, evidenced by the fact that so many Mongol soldiers were already Muslims. But now Ghazan moved decisively to Islamize the state, and this came initially at the expense of the Mongol's long history of religious tolerance.

Within a year, Ghazan had apparently realized that persecuting large numbers of his people because of their faith was not the way to unite the population of the Ilkhanate behind him. For instance, he cracked down on periodic pogroms that flared up within the Islamic populace, and even revoked the ancient tax that Muslims had long used to encourage conversion, the *jizya*.

Nor did Ghazan's personal faith prevent him from waging war against fellow Muslims. Because of a civil war within the Jochid *ulus* in the north, Ghazan was free to launch a concerted assault against the Muslim Mamluks in Arabia and the Middle East. In 1299, his armies defeated Mamluk forces near Homs and captured Damascus. Further invasions followed in 1300 and 1303, although the latter ended in defeat for the ilkhan's forces.

Ghazan also attempted to restore the agricultural infrastructure of his realm and protect and encourage small-scale farmers, although this required a major mindset change on the part of the Mongol military, which had always regarded the peasants as fair game.

Ghazan also embarked on a series of reforms that included prescribing rates and methods of payment of taxation, the reorganization of the *jam* communications network, and the standardization of coinage, weights, and measures. Another feature was reforms of the judiciary, including more equitable payment for judges. There were also incentives to recultivate agricultural land that had been neglected for decades.

Next, Ghazan turned to the problem of how to pay the army. He adopted an Islamic method of military administration by offering land grants to Mongol soldiers, who now received regular income from the revenues produced by farmers and villages in their personal domains.

Ghazan also minted new coins in his name, often with Islamic inscriptions on them. Economic activity was stabilized by this introduction of silver coinage currency after the disastrous attempts by earlier ilkhans to introduce paper money. These economic reforms also helped revive caravan trade along the ancient Silk Roads routes, which in turn contributed to a general reconnection of the Mongol khanates during a period often referred to as the Pax Mongolica, or Mongol Peace.

Oljeitu, Abu Said, and Choban's Reigns

Ghazan died from an illness in 1304, and he was succeeded by his brother Oljeitu, who went on to rule for the next 12 years. One of Oljeitu's first decisions was to move the capital from Tabriz to Sultanniya in northwestern Iran, a region that was better suited for hunting and other traditional Mongol pastimes.

Oljeitu's reign was largely peaceful, and trade flourished within the realm. However, in the midst of this apparent golden age, Oljeitu died from a stomach illness in 1316. He was succeeded by the 12-year-old Abu Said and his emir, Choban.

Two years into their reign, Abu Said and Choban were persuaded by the vizier Alisah to execute Rashid al-Din. The charge leveled against him was that he had murdered his lord Oljeitu. Rashid denied this, but he did admit giving Oljeitu a laxative to help purge his stomach ailment. His rivals, many of them jealous of his power and resentful of his Jewish heritage, used this admission to meticulously build a case against him. In the end, Abu Said and Choban had Rashid al-Din executed in July 1318.

Despite the execution of Rashid al-Din, most historians view the reign of Abu Said as a success, a continuation of the golden age that had preceded it. Abu Said even finally succeeded in signing a peace treaty with the Mamluks in 1322, who had been enemies of the Mongols since 1260.

However, the idea of a golden age might have emerged in retrospect because of the chaos that immediately followed Abu Said's death in 1335. Abu Said left no male heir, and the Ilkhanate immediately devolved into chaos, with eight different Chinggisid princes claiming the throne between 1335 and 1344.

THE MONGOLS IN PERSIA AND THE MIDDLE EAST
LECTURE 16 TRANSCRIPT

One of the most important primary sources for the story of Mongol rule in Persia is Rashid al-Din. Born in Hamadan in 1247, the son of a Jewish apothecary, he became a physician, then later converted to Islam around the age of 30 and ended up as grand vizier to two of the most powerful and successful of all the Mongol rulers of the Ilkhanate, Ghazan and his brother Oljeitu.

We will return to the story of Rashid al-Din's political influence later in this lecture, but of greatest importance to historians of the Mongol era is the superb work of history he wrote titled the *Jami al-tawarikh*, or the *Compendium of Chronicles*. All Mongol scholars would agree with cultural historian Thomas Allsen in assessing the work as "unprecedented in its scope and unique in its research methods."

This is how Rashid al-Din himself describes his approach to the writing of history, an approach that was only made possible because of the unification of much of Eurasia by Chinggis Khan and his successors:

Until now, no work has been produced in any epoch which contains a general account of the history of the inhabitants of the regions of the world and different humans species. Today, thanks to God, the extremities of the inhabited earth are under the dominion of the house of Chinggis Khan, and philosophers, astronomers, scholars and historians from North and South China, India, Kashmir, Tibet, the lands of the Uyghurs, other Turkic tribes, the Arabs and Franks, all belonging to different religions and sects, are united in large numbers in the service of heaven. And each one has manuscripts on the history, chronology and articles of faith of his own people and each has knowledge of some aspects of this. Wisdom demands that there should be prepared from the details of these chronicles an essentially complete work that will bear our august name. This book, in its totality, will be unprecedented—an assemblage of all branches of history.

In order to complete his magnum opus, Rashid al-Din had a special intellectual quarter constructed in the Ilkhanate capital city of Tabriz, fittingly named the Rab-i-Rashidi, or Rashid's Quarter. This district became home to fellow historians, philosophers, scientists, artists, agricultural specialists, and many other scholars from all over the Mongol Empire. So Chinese, Persian, and Italian scholars, to name but a few, worked together on a range of intellectual pursuits, but most particularly on helping Rashid al-Din compile his *Compendium*, of which some 20 lavishly illustrated copies were made during his lifetime. The fact that Rashid al-Din did all this while still functioning as the highest administrator in Mongol-controlled Persia says much about the energy, intelligence, and work ethic of this extraordinary man.

The *Jami al-tawarikh* was probably completed in 1308, and it does indeed recount the histories of a wide range of peoples and regions within Eurasia, as Rashid al-Din explicitly set out to do. But Mongol scholars are particularly grateful that the author kept much of his focus firmly on the rise of the Mongol Empire. Throughout this course, we have been dependent on a handful of crucial primary sources to help us recount different aspects of the extraordinary history of the Mongols: *The Secret History*, of course; *The History of the World Conqueror* by Juvaini; the annals of the Yuan Dynasty; Korean and Japanese histories and illustrations; along with a wide assortment of chronicles by Russian, European, and Islamic observers.

But arguably none of these sources is more important than Rashid al-Din's *Compendium of Chronicles*. The historian had access to now lost Mongol documents and accounts, and he was also able to personally interview many Mongol elites of his time, including an ambassador from the great khan in China, Bolod Chingsang, who was one of the most highly placed Mongols in the Yuan administration. So, with Rashid al-Din as our guide, and always conscious of the fact that he, like all historians, had certain inherent biases, we turn in this lecture to the story of Mongol rule in Persia and the Middle East, a region known as the Ilkhanate.

The fact that the Mongol rulers of this huge, multicultural, multiethnic state actually referred to their realm as the Ilkhanate is in itself quite fascinating. You might remember that it was Mongke Khan who bestowed upon his brothers Qubilai and Hulagu the title of ilkhan, which explicitly placed them in a subordinate position to the great khan himself. We have also seen that after Mongke's death, Qubilai abandoned the title and declared himself to be great khan instead, and also emperor of the Yuan Dynasty. But it is fascinating that Hulagu continued to use the title of ilkhan even as the Mongol Empire disintegrated into distinct states ruled by descendants of the four sons of Chinggis. As far as we are aware, no other Mongol prince from the Chagatayid, Ogedeid, and Jochid lineages ever referred to himself as ilkhan.

The first phase of the story of the Ilkhanate concerns the reign of Hulagu, who, although he had been successful with the siege of Baghdad, had tasted defeat at the hands of the Mamluks at the Battle of Ain Jalut. Soon after this loss, the city of Mosul rebelled against the Mongols, while other regional leaders began forming alliances against them, including the daughter of an old and formidable enemy of the Mongols, none other than Jalal al-Din, son of the Khwarazm-Shah.

Hulagu and Mongol forces immediately besieged Mosul, which fell after six months and suffered the usual massacre and devastation. Rashid al-Din offers a gruesome account of the death of the ruler of Mosul, Malik Salih, at the hands of Hulagu. He was covered in sheep's fat and left tied up in the summer sun until maggots appeared in the fat and devoured the poor man to death from the outside in, an agonizing process that apparently took a month to complete.

With the formerly unified Mongol Empire now disintegrating into civil war, Hulagu decided to appoint Persian administrators to run his Ilkhanate very much in the manner that its inhabitants would have been used to, while at the same time still retaining some Mongol political and cultural traditions. Hulagu also bestowed lands within his realm on his sons and other Mongol elites, including both Mongol and allied Turkic military commanders.

Despite the splintering of the Mongol realm, the Chinggisid princes still believed in the Mongols' Mandate of Heaven to conquer the whole world, virtually the last message Chinggis Khan had passed on to his sons at his death. But opportunities for expansion were now limited to the fringes of empire, as we saw with Qubilai in east and southeast Asia. Expansion was made particularly difficult for the Ilkhanate, which was hemmed in by the Chagatayid *ulus* in central Asia to the east, and the Jochid *ulus* to the north.

In addition to these geopolitical restrictions, the regions that now composed the Ilkhanate had suffered decades of destruction and depravation during various Mongol campaigns of conquest. Hulagu did his best to rebuild some cities, including Baghdad, but the widespread destruction of the ancient qanat irrigation systems meant that farming was now much more difficult, and many small-scale peasant farmers simply slipped away from the land.

Aware of these problems, and at war almost from the beginning of his reign with the Jochids to the north, Hulagu allowed many regions within the Ilkhanate to remain semi-autonomous. In keeping with the Mongols' genuinely tolerant attitude to all religions, Hulagu also sanctioned and protected the worship of all religions that were practiced within the Ilkhanate. Hulagu's wife, Dokuz Khatun, was a Nestorian Christian, and she personally supervised the construction of a number of churches. But at no stage was the Muslim majority of the region suppressed, although their monopoly on power was somewhat undermined by the more equitable favor extended to other religions.

Hulagu also supported a range of intellectual and cultural pursuits, the beginning of Mongol patronage of arts and sciences that would become an enduring hallmark of the Ilkhanate. One of the scientists Hulagu supported was Nasir al-Din al-Tusi, who used the observatory Hulagu had constructed for him to make some extraordinarily accurate discoveries about the movements of the planets, which he used to critique the long-standing Ptolemaic model.

Rashid al-Din was later rather caustic in his comments on Hulagu's support of some of these scientific endeavors, particularly of alchemy, or the transmutation of metals. As a professional administrator, Rashid was careful with state resources, so it is hardly surprising he wrote: "In transmutation they had no luck, but they were miracles of cheating and fraud, squandering and wasting the stores of the workshops of lordly power."

While these various reforms were going on, in 1262, war broke out with the descendants of Jochi over control of the region of modern Azerbaijan in the north, but it was a scrappy conflict with few concrete gains on either side. Before it was concluded, however, Ilkhan Hulagu died from some unknown illness in February 1265. His wife Dokuz Khatun died four months later. There is some evidence from Rashid al-Din to suggest that Hulagu's funeral involved human sacrifices—as far as we know, the only ilkhan funeral ever to do so—but the circumstances behind this are unclear.

Hulagu was succeeded by his son Abaqa, who ruled for the next 17 years and essentially maintained Hulagu's approach to government. Wars with the Jochids continued in the north, and new conflicts broke out with the Mamluks in the west and the Chagatayids in the east. Abaqa employed his father's vizier, so administration of the state continued without much disruption, but as Tim May points out, because of the ongoing wars, "the state remained subservient to military needs and was largely a ramshackle assemblage of methods without well-developed institutions." The longer-term effect of the wars was to devastate the borderlands between the competing states and to drain the treasury, which was hard-pressed to pay for them.

As well as waging wars simultaneously on several fronts, Abaqa also engaged in diplomatic exchanges with European rulers, including the pope, hoping to forge alliances against the Mamluks. Abaqa also sent emissaries to China acknowledging Qubilai Khan as the legitimate great khan of the Mongol realm, and these connections between the Ilkhanate and the Yuan Dynasty resulted in some quite extraordinary cultural exchanges, which we shall return to later in the course.

The dynamic and capable Abaqa died, probably of the "Mongol Disease"—alcohol poisoning—on April 1st, 1282, which meant a *quriltai* had to be convened to choose a successor. Of course, now that the Mongol world was divided into four khanates, the *quriltai* became much smaller and more regionally focused. It also meant that, where in the past, khans might be sought from any of the *altan urugh*, or Golden Family princes, now the only Chinggisid descendants considered for the throne were those from families that controlled the individual khanates. So narrow had the pool of potential rulers become that for the *quriltai* convened following the death of Abaqa, only direct descendants of Hulagu were considered, and even other Toluids were excluded.

The eventual successor to Abaqa was Teguder, the seventh son of Hulagu, who came to the throne in 1282. Teguder had converted from Christianity to Islam during his youth and preferred to be known by his Muslim name, Ahmad, which angered many Mongols. Court intrigued hampered Ahmad's efforts to govern, and various Muslim advisers, including the historian Ata-Malik Juvaini, conspired with Ahmad—and with Arghun, the son of Abaqa—in their jockeying for power.

Rashid al-Din informs us that at one stage, Ahmad became convinced that a senior administrator, Majd al-Mulk, had to be executed because he had been conspiring with Arghun. He describes the death of al-Mulk thus: "Ahmad's decree was issued for him to be turned over to his adversaries to be put to death ... and he was turned over at night to a crowd that tore him from limb to limb." This occurred in August 1282, during Ahmad's first months of rule.

After this, the conflict between Ahmad and Arghun intensified, with followers of each man being captured and often tortured or humiliated by followers of the other. Tensions now turned into open rebellion, and several Mongol military commanders went over to Arghun, concerned that Ahmad was trying to turn the Ilkhanate into an Islamic state. But as Thomas Allsen points out, despite his conversion, Ahmad Teguder remained committed to Mongol norms and rules and might have used Islamic formulas and inscriptions in an attempt to broaden his legitimacy amongst the largely Muslim population of the Ilkhanate.

This theory is borne out by the different coins Ahmad had struck during his reign. On one type, he used the Mongol formula: "Struck by Ahmad in the name of the Qaghan." On another, he had the same formula, but with his name spelled in Arabic. And on a third coin type, he had "Khan the Supreme Ahmad" on the obverse and "There is no god but Allah, Muhammad is the Prophet of God, Sultan Ahmad" on the reverse.

But these ideological shifts, whatever their intention, angered many Mongols, including apparently Yuan emperor Qubilai Khan himself, who decided to throw his support behind Arghun. Ahmad actually captured Arghun in a campaign in the Amu Darya valley. He was urged to execute Arghun but hesitated, perhaps unwilling to shed the blood of his nephew, who was liberated soon after by supporters of Arghun. Arghun then promptly seized Ahmad's camp, which meant that, as Tim May puts it, "the loyalty of the entire Ilkhanate shifted." Ahmad Teguder was captured and executed in 1284, along with his remaining supporters.

Ahmad was succeeded, not surprisingly, by his nephew Arghun, who for the seven years of his reign pulled back from any attempts to create an Islamic state and also from military expansion and focused instead on trying to create more effective civil administration. With this in mind, he placed his trust in senior administrators such as Buqa Noyan, and after his demise in January 1289, in a Jewish physician named Sa'd-al-Dawla, who proved remarkably competent despite the outrage some other Islamic administrators felt about having a Jew in a position of power over them.

Although Arghun preferred to focus his attention on matters of administration, he was forced into war when a Jochid army invaded the Ilkhanate in March 1288. Arghun proved his military competence by personally leading his army to victory over his enemies. He preferred not to engage the Ilkhanate's old enemy the Mamluks directly, but continued his predecessors' policies of using diplomacy against them. It was in this context that he dispatched a remarkable Nestorian monk named Rabban Sawma as an ambassador to Europe. We shall return to Rabban Sawma's journey, and the extensive account that he left of it, in a future lecture.

Arghun died on March 10th, 1291, probably from mercury and sulfur poisoning, as he drank medicines prescribed by Buddhist or Jewish doctors. Two contenders now vied for the throne: Arghun's brother Gaikhatu and his cousin Baidu. Gaikhatu emerged successful and was elected ilkhan on July 23rd, 1291. Gaikhatu then promptly left for Anatolia (modern Turkey), which gave the Mamluks the chance to raid Ilkhanate territories along the Euphrates River Valley. The Mamluks withdrew soon after, and the Jochids to the north also agreed to a détente, so Gaikhatu did not face any more serious military conflicts during his reign.

While relations with Mamluks, Chagatayids, and Jochids were strained, the Ilkhanate maintained strong diplomatic relations with the Yuan court in China despite changes in leadership. Just before he died, Arghun had sent a diplomatic mission to Beijing seeking a Chinese wife to further reinforce the Yuan/Ilkhanate alliance. Qubilai Khan sent a Mongolian noblewoman named Kokejin to Arghun, and he also sent Marco Polo and his father and uncle to accompany her on her journey. Most of this journey took place by ship because ongoing conflict within the Chagatayid *ulus* of central Asia made the overland route too dangerous.

Marco Polo provides few details of the long and often harrowing voyage from China, but when the travelers arrived at the Persian Gulf port of Hormuz early in 1294, they found that Arghun was dead and Gaikhatu was on the throne instead. The party received a hospitable welcome nonetheless, and according to Mongol custom, Kokejin was now betrothed to Arghun's son Ghazan, who was destined to become the greatest of the ilkhans.

The Polos were well treated by Gaikhatu, who sent them home with tablets of authority issued in the name of the great khan. According to Marco, the princess Kokejin had become so enamored with the Polos that she wept long and hard when they departed. The Polos made it safely back to Venice in 1295 after an absence of 24 years, but sadly, Kokejin herself died within three years at the age of 22.

As the Polos were arriving back in Venice, support for the rule of Gaikhatu was waning. His attempts to reform the economy by introducing paper money (something that been done effectively in the Yuan Dynasty in China) proved disastrous, and his cousin Baidu, still nursing a grudge that Gaikhatu had been elected ilkhan over him, sowed discontent amongst the Mongol elites, even accusing Gaikhatu of debauchery. The rebellion of Baidu that followed proved, as Tim May succinctly puts it, "short, swift and successful." On March 24th, 1295, Gaikhatu and his supporters were executed.

Baidu seized the throne but was almost immediately challenged by Arghun's son Ghazan. Rashid al-Din informs us that because Ghazan converted to Islam just before a decisive battle against Baidu, many of the Muslim soldiers in Baidu's army defected to Ghazan, and with these reinforcements, Ghazan was able to defeat Baidu, evict him from the throne, and execute him.

Actually, this conversion story as recounted by Rashid al-Din is even more dramatic. On the eve of battle, storms sprang up that rendered Ghazan's battle plans useless, and at the same time, he realized that Baidu's forces greatly outnumbered his. His general Nawruz convinced Ghazan to convert, and then, after duly observing Ramadan, his Muslim army easily destroyed that of Baidu. Of course, Rashid al-Din was an excellent propagandist both for Ghazan and for his faith of Islam, so we need to treat his account with caution, but there is no doubt Ghazan won a decisive victory over his rival.

Ghazan was to prove exactly the right man for the job at the right time. His accession to the throne of the Ilkhanate led to, as David Morgan puts it, "the most sustained attempt to right the wrongs of the previous seven decades" of misrule. Mongol historians agree that Ghazan combined the skills of an excellent military leader with those of a skilled administrator—as we have seen throughout this course, a rare enough combination amongst

Mongol elites. Ghazan's reforms were to prove sweeping and effective, and as a result of Ghazan's rule, the Ilkhanate was effectively transformed from a Mongol khanate into an Islamic empire.

Ghazan's reforms were clearly critical to this transformation, but the deeper Islamization of the Mongol state in Persia had undoubtedly begun much earlier, evidenced by the fact that so many Mongol soldiers were already Muslims. But now Ghazan moved decisively to Islamize the state, and this came initially at the expense of the Mongols' long history of religious tolerance. Early in his reign, Ghazan issued a harsh edict, the effects of which were reported by Rashid al-Din: "All the Buddhist temples and houses of worship, as well as Christian churches and Jewish synagogues, were to be destroyed in Tabriz, Baghdad and other Islamic places, and for that victory most of the people of Islam rendered thanks since God had not seen fit to grant this wish to past generations."

Yet, within a year, Ghazan had apparently rethought this policy of intolerance and realized that persecuting large numbers of his people because of their faith was not the way to unite the population of the Ilkhanate behind him. So he gave the Georgians and Armenians the right to build new churches, established a cordial relationship with the Nestorian hierarchy, cracked down on periodic pogroms that flared up within the Islamic populace, and even revoked the ancient tax that Muslims had long used to encourage conversion, the jizya.

Nor did Ghazan's personal faith prevent him from waging war against fellow Muslims. He was a Mongol, after all, and war and conquest is what Mongols had always done. Because of a civil war within the Jochid *ulus* in the north, Ghazan was free to launch a concerted assault against the Muslim Mamluks in Arabia and the Middle East. In 1299, his armies defeated Mamluk forces near Homs and captured the city of Damascus. Further invasions followed in 1300 and 1303, although the latter ended in defeat for the Ilkhans.

Ghazan also attempted to restore the agricultural infrastructure of his realm and protect and encourage small-scale farmers, although this required a major mindset change on the part of the Mongol military which had always regarded the peasants as fair game. Rashid al-Din, who was now employed as Ghazan's *sahib divan*, or senior administrator, relates a speech Ghazan is supposed to have given to his Mongol commanders as part of his attempt to persuade them to think differently about the peasants, a sort of level-headed argument that he hoped would appeal to Mongol common sense:

> I am not protecting the Persian peasantry. If it is expedient, then let me pillage them all, there is no one with more power to do so than I. Let us rob them together. But if you expect to collect provisions and food in the future I will be harsh with you. And you must consider: if you commit extortion against the peasants, take their oxen and seed, and cause their crops to be consumed, what will you do in the future?

Having done his best to persuade other Mongols to support his vision, Ghazan now embarked on a series of reforms that included prescribing rates and methods of payment of taxation; the reorganization of the *Jam* communications network; the standardization of coinage, weights and measures; reforms of the judiciary, including more equitable payment for judges; and incentives to recultivate agricultural land that had been neglected for decades.

Ghazan next turned to the vexed problem of how to pay the army. Following Rashid al-Din's advice (or so the historian informs us), Ghazan adopted an Islamic method of military administration by offering land grants to Mongol soldiers, who now received regular income from the revenues produced by farmers and villages in their personal domains. This was also obviously a brilliant part of his attempts to protect the peasants against pillaging: The income of his soldiers now depended on the success of the farmers.

Ghazan also minted new coins in his name, often with Islamic inscriptions on them, and economic activity was stabilized by the introduction of silver coinage currency after the disastrous attempts by earlier ilkhans to introduce paper money. These economic reforms also helped revive caravan trade along the ancient Silk Roads routes, which in turn contributed to a general reconnection of the Mongol khanates during a period often referred to as the Pax Mongolica, the Mongol Peace.

Although some historians prefer not to use the term *Pax Mongolica* anymore, there's evidence supporting its existence during the late 13th and early 14th centuries. Despite frequent periods of conflicts between the four major khanates of the empire, conditions were such that a slew of extraordinary diplomats, missionaries, ambassadors, and adventurers like Rabban Sawma and the Polos were able to travel back and forth across Eurasia in a way that had rarely been experienced before, and which arguably has never been experienced since, safe under the protection of the various Chinggisid elites. This is a crucial topic we will return to very soon, and also assess again in our last lecture on the impact of the Mongols on world history.

Ghazan Khan died from some illness in 1304 and was succeeded by his brother Oljeitu, who went on to rule for the next dozen years. One of Oljeitu's first decisions was to move the capital from Tabriz to Sultaniyya in northwestern Iran, a region that was better suited for hunting and other traditional Mongol pastimes.

Oljeitu followed a long and torturous path in his personal religious faith. He was baptized as a Christian while still a child, later converted to Buddhism and adopted the Mongolian Buddhist name Oljeitu, and then converted to Sunni Islam, which he soon abandoned because of his disgust over the constant bickering between religious authorities over what seemed to him to be inconsequential points of theological difference. So Oljeitu became a Buddhist again, but realizing this was not politically advisable in a majority Muslim khanate, he finally converted to Shia Islam in 1309.

Oljeitu's reign was largely peaceful, and trade flourished within the realm. Further evidence of the operation of a Pax Mongolica comes in the form of a letter Oljeitu wrote to King Philip IV of France in which he stated that the realms of the descendants of the four sons of Chinggis had now settled their differences and were reunited in their recognition that the son of Qubilai should succeed him as great khan of the Mongol Empire. Then, in the midst of this apparent golden age, Oljeitu died from some stomach illness in 1316, to be succeeded by the 12-year-old Abu Said and his emir, Choban.

Two years into their reign, Abu Said and Choban were persuaded by vizier Alisah to execute the grand vizier of the Ilkhanate under both Ghazan and Oljeitu, and our crucial source for much of the story we have unfolded in this lecture, Rashid al-Din. The charge leveled against him was that he had murdered his lord Oljeitu. Rashid denied this, but did admit giving Oljeitu a laxative to help purge his stomach ailment. His rivals, many of them jealous of his power and prestige, and resentful of his Jewish heritage, used this admission to meticulously build a case against him. In the end, Abu Said and Choban had the great vizier executed in July 1318.

Despite the execution of Rashid al-Din, most historians now view the reign of Abu Said as a success, a continuation of the golden age that had preceded it, although without the meticulous records of a historian like Juvaini or Rashid al-Din, many of the details of his reign remain obscure. Abu Said even finally succeeded in signing a peace treaty with the Mamluks in 1322, who had been enemies of the Mongols since 1260—no mean achievement. Yet the idea of a golden age might have emerged in retrospect because of the chaos that immediately followed Abu Said's death in 1335.

Abu Said left no male heir, and the Ilkhanate immediately devolved into chaos, with eight different Chinggisid princes claiming the throne between 1335 and 1344. As David Morgan notes, "we appear to have here the perplexing phenomenon of an empire which fell without having previously declined."

We shall return to the story of the dramatic fall of the Ilkhanate, part of an empire-wide decline, in a future lecture. But first, we have to complete our survey of the division of Chinggis's empire into four khanates by tracing the story of the descendants of Chinggis Khan's oldest son, Jochi, in carving out their own substantial state in Russia, a state popularly known as the realm of the Golden Horde.

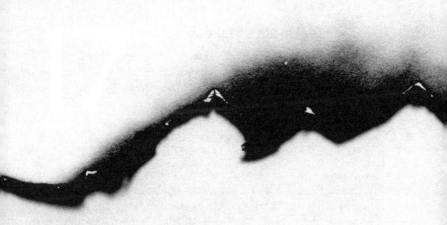

THE MONGOLS IN RUSSIA:
THE GOLDEN HORDE

B atu Khan, the son of Chinggis Khan's oldest son, Jochi, was a Mongol force of nature. Following a series of successes, Batu came to be in control of a vast realm that stretched from the Irtysh River in Siberia across all of eastern Siberia, the steppes of modern Kazakhstan, and the plains of southern Russia as far as the Dniester River. Batu's hordes regularly nomadized much further to the west. In the south, Batu's lands included the Crimean Peninsula, the northern reaches of the Caucasus Mountains, and the northern regions of Khwarazm west of the Aral Sea. In the north, the territory extended deep into Siberia, covering all the Rus principalities, and to the northwest as far as the Volga River.

From the 13th century to the 15th century, this enormous realm was known simply as the *ulus* or khanate of the Jochids—that is, the state or nation that belonged to Batu and the descendants of Jochi. Ever since the 16th century, though, it has been known as the realm of the Golden Horde.

The Golden Horde's Makeup

Of the four khanates of the Mongol empire, the Golden Horde was destined to survive the longest, well into the 16th century.* Throughout the long history of the Golden Horde, the Mongols were decidedly in the minority in their enormous realm. When Chinggis Khan originally divided his empire among his sons before his death, he apportioned to the Jochids some 9,000 soldiers and the families that supported them. Assuming an average of five persons per household, that would mean a maximum of 45,000 Mongols.

The population of the khanate of the Golden Horde included Greeks, Armenians, Russians, Jews, and Italians, but by far the greatest percentage consisted of various Turkic-speaking seminomadic groups who had made the steppes their own: the Kipchaks, the Cuman, and the Bulgars. This made a degree of Turkification of the Mongols inevitable and even quite rapid. By as early as the 1280s, Turkish script had replaced Mongolian on Mongol coins.

Batu chose to make the lower reaches of the Volga River the administrative center of his realm. Although he generally preferred to remain in his camp, in the early 1250s, Batu had a capital city constructed at Sarai in the Volga Delta. The location of Sarai was important because the lower Volga was central to transregional land and river trade and also close to important Black Sea ports like Sudak and Kaffa.

Batu and his successors did their best to encourage commerce, including granting all sorts of privileges and tax concessions to the mostly Muslim merchants. The wealth that flowed through the realm of the Golden Horde as a result of thriving trade meant that the region recovered quite quickly from the devastation of the previous Mongol invasion.

Political Machinations and Successions

As Batu's power and influence expanded, his relationship with the Mongol leader Guyuk Khan deteriorated. Sorkaktani, the widow of Chinggis Khan's youngest son Tolui and an ally of Batu, warned Batu that Guyuk was planning to destroy him. Guyuk indeed summoned Batu to appear before him, but Batu hesitated, and Guyuk died before the meeting could take place.

---

* Smaller Mongol successor states persisted into the 18th and even 19th centuries.

Following the death of Guyuk, Batu could have moved to assert his own claims to be elected great khan, but he was apparently happy in his realm and supported the regency of Oghul Qaimish. He later helped promote the claims of Mongke, who was elected great khan in 1251.

During the reign of Mongke, Batu's prestige and reputation as kingmaker reached its zenith. He ruled his vast *ulus* well, and he left a thriving state to his younger brother Berke. When Batu died in 1255, aged just 48, it would be Berke's job to guide the fortunes of the Jochid *ulus* into the post-dissolution phase of the Mongol empire.

Berke's Reign

An important part of the administration of the Mongol empire undertaken by Mongke Khan was an empire-wide census that was conducted between 1252 and 1259 to better regulate the collection of taxes. The Jochids supported this census, but the officials appointed by Mongke to carry out the census met stiff opposition within the Russian states of the Golden Horde. Some census officials were assassinated, but with the support of Berke, eventually the Russians were brought under control and taxation within the Golden Horde was regulated.

The Golden Horde army defeats the Ilkhanate at the battle of Terek in 1262

With the administration of his state in good order, in 1262, Berke started a war with Hulagu and the Ilkhanate in the south. Berke was intent on taking control of lush grasslands in parts of Azerbaijan and Iran that he believed had been granted to the Jochids by Chinggis Khan himself. Hulagu pushed back and invaded parts of the Jochid realm. An uneasy stalemate ensued with the Caucasus Mountains becoming the front line between the two sides.

To break the stalemate, Berke agreed to an alliance with Sultan Baybars, the leader of the Mamluks of Egypt. As a result of the alliance between Berke and Sultan Baybars, diplomatic exchanges became regular between Egypt and the Golden Horde, and a second front was opened in the war with the Ilkhanate.

Ilkhan Hulagu died in 1265, and his sons immediately took up the war with the Jochids. Berke led his forces into battle with Hulagu's son and successor Abaqa near the modern city of Tbilisi, but just as the armies were about to engage, Berke died. He was succeeded two years later by Mongke Temur, a descendant of Batu.

Mongke Temur's Reign and Successors

Mongke Temur proclaimed to the rest of the Mongol world the de facto independence of the Golden Horde by being the first khan to issue silver and copper coins in his own name. The Golden Horde's support for trade continued under Mongke Temur, particularly after he signed a peace agreement with Ilkhan Abaqa that lasted from 1268 to 1269.

During the détente with the Ilkhanate, Jochid forces returned to eastern Europe to raid and pillage in Hungary and Poland. The kingdom of Bulgaria, which had submitted to the Mongols during their earlier invasion of Eastern Europe, remained loyal to the Golden Horde, permitting Mongol armies to pass through its territory to bypass the Byzantine Empire.

Mongke Temur died in 1280 and was succeeded by his younger brother Tode Mongke. But Tode was an ineffectual ruler, and seven years later, he abdicated. His nephew Tole Buqa became khan. Both khans were easily manipulated by Noghai, an emir who now emerged as the new power of the Golden Horde.

Tode Mongke

Noghai's Actions

In the two decades following the death of Mongke Temur, Noghai exploited the weaker khans of the Golden Horde to such an extent that by 1286, he was even issuing coins in his own name. Noghai had converted to Islam in 1270, and he used this ideological shift in an attempt to reignite the alliance with the Mamluks.

However, Sultan Baybars was now less inclined to become involved in Mongol politics and demurred. The wars continued, nonetheless. Although there were no major victories on either side, Noghai's strategic and military experience ensured that Ilkhan Abaqa was unable to make any significant gains of territory.

Khan Tole Buqa eventually decided to raise troops against Noghai, which led to civil war between the two factions. Noghai appointed Toqta, the son of Mongke Temur, to lead the fight against Tole Buqa, but in 1291, Toqta executed the khan and claimed the throne for himself.

For the first few years of his reign, Toqta was happy to allow Noghai to rule his own lands and pursue his own strategic interests. But as Toqta grew older and more assertive, he gradually built his own strategic alliances to form a powerful coalition against Noghai, including marrying a Byzantine princess of his own. By 1297, the Golden Horde had devolved into open civil war again.

The war lasted for years and was incredibly violent and disruptive, affecting both nomadic and sedentary populations of the khanate. Toqta fought to regain control of Noghai's realm between the Don and Dnieper Rivers, while Noghai fought for his lands and his powerful position within the Golden Horde. The ultimate showdown between the two occurred in the either 1299 or 1300 at Kugenlik. Noghai died on the battlefield, and Toqta emerged victorious as the sole Khan of the Golden Horde.

Toqta and Ozbeg's Reigns

Toqta's long reign of 22 years stabilized the Golden Horde. He intervened in small-scale civil wars between the various Rus princes, who generally welcomed these interventions and his support. The reign of Toqta also benefitted from a general peace that prevailed between all the khanates. It was the stable and prosperous reign of Toqta that made possible the subsequent golden age of the Golden Horde, which reached its zenith during the 30-year reign of Toqta's nephew Ozbeg Khan.

Ozbeg, who ruled from 1312 to 1342, was an energetic and clearheaded ruler who managed domestic and foreign affairs with intelligence and efficiency. He was by all accounts a devout Muslim, and under him, the Islamization of the Jochid khanate continued among both elites and common Mongols. Still, the Mongols generally maintained their policy of religious tolerance.

The reign of Ozbeg also had a favorable impact on the fortunes of the Russian princes. The most important position of authority in the Russian world was that of the grand prince of the city of Vladimir, and since the advent of the Golden Horde, the right to bestow this position had belonged to the Mongol khan. This led to intense diplomatic jockeying to gain the favor of the khan, and also to all sorts of corrupt behavior among the princes themselves.

In the 1320s, the grand prince of Moscow was appointed grand prince of Vladimir by Ozbeg, which gave him the right to collect the taxes his fellow princes owed to the Mongols. Because the Grand Prince was permitted to keep a share of the tax revenue, this meant that his status and wealth grew exponentially, as did the fortunes of his home city of Moscow.

Janibeg's Reign

With the death of Ozbeg in 1342, his son Tinibeg came to the throne, only to die mysteriously a few months later. He was replaced by his brother Janibeg, who ruled until 1357. Janibeg soon found himself involved in a violent struggle that broke out between Italian and Muslim merchants in the Black Sea trading city of Tana, which escalated into violent street brawls. Determined to protect his Muslim populations, Janibeg prepared to besiege the city of Kaffa, to which both Venetian and Genovese merchants had fled in the aftermath.

The siege dragged on from 1346 into 1347, with both sides negotiating for favorable terms to end it. However, by early 1348, the Black Death had devastated Italy, and it arrived in England by June of that same year. In the end, Europe lost a total of 25 million humans to the plague, between a third and a half of the total population.

Janibeg spent the rest of his time as Khan of the Golden Horde dealing with plague and various other problems that arose. In the final year of his reign, 1357, he briefly enjoyed a triumph that had eluded the khans of the Golden Horde ever since Berke: He finally captured the lush pastures of Azerbaijan from the Ilkhans. But the Ilkhanate was already in serious decline by this stage; and Janibeg only had a brief moment to celebrate this victory before he died.

After Janibeg

The Golden Horde now fell into anarchy. During the two decades between 1359 and 1380, some 25 different khans claimed the throne. Geographically, the empire began to fall apart. Lithuania expanded its territory at the expense of the Mongols, even taking control of the great city of Kiev. In the south, the city of Urgench in Khwarazm, on the banks of the Amu Darya, broke away from the Golden Horde, as did the Volga Bulgars.

Italian and Genoese merchants in the Crimea ceased paying their taxes to the Golden Horde. The embryonic Russian state also increased its power and autonomy during this period, particularly during the reign of Dmitri Donskoi between 1362 and 1389.

THE MONGOLS IN RUSSIA: THE GOLDEN HORDE

LECTURE 17 TRANSCRIPT

Batu Khan, the son of Chinggis Khan's oldest son, Jochi, was a Mongol force of nature. Rashid al-Din wrote that Jochi fathered 40 sons before his death in 1227, although the chronicler names only 14. Of these, four in particular stand out because they later founded their own dynasties: Orda, Batu, Shiban, and Toqa Temur. Although he was Jochi's oldest son, Orda was apparently more than happy to support his father's decision to name Batu as his heir, particularly as Chinggis Khan also supported the decision.

The two oldest brothers worked well together in administering the lands and the several thousand households Chinggis Khan bequeathed to the descendants of Jochi. Using techniques of steppe imperial administration introduced by the Xiongnu 1,500 years earlier, Orda and his White Horde ruled the left wing of the realm, essentially the lands between the Volga River and Lake Balkhash in Siberia, while Batu controlled the right wing, which was everything west of the Volga River. Both Batu and Orda were fully supported in the ownership and administration of their realm by subsequent khans Ogedai and Mongke.

When Ogedai came to the throne, he commanded Batu to join the military campaigns against the Jin Dynasty in China, while Orda was sent to campaign against various nomadic tribes on the steppe. Batu performed well in China, and at the *quriltai* convened in 1235 following the defeat of the Jin, Ogedai appointed Batu as the military commander of the vast Mongol force of perhaps 150,000 soldiers that he dispatched to Russia and Europe. This was an invasion force led by a glittering array of Mongol princes under the overall command of Batu and General Subedei, and Batu was determined to play his role in making it a success.

It was Batu who took command of the forces sent against the Rus principalities, which resulted in the fall of the city of Ryazan in December 1237. During the early months of 1238, Batu divided his forces into smaller units which captured and ransacked 14 additional Rus cities. Only Smolensk escaped destruction, because it submitted to Batu and agreed to pay tribute. In the summer of 1238, Batu led his troops on a devastating raid into Crimea and also crushed Kipchak resistance on the adjacent steppe. Batu was also at the forefront of the sacking of the Ukrainian towns of Chernigov and Pereyaslav in the winter of 1239 and the siege and devastation of the great city of Kiev in December 1240.

A group of Kipchaks had fled before the Mongol onslaught and sought refuge with the king of Hungary, who permitted them to settle in his kingdom despite their unruly behavior. The Mongols regarded these refugees as their property, and Batu sent five different messengers to Hungarian king Bela IV demanding their return. The king had all of them killed. With the way into central and western Europe now wide open to them, an enraged Batu famously declared that the Mongols would now invade and would not stop until they had reached "the ultimate sea," probably a reference to the Atlantic. It is difficult to interpret this any other way than that Batu was now determined to personally conquer all of Europe.

The Mongols immediately invaded Poland and Hungary and, as we have seen, destroyed both kingdoms along with the flower of European knighthood in a series of brilliantly conducted battles and sieges. Again, Batu was the engine driving several of these campaigns, successfully conducting the siege of Pest, then working with Subedei to defeat the knights of King Bela and his allies at the Battle of Mohi on April 11th, 1241.

Following these successes, the Mongols began drawing up serious plans to invade Austria, Italy, and Germany. Batu even sent a letter to Frederick II, the Holy Roman Emperor himself, demanding that he step down because "I am coming to usurp your throne!" But as we know, even as Mongol forces were spotted on the outskirts of Vienna, Europe was saved from further devastation by the sudden death of Ogedai and the need for Subedei and the Mongol princes to return to the homeland for a *quriltai*, which most did in the spring of 1242.

Although Batu did withdraw from Hungary, he did not return to Mongolia for the *quriltai*, preferring instead to remain in his camp on the banks of the Volga River. Batu's refusal to return delayed the gathering for several years. Eventually, Guyuk was elected khan in 1246, and although Batu did not support the selection, his elite status meant that Batu was nonetheless acknowledged by all Mongols as supreme ruler of all the western regions of the Mongol Empire.

This meant that Batu was in control of a vast realm that stretched from the Irtysh River in Siberia across all of eastern Siberia, the steppes of modern Kazakhstan, and the plains of southern Russia as far as the Dniester River, although Batu's hordes regularly nomadized much further to the west. In the south, Batu's lands included the Crimean Peninsula, the northern reaches of the Caucasus Mountains, and the northern regions of Khwarazm west of the Aral Sea. In the north, the realm of the Jochids extended deep into Siberia, included all the Rus principalities, and to the northwest as far as the Volga River.

From the 13th to the 15th century, this enormous realm was simply known as the *ulus*, or khanate, of the Jochids— that is, the state or nation that belonged to Batu and all the descendants of Jochi. But ever since the 16th century, it has been known as the realm of the Golden Horde, after Russian chroniclers started naming the khanate the Zolotaia Orda, or the Golden Camp.

Of the four khanates of the Mongol Empire, the Golden Horde was destined to survive the longest, well into the 16th century. Smaller Mongol successor states persisted long after this again, well into the 18th and even 19th centuries. The Golden Horde is the subject of this lecture, the last in our survey of the four khanates the Mongol Empire was divided into following the death of Mongke Khan.

Throughout the long history of the Golden Horde, the Mongols were decidedly in the minority in their enormous realm. When Chinggis Khan originally divided the empire amongst his sons before his death, he apportioned to the Jochids some 9,000 soldiers and the families that supported them. If we assume an average of five persons per household, that would mean a maximum of 45,000 Mongols.

The population of the khanate of the Golden Horde included Greeks, Armenians, Russians, Jews, and Italians, but by far the greatest percentage consisted of various Turkic-speaking semi-nomadic groups who had made the steppes their own: the Kipchaks, the Cuman, and the Bulgars. This made a degree of Turkification of the Mongols inevitable and even quite rapid. Evidence of this can be seen in the fact that by as early as the 1280s, during the reign of Tode Mongke, Turkish script had replaced Mongolian on Mongol coins.

Batu chose to make the lower reaches of the Volga River the administrative center of his realm. The left bank of the river in particular was an ideal place to establish his large camp, surrounded by the camps of his nomadic followers and troops. During the spring and summer, the nomads could graze their herds extensively within the river valley north as far as the modern Russian city of Saratov. And during the winter months, they could graze in the enormous delta grasslands of the Volga to the south, a region known as Astrakhan.

Although he generally preferred to remain in his camp, in the early 1250s, Batu had a capital city constructed at Sarai in the Volga Delta. The location of Sarai was important because the Lower Volga was central to transregional land and river trade. Batu and his successors, like all Mongol princes throughout the empire, did their best to encourage commerce every way they could, including granting all sorts of privileges and tax concessions to the mostly Muslim merchants.

The wealth that flowed through the realm of the Golden Horde as a result of thriving trade meant that the region recovered quite quickly from the devastation of the previous Mongol invasion. Even the Persian historian Minhaj-i-Sarif Juzjani—who, unlike Juvaini and Rashid al-Din, was no apologist for the Mongols—wrote in his major work the *Tabaqat-i-Nasiri* that "Batu was a just ruler and a friend of the Muslims."

Batu also enjoyed the role as kingmaker within his realm, granting regional authority to various local rulers such as Yaroslav II of the city of Vladimir, who was given the right to rule over all the city-states of Kievan Rus. This was just the beginning of an almost feudal relationship that Batu established with many Russian princes who all now acknowledged Batu as their supreme ruler and personally went to his camp to pay their respects.

As Batu's power and influence expanded, his relationship with Guyuk Khan deteriorated. Sorkaktani, the widow of Chinggis Khan's youngest son, Tolui, and an ally of Batu, warned Batu that Guyuk was planning to destroy him. Guyuk indeed summoned Batu to appear before him, but Batu hesitated, and Guyuk died before the meeting could take place. Following the death of Guyuk, Batu could have moved to assert his own claims to be elected great khan, but he was apparently happy in his realm and supported the regency of Oghul Qaimish. He later helped promote the claims of Mongke, who was elected great khan in 1251. During the reign of Mongke, Batu's prestige and reputation as kingmaker reached its zenith. He ruled his vast *ulus* well and left a thriving state to his younger brother Berke. When the force of nature that was Batu Khan died in 1255, aged just 48, it would be Berke's job to guide the fortunes of the Jochid *ulus* into the post-dissolution phase of the Mongol Empire.

Actually, Berke was the third in line for succession, but Batu's oldest son, Sartaq, and grandson Ulagchi had both passed away under mysterious circumstances. By the time he assumed the throne in 1257, Berke was a mature and experienced leader. He was also a Muslim, and although the deeper effects of this were not felt in his lifetime, perhaps the most historically significant decision Berke made was to turn the Golden Horde into a Muslim state. Many historians credit Berke as the true founder of the Golden Horde. As Istfan Vasary, a noted specialist on the Golden Horde, puts it, "Batu created the framework of the empire while Berke organized the Golden Horde into an actual state."

An important part of the administration of the Mongol Empire undertaken by Mongke Khan was an empire-wide census that was conducted between 1252 and 1259 to better regulate the collection of taxes. The Jochids supported this census, but the officials appointed by Mongke to carry out the census met stiff opposition within the Russian states of the Golden Horde. Some census officials were assassinated, but with the support of Berke, eventually the Russians were brought under control, and taxation within the Golden Horde was regulated.

With the administration of his state in good order, in 1262, Berke started a war with Hulagu and the Ilkhanate in the south. Some sources see a religious motivation in this, that the Muslim Berke attacked Hulagu because he had executed the Abbasid caliph. But this was more about territory than ideology; Berke was intent upon taking control of lush grasslands in parts of Azerbaijan and Iran that he believed had been granted to the Jochids by Chinggis Khan himself. Hulagu pushed back and invaded parts of the Jochid realm. An uneasy stalemate ensued with the Caucasus Mountains becoming the front line between the two states.

To break the stalemate, Berke agreed to an alliance with Sultan Baybars, the leader of the Mamluks of Egypt. The sultan agreed that an alliance made sense because both men were defenders of the true faith. This meant that a military alliance was now established between one Mongol khanate and former enemies against another Mongol khanate. To his Muslim populace, Berke used the religious argument to justify the alliance with Muslims against fellow Mongols, but to his Mongol populace, he used a more traditional argument claiming Hulagu had contravened the laws of the Yasa in seizing Jochid steppeland and killing Jochid commanders.

As a result of the alliance between Berke and Sultan Baybars, diplomatic exchanges became regular between Egypt and the Golden Horde, and a second front was opened in the war with the Ilkhanate.

Ilkhan Hulagu died in 1265, and his sons immediately took up the war with the Jochids. Berke led his forces into battle with Hulagu's son and successor Abaqa near the modern city of Tbilisi, but just as the armies were about to engage, Berke died. He was succeeded two years later by Mongke Temur, a descendant of Batu. Mongke Temur proclaimed to the rest of the Mongol world the de facto independence of the Golden Horde by being the first khan to issue silver and copper coins in his own name.

The Golden Horde's support for trade continued under Mongke Temur, particularly after he signed a peace agreement with Ilkhan Abaqa that lasted from 1268 to 1269. Italian merchants from rival city-states Venice and Genoa now expanded commercial colonies in Crimea, on the shores of the Black Sea. These functioned as transit stations for the movement of high-value goods such as silk, spices, and slaves from central Asia on towards Europe.

The most important of these Crimean trade colonies was Kaffa, the modern city of Feodosiya. The Venetians controlled Kaffa initially, but their old rivals the Genoese drove them out. The capital of Sarai also thrived under Mongke Temur. There was so much commercial activity in the Golden Horde that separate merchant quarters were established in the city, for Venetians and Genoese certainly, but also for traders from Armenia, Persia, and Mamluk Egypt.

During the détente with the Ilkhanate, Jochid forces returned to eastern Europe to raid and pillage in Hungary and Poland. The Kingdom of Bulgaria, which had submitted to the Mongols during their earlier invasion of eastern Europe, remained loyal to the Golden Horde, permitting Mongol armies to pass through its territory to bypass the Byzantine Empire, and even allowing the Mongols to occasionally meddle in internal Bulgarian succession matters. Mongol armies also assisted Russian forces in campaigns against Teutonic Knights and armies from Lithuania.

Mongke Temur died in 1280 and was succeeded by his younger brother Toda Mongke. But Toda was an ineffectual ruler, and seven years later, he abdicated in favor of his nephew Tole Buqa. Both khans were easily manipulated by Noghai, an emir who now emerged as the new power of the Golden Horde. Noghai was a lesser Jochid prince who had distinguished himself in military campaigns against the ilkhans in the 1260s and on campaigns though Bulgaria and into the fringes of the Byzantine Empire. He had worked closely with Berke, but by the time of the khan's death had become a semi-autonomous ruler controlling his own lands between the Don and Dnieper Rivers.

Noghai was a clever strategic thinker who came to play a key role in political affairs in Hungary and the Balkans. Byzantine emperor Michael VIII Palaiologos was so impressed with Noghai that he married his daughter Euphrosyne to Noghai in 1272. The alliance proved useful to the Byzantines because Noghai later used Mongol troops to crush an anti-Byzantine revolt in Thessaly. Noghai also became the key power in the relationship between the Bulgars and the Byzantines.

In the two decades following the death of Mongke Temur, Noghai exploited the weaker khans of the Golden Horde to such an extent that by 1286, he was even issuing coins in his own name. Noghai had converted to Islam in 1270, and he used this ideological shift in an attempt to reignite the alliance with the Mamluks against the Ilkhanids. But Sultan Baybars was now less inclined to become involved in Mongol politics and demurred. The wars between the Jochids and ilkhans continued, nonetheless. Although there were no major victories on either side, Noghai's strategic and military experience ensured that Ilkhan Abaqa was unable to make any significant gains of territory.

Although Noghai was the real power behind the throne, during the reign of Toda Mongke, significant religious and cultural changes occurred in the Golden Horde that were largely beyond Noghai's control. Tode Mongke was apparently a devout Muslim who preferred the mystical Sufi strain of Islam, although many other religious leaders and experts were also welcomed in his court. Conversions were not forced upon the populace, but many Mongols and Turks did eventually convert to Islam.

Turkic language also gradually supplanted Mongol during the reign of Toda Mongke. Mongolian was still used in court, but as noted earlier, Turkic inscriptions now appeared on Golden Horde coinage, and Turkic dialects such as Kipchak and Uyghur became the everyday lingua franca. As Tim May reminds us, by the reign of Toda Mongke, a whole generation had passed since the Mongol Empire had splintered, so fewer and fewer Mongols were arriving from the east to "refresh the Mongolian identity."

Kingmaker Noghai replaced Toda Mongke with Tole Buqa in 1287. Noghai's personal realm was now so powerful and independent that the Russian subjects of the Golden Horde believed Noghai was the true khan. Bulgarian elites would deal only with Noghai, and many other European rulers also assumed that Noghai was the ruler of the Golden Horde. Khan Tole Buqa decided enough was enough and tried to raise troops against Noghai, which led to civil war between the two factions. Noghai appointed Toqta, the son of Mongke Temur, to lead the fight against Tole Buqa, but in 1291, Toqta executed the khan and claimed the throne for himself.

For the first few years of his reign, Toqta was happy to allow Noghai to rule his own lands and pursue his own strategic interests. But as Toqta grew older and more assertive, he gradually built his own strategic alliances to form a powerful coalition against Noghai, including marrying a Byzantine princess of his own. By 1297, the Golden Horde had devolved into open civil war again.

The war lasted for years and was incredibly violent and disruptive, affecting both nomadic and sedentary populations of the khanate. Toqta fought to regain control of Noghai's realm between the Don and Dnieper Rivers, while Noghai fought for his lands and his powerful position within the Golden Horde. The ultimate showdown between the two occurred in the either 1299 or 1300 at Kugenlik. Noghai died on the battlefield, and Toqta emerged victorious as the sole khan of the Golden Horde.

Toqta now strengthened the central authority of the khan by moving to reassert control over various merchant communities, particularly those established by Genoese on the Black Sea coast. As Toqta saw it, not only were the Genoese essentially allies of the ilkhans, but they were also arrogant in their dealings with Mongols, even capturing Mongol children and selling them into slavery.

Determined to teach them a lesson, in 1307, Toqta arrested Genoese merchants in Sarai and confiscated their goods, and also sacked the well-defended town of Kaffa after an eight-month siege, driving out the Genoese. But trade was too important for the Golden Horde for this situation to last long, and he soon invited the merchants back to their cities, although he felt he had made the point to them about who was actually in charge of their activities.

Toqta's long reign of 22 years stabilized the Golden Horde. He intervened in small-scale civil wars between the various Rus princes, who generally welcomed these interventions and his support. The reign of Toqta also benefitted from a general peace that prevailed between all the khanates, a new phase of the Pax Mongolica in which diplomatic contacts and trade flourished across Eurasia. It was the stable and prosperous reign of Toqta that made possible the subsequent Golden Age of the Golden Horde, which reached its zenith during the 30-year reign of Toqta's nephew Ozbeg Khan.

Ozbeg, who ruled from 1312 to 1342, was an energetic and clear-headed ruler who managed domestic and foreign affairs with intelligence and efficiency. He was by all accounts a devout Muslim, and under him, the Islamization of the Jochid khanate continued amongst both the elites and the common Mongols until the Golden Horde truly became part of the Dar al-Islam. Yet even now, a century after the death of Chinggis Khan, and despite Ozbeg's absolute commitment to Islam, the Mongols generally maintained their policy of religious tolerance, and, as Vasary puts it, "the non-Muslim communities, especially the Orthodox and the Catholics, were able to live undisturbed for the most part."

The reign of Ozbeg also had a favorable impact on the fortunes of the Russian princes. The most important position of authority in the Russian world was that of the grand prince of the city of Vladimir, and since the advent of the Golden Horde, the right to bestow this position had belonged to the Mongol khan. This led to intense diplomatic jockeying to gain the favor of the khan, and also to all sorts of corrupt behavior amongst the princes themselves.

In the 1320s, the grand prince of Moscow was appointed grand prince of Vladimir by Ozbeg, which gave him the right to collect the taxes his fellow princes owed to the Mongols. Because the grand prince was permitted to keep a share of the tax revenue, this meant that his status and his wealth grew exponentially, as did the fortunes of his home city of Moscow.

Although some historians, such as Golden Horde specialist Charles Halperin, have argued that "Russia itself was peripheral to the Horde, not only geographically but also politically and economically," most today believe that the rule of the Golden Horde was instrumental in the rise of Moscow and of the strengthening of the Russian state that followed.

Vasary is representative of this view in arguing that "this economic revival of northeastern Russia paved the way for the political rise of Muscovy in the following centuries."

With the death of Ozbeg in 1342, his son Tinibeg came to the throne, only to die mysteriously a few months later and be replaced by his brother Janibeg, who ruled until 1357. Janibeg soon found himself involved in a violent struggle that broke out between Italian and Muslim merchants in the Black Sea trading city of Tana, which escalated into violent street brawls. Determined to protect his Muslim populations, Janibeg prepared to besiege the city of Kaffa, to which both Venetian and Genovese merchants had fled in the aftermath.

The Mongols had sacked Kaffa before, but this was to be a far more serious siege because the Genoese had greatly strengthened the city's defenses and also destroyed a small Mongol navy a few years earlier. This meant they could easily flee the city by ship across the Black Sea were it to fall to Janibeg. The siege dragged on from 1346 into 1347, with both sides negotiating for favorable terms to end it. But then, in one of the most famous incidents in the long history of siege warfare, the conflict took an extraordinary turn when the Mongols started using their catapults to fire dead human bodies across the walls and into the streets of the city.

Now, to be completely honest, we have no way of knowing if the reports of this startling new tactic are completely correct. As Tim May puts it, "it is bizarre enough to be fiction, yet a pragmatic enough action to be accurate." Sometime in the mid-14th century, bubonic plague had broken out in parts of the Mongol realm, carried by fleas who lodged on animals and humans, and it was dead bodies infected with plague that the Mongols now decided to fire into the Italians as an early example of biological warfare.

The Genoese residents of Kaffa were terrified as these diseased bodies covered in puss and blisters fell amongst them, and immediately took to their ships and sailed back across the Black Sea to Constantinople, from where the disease quickly spread to Egypt and Sicily. Jack Weatherford argues that the closed confines of the ships was the perfect incubator for the plague. As he puts it, "freed from the comparatively slow movement on the trading routes, where the disease had to wait for precisely the right cart or cargo of goods, the plague spread with the speed of the wind in its sails."

By early 1348, the Black Death had devastated Italy, and it arrived in England by June of that same year. In the end, Europe lost a total of 25 million humans to the plague, between a third and a half of the total population. The worldwide political, economic, and social impacts of the Black Death of the mid-14th century have been well documented and are beyond the scope of this lecture. But as we consider all the extraordinary ways the Mongols influenced the subsequent course of world history, the role of the Mongol Empire in facilitating the spread of the disease across Eurasia was surely one of the most profound.

Janibeg spent the rest of his life as khan of the Golden Horde dealing with plague and various other problems that arose. In the final year of his reign, 1357, he briefly enjoyed a triumph that had eluded the khans of the Golden Horde ever since Berke: He finally captured the lush pastures of Azerbaijan from the ilkhans. But the Ilkhanate was already in serious decline by this stage, and Janibeg only had a brief moment to celebrate this victory before he died on the return journey to Sarai.

The Golden Horde itself now fell into anarchy. During the two decades between 1359 and 1380, some 25 different khans claimed the throne. As Vasary puts it, "intrigue, murder and usurpation became commonplace." The coins issued by the various pretenders tell a sorry tale of anarchy. Between November 1360 and October 1361, for example, silver coins were minted in the capital Sarai by six different khans.

Geographically, too, the empire began to fall apart. Lithuania expanded its territory at the expense of the Mongols, even taking control of the great city of Kiev. In the south, the city of Urgench in Khwarazm, on the banks of the Amu Darya, broke away from the Golden Horde, as did the Volga Bulgars. Italian and Genoese merchants in the Crimea ceased paying their taxes to the Horde.

The embryonic Russian state also increased its power and autonomy during this period, particularly during the reign of Dmitri Donskoi between 1362 and 1389. Dmitri also stopped paying tribute to the Golden Horde. Current Golden Horde ruler Mamai responded by sending a punitive force against him in 1373, which Dmitri defeated. More conflicts followed until the matter came to a head in September 1380. An allied Russian army headed south from Moscow, crossed the Don, and decisively defeated Mongol forces on the field of Kulikovo. This was the first Russian victory over the Mongols in more than 150 years, since their troops had first been defeated by armies fighting under Chinggis Khan himself back in 1223.

Despite these various calamities, this was not the end of the Golden Horde, nor of Mongol rule of vast regions of Eurasia. As we will see in a group of lectures towards the end of this course, Jochid fortunes were revived under the capable leadership of Toqtamish, until he was dragged into a life-and-death struggle with the emerging regional ruler named Timur, also called Timur-i Lang, or Tamerlane in the West.

Although not a Chinggisid prince, Timur claimed descent from Chinggis Khan through marriage, and after his epic struggle with Toqtamish went on to create his own enormous Timurid Empire. Chinggis Khan undoubtedly deserves the title of the greatest conqueror in world history, but one could mount a strong argument that Timur runs a close second.

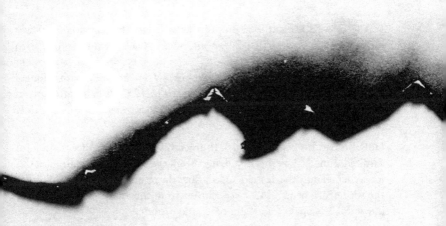

THE PAX MONGOLICA:
EURASIA RECONNECTED

In April of 1246, Friar John of Plano Carpini, an envoy dispatched by Pope Innocent IV to the court of Guyuk Khan, arrived at the camp of Batu, khan of the Golden Horde. The envoy's journal provides one of the first accounts by a European of conditions inside the Mongol empire during the Pax Mongolica, or Mongol Peace. Despite ongoing conflict between the four khanates, the overall effect of the Pax Mongolica was to create conditions of stability and genuine security that made it possible for papal envoys, merchants, missionaries, and adventurers to travel from one end of Eurasia to the other in relative safety.

Early Interactions

Friar Carpini's journey was probably not the first interaction Europeans had with the Mongol world. Eight years earlier in 1238, Matthew of Paris mentions an embassy that arrived from somewhere in the Middle East to ask both the King of France and the King of England for their assistance against the Mongols. These envoys might have come from the Nizari Assassins, who were facing an existential threat from Hulagu. It is difficult to verify the existence of this embassy. If the Assassins did approach European monarchs for aid, their pleas fell on deaf ears. Few in Western Europe would have even heard of the Mongols in 1238, let alone be concerned about them.

In the mid-13th century, European knowledge of Asia in general was minimal. Probably the first European to bring back accurate information about the Mongols was Friar Julian of Hungary, who was twice sent as an envoy of the Hungarian King Bela IV to intercede with Mongol commanders. He went in 1234 and again in 1237. Julian's attempts at diplomacy failed, and Batu's destruction of the city-states of Rus certainly made European leaders sit up and take notice.

Holy Roman Emperor Frederick II urged his fellow heads of state to form a united front against this new danger from the east. However, his plea was ignored, and only the death of Ogedai and the return of most Mongols from the western front in 1242 saved Europe from the awful penalty it would inevitably have paid for its ignorance and disunity.

Innocent IV's Envoys

The destruction of Hungary and Poland at the hands of the Mongols was nonetheless a severe wakeup call, particularly as European leaders had no way of knowing when or if the Mongols would return in force. Once Innocent IV was elected pope in 1243, he decided to take action. After discussing the matter at the Council of Lyon in 1245, he dispatched envoys to the Mongols.

Two Dominican embassies were sent to the Middle East to make contact with the Mongols, but neither enjoyed much success. But a third mission, led by Friar John of Plano Carpini, followed a more northerly route. The mission made it to the camp of Batu and eventually across the Mongol empire to the camp of Guyuk, just in time to see him enthroned as Great Khan.

Carpini was impressed with Batu and with Guyuk, and with the hospitable manner in which he and his colleagues were received throughout the empire. Guyuk wanted to send Mongol envoys back to Europe with Carpini's party on their return, but Carpini, accurately judging the hostile attitude of his fellow Europeans, demurred.

Guyuk sent a letter to the pope instead, demanding that he and other European leaders present themselves at his court and make their formal submission to the Mongols. Although Carpini gathered useful information about Mongol political and military organization, this was hardly a reassuring outcome.

William of Rubruck's Travels

A year after Carpini's return, King Louis IX of France, in preparation for a crusade he was about to lead in Egypt, received ambassadors from a Mongol general who commanded Mongol forces in the Middle East. The Mongols proposed some sort of alliance with Louis's crusading forces against the Muslims, but any such possibility fell apart after the death of Guyuk and the subsequent struggle for political power that consumed the Mongol world. This experience put Louis off dispatching any more formal embassies, so when a Flemish Franciscan monk named William of Rubruck decided to travel deep into the Mongol empire, he did so with Louis's blessing but at his own expense.

Rubruck decided to undertake his mission to the Mongols primarily in the hope of converting them to Christianity. He set out in 1253 and, like Carpini, traveled through the realm of the Golden Horde then on across central Asia. Rubruck compiled detailed reports of many aspects of Mongol life, including their religious and funeral practices, the functioning of Nestorian and Buddhist communities within the empire, and food and alcohol preferences.

Marco Polo's Travels

The next European to travel deep into the Mongol empire would become the most famous of all, Marco Polo. He was born in 1254 into a successful Venetian commercial family. His father, Niccolò, and uncle, Maffeo, established successful partnerships in Constantinople and the Middle East. In 1260, alert to a significant political change they saw coming in the Byzantine Empire, they liquidated their assets in Constantinople where they were living, invested in jewels, and traveled to the Volga River heartland of the Golden Horde, then under the control of Berke Khan.

Berke was very pro-commerce, and the Polos became successful businessmen within the Golden Horde. When political developments in Venice made it unwise for them to return home, they decided to travel eastward instead, deeper into the Mongol realm. They eventually went all the way to Beijing where, according to Marco Polo's later account, they met with Qubilai Khan himself. Niccolò and Maffeo Polo then returned to Venice, where in 1269 they met for the first time the 15-year-old Marco.

Two years later Niccolò, Maffeo and Marco Polo set out from Acre with holy oil and a letter from the pope. They were traveling back to the court of Qubilai Khan. They originally planned to make the journey by sea, but the unseaworthiness of the ships they found at the Persian Gulf port of Hormuz convinced them that an overland journey would be safer. They followed the ancient Silk Roads route across Persia, central Asia, and western China, eventually arriving after many adventures at the palace of Qubilai Khan in 1275, some four years after they had set out.

Now 21, Marco had acquired several languages and a great deal of useful information on the journey, and Qubilai apparently recruited him into his household staff as an adviser. According to Marco, he personally undertook several diplomatic missions for the khan in southern China. The Polos finally left China 17 years after serving as escorts for a Yuan princess named Kokejin, who Qubilai sent to become wife to Ilkhan Arghun. After an epic two-year voyage from China to Hormuz, they duly passed on the princess to the Ilkhan before arriving home in 1295.

Marco Polo and his brothers presenting the pope's letter to Qubilai Khan

Marco's Account

Scholars have struggled for centuries to make sense of the account of his journey that Marco later dictated to a cellmate. (He was thrown in jail in Genoa some years later.) His positive description of the sophisticated civilization in China seemed in stark contrast to Carpini's and Rubruck's accounts of the so-called barbarian Mongols. Scholars also wondered why, if Marco did visit China, he never mentioned the Great Wall, nor the drinking of tea, nor the use of chopsticks, nor indeed the practice of foot-binding, which was widely practiced among Chinese women during the period.

More recently, historians have been increasingly reassured by the level of accurate detail in Marco's account and the limited number of extraordinary or impossible fables he includes. Indeed, as more details have become known about administration, currency, and taxation in the Mongol khanates, Marco's account is seen as increasingly accurate. Historians also point out that Marco spent his time with Mongols in China, and Mongols did not drink tea or use chopsticks, let alone bind the feet of their independent young women.

John of Montecorvino

As the Polos were sailing back across the Indian Ocean from China, another European, John of Montecorvino, was just arriving in the Yuan capital of Khanbaliq (modern Beijing). John, who was born in 1247, was a dedicated Franciscan missionary who spent much of his life working as an envoy for both the Byzantine emperor and the pope.

He came to the attention of Ilkhan Arghun, who asked the pope to send a Catholic mission to Khanbaliq to meet with Qubilai Khan. Pope Nicholas IV commissioned John of Montecorvino to undertake this epic journey. Duly armed with letters from the pope to most of the leading Mongol rulers—Ilkhan Arghun, Khan Qaidu of the Chagatayid khanate, and Qubilai Khan himself—John set out from Persia in 1289 accompanied by a small entourage.

Pope Nicholas IV

John's party sailed across the Arabian Sea to Madras in India. After spending more than a year preaching in India, John sailed on again from Bengal to China, arriving in 1294 just as the Polos were returning home in Venice, but also just after the death of Qubilai. The new khan Temur was no fan of Christianity, but he did not impede John and his party, allowing them to stay in Khanbaliq despite the objections of the Nestorian Christians who were already well established there.

By 1299, John had built his first church in the capital, and within six years he had constructed a second, much larger and more conspicuously located Catholic complex in front of the gates of the imperial palace itself. John took his missionary activities seriously, instructing hundreds of boys in Greek and Latin and training them to serve in Catholic masses.

He also mastered the Uyghur language that was widely spoken among the Mongols in the city, and even had the New Testament translated into Uyghur. He later claimed to have converted some 6,000 Chinese and other peoples to Catholicism. John was eventually promoted to the position of bishop of Khanbaliq after sending detailed reports of his activities back to Rome in 1305 and 1306. John continued his missionary work in Khanbaliq for another two decades, eventually dying in his adopted city in 1328.

Rabban Sawma

So far, this lecture has considered envoys who made journeys eastward from Europe into the Mongol empire before, in most cases, returning home. However, there was at least one extraordinary individual who made the journey in the opposite direction, a cleric named Rabban Sawma.

Rabban Sawma was born in approximately 1220 into a wealthy family in the city that became Khanbaliq. Some sources suggest he was a Uyghur, others a member of a Turkic tribe allied with the Mongols. In his early 20s, he abandoned his wealth and became an ascetic monk in the Nestorian Christian faith.

Several decades later, Sawma and one of his younger students decided to undertake a pilgrimage to Jerusalem, traveling along the old Silk Roads routes. But once they entered the lands controlled by the ilkhans, they were dissuaded from traveling on through the Crusades-ravaged Middle East. They were later sent by the Nestorian patriarch to the court of Ilkhan Arghun as the patriarch's envoys.

Arghun was involved in a two-front war with the Golden Horde and the Mamluks, so he decided in 1287 to send the now-67-year-old Sawma on a mission to Europe as his envoy. The hope was that he might be able to secure some strategic alliances with European leaders against the Mamluks in Egypt.

Sawma was accompanied by a large retinue of aides, including translators, a representative from a leading Genoese bank, and some 30 horses. He traveled overland through Armenia to the Black Sea, then by ship to Constantinople, where he was greatly impressed by the magnificent Hagia Sophia. Sailing on to Italy, he even reported on an eruption of Mount Etna that happened to occur on June 18, 1287, as he passed through the Straits of Messina.

Hagia Sophia

The next stop for Sawma was Rome, but the pope had just died, so Sawma had discussions with the cardinals instead before wintering in Genoa. Early in 1288, he traveled on to Paris, where he stayed for a month with King Philip the Fair. The king seems to have genuinely taken to the traveling cleric, giving him presents and agreeing to send some of his representatives back to Khanbaliq when Rabban Sawma returned.

The French region of Gascony was under English control in 1288, but this did not prevent Rabban Sawma from traveling on to Bordeaux for an audience with the English King Edward I, who even celebrated mass with the Mongol envoy. By Palm Sunday of 1288, Sawma was back in Rome, enjoying communion with the newly elected Pope Nicholas IV. Thereafter, Rabban Sawma made his return to Baghdad late in 1288. He spent most of the rest of his life in that city, where he wrote and published his account of his travels.

King Edward I

THE PAX MONGOLICA: EURASIA RECONNECTED

LECTURE 18 TRANSCRIPT

In April of 1246, Friar John of Plano Carpini, an envoy dispatched by Pope Innocent IV to the court of Guyuk Khan, arrived at the camp of Batu, khan of the Golden Horde and scion of Chinggis Khan's eldest son, Jochi. This is how Carpini describes his audience with Batu:

> This Batu holds his court right magnificently, for he has door-keepers and all the other officials like unto their Emperor. He sits also in a raised place, as on a throne, with one of his wives. But everyone else of his family, as well as his brothers and sons as others of lesser degree, sit lower down on a bench in the middle of the tent. He has tents made of linen. They are large and quite handsome, and used to belong to the King of Hungary. When we had stated our object we took a seat to the left, for thus do all the ambassadors. In the middle of the dwelling near the door is a table, on which is placed drink in gold and silver vases; and Batu never drinks, nor does any prince of the Mongols, especially when they are in public, without there being singing and guitar playing. This Batu is kind enough to his own people, but he is greatly feared by them. He is, however, most cruel in fight; he is very shrewd and extremely crafty in warfare, for he has been waging war for a long time.

Carpini's journal provides one of the first accounts we have by a European of conditions inside the Mongol Empire during the Pax Mongolica. Despite ongoing conflict between the four khanates, the overall effect of the Mongol Peace was to create conditions of stability and genuine security that made it possible for papal envoys, merchants, missionaries, and just plain old adventurers to travel from one end of Eurasia to the other in relative safety.

The Pax Mongolica also facilitated the transfer of many material goods and intellectual ideas from Yuan China in the east to the Ilkhanate, and eventually on to Europe, and these cultural transfers are arguably of even greater consequence than the journals produced by various travelers. We will return to these cultural exchanges in the final lecture of the course as we try and assess the impact of the Mongols on world history.

But in this lecture, we follow in the footsteps of a ragtag group of travelers who gave Europeans their first glimpse of the extraordinary cultural diversity of Asia under Mongol hegemony.

Friar Carpini's journey was probably not the first interaction Europeans had with the Mongol world. Eight years earlier in 1238, Matthew of Paris mentions an embassy that arrived from somewhere in the Middle East to ask both the king of France and the king of England for their assistance against the Mongols. These envoys might have come from the Nizari Assassins, who, as you might remember, were facing an existential threat from Hulagu. It is difficult to verify the existence of this embassy—Matthew's is the only reference we have to it—but some numismatic evidence does seem to support it.

If the Assassins did approach European monarchs for aid, their pleas fell on deaf ears. Few in Western Europe would have even heard of the Mongols in 1238, let alone be concerned about them. But Batu and Subedei had just begun their destructive campaign against the princedoms of Rus, so it would not be long before Mongol hordes would come storming into Hungary and Poland, smashing any ignorance or sense of complacency European rulers might have held.

It is fair to say that in the mid-13th century, European knowledge of Asia in general was minimal. Despite the operation of the Silk Roads exchange networks on and off for 1,200 years by this point, merchants in the center of Eurasia—like the Kushans, Parthians, Sogdians, and Turks—had done their best to ensure that the two ends of the network never met, thus safeguarding their monopolies and sources of wealth. Only with the advent of the Mongol Empire was Eurasia genuinely unified for the first time in history, making it possible for intrepid travelers to make epic journeys from Europe to China and back again. However, although they produced detailed, first-hand reports on what they found there, they were not always believed by European audiences, as Marco Polo found out to his chagrin.

One example of just how profound European and Russian ignorance was of the Mongols can be read in the utter shock Russian chroniclers felt at the sudden appearance of Mongol soldiers in their midst during Chinggis Khan's Khwarazm campaign 15 years before Batu's and Subedei's invasion. Back in 1223, the Mongol generals Jebe and Subedei had encountered a Russian army camped on the Kalka River and utterly destroyed it. The Russians were completely in the dark as to who the Mongols were and where they had come from.

Probably the first European to bring back accurate information about the Mongols was Friar Julian of Hungary, who was twice sent as an envoy of the Hungarian King Bela IV to intercede with Mongol commanders, in 1234 and again in 1237. Julian's attempts at diplomacy failed, and Batu's destruction of the city-states of Rus certainly made European leaders sit up and take notice. We know this because a number of letters now began to circulate between concerned kings, princes, and religious leaders, letters that Matthew of Paris preserved in his *Chronica Majora*.

The author of one of these letters was none other than the Holy Roman Emperor himself, Frederick II, who urged his fellow heads of state to form a united front against this new danger from the east. This was the same monarch Batu would later send a letter to insolently demanding that Frederick step down from the throne because Batu was about to usurp it. Frederick's plea for a united European front against the Mongols was ignored, and only the death of Ogedai and the return of most Mongols from the western front in 1242 saved Europe from the awful penalty it would inevitably have paid for its ignorance and disunity.

The destruction of Hungary and Poland at the hands of the Mongols, not to mention the death of tens of thousands of European knights, was nonetheless a severe wake-up call, particularly as European leaders had no way of knowing when or if the Mongols would return in force. Once Innocent IV was elected pope in 1243, he decided to take action. After discussing the matter at the Council of Lyon in 1245, he dispatched envoys to the Mongols.

Two Dominican embassies were sent to the Middle East to make contact with the Mongols, but neither enjoyed much success. But a third mission, led by the Franciscan friar John Carpini, followed a more northerly route, and not only made it to the camp of Batu, but eventually a long way across the Mongol Empire to the camp of Guyuk, just in time to see him enthroned as great khan.

Carpini was impressed with Batu and with Guyuk, and with the hospitable manner in which he and his colleagues were received throughout the empire. Of Guyuk, he wrote: "This emperor is maybe forty or forty-five years old.

He is of medium stature, very prudent and extremely shrewd, and serious and sedate in his manners; and he has never been seen to laugh lightly or show any levity."

Guyuk wanted to send Mongol envoys back to Europe with Carpini's party on their return, but Carpini, accurately judging the attitude of his fellow Europeans, demurred because "we feared lest they be put to death, as our people for the most part are arrogant and hasty." Guyuk sent a letter to the pope instead, demanding that he and other European leaders present themselves at his court and make their formal submission to the Mongols. So although Carpini gathered all sort of useful information about Mongol political and military organization, this was hardly a reassuring outcome.

A year after Carpini's return, King Louis IX of France, in preparation for a crusade he was about to lead in Egypt, received ambassadors from Mongol general Eljigedei, the commander of Mongol forces in the Middle East. The Mongols proposed some sort of alliance with Louis's crusading forces against the Muslims, but any such possibility fell apart after the death of Guyuk and the subsequent struggle for political power that consumed the Mongol world. This experience put Louis off dispatching any more formal embassies. So when a Flemish Franciscan monk named William of Rubruck decided to travel deep into the Mongol Empire, he did so with Louis's blessing but at his own expense.

Rubruck had participated in King Louis's crusade and decided to undertake his mission to the Mongols primarily in the hope of converting them to Christianity. He set out in 1253 and, like Carpini, traveled through the realm of the Golden Horde then on across central Asia. Rubruck has the distinction of being the first European to visit the Mongol capital of Karakorum in the Orkhon River Valley of Mongolia. You might remember that he was not particularly impressed with the size of the city, famously declaring it to be no larger than the Parisian suburb of St. Denis.

But Rubruck was a keen observer and something of an anthropologist, and he compiled detailed reports on many aspects of Mongol life: their religious and funeral practices, for example; the functioning of Nestorian and Buddhist communities within the empire; food and alcohol preferences, including the Mongols' penchant for the powerful alcoholic drink made from fermented mare's milk, kumiss; and so much more. Rubruck even got to participate in a religious debate in court and was convinced Mongke Khan was on the verge of converting to Christianity, although in this, he was disappointed. Like his predecessor, Guyuk, Mongke also wrote a letter to be carried back to Europe by Rubruck, addressed to King Louis of France. It read in part:

The commandment of the eternal God is, in Heaven there is only one eternal God, and on earth there is only one lord, Chinggis Khan. This is the sword of the Son of God because Temujin means "sound of iron." Our country is far off, our mountains are strong, our sea is wide, and if in this belief you make war against us, you shall find out what we can do.

Rubruck's account was detailed, accurate, and shrewd, but it was also destined for obscurity. This was a shame because, as David Morgan notes, "it is arguably the most accurate account of the Mongols we have from any European pen." The next European to travel deep into the Mongol world would become the most famous of all, Marco Polo. We have already had much to say about Marco and his observations on Mongol-controlled central Asia and China, but it is worth briefly considering his journey again here.

Marco was born in 1254 into a successful Venetian commercial family. His father and uncle established successful partnerships in Constantinople and the Middle East. In 1260, alert to a significant political change they saw coming in the Byzantine Empire, they liquidated their assets in Constantinople where they were living, invested in jewels, and traveled to the Volga River heartland of the Golden Horde, then under the control of Berke Khan.

As we've seen, Berke was very pro-commerce, and the Polos became successful businessmen within the Golden Horde. When political developments in Venice made it unwise for them to return home, they decided to travel eastwards instead, deeper into the Mongol realm, eventually all the way to Beijing, where, according to Marco Polo's later account, they met with Qubilai Khan himself. The khan gave the Polo brothers a letter to the pope requesting that he send to China 100 Christians with expertise in the sciences and also a quantity of oil from a holy lamp in Jerusalem. Niccolò and Maffeo Polo then returned to Venice, where in 1269 they met for the first time the 15-year-old Marco.

Two years later, Niccolò, Maffeo, and Marco Polo set out from Acre, without the 100 scholars but with the holy oil and a letter from the pope, to travel back to the court of Qubilai Khan. They originally planned to make the journey by sea, but the unseaworthiness of the ships they found at the Persian Gulf port of Hormuz convinced them that an overland journey would be safer. So they followed the ancient Silk Roads route across Persia, central Asia, and western China, eventually arriving after many adventures at the palace of Qubilai Khan in 1275, some four years after they had set out.

Now 21, Marco had acquired several languages and a great deal of useful information on the journey, and Qubilai apparently recruited him into his household staff as an adviser. According to Marco, he personally undertook several diplomatic missions for the khan in southern China. The Polos eventually left China 17 years later, serving as escorts for a Yuan princess named Kokejin, who Qubilai sent to become wife to Ilkhan Arghun. After an epic two-year voyage from China to Hormuz, they duly passed on the princess to the ilkhan before arriving home in 1295. Marco writes that Kokejin was so sad to see them leave that she wept copious tears.

Scholars have struggled for centuries to make sense of the account of this journey that Marco later dictated to a cell mate after he was thrown in jail in Genoa some years later. His positive description of the sophisticated civilization of China seemed in stark contrast to Carpini's and Rubruck's accounts of the "barbarian" Mongols. Scholars also wondered why, if Marco did visit China, he never mentioned the Great Wall, nor the drinking of tea, nor the use of chopsticks, nor indeed the practice of footbinding, which was widely practiced amongst Chinese women during the period.

More recently, historians have been increasingly reassured by the level of accurate detail in Marco's account, and the limited number of extraordinary or impossible fables he includes. Indeed, as more details have become known about administration, currency, and taxation in the Mongol khanates, Marco's account is seen as increasingly accurate. Historians also point out that Marco spent his time with Mongols in China, and Mongols did not drink tea or use chopsticks, let alone bind the feet of their independent young women.

As further confirmation that the Polos did indeed undertake their epic journey, in the 1970s, two independent documents, one Chinese and one Persian, were unearthed that support the account of the Polos' voyage to Hormuz in the company of Princess Kokejin. So I think it safe to include the extraordinary Polo family in our list of Europeans who took advantage of the Pax Mongolica to travel extensively in Eurasia in the 13th century.

As the Polos were sailing back across the Indian Ocean from China, another European, one John of Montecorvino, was just arriving in the Yuan capital of Khanbaliq (modern Beijing). John, who was born in 1247, just one year after Friar John of Plano Carpini's visit to the camp of Batu, was a dedicated Franciscan missionary who spent much of his life working as an envoy for both the Byzantine emperor and the pope, doing what he could to calm the religious discord that existed between the Catholic and Orthodox realms, and also working to spread the faith in the Middle East and Persia.

This brought him to the attention of Ilkhan Arghun, who asked the pope to send a Catholic mission to Khanbaliq to meet with Qubilai Khan. Pope Nicholas IV commissioned John of Montecorvino to undertake this epic journey. Duly armed with letters from the pope to most of the leading Mongol rulers—to Ilkhan Arghun, to Khan Qaidu of the Chagatayid khanate, and to Qubilai Khan himself—John set out from Persia in 1289, accompanied by a small entourage.

Apparently, the vessels they encountered in the Persian Gulf were more seaworthy than those the Polos had inspected 18 years earlier, so John's party sailed across the Arabian Sea to Madras in India. After spending more than a year preaching in India, John sailed on again from Bengal to China, arriving in 1294, just as the Polos were returning home in Venice, but also just after the death of Qubilai. The new khan Temur was no fan of Christianity, but he did not impede John and his party, allowing them to stay in Khanbaliq despite the objections of the Nestorian Christians who were already well established there.

By 1299, John had built his first church in the capital, and within six years, he had constructed a second, much larger and more conspicuously located Catholic complex in front of the gates of the imperial palace itself, complete with a bell tower and three bells. John took his missionary activities seriously, instructing hundreds of boys in Greek and Latin and training them to serve in Catholic masses and sing in the church choir. He also mastered the Uyghur language that was widely spoken amongst the Mongols in the city, and even had the New Testament translated into Uyghur. He later claimed to have converted some 6,000 Chinese and other peoples to Catholicism.

John was eventually promoted to the position of bishop of Khanbaliq after sending detailed reports of his activities back to Rome in 1305 and 1306. The letters make fascinating reading. At one point, he discusses the options for travel from Europe to China early in the 14th century, which provides further evidence of the uneasy relationship between the khanates at that time, blighted by a civil war in the Golden Horde between Toqtu and Noghai, and ongoing campaigns by Ilkhan Ghazan against the Mamluks:

> As for the road hither, I may tell you that the way through the land of the Goths, subject to the emperor of the Northern Tartars [that is, the khan of the Golden Horde] is the shortest and safest; and by it the friars might come in five or six months. The other route again is very long and very dangerous, involving two sea voyages. But on the other hand, the first-mentioned route has not been open for a considerable time, on account of wars that have been going on.

John concludes by expressing his awe for the Mongol emperor of Yuan China: "As far as I ever saw or heard tell, I do not believe that any king or prince in the world can be compared to the majesty of the khan in respect of the extent of his dominions, the vastness of his population, or the amount of his wealth."

John continued his missionary work in Khanbaliq for another two decades, eventually dying in his adopted city in 1328. He was without doubt one of the most effective of the many Christian missionaries who, over the course of the next several centuries, would attempt to convert the Chinese people to Christianity.

So far, we have considered envoys who made journeys eastwards from Europe into the Mongol Empire before, in most cases, returning home. But it was not all one-way traffic, and there was at least one extraordinary individual we know of who made the journey in the opposite direction, a cleric named Rabban Sawma.

Rabban (or Master) Sawma was born into a wealthy family in the city that became Khanbaliq, in the year 1220 or thereabouts. Some sources suggest he was a Uyghur, others a member of a Turkic tribe allied with the Mongols. In his early 20s, he abandoned his wealth and became an ascetic monk in the Nestorian Christian faith.

Several decades later, Sawma and one of his younger students decided to undertake a pilgrimage to Jerusalem, traveling along the old Silk Roads routes. But once they entered the lands controlled by the ilkhans, they were dissuaded from traveling on through the Crusades-ravaged Middle East, and were later sent by the Nestorian patriarch to the court of Ilkhan Arghun instead, as the patriarch's envoys.

It so happened that at this moment, Arghun was involved in a two-front war with the Golden Horde and the Mamluks, so he decided in 1287 to send the now 67-year-old Master Sawma on a mission to Europe as his envoy, in the hope he might be able to secure some strategic alliances with European leaders against the Mamluks in Egypt.

From the detailed account he compiled of his journey to Europe, we know that Sawma was accompanied by a large retinue of aides, including translators, a representative from a leading Genoese bank, and some 30 horses. He traveled overland through Armenia to the Black Sea, then by ship to Constantinople, where he was greatly impressed by the magnificent Hagia Sophia. Sailing on to Italy, he even reported on an eruption of Mount Etna that happened to occur on June 18, 1287, as he passed through the Straits of Messina.

Next stop for Master Sawma was Rome, but the pope had just died, so Sawma had discussions with the cardinals instead before wintering in Genoa. Early in 1288, he traveled on to Paris, where he stayed for a month with King Philip the Fair, who seems to have genuinely taken to the traveling cleric, giving him presents and agreeing to send some of his representatives back to Khanbaliq when Rabban Sawma returned. Philip was good to his word, and two French clerics and a crossbowman, presumably to provide protection, did indeed later accompany Sawma on his journey back to Persia.

The French region of Gascony was under English control in 1288, but this did not prevent Rabban Sawma from traveling on to Bordeaux for an audience with the English king Edward I, who even celebrated mass with the Mongol envoy. Sawma reports that "King Edward gave us many gifts and money for the expenses of the road." By Palm Sunday 1288, Sawma was back in Rome enjoying communion with the newly elected Pope Nicholas IV. Thereafter, Rabban Sawma made his return to Baghdad late in 1288 and spent most of the rest of his life in that city, where he wrote and published his account of his travels.

As Jack Weatherford points out, "Rabban Sawma had probably traveled farther than any official envoy in history, covering some seven thousand miles on the circuitous land route from the Mongol capital, through the major cities of the Middle East, and on to the capitals of Europe." Although the secular and religious elites of Europe received Rabban Sawma openly and hospitably in their courts, he ultimately failed to secure any military alliances between the Ilkhanate and European states. But Sawma does have the distinction of being the most famous envoy the Mongols ever sent to the West, and the account of his travels amongst the Europeans is a nice counter to European observations of the Mongols.

His account also provides further evidence of the religious tolerance of the Mongols, so unlike the attitude of contemporary Europeans. Coming from the religiously diverse Mongol Empire, Rabban Sawma was genuinely shocked by the fact that only the narrow Catholic version of Christianity was tolerated and accepted in Europe. He couldn't help but contrast this with the attitude of his patron, Ilkhan Arghun.

Arghun was a Muslim, of course, but deeply committed to religious tolerance and diversity, as were virtually all of the Mongol khans, beginning with Chinggis. One example of this: Arghun employed a Jewish physician to be his chief adviser despite objections from his Muslim administrators. And despite Arghun's own spiritual loyalties to Islam, Rabban Sawma deeply appreciated Arghun's attitude towards his Christian subjects, which he describes in a chapter entitled "The Good Acts of Khan Arghun." Let me quote from Sawma:

> Arghun set up a church in a tent so close to the door of the throne room that the ropes of the curtains intermingled with those of his house. And he made a great feast which lasted three days, and Arghun himself brought food to the Catholics, and handed the cup of drink to him and all the members of his company. But when the state of affairs which we have mentioned had remained thus for a short time, God removed Khan Arghun to the seat of joys and to the Abrahamic bosom. And at his departure grief fettered the whole Church.

Well, this lecture is nearly over, so I barely have time to mention arguably the greatest Pax Mongolica traveler of all, Ibn Battuta. During a 28-year career of dedicated travel, Battuta visited virtually every Islamic state that existed in the world and all four of the Mongol khanates. Scholars estimate that he traveled some 75,000 miles in his lifetime, many times more than Marco Polo or Rabban Sawma.

Ibn Battuta was born in Morocco, and in 1325, aged 21, he decided to undertake the hajj to Mecca, one of the solemn obligations of all Muslims. But somewhere along the way, Battuta was bitten by the travel bug and spent the next couple of years visiting Cairo, Jerusalem, Damascus, and Medina, finally completing the hajj in 1326.

Next he traveled east through the Ilkhanate, passing through Persia and Iraq before undertaking a sea voyage through the Red Sea, down the East African coast, and across the Arabian Sea. He then spent a year back in Constantinople before traveling by caravan overland along the ancient Silk Roads routes through the realm of the Golden Horde, and also the Chagatayid khanate, where he commented on the vibrancy of some ancient trading cities like Khiva, but also the lack of recovery in others like Bukhara.

He praised the emir of Khiva, who was "untiringly taking care of law and order," and reported that the city was so full of people that it was almost impossible to find one's way in the crowd. But of Bukhara, he wrote "the mosques, colleges and bazaars are in ruins … there is not one person in it today who possesses any learning." Once one of the great intellectual cities of the Islamic world, Bukhara was clearly still struggling to recover from the Mongol devastation that had first occurred during the Khwarazmian campaign of the 1220s, more than a century earlier.

Ibn Battuta journeyed south from central Asia to India, spending some time in Delhi before embarking by ship for China via Sri Lanka and the Maldives. He arrived in Yuan China in 1345 and spent a year visiting all the great port cities, along with Beijing and the Great Wall. Then he sailed back to Hormuz in the Persian Gulf via Sumatra and India.

Traveling through Persia in 1348, he was shocked at how the formerly mighty Ilkhanate was falling apart. He hastened on to Syria, then in the grip of the Black Death. After 28 years of sustained travel, he finally returned to Morocco in 1354 at the age of 49. It was in Tangier that he dictated the account of his travels, the *Rihla*, or *Journey*, which has been a major source for historians ever since.

During the Pax Mongolica, then, Europe, the Islamic world, and Asia were closer than ever before. With vast regions of Eurasia under Mongol law, travelers could undertake epic journeys from Rome or Morocco clear across the continent to China and back again. Frankly, it would never be this easy to cross the Eurasian continent again; imagine the logistical challenges of trying to follow in Ibn Battuta's footsteps today!

But the Pax Mongolica, like all great ages of human history, was fragile, and as Ibn Battuta noted, was already starting to unravel in 1348. In our next lecture, we'll trace the rapid disintegration of the Mongol Empire and the end of the Mongol Peace.

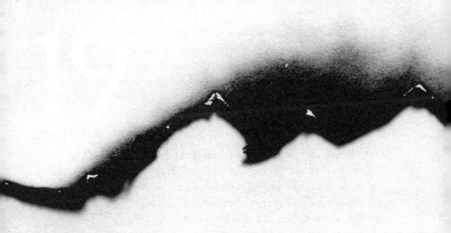

THE COLLAPSE OF THE MONGOL EMPIRES

The disintegration of the Mongol regime is the subject of this lecture. The collapse occurred quickly in the Persian Ilkhanate and Yuan China, in 1335 and 1368 respectively. A much more gradual disintegration of the Chagatayid khanate and the Golden Horde also occurred, as the Mongols splintered into smaller more autonomous units.

Persia

Persia saw a rapid decline of Mongol rule. Ilkhan Abu Said died in 1335. He left no male heir, and no other descendants of Hulagu emerged with the strength or credibility to claim the throne. The Toluid elites within the Ilkhanate elected Arpa Khan, a distant descendant of Ariq Boke who had waged civil war against Qubilai Khan several decades earlier. During his brief reign, rebellions broke out all over the Ilkhanate, and rebel commanders captured and executed Arpa Khan on May 15, 1336, only a year after he had been elected ilkhan.

These rebel commanders were military officers who now revealed their own ambitions for power by trying to find a puppet Chinggisid they could promote to the throne.

The various factions fought bitterly, and in the chaos, eight different Chinggisid princes were promoted to the throne between 1335 and 1344. Each ruled from a different regional base. Centralized power was never restored, which meant that the Ilkhanate effectively ceased to exist with the death of Abu Said in 1335.

China

This lecture turns to Mongol-controlled China next. Qubilai Khan died in February 18, 1294. He had outlived most of his sons, including his designated successor, Jingim, who had died 10 years earlier. The most viable contender was Qubilai's grandson Temur Oljeitu, the son of Jingim, and he was duly elected khan of the Yuan dynasty in 1295.

During the early years of his reign, Temur Oljeitu maintained many of his grandfather's policies and continued the war against the Ogedeid leader Qaidu, who was attacking the western regions of the Yuan Empire. When Qaidu died in 1301, the war petered out.

Undoubtedly the biggest problems Temur faced were fiscal; expenditure had far outpaced income for years, and the Yuan dynasty's coffers were rapidly depleting. This problem was exacerbated by the various intrigues and squabbling that broke out among the Mongol elites in China after Temur died in 1307.

Following the death of his primary wife, Temur had promoted another wife named Buluqan as empress. Various factions emerged during the regency of Buluqan, and in the intense jockeying for power that ensued, violence broke out. In the end, it was a nephew of Temur Oljeitu, Qaishan, who seized the throne because of his sharper military acumen and more widespread support. Under his ineffective rule, the fiscal problems of the empire only worsened.

When Qaishan died in 1311, his younger brother Ayurbarwada assumed the throne, and his first action was to violently purge many of Qaishan's supporters from their positions within government. Ayurbarwada had received a good Confucian education, and he spoke and wrote Chinese. He spent the early years of his reign trying to balance the budget, and he also reintroduced the Confucian civil service exam.

Ayurbarwada's death in 1320, when he was aged just 35, prevented any serious reforms. His 17-year-old son Shidebala assumed the throne without opposition, but he was assassinated three years later. He was followed in 1323 by the older and more experienced Yesun Temur, who tried to calm religious and ethnic tensions within the empire.

After the death of Yesun Temur in 1328, violence again broke out between various contenders. A powerful Kipchak military commander named El Temur emerged as the real power behind the throne, supported by his Merkit chancellor Bayan. The two promoted puppet emperors to the throne like Qoshila, who lasted only six months, and Tuq Temur, who ruled through to 1332. Rebellions broke out at regular intervals, which El Temur and his troops attempted to crush. Instability only worsened when Tuq Temur died without an heir in September 1332, to be replaced by a six-year-old puppet of El Temur who died of illness just 53 days later.

Tuq Temur

Control Disintegrates in China

At this moment, a Chinggisid prince named Toghon Temur, who had been exiled in Korea, returned to take up the throne. And though his reign of 35 years might have indicated a return to stability, it was blighted from the beginning.

Mongol control disintegrated in southern China first, where numerous rebellions broke out. The ancient heartland of Mongolia itself broke away from the Yuan next, because the Yuan royal family was now viewed as more Chinese than Mongol by many conservative Mongols.

Corruption became rampant throughout the bureaucracy. El Temur's former chancellor Bayan led a coup in 1335 and personally took control of government for five years, but his attempts at reform failed. Bayan's nephew subsequently led a coup against him, and Bayan died in exile.

Additionally, a series of natural disasters occurred throughout the empire. Massive floods caused devastation along the Yellow River valley, and then a particularly virulent epidemic of bubonic plague broke out and devasted China between 1353 and 1354.

In the midst of this chaos, a particularly dangerous rebellion broke out in the south in the year 1352, led by a young Buddhist rebel named Zhu Yuanzhang. Called the Red Turban movement for the color of the ribbons they used to tie back their hair, Zhu Yuanzhang's rebel army consistently defeated Mongol forces throughout the 1360s as they drove north. Finally, in 1368, the Red Turbans captured the Yuan capital and drove Toghon Temur and his family out of the palace. After a rule of 98 years, the Yuan dynasty now officially ceased to exist.

The Mongols departed China for good, to return to the steppes from whence they had come. Some scholars estimate that up to 60,000 Mongols

Zhu Yuanzhang

returned to the Mongolian heartland from China, which led to an outbreak of intense intertribal conflicts with those that had remained behind.

In China, meanwhile, Buddhist rebel leader Zhu Yuanzhang, better known to world history by his imperial reign name of Hongwu, quickly established the new Ming dynasty. It would go on to rule China until 1644.

Korea

In Korea, too, the end of Mongol domination had momentous consequences that included a change of dynasties. King Kongmin of the Goryeo dynasty held the throne through the last phase of Mongol rule, from 1351 to 1374. He became the first ruler in more than a century to openly oppose the Mongols, and he was also determined to destroy the power of those Korean families who had been enriching themselves by working closely with the Mongols.

When the Ming dynasty was declared in China in 1368, Kongmin immediately adopted a pro-Ming, anti-Mongol policy. But his decision exacerbated the general chaos that now enveloped the final years of Goryeo rule, even as the Mongols were being driven out.

King Kongmin was assassinated in 1374, and peasant revolts broke out all over the peninsula. The peasants had been bearing a double burden of taxation by the Goryeo state and by the Mongols. Then Japanese pirates known as the *waegu* began raiding the Korean coast, devastating the villages.

As the Mongols retreated northward to the steppe and were no longer a problem for the Goryeo military, two commanders were appointed to lead the Goryeo armed forces against the pirates: Choe Yong and Yi Song-gye. Their success led to both commanders gaining high status and influence in the Goryeo capital. However, the two fell out over the question of whether to attack or support the Chinese Ming dynasty, which had just declared its intention of taking over part of Goryeo's northeastern territory.

While Choe Yong was leading an expedition against the Ming forces, Yi Song-gye, who was pro-Ming, led his forces into the capital and staged a military coup against both Choe Yong and the king. Yi Song-gye quickly established a new dynasty, the Choson dynasty. This was the last dynasty to rule Korea, and it lasted from 1392 until 1910, when Korea was annexed by the rising power of Japan.

The Golden Horde

In the steppes of Russia, meanwhile, the Golden Horde maintained its authority much longer than any of the other khanates. However, by the end of the 14th century, it was clearly also in decline. In 1438, the Golden Horde was divided into two states: the khanates of Kazan and the so-called Great Horde. Another division occurred five years later, leading to the breakaway of two smaller states: the khanates of Astrakhan and of Crimea.

Some historians date the official end of the Golden Horde to the defeat of the Great Horde by Khan Mengli Girai of the Crimean khanate in 1502, particularly as Mengli had previously accepted a position of subordination to the burgeoning empire of the Ottoman Turks in 1475.

Farther north, the expansion of the Russian state under Ivan the Terrible absorbed the khanate of Kazan in 1552 and the khanate of Astrakhan in 1556. But the Crimean khanate managed to remain semi-independent for more than another century, until it was finally annexed by Catherine the Great of Russia in 1783.

The Tatars of Crimea were descendants of the Golden Horde who continued to exist as a discrete community through to the middle of the 20th century. This lasted until May 1944, when Joseph Stalin and his henchman Lavrenty Beria used cattle trains to deport 191,044 Tatars eastward into central Asia and the Siberian steppe.

THE COLLAPSE OF THE MONGOL EMPIRES

LECTURE 19 TRANSCRIPT

As historian John Man reminds us, by 1300, the Mongols were in control of one-sixth of the land area of earth, and one man, Qubilai, the grandson of Mongol founder Chinggis Khan, was nominally master of this enormous realm. But, as we have seen, tensions between the descendants of the four sons of Chinggis Khan led to jealousy, family squabbles, and often outright war. As the various lineages settled into their own khanates, most of them gradually adopted the languages, religions, and cultural attitudes of the various peoples they now ruled, which meant that over time, they became less and less connected to the Mongolian heartland and to the great khan who had created the empire. As Man concludes, "a detailed history of them all would be like describing three-dimensional chess. Such a huge and varied entity could never hold together."

It is the disintegration of the Mongol Empire that is the subject of this lecture. We shall see just how quickly collapse occurred in the Persian Ilkhanate and in Yuan China, in 1335 and 1368 respectively. And we shall also observe the much more gradual disintegration of the Chagatayid Khanate and the Golden Horde as the Mongols splintered into smaller, more autonomous units.

But as we explore the fate of the four khanates, the overall arc is one of decline and dissolution, with many Mongols simply slipping back to the steppe to resume their ancestral way of life, as many still do today in the modern nation of Mongolia. Thinking in particular of the end of the Yuan Dynasty, Jack Weatherford suggests it was as though "the entire Chinese episode from 1211 to 1368 had been merely an extended stay at their southern summer camp."

Let's begin in Persia and follow the rapid decline of Mongol rule there. When we were last in the Ilkhanate, we saw how Ilkhan Abu Said and his adviser Choban had decided to execute the great administrator and historian Rashid al-Din in July of 1318. Despite the execution of his vizier, Abu Said's reign is now viewed as a success by historians, a continuation of the golden age that had preceded it. Yet this idea of a golden age must be considered in the context of the chaos that immediately followed Abu Said's death in 1335. Abu Said had left no male heir, and no other descendants of Hulagu emerged with the strength or credibility to claim the throne.

The Toluid elites within the Ilkhanate elected Arpa Khan, a distant descendant of Ariq Boke who had waged civil war against Qubilai Khan several decades earlier. Arpa Khan tried to lend more legitimacy to his reign by marrying Abu Said's sister Sati Beg, and also by enjoying some early military success against armies of the Golden Horde. But during his brief reign, rebellions broke out all over the Ilkhanate, and rebel commanders captured and executed Arpa Khan on May 15th, 1336, only a year after he had been elected ilkhan.

These rebel commanders were military officers who now revealed their own ambitions for power by trying to find a puppet Chinggisid they could promote to the throne. The various factions fought bitterly, and in the chaos, no less than eight different Chinggisid princes were promoted to the throne between 1335 and 1344, each ruling from a different regional base within the Ilkhanate.

Inevitably, the once powerful and unified khanate rapidly devolved into a series of small regional states manipulated by the military commanders of the former Ilkhanate army. Centralized power was never restored, which meant that the Ilkhanate effectively ceased to exist with the death of Abu Said in 1335. As I noted in the previous lecture, so rapid was the demise of the Ilkhanate that, as David Morgan concludes, "we appear to have here the perplexing phenomenon of an empire which fell without having previously declined."

To Mongol-controlled China next, whose fortunes we have previously followed up to the death of Qubilai Khan on February 18th, 1294. Qubilai had lived a long life, and indeed outlived most of his sons, including his designated successor, Jingim, who had died 10 years earlier. The most viable contender was Qubilai's grandson Temur Oljeitu, the son of Jingim, and he was duly elected khan of the Yuan Dynasty in 1295. Temur's tenure as emperor is assessed favorably by modern historians, although he had to spend most of his 12-year reign correcting problems that Qubilai had caused during the previous decade of alcoholic neglect. Qubilai probably also suffered from severe depression towards the end of his reign following the death of his primary wife and chief companion and council, Chabi.

During the early years of his reign, Temur Oljeitu maintained many of his grandfather's policies and also continued the war against the Ogedeid leader Qaidu, who was attacking the western regions of the Yuan Empire. When Qaidu died in 1301, the war petered out. This no doubt relieved

Temur Oljeitu, who was not a military commander, nor was he interested in expanding the empire beyond its already considerable dimensions. He canceled plans Qubilai had drawn up for yet another attempted invasion of Japan, for example.

But Temur was decidedly interested in expanding trade across Eurasia, and to this end, he was a strong advocate for the Pax Mongolica. He worked diligently with his cousins all over the Mongol world to create genuine peace between the four khanates. His efforts were appreciated by most of the Chinggisids, and he was recognized as nominal great khan of the entire Mongol Empire during the last years of his reign, although of course, in reality, he only actually ruled the Yuan Dynasty.

Temur's domestic policies were also focused on stability. Many Mongols now lived in China, and indeed all over the Yuan Empire, but many others had remained in Mongolia, where they had grown resentful of the sedentary and increasingly Sinicized lifestyle adopted by Qubilai and other Mongol elites in China. Temur sent them gifts to try to mend various fractures that had emerged under Qubilai, but these gifts ended up being an expensive drain on the treasury. Partly to increase revenue, Temur also tried to root out corruption within the empire. Yuan Dynasty records show that a staggering 18,373 officials were convicted of corrupt behavior, although in most cases their punishment was lenient.

Undoubtedly the biggest problems Temur faced were fiscal; expenditure had far outpaced income for years, and the Yuan Dynasty's coffers were rapidly depleting. This problem was exacerbated by the various intrigues and squabbling that broke out amongst the Mongol elites in China after Temur died in 1307.

Following the death of his primary wife, Temur had promoted another wife named Buluqan as empress. She had spent the last years of Temur's reign acquiring wealth by confiscating the assets of those accused of corruption, and this had allowed her to amass considerable prestige and power. She used this power to try and promote her son Deshou as successor to Temur Oljeitu, and to this end had relocated potential rivals to far-flung places all over the empire. But Deshou died the year before Temur, so when Khan Temur died, there was literally a race for the throne as potential successors all converged on the palace.

Various factions now emerged during the regency of Buluqan, and in the intense jockeying for power that ensued, violence broke out. In the end, it was a nephew of Temur Oljeitu, Qaishan, who seized the throne because of his sharper military acumen and more widespread support.

Qaishan was a soldier who had spent much of his life leading Mongol armies in campaigns on the steppe. So it was no surprise that once he seized power, he tried to rule as an old-fashioned Mongol steppe khan, living in his camp and using advisers to impose his will on the empire. But as Tim May points out, "the empire was too vast and too diverse to be ruled as such," and under his ineffective rule, the fiscal problems of the empire only worsened.

When Qaishan died in 1311, his younger brother Ayurbarwada peacefully assumed the throne, although his first action was to violently purge many of Qaishan's supporters from their positions within government. Ayurbarwada had received a good Confucian education, and also, almost uniquely amongst all the Yuan Dynasty khans, he spoke and wrote Chinese.

He spent the early years of his reign trying to balance the budget by trimming expenditure, and he also reintroduced the Confucian civil service exam to recruit good ethical men to positions of authority within the bureaucracy. However, he also made sure that the two top classes of the Yuan world—the Mongols and the Semuren, or foreigners—received preferential treatment in taking the test.

Perhaps the fortunes of the Yuan Dynasty might have improved had Ayurbarwada enjoyed a long reign, but his death in 1320, aged just 35, prevented any serious reforms. His 17-year-old son Shidebala assumed the throne without opposition but was assassinated three years later. He was followed in 1323 by the older and more experienced Yesun Temur, who tried to calm religious and ethnic tensions within the empire by promoting Muslims to positions of authority, while also leaving many Confucians in important posts and showering gifts and attention on various Tibetan Buddhist sects.

But Jack Weatherford argues that during the late period of the Yuan, the Mongol elites actually became increasingly less tolerant of religious diversity and showed increasing favor to Tibetan Buddhism. As a result of this, he notes, although the Chinese had always distrusted the various foreigners the Mongols had placed over them, the "Tibetan Buddhist monks in particular became the object of hatred, since local people along the newly opened route to Tibet carried the obligation not merely of feeding, housing and transporting the monks, but of carrying the goods for them as well."

Increasingly isolated from the Chinese, the Yuan royals sought spiritual guidance from these Tibetan monks, and somewhat bizarrely, the monks promoted Tantric sexual acts amongst the Mongols as a way of achieving spiritual liberation. Here's Weatherford again: "This not only produced a vigorous display of sexual art, but it also encouraged the royal family to engage in elaborate sexual dances and rituals that centered on the eager participation of the Great Khan himself under the watchful eye of the lamas." This led to rumors of debauchery and even human sacrifice within the palace, which further damaged the reputation of the Mongols amongst the Chinese.

After the death of Yesun Temur in 1328, violence again broke out between various contenders. A powerful Kipchak military commander named El Temur emerged as the real power behind the throne, supported by his Merkit chancellor Bayan. The two promoted puppet emperors to the throne, like Qoshila, who lasted only six months, and Tuq Temur, who ruled through to 1332. Rebellions broke out at regular intervals, which El Temur and his troops attempted to crush. Instability only worsened when Tuq Temur died without an heir in September 1332, to be replaced by a six-year-old puppet of El Temur who died of illness just 53 days later.

At this moment, a Chinggisid prince named Toghon Temur, who had been exiled in Korea, returned to take up the throne, and while his long reign of 35 years might indicate a return to stability, it was blighted from the beginning, because, as Tim May puts it, "Toghon Temur inherited a disaster." Toghon Temur was destined to be the last Mongol who would ever rule China.

Mongol control disintegrated in southern China first, where numerous rebellions broke out. The ancient heartland of Mongolia itself broke away from the Yuan next, because the Yuan royal family was now viewed as more Chinese than Mongol by many conservative Mongols.

Corruption became rampant throughout the bureaucracy as the modified version of the Confucian civil service exam failed to produce administrators of character. El Temur's former chancellor Bayan led a coup in 1335 and personally took control of government for five years, but his attempts at reform failed. Bayan's nephew led a coup against him, and Bayan died in exile.

As Toghon Temur tried to hold on to the reins of government, a series of natural disasters occurred throughout the empire. Massive floods caused devastation along the Huang He (or Yellow River) valley, and then a particularly virulent epidemic of bubonic plague broke out and devasted China between 1353 and 1354. This killed so many Chinese that David Morgan argues it "may well be among the principal reasons for the demographic decline in Mongol China." To make matters worse, the Grand Canal connecting the Yangtze with the Huang He had fallen into such a poor state of repair that food supplies from the south could now barely reach the north, a problem exacerbated by widespread piracy.

In the midst of this chaos, a particularly dangerous rebellion broke out in the south in the year 1352, led by a young Buddhist rebel named Zhu Yuanzhang. Called the Red Turban movement for the color of the ribbons they used to tie back their hair, Zhu Yuanzhang's rebel army consistently defeated Mongol forces throughout the 1360s as they drove north. Finally, in 1368, the Red Turbans captured the Yuan capital and drove Toghon Temur and his family out of the palace. After a rule of 98 years, the Yuan Dynasty now officially ceased to exist. The Mongols departed China for good, to return to the steppes from whence they had come.

Some scholars estimate that up to 60,000 Mongols returned to the Mongolian heartland from China, which led to an outbreak of intense intertribal conflict with those that had remained behind in what had become a backwater of the Yuan Dynasty. Veronika Veit, a noted expert on Mongol regimes in the steppe after the collapse of the Yuan, writes that the period between 1368 and 1636 is often described as a Mongol dark age, a categorization first applied by 19th-century Russian historian A. M. Pozdneev.

The label "dark" works in various ways. Dark because the glory days of the Mongols and Chinggisids were essentially over. Dark because ruthless and often brutal intertribal conflict and warfare returned to the steppes, the sort of endemic conflict that only a leader of the strength and skill of Chinggis Khan had been able to quell. And dark because there are few, if any, sources surviving that historians can use to shed light on the period. What we can definitively say, however, is, in the words of Veronika Veit, that the return of intertribal rivalries "eventually destroyed all chances for the Mongols to present a united front, not only with regard to China, but also with regard to their own personal fate."

In China, meanwhile, Buddhist rebel leader Zhu Yuanzhang, better known to world history by his imperial reign name of Hongwu, quickly established the new Ming Dynasty, which would go on to rule China until 1644. Hongwu personally guided the fortunes of the Ming Dynasty from 1368 to 1398. As founder of the dynasty, he chose the name Ming, which means "brilliant," and after driving the Mongols out, he set to work to build a tightly centralized Chinese-run state. But as could only be expected, an event as traumatic as the Mongol conquest and rule of China inevitably had profound historical consequences, both for China, and indeed for the world.

Hongwu and his successors stabilized the government and defended China from further invasion for almost three centuries. They did this partly by adopting a defensive policy based on the reconstruction of the Great Wall of China to ensure that neither the Mongols nor any other militarized nomadic confederations would ever invade China again. It was the first emperor of unified China, Qin Shi Huangdi, who in the 3rd century BCE had first connected many of the smaller Zhou Dynasty walls together to create the first Great Wall system. Later dynasties like the Han had maintained and extended the fortifications, but by the time of the Ming, these ancient walls had largely fallen into ruin.

In their determination to ensure the Mongols would never return, the Ming government made the reconstruction of the Great Wall a major defensive priority. Hundreds of thousands of workers were employed to labor throughout the late 15th and early 16th centuries to build a truly formidable stone and brick barrier that in the end ran for some 1,550 miles. This Ming Great Wall averaged about 30 feet in height, included watch and signal towers at regular intervals, and accommodations for troops stationed along the extensive border. If you have walked on the section of the Great Wall near Beijing, then you have certainly walked on part of the Ming Great Wall.

The rule of the Ming and subsequent Qing Dynasties undoubtedly created stability that led to a revival of core Chinese cultural values, but this came at an enormous cost. Some scholars have even argued that the ultimate consequence of the Ming reaction to the Mongol century was the surrender of Chinese power, innovation, and global leadership five centuries later to the new and rising power of the world, the Europeans.

The argument for this surrender of Chinese global leadership goes something like this: During their reign, the Mongols had largely ignored Chinese political and cultural traditions. They dismantled the Confucian exam system and replaced Chinese bureaucrats with central Asian, Persian, and other foreign administrators, many of whom were Muslims. So when the Yuan century was finally ended, the Ming emperors who followed attempted to erase all signs not only of Mongol, but indeed of any foreign influence, and restore traditional forms of culture and governance to China.

For inspiration, they looked back to the great Chinese dynasties that had preceded the Mongols. Like the Tang Dynasty, in particular, which had ruled China for almost three centuries from 618 to 907 CE, the Ming built a centralized imperial state, they revived the Confucian civil service exam and the notion of the scholar-bureaucrat, and they promoted Confucian values at the expense of "foreign" ideas. The rulers of the Qing Dynasty that followed the Ming, although they themselves were Manchus of nomadic origin and thus technically outsiders, also worked hard to promote traditional Chinese ways.

Both the Ming and Qing Dynasties were thus deeply conservative; their focus was on maintaining stability and tradition in a huge agrarian society, and to a certain extent on isolating and protecting China from "unwholesome" outside influences. By adopting policies that favored classical Chinese traditions, these two dynasties collectively maintained a successful and stable state for half a millennium, something that was certainly appreciated by Chinese intellectuals, and of course the common people at the time.

But some modern historians have now come to view the Ming and Qing Dynasties as deadweights that effectively slowed Chinese innovation and entrepreneurship just when real global competition from European states was appearing. It is a profound irony, for example, that at the same moment tiny European countries like Portugal began to send their fleets into the Indian Ocean and eventually on to east Asia, the Ming government had already withdrawn its own powerful fleet from the seas.

And just as Europeans began putting Chinese inventions like printing, gunpowder, and the compass to good use, inventions that had spread from east to west as a result of the Pax Mongolica, China gave up its position of global scientific leadership. Undoubtedly, the Ming Dynasty preserved peace within China and much of east Asia for centuries, an achievement for which they deserve enormous credit. But ultimately, the peaceful and conservative stagnation of China under the Ming was to have disastrous consequences for China under the succeeding Qing Dynasty.

In Korea, too, the end of Mongol domination had momentous consequences that included a change of dynasties. King Kongmin of the Koryo Dynasty held the throne through the last phase of Mongol rule, from 1351 to 1374. He became the first ruler in more than a century to openly oppose the Mongols, and he was also determined to destroy the power of those Korean families who had been enriching themselves by working closely with the Mongols.

When the Ming Dynasty was declared in China in 1368, Kongmin immediately adopted a pro-Ming, anti-Mongol policy. But his decision exacerbated the general chaos that now enveloped the final years of Koryo rule, even as the Mongols were being driven out. King Kongmin was assassinated in 1374, and peasant revolts broke out all over the peninsula. Remember, it was the peasants that had been bearing a double burden of taxation by the Koryo state and by the Mongols.

Then Japanese pirates known as the *waegu* began raiding the Korean coast, devastating the villages. The *waegu* were only lightly armed, but their ability to unexpectedly turn up and raid the coast at will forced many peasants to flee inland and abandon the rich coastal farmlands. Repeated diplomatic representations to the Japanese government failed to end the attacks, so the Koryo decided to launch a military campaign against them.

As the Mongols retreated northwards to the steppe and were no longer a problem for the Koryo military, two commanders were appointed to lead the Koryo armed forces against the pirates: Choe Yong and Yi Song-gye. Their almost immediate success against the *waegu* led to both commanders gaining high status and influence in the Koryo capital. But the two military leaders, comrades up to this point, fell out over the question of whether to attack or support the Chinese Ming Dynasty, which had just declared its intention of taking over part of Koryo's northeastern territory.

While Choe Yong was leading an expedition against the Ming forces, Yi Song-gye, who was pro-Ming and opposed to the expedition, surprised everyone by suddenly leading his forces back into the capital and staging a military coup against both Choe Yong and the king. Yi Song-gye quickly established a new dynasty, the Choson Dynasty. The Choson, the last dynasty to rule Korea, lasted for more than 500 years, from 1392 until the 22nd of August, 1910, when Korea was annexed by the rising power of Japan.

In the steppes of Russia, meanwhile, the Golden Horde maintained its authority much longer than any of the other khanates, although by the end of the 14th century, it was clearly also in decline. In 1438, the Horde was divided into two states: the Khanates of Kazan and the so-called Great Horde. Another division occurred five years later, leading to the breakaway of two smaller states: the Khanates of Astrakhan and of Crimea.

Some historians date the official end of the Golden Horde to the defeat of the Great Horde by Khan Mengli Girai of the Crimean Khanate in 1502, particularly as Mengli had previously accepted a position of subordination to the burgeoning empire of the Ottoman Turks in 1475. Further north, the expansion of the Russian state under Ivan the Terrible absorbed the Khanate of Kazan in 1552 and the Khanate of Astrakhan in 1556.

But the Crimean Khanate managed to remain semi-independent for more than another century, "the last vestige of the Eurasian empire of Chinggis Khan" as David Morgan describes it, until it was finally annexed by Catherine the Great of Russia in 1783. But was this truly the end of the story of Mongols in Russia? The Tatars of Crimea, as they were known, descendants of the Golden Horde, continued to exist as a discrete community through to the middle of the 20th century, until in May 1944, Joseph Stalin and his henchman Beria used cattle trains to deport 191,044 Tatars eastwards into central Asia and the Siberian steppe.

Why did the Golden Horde last so much longer than the other khanates? John Man and David Morgan agree that in the case of the other three khanates, the Mongols, although overlords, were so interfused with the peoples, languages, and cultures of the regions they conquered that they were in a way "contaminated" by them. But the Golden Horde always remained semi-nomadic, closer to the lifestyles of their Mongol predecessors and the effective armies this lifestyle had created. They gained their wealth through tribute and raiding and facilitating commercial activities within their realm, but never adopted the lifestyles of the Russians or other sedentary peoples that flourished within their realm. Thus, they were able to maintain their independence until they came up against the much greater military power of the expansive Russian Empire under rulers like Catherine.

By way of conclusion, and to set ourselves up for the next group of four lectures, we need to briefly consider events in Transoxiana, today's Amu Darya region, in what had been part of the Chagatayid and Ogedeid khanates of central Asia. By the 1340s, the region had divided in two. The western territory was ruled by the Qara'unas, descendants of a large Mongol garrison that had been stationed in parts of Afghanistan decades earlier; and an eastern territory ruled by a Chinggisid prince named Tughluq Temur Khan, who ruled from Kashgar with the help of the powerful Dughlat tribe. The western realm retained the name Ulus Chagatai, while the eastern realm was called Moghulistan.

The Ulus Chagatai was essentially a tribal confederation where leadership, as the specialist on this region and period Beatrice Forbes Manz reminds us, "was often contested and tribes were frequently split in their loyalties, with rivals for power backing different candidates for central rule." Losers in the struggle for power would often seek external alliances for support, while power brokers in the competing tribes would try and legitimize their claims by finding some puppet prince who could prove descent from Chinggis Khan himself through his second son, Chagatai.

It was in this atmosphere that three particularly powerful tribes emerged, each claiming descent from Chagatai: the Jalayir, the Suldus, and the Barlas tribes. Although the former Chagatayid khanate was split into an eastern and a western realm, tribal leaders still harbored hopes of reuniting the two and recreating a unified khanate. In 1361, one Tughluq Temur Khan came to power and attempted to reunite the realm under his leadership. Some tribal leaders joined him, but others refused to, including the chief of the Barlas tribe, Hajji Beg.

It was at this moment that a minor tribal ruler named Timur first enters the pages of history. Timur was probably around 30 years of age at this point, and he was able to persuade Tughluq Temur Khan to make him leader of the Barlas, even though by lineage, he was not part of the ruling elite. In a manner very similar to his hero Chinggis Khan, Timur then began assembling a web of alliances with other tribes, most critically with Amir Husayn, the leader of the Qara'unas.

Over the years that followed, Amir Husayn and Timur both amassed considerable power. Often they worked together, but late in the 1360s, Timur staged a rebellion against Amir Husayn. Timur then convened a *quriltai* and had his Chinggisid puppet prince Soyur-Ghatmish declared khan of the Ulus Chagatai. Timur chose the city of Samarkand to be his base, and he entered the Chinggisid aristocracy by wedding princess Saray Malik. Timur then built a formidable army and set out to emulate the success of Chinggis Khan by creating his own enormous empire.

By 1370, Timur was in control of the entire region of the former Chagatayid Khanate. Six hundred and fifty years later, his name still resonates in central Asia, where he is seen as the heroic founder and unifying figure of the modern nation of Uzbekistan.

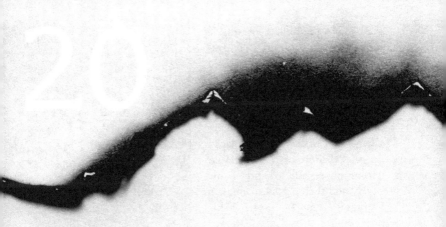

TIMUR THE LAME,
A.K.A. TAMERLANE

The lecture tells the beginning of the story of Timur and his Timurid successors. Timur was the final and formidable representative of nomadic power. Following the disintegration of the Mongol khanate in central Asia, three powerful tribes emerged, each of them claiming to be descended from Chinggis Khan's second son, Chagatai. The three tribes were the Jalayir, the Suldus, and the Barlas. The leaders of each hoped to reunite the now-splintered khanate under their hegemony.

Timur was born in the region known historically as Transoxiana. At around the age of 30, Timur entered the realms of recorded history engaged in an effort to use tribal politics to increase his own power within the Barlas tribe.

Timur's Early Activities

Following the tremendous success of the Mongols, Timur and all tribal leaders knew that it was essential to have the support of a Chinggisid prince if any attempt to gain power was to be successful. After defeating his rivals and declaring himself leader of the Barlas, Timur promoted a Chinggisid puppet prince as khan. Timur also entered into the Chinggisid royal line by wedding princess Saray Malik.

He had already built a formidable nomadic army and a loyal following, and he was determined to increase his power within the crumbling Chagatai state. With his legitimacy enhanced through his Chinggisid wife and the puppet Chagatayid prince he had placed on the throne of Transoxiana, Timur chose Samarkand as his capital and then set out to emulate Chinggis Khan by creating his own empire.

In the early 1360s, Timur formed an alliance with Amir Husayn, ruler of the Qara'unas Mongols. Both men spent some time in the region of Khurasan to the west of Transoxiana, working as virtual mercenaries for local leaders. In 1364, the two commanders attacked a Moghul army in Transoxiana, but the following year, Amir Husayn presumptuously declared himself ruler of the entire Chagatai territory.

He was immediately opposed by other tribal chiefs, including Timur, which led to a protracted war between the two former allies. Three years later, Timur led a successful rebellion against Amir Husayn, who was killed soon afterward. Timur then appointed a close ally, Amir Cheku, as new commander of Amir Husayn's Qara'unas troops, thus considerably enhancing the size of his army.

TIMUR'S FAITH AND PERSONALITY

All available evidence indicates that Timur was a Muslim, possibly a member of the Naqshbandi school of Sufism. While Timur was a strong supporter of Islam, his faith does not seem to have mitigated in any way his penchant for warfare and conquest.

Timur was a military genius very much in the mold of Chinggis Khan, but various contemporary sources also comment on Timur's intelligence more generally. As well as his native Chagatayid language, Timur also learned to speak Persian, Mongolian, and various Turkic dialects.

Timur's Strategies and Advances

In his early campaigns, Timur seems to have intentionally set out not only to emulate Chinggis Khan but also to draw strategically on the legacy of the Mongols. This included the eradication of any rival tribal claimants for power in the region, much as Chinggis Khan had done in his rise to power.

For instance, Timur attempted to destroy the leader of the Dughlat tribe, Qamar al-Din, who had staged a rebellion against the clans descended from the Chagatayids. This took multiple campaigns, but by 1378, Timur had succeeded in driving Qasar al-Din into exile.

Timur's power and prestige continued to increase with each victory over a rival. His prestige was further enhanced when, in 1375, Timur gave refuge to a prince of the Jochid lineage named Toqtamish, a pretender to the throne of the Mongol Blue Horde that ruled lands to the north of Timur's growing empire.

Timur launched an invasion of Khwarazm in 1379 and 1380, during which he razed the city of Urgench to the ground and divided its population in the manner of the Mongols. He sent scholars and artisans back to his capital of Samarkand but destroyed the rest.

In 1381, Timur installed his third son, Amiranshah, as governor of Khurasan, then set out to destroy any rivals to that position by attacking other regional powers. This included the Khartids, who ruled as the kings of Herat in modern Afghanistan. Timur defeated them in 1381, then removed them completely in 1383, placing the region under his control.

Campaigns to the West and North

With his position now secure in central Asia and with Toqtamish a close ally along the northern borders, Timur turned his gaze toward the west, to the territories of the former Mongol Ilkhanate. He first invaded the region of Mazandaran in 1384, and he installed a puppet Chinggisid prince named Luqman on the throne. After this, he captured the city of Soltaniyeh, about 150 miles northwest of Tehran. In doing so, Timur clearly proclaimed himself as heir to the Ilkhanate in addition to the *Ulus Chagatai*.

While Timur was actively campaigning in the former Ilkhanate, further north, his protégé and ally Toqtamish was busy with his own campaigns. This led to him taking control of the Mongol Golden Horde itself. Once secure as khan of the Golden Horde, Toqtamish suddenly turned against Timur.

Timur versus Toqtamish

In 1382, Toqtamish had formed an alliance with the Mamluk sultans of Egypt and Syria. During the winter of 1385–1386, Toqtamish attacked the populous city of Tabriz in Iranian Azerbaijan, thus reasserting the old claim of the Golden Horde to rule the Caucasus.

The attack on Tabriz led to the outbreak of war between Toqtamish and Timur, a war that would occupy both men for a decade. In the spring of 1386, Timur set out on an invasion of Iran, the first major campaign of genuine imperial conquest of his rule.

Timur enjoyed immediate success on his Iranian campaign by defeating another Turko-Mongol ruler named Ahmad Jalayir in Azerbaijan. The following year, Toqtamish launched his first direct attack on Timur. Timurid propagandists and historians later claimed this ended in victory for Timur, but evidence tells a different story, because Toqtamish continued to issue coins in his name in major Azerbaijan cities like Baku and Darband for the next several years.

At the urging of Toqtamish, Timur's enemies began to form alliances against him. Late in 1387, Timur learned that Toqtamish had allied with Timur's old enemy Qamar al-Din and other dissident tribal leaders, and their combined armies had attacked the Timurid heartland of Transoxiana, ravaging it as far as the Oxus River.

Timur immediately marched eastward and attacked the Sufi dynasty ruling Khwarazm, which had also gone over to Toqtamish. The city of Urgench found itself squarely in Timur's sights for a second time in eight years; it was razed again. Timur next marched against the khan of the eastern Chagatayid realm who had also supported Toqtamish, campaigning against him as far north as Lake Zaysan in modern Kazakhstan.

Timur spent the late spring of 1390 preparing for what he hoped would be the decisive campaign against Toqtamish. He passed the winter of 1390–1391 in Tashkent, then confronted Toqtamish at the Battle of the Kondurcha River on June 18, 1391. This occurred in what is today the Samara Oblast of Russia.

Toqtamish's cavalry tried to encircle Timur's army and attack its flanks, but Timur's cavalry stood its ground and then launched a decisive frontal attack. The forces of the Golden Horde were put to flight all the way up to the Volga River.

The Conflict Concludes

The following year, in the autumn of 1392, Timur set out on another major campaign into Persia. Toqtamish spent the years of Timur's absence in Persia rebuilding his forces, being careful to avoid any direct confrontation with Timurids in the meantime. By the spring of 1395, Toqtamish was ready, and he renewed hostilities by attacking Timurid forces at Shirvan in the eastern Caucasus. Timur immediately marched against him and reconquered all the territories Toqtamish had captured.

Battle of Shirvan

The final confrontation between the two men occurred at the Battle of the Terek River on April 15, 1395. The cavalry of Toqtamish and his allies focused their attack on the right flank and center of Timur's army. At a critical moment, some of the emirs who had allied with the Golden Horde went over to Timur, allowing the Timurid forces to turn the tables and attack and destroy the left flank of Toqtamish's army.

Toqtamish and the remnants of his army fled north to the Volga River, pursued by Timur and his victorious army, which destroyed city after city as they marched almost all the way to Moscow. That city was only saved from destruction by events that pious Muscovites saw as miraculous, and which have only added to the legend of Timur.

As Timur's army approached, Prince Vasily I, the ruler of Moscow, led his badly outnumbered army out to engage the Timurid forces. While Prince Vasily waited to confront the enemy, Russian Orthodox clerics decided to seek help from God by transporting a sacred icon, a beautiful medieval painting titled *Theotokos of Vladimir*, from the town of Vladimir to Moscow.

As the relic passed through villages along the way, pious Russians prayed for deliverance. According to contemporary accounts, Prince Vasily himself spent a night weeping in prayer over the icon. The people's prayers would appear to have been answered: On August 26, Timur suddenly packed up his army and left.

Timur wanted to return to Samarkand and then regroup for a major campaign into Persia. In the aftermath of the Battle of the Terek River, Toqtamish was deposed as khan of the Golden Horde and replaced by Edigu. Toqtamish fled into the steppes of Ukraine and formed an alliance with the grand duke of Lithuania. The two confronted a Timurid army in 1399, this time led by two of Timur's generals, and were utterly crushed. Toqtamish survived again and now fled into Siberia, where he was eventually killed by the troops of Edigu sometime in 1406.

These events effectively marked the end of the Golden Horde, which now splintered into a series of smaller khanates. Timur was content with having destroyed the power of the Golden Horde, and he made no attempt to establish control over its former territories.

TIMUR THE LAME, A.K.A. TAMERLANE

Early in Christopher Marlowe's play on the life of Timur, or Tamburlaine as the author names him, the protagonist recites the following lines to a high-born woman named Zenocrate, the daughter of the Sultan of Egypt:

> I am a lord, for so my deeds shall prove;
>
> And yet a shepherd by my parentage.
>
> But, lady, this fair face and heavenly hue
>
> Must grace his bed that conquers Asia,
>
> And means to be a terror to the world …
>
> And, madam, whatsoever you esteem
>
> Of this success, and loss unvalued,
>
> Both may invest you empress of the East;
>
> And these that seem but silly country swains
>
> May have the leading of so great a host
>
> As with their weight shall make the mountains quake,
>
> Even as when windy exhalations,
>
> Fighting for passage, tilt within the earth.

On the title page of the first edition of *Tamburlaine the Great*, published in 1590, Marlowe introduces his hero thus: "Tamburlaine the Great. Who from a Scythian Shepheard by his rare and wonderful Conquests, became a most puissant and mighty Monarque. And, for his tyranny and terror in Warre, was termed the Scourge of God."

Marlowe's play was probably written in 1587, some 180 years after the death of Timur in 1405. But the conqueror's name had continued to resonate in European circles over the decades almost as forcefully as it had done during Timur's lifetime. *Tamburlaine the Great* is regarded as a milestone in Elizabethan theater, and, published early in his career, it announced in Christopher Marlowe the arrival of a dramatist of exceptional talent.

Critics find woven throughout the play some of the ideals of Renaissance humanism, ideals that profoundly resonated within the court of Elizabeth I in the late 16th century. Of particular importance to Renaissance humanists was the unlimited potential of humans. We know that Timur was of Turkic-Mongol heritage and born into medium-level tribal nobility, but Marlowe has him descended from a lowly Scythian shepherd to make the point that Timur was a man who rose from humble stock to become one of the great conquerors in world history. And despite the fact that Timur was a Muslim, some critics also see in the play a promotion of atheism, arguably another ideal of Renaissance humanism, and a charge that was often leveled against Christopher Marlowe himself.

The first part of *Tamburlaine the Great* was probably performed the same year it was written, 1587, by a group of players known as the Admiral's Men. The play was so successful with the public that Marlowe almost immediately wrote a sequel, *Tamburlaine the Great Part Two*. The play was also influential on other Elizabethan dramatists, including William Shakespeare himself. Modern Shakespeare historian Stephen Greenblatt believes that *Tamburlaine* was probably one of the first plays the young Shakespeare saw upon arriving in London from Stratford. The experience inspired Shakespeare to write his first plays about Henry VI in the late 1590s. Some scholars even wonder whether Shakespeare may have written Henry VI Part 1 in collaboration with Christopher Marlowe himself.

But I digress. We are getting a long way away from medieval central Asia here, and the rise of the great conqueror Timur, whose career is our focus in this final group of lectures. Timur was the last of the great militarized nomadic conquerors, a mantle that could be traced back through all the Mongol khans to the leaders of the great Turkic empires, and before them to the Xiongnu and the powerful Shanyu Modu who had so terrorized the Han Chinese 1,500 years earlier.

Timur was as relentless in his campaigns as any of his conquering predecessors, bristling with restless energy and determined to emulate the success of his hero Chinggis Khan. Noted Timur specialist Beatrice Forbes Manz describes his career like this: "From 1382 to 1405 his great armies crisscrossed Eurasia from Delhi to Moscow, from the Tien Shan Mountains of Central Asia to the Taurus mountains in Anatolia, conquering and reconquering, razing some cities, sparing others. His activity was relentless and unending." It is the story of Timur and his Timurid successors that we unfold in this last part of the course. As the final and formidable representative of nomadic power, Timur provides a fitting end to our story.

In the previous lecture, we saw how following the disintegration of the Mongol khanate in central Asia, the Ulus Chagatai, three powerful tribes emerged, each of them claiming to be descended from Chinggis Khan's second son, Chagatai. The three tribes were the Jalayir, the Suldus, and the Barlas. The leaders of each hoped to reunite the now splintered khanate under their hegemony, but each time one tribe attempted to do so, the others refused to acknowledge their supremacy.

At around the age of 30, Timur enters the realms of recorded history engaged in an effort to use tribal politics to increase his own power within the Barlas tribe. Following the tremendous success of the Mongols, Timur and all tribal leaders knew that it was essential to have the support of a Chinggisid prince if any attempt to gain power was to be successful. So after defeating his rivals and declaring himself leader of the Barlas, Timur promoted a Chinggisid puppet-prince named Soyur-Ghatmish as khan of the Ulus Chagatai. Timur also entered into the Chinggisid royal line by wedding princess Saray Malik. This marriage gave Timur the right to use the title *gurgan*, or royal son-in-law, a title that only those related to the Chinggisids could claim.

This part of the story of Timur we have already recounted, but let's go back to the beginning now and explore what we know about the early life of Timur before he first came to the notice of chroniclers. I should warn you, though, it is very difficult to separate fact from legend in recounting the early decades of Timur's life, partly because Timur employed his own historians to tell the story of his life the way he wanted it told.

We can be certain that Timur was born in the region known historically as Transoxiana, essentially the lands between the Oxus and Jaxartes Rivers, located in the nations of Uzbekistan and Turkmenistan today. But Transoxiana was not just any region of the former Ulus Chagatai; it was its wealthy, multicultural heartland and key to the conduct of Silk Roads trade for millennia. Chinggis Khan himself had first led Mongol armies into the region back in the 1220s, during his Khwarazmian campaign, sacking the two great cities of Samarkand and Bukhara. Now, more than a century later, the region had recovered much of its former glory and wealth. An early 20th-century historian of the Mongols and Timurids, Michael Prawdin, describes the region like this:

Transoxiana is a wealthy and fertile land with big cities and a highly developed civilization, abundant orchards and vineyards, rows of mulberry trees for sericulture, rich pastures for cattle. Across Transoxiana ran the most important Asiatic trade-route which led from Western Asia to China. The merchants, the handicraftsmen, and the peasants were Persians; the warriors, whose horses, camels and weathers were herded by slaves in the valleys, were Mongols, Tartars, men of Turan, nomads.

Timur was born into the Barlas, one of many tribes that nomadized in the region. He later claimed that his birth date was April 9th, 1336, although as we shall see shortly, this was a date chosen for convenience rather than historical accuracy. Most modern historians believe Timur was born sometime in the 1320s.

Timur was born in a village near the city of Kesh, known as Shahrisabz, or Green City, today, a city about 50 miles south of Samarkand that I have had the pleasure of visiting on several occasions. Shahrisabz is well named because an abundance of water flowing from surrounding snow-covered mountains makes the region flourish. Ancient Kesh, modern Shahrisabz, is also the town Timur would choose for his own mausoleum, but as we will see in a later lecture, fate in the form of winter snows on passes into Kesh intervened, and Timur was ultimately buried in Samarkand.

Timur's father was a minor chieftain of the Barlas tribe, although the Barlas had been living in the midst of a Turkic political and cultural environment for so long that it is more accurate to refer to the Barlas, and thus to Timur himself, as Turkic-Mongol. We should add that Timur was also a Muslim, so here was a man with multiple and sometimes conflicted identities.

Legend has it that that Timur's father, Teragai, had a dream not long before his son was born. In the dream, Teragai saw a young man handing him a sword. He took the sword and swung it through the air, and it shed a bright illumination on the entire world. Teragai sought an interpretation of the dream from a local sheik. According to Michael Prawdin, the sheik replied: "A son will be born to you who, with the might of his sword, will conquer the whole world, converting all men to Islam, and cleansing the earth from the darkness of innovation and errors."

When the boy was born, his parents chose the name Timur, or Demir in the local Chagatayid-Turkic language, which means "Iron." Timur was intent on showing how much he deserved that name almost from birth. Some sources relate that when Timur was aged eight or nine, he, his brothers, and mother were captured by a Mongol army and taken to Samarkand as prisoners. If true, this would have occurred during the reasonably successful reign of Chagatayid khan Kebek, under whom peace was generally maintained throughout the khanate and trade flourished with Yuan China. This increase in trade apparently aided the teenage Timur, who, according to historians, formed a small band of loyal followers who together began raiding commercial caravans, stealing their goods and particularly their animals.

But sometime during this period of his life, Timur apparently went too far in his rustling activities. According to his biographers, he tried to steal sheep from a well-armed shepherd. The shepherd unleashed his arrows at Timur and shot him twice, once in the hand and once in the leg. The injuries were serious, and Timur was to carry the legacy of them for the rest of his life. He lost two fingers from his right hand, but even worse damage was done to his leg, which was partly paralyzed.

Historian Peter Jackson thinks it far more likely that Timur received his wounds later, while campaigning in eastern Persia, but either way, after suffering these injuries, he walked with a pronounced limp, which is why he eventually became known in central Asia as Timur-i Lang, and in European chronicles as Timur the Lame, shortened to Tamerlane, and later modified by Christopher Marlowe to Tamburlaine.

All the evidence we have suggests that Timur was a Muslim, possibly a member of the Naqshbandi school of Sufism, a connection that profoundly influenced Timur's approach to his Islamic faith. Bakhautdin Naqshbandi was born into a family of weavers probably in 1318, just a few years before Timur's birth. He was an excellent weaver, but also a zealous student of Islamic scripture with outstanding teachers. Naqshbandi eventually abandoned his profession and established his own Sufi school based on the principal of *faqr*, or voluntary poverty. Thereafter, Naqshbandi adopted a modest life, sleeping on a plain mat in the summer and straw in the winter. He died in 1389, but not before seeing his Naqshbandi Sufi order grow to great prominence in central Asia. Their motto was "Seclusion from society, traveling about the motherland, outwardly with people, inwardly with God."

I have visited the tomb of Bakhautdin Naqshbandi on the outskirts of Bukhara on several occasions, and it is a deeply spiritual and inspirational place. Timur was also influenced by his chief spiritual mentor Sayyid Baraka, who was so important to Timur that he is buried beside him in the great mausoleum of the Gur i-Emir in Samarkand.

But while Timur was a strong supporter of Islam who liked to engage in religious debates and was even accompanied by a portable mosque on his campaigns, his faith does not seem to have mitigated in any way his penchant for warfare and conquest. As Christopher Marlowe indicated in his play, Timur justified his violent conquests by claiming to be the Scourge of God, just as Chinggis Khan had done a century earlier to the elites of Bukhara after he had sacked their city.

Perhaps we should say a little more here about the personality of Timur. Beyond doubt, he was a military genius very much in the mold of Chinggis Khan, but in the rest of this lecture and the next, we will unfold the story of his many campaigns and victories. But various contemporary sources also comment upon Timur's intelligence more generally, including the Arab writer and traveler Muhammad Ibn Arabshah, who lived during the reign of Timur and commented on his exceptional linguistic ability. As well as his native Chagatayid language, Timur also learned to speak Persian, Mongolian, and various other Turkic dialects.

Other sources comment on how comfortable Timur felt conversing with some of the great scholars of his time, including the renowned Persian poet Hafez, whose collected works are regarded as the pinnacle of Persian literature. Several sources inform us that Timur was a superb chess player and that he even invented a new and much larger version of the game with many more squares and new pieces including elephants and camels. So clearly Timur's intelligence extended well beyond the art of war.

But speaking of the art of war, let's pick up our story again with Timur aged in his 30s. He had already built a formidable nomadic army and a loyal following and was determined to increase his power within the crumbling Ulus Chagatai. With his legitimacy enhanced through his Chinggisid wife and the puppet Chagatayid prince he had placed on the throne of Transoxiana, Timur chose Samarkand as his capital and then set out to emulate Chinggis Khan by creating his own empire. And much like Chinggis Khan, it was from the ranks of his early and loyal supporters and family members that Timur recruited his most important commanders and most trusted lieutenants, who he appointed to positions of power within all the regions he conquered.

In the early 1360s, Timur formed an alliance with Amir Husayn, ruler of the Qara'unas Mongols. Both men spent some time in the region of Khurasan to the west of Transoxiana, working as virtual mercenaries for local leaders. In 1364, the two commanders attacked a Moghul army in Transoxiana, but the following year, Amir Husayn presumptuously declared himself ruler of the entire Ulus Chagatai. He was immediately opposed by other tribal chiefs, including Timur, which led to a protracted war between the two former allies. Three years later, Timur led a successful rebellion against Amir Husayn, who was killed soon afterwards. Timur then appointed a close ally, Amir Cheku, also of the Barlas tribe, as new commander of Amir Husayn's Qara'unas troops, thus considerably enhancing the size of his army.

In his early campaigns, Timur seems to have intentionally set out not only to emulate Chinggis Khan but also to draw strategically on the legacy of the Mongols. This included the eradication of any rival tribal claimants for power in the region, such as Chinggis Khan had done in his rise to power.

Between 1370 and 1372, Timur attempted to destroy the leader of the Dughlat tribe, emir Qamar al-Din, who had staged a rebellion against the clans descended from the Chagatayids. From his secure base in the region of Moghulistan, Qamar al-Din had gone so far as to claim the title of khan. Timur immediately marched against him, but the climate and environment of Moghulistan made it difficult for the army to make headway, and Timur temporarily gave up the chase.

The following year, Timur launched what would turn out to be the first of several campaigns against the Qunqirat Sufi dynasty in Khwarazm. Calling again on the legacy of the Mongols, Timur justified this campaign by arguing that Chinggis Khan had specifically bequeathed the revenues of the two principal cities of Khwarazm, Khiva and Khat, to Chagatai and his descendants. As Timur had installed his puppet Chagatayid prince on the throne, this was justification enough, although clearly it was simply a convenient reason to attack potential rivals.

Timur launched another campaign against Qamar al-Din in 1375, and this occupied him for the next three years. As part of this campaign, he appointed his eldest son, Umar Shaykh, governor of the richest part of

Qamar al-Din's realm, the Fergana Valley in modern Uzbekistan. This so enraged Qamar al-Din that he formed an alliance with other dissident princes of the Ulus Chagatai, and for a time, Timur was hard-pressed to defend his territories against them. But by 1378, Timur had succeeded in driving Qamar al-Din into exile and taking control of his lands.

Timur's power and prestige, not to mention his wealth, continued to increase with each victory over a rival. His prestige was further enhanced when, in 1375, Timur gave refuge to a prince of the Jochid lineage named Toqtamish, a pretender to the throne of the Mongol Blue Horde that ruled lands to the north of Timur's growing empire. Timur used his forces and his strategic alliances to help Toqtamish win the throne of the Blue Horde in the winter of 1379. Now, with a Jochid prince as his protégé in the north and a Chagatayid pretender prince on the throne of Transoxiana, Timur presented himself to rivals and allies alike as a great conqueror in the mold of Chinggis Khan and the champion of the continuing Chinggisid right to rule in central Asia.

Timur launched an invasion of Khwarazm in 1379 and 1380, during which he razed the city of Urgench to the ground and divided its population in the manner of the Mongols, sending scholars and artisans back to his capital of Samarkand but destroying the rest. As Beatrice Forbes Manz points out, "this action marked a radical departure from his earlier campaigns, and was probably designed to evoke the Mongol conquests."

This was a pattern of harsh and violent conquest that would now mark most of Timur's remaining campaigns and would be principally responsible for his reputation for brutality, a reputation that continues to the present day. But it is intriguing to speculate on how much of this behavior was a product of Timur's own psyche and how much was an explicit evocation of the legacy of Chinggis Khan, and of himself as worthy successor.

In 1381, Timur installed his third son, Amiranshah, as governor of Khurasan, then set out to destroy any rivals to that position by attacking other regional powers, including the Khartids, who ruled as the kings of Herat in modern Afghanistan. Timur defeated them in 1381, then removed them completely in 1383, placing the region under Chagatayid—and this his own—control.

With his position now secure in central Asia, and with Toqtamish a close ally along the northern borders, Timur turned his gaze towards the west, to the territories of the former Mongol Ilkhanate. He first invaded the region of Mazandaran in 1384 and installed another puppet Chinggisid prince named Luqman on the throne. He allowed Luqman to retain the ilkhanid title of *padshah*, but it was clear to everyone, including Luqman, that he now ruled as a vassal of Timur.

After this, he captured the city of Soltaniyeh, about 150 miles northwest of Tehran, the city where all the late ilkhans had been enthroned and where former ilkhan Oljeitu was buried in a royal mausoleum. In doing so, Timur clearly proclaimed himself as heir to the Ilkhanate in addition to the Ulus Chagatai. This was also why Timur later chose his own birth date, to support his claim to the Ilkhanate. As Beatrice Forbes Manz points out, the selection of the year 1336 for his birth date legitimized his claim to the throne because it was one year after the death of the last ilkhan, Abu Said, who had died in 1335. Timur thus implicitly laid claim to the ilkhanid inheritance.

While Timur was actively campaigning in the former Ilkhanate, further north, his protégé and ally Toqtamish was busy with his own campaigns, which led to him taking control of the Mongol Golden Horde itself. But once secure as khan of the Golden Horde, Toqtamish suddenly turned against Timur, perhaps genuinely offended that this Barlas outsider was now laying claim to the legacy of the Chinggisids in two former khanates. As a descendant of Chinggis Khan's oldest son Jochi, Toqtamish might well have been outraged by the actions of Timur, who was only related to the Chinggisids by marriage. Beatrice Forbes Manz notes that "as a descendant of Chinggis Khan [Toqtamish] could claim a higher station in the Turco-Mongolian world."

In 1382, while Timur had been fighting the Khartids of Herat, Toqtamish, had formed an alliance with the Mamluk sultans of Egypt and Syria, the same Mamluks whose forces had defeated a Mongol army under Hulagu at the Battle of Ain Jalut more than a century earlier, in 1260. During the winter of 1385–86, Toqtamish attacked the populous city of Tabriz in Iranian Azerbaijan, thus reasserting the old claim of the Golden Horde to rule the Caucasus.

The attack on Tabriz led to the outbreak of war between Toqtamish and Timur, a war that would occupy both men for a decade. In the spring of 1386, Timur set out on an invasion of Iran, the first major campaign of genuine imperial conquest of his rule. We will have more to say about the great campaigns of Timur in the next lecture, but here we remain intent on tracing the conflict between the two former allies and the role this played in the rise of Timur.

Timur enjoyed immediate success on his Iranian campaign by defeating another Turkic-Mongol ruler named Ahmad Jalayir in Azerbaijan. But the following year, Toqtamish launched his first direct attack on Timur. Timurid propagandists and historians later claimed this ended in victory for Timur, but numismatic evidence tells a different story, because Toqtamish continued to issue coins in his name in major Azerbaijan cities like Baku and Darband for the next several years.

At the urging of Toqtamish, Timur's enemies old and new now began to form alliances against him. Late in 1387, Timur learned that Toqtamish had allied with Timur's old enemy Qamar al-Din and other dissident tribal leaders, and their combined armies had attacked the Timurid heartland of Transoxiana, ravaging it as far as the Oxus River. Timur immediately marched eastwards and attacked the Sufi dynasty ruling Khwarazm, which had also gone over to Toqtamish. The poor city of Urgench found itself squarely in Timur's sights for a second time in eight years; it was razed to the ground again, and large numbers of its people deported. Timur next marched against the khan of the eastern Chagatayid realm, who had also supported Toqtamish, campaigning against him as far north as Lake Zaysan in modern Kazakhstan.

Timur spent the late spring of 1390 preparing for what he hoped would be a decisive campaign against Toqtamish. He passed the winter of '90–91 in Tashkent, then confronted Toqtamish at the Battle of the Kondurcha River on June 18th, 1391, in what is today the Samara Oblast of Russia. Toqtamish's cavalry tried to encircle Timur's army and attack its flanks, but Timur's cavalry stood its ground and then launched a decisive frontal attack. The forces of the Golden Horde were put to flight all the way up to the Volga River. Although most of the Horde's cavalry escaped, Timur claimed victory. Timur collected a massive amount of booty from this victory, then returned to Samarkand.

The following year, in the autumn of 1392, Timur set out on another major campaign into Persia, which we will discuss in detail in the next lecture. Toqtamish spent the years of Timur's absence in Persia rebuilding his forces, being careful to avoid any direct confrontation with Timurids in the meantime. By the spring of 1395, Toqtamish was ready, and he renewed hostilities by attacking Timurid forces at Shirvan in the eastern Caucasus. Timur immediately marched against him and reconquered all the territories Toqtamish had captured.

The final confrontation between the two men occurred at the Battle of the Terek River on April 15th, 1395. The Terek is one of the major rivers of the Caucasus, flowing eastwards through Georgia and Russia and into the Caspian Sea. The cavalry of Toqtamish and his allies focused their attacks on the right flank and center of Timur's army. But at a critical moment, some of the emirs who had allied with the Golden Horde went over to Timur, allowing the Timurid forces to turn the tables and attack and destroy the left flank of Toqtamish's army.

Toqtamish and the remnants of his army fled north to the Volga River, pursued by Timur and his victorious army, which destroyed city after city as they marched—Azaq, Majar, Sarai, and Ukek—almost all the way to Moscow, which was only saved from destruction by events that pious Muscovites saw as miraculous, and which have only added to the legend of Timur.

As Timur's army approached, Prince Vasily I, the ruler of Moscow, led his badly outnumbered army out to engage the Timurid forces. While Prince Vasily waited to confront the enemy, Russian Orthodox clerics decided to seek help from God by transporting a sacred icon, a beautiful medieval painting titled *Theotokos of Vladimir*, from the town of Vladimir to Moscow.

The word *Theotokos* is the Greek name for the Virgin Mary and literally means the "Birth-Giver of God." As the sacred relic passed through the villages along the way, pious Russians prayed for deliverance. According to contemporary accounts, Prince Vasily himself spent a night weeping in prayer over the icon. The people's prayers would appear to have been answered, because on August 26th, Timur suddenly packed up his army and left.

Timur had had enough of chasing the defeated Golden Horde; he wanted to return to Samarkand and then regroup for a major campaign into Persia. But because of this miraculous deliverance, Russians have celebrated the feast day of Theotokos ever since. And if you want to see this superb icon, you will need to visit the Tretyakov Gallery in Moscow, which I can personally attest is one of the great art galleries of the world.

In the aftermath of the Battle of the Terek River, Toqtamish was deposed as khan of the Golden Horde and replaced by Edigu. Toqtamish fled into the steppes of Ukraine and formed an alliance with the Grand Duke of Lithuania. The two confronted a Timurid army in 1399, this time led by two of Timur's generals, and were utterly crushed. Toqtamish survived again and now fled into Siberia, where he was eventually killed by the troops of Khan Edigu sometime in 1406.

These events effectively marked the end of the Golden Horde, which now splintered into a series of smaller khanates, as we saw in the previous lecture. Timur was content with having destroyed the power of the Golden Horde and made no attempt to establish control over its former territories.

The war with Toqtamish was just one of the many problems that occupied the strategic thinking of Timur. In the next lecture, we will follow Timur on the major campaigns that made him infamous throughout Eurasia and brought him very much to the attention of the pope and various kings and princes of Europe.

These campaigns include two invasions of Persia and the destruction of Baghdad; an invasion of India and the sacking of Delhi; a campaign into Anatolia, where he defeated the powerful army of Ottoman sultan Bayezid I, and thus inadvertently delayed the fall of Constantinople to the Ottomans by a half century; and his final planned assault on the Ming Dynasty in China.

But before we go, let's leave the last words in this lecture to Christopher Marlowe's Tamburlaine the Great, who exhorts a Persian prince to join him in his campaigns of conquest with the following prophetic lines:

> Forsake thy king, and do but join with me,
>
> And we will triumph over all the world:
>
> I hold the Fates bound fast in iron chains,
>
> And with my hand turn Fortune's wheel about;
>
> And sooner shall the sun fall from his sphere
>
> Than Tamburlaine be slain or overcome.

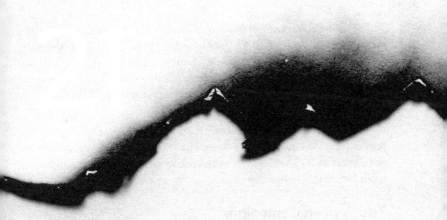

TIMUR'S MAJOR CAMPAIGNS

This lecture follows Timur on the major campaigns that made the construction of his vast steppe and desert empire possible. These campaigns also financed the construction of Timur's many building projects in Samarkand, because from each of them he returned with masses of treasure.

Timur's Success

Timur's success as a conqueror was made possible by the formidable army he constructed and the effective way he used this to topple various regional powers before appointing his sons or other trusted lieutenants to rule their kingdoms. Rulers who swore allegiance to Timur, either voluntarily or after being defeated by him, were expected to contribute additional troops for his campaigns, and Timur would also conscript local nomadic contingents into his cavalry as he passed through a region.

In addition, when the Mongols had ruled the sedentary populations of Persia and the Middle East during the Ilkhanate era, they had created regional armies called *cherig*. Timur made use of these by assigning them to his regional governors to help them quell any uprisings.

Timur tended to make most major military decisions himself, trusting to his tactical genius and his flair for improvisation. As he set out on a campaign, Timur rode at the head of a single invading army, but as the campaigns developed, he often divided his forces into various contingents and dispatched them in several different directions at once.

Timur also maintained tight control over his troops, allowing them to undertake massacres of defeated urban populations only after he had selected specific cities to suffer them. His army did pillage various regions, but Timur sometimes had his men work to restore damaged agricultural lands before they moved on.

The Persian Campaigns

Persia was the heartland of the former Ilkhanate, and Timur's campaigns into that region were sandwiched between his long conflict with Toqtamish. Following the death of the last ilkhan, Abu Said, various factions had moved into the power vacuum in Persia and created a number of regional states. Timur decided to add the Ilkhanate to his burgeoning empire. He did so initially by destroying the states that ruled the eastern portions of the former Ilkhanate, particularly the region of Khurasan and the cities of Kandahar and Herat, which he captured in 1381.

With these regions secure, in 1383, Timur marched west into Persia proper, capturing Tehran, which surrendered to him and so was spared any general massacre. Other towns like Sultaniya were not so lucky. When Khurasan revolted against Timurid rule in 1384, Timur destroyed the town of Isfizar and cemented many of its residents into the walls of the city alive. After completing this phase of the campaign, Timur returned to Samarkand for a year before marching into the Caucasus in pursuit of Toqtamish again, which occupied him for the next several years.

When Timur returned to Persia in the late 1380s, he was pleased to find that the cities and regions he had conquered earlier had generally remained loyal to him. On this second phase of the Persian campaign, Timur first focused on the important southern cities of Isfahan and Shiraz.

As Timur approached Isfahan in 1387, the city sent out emissaries to greet him, and they offered the immediate surrender of the city. Timur accepted the surrender, but soon afterward a revolt broke out among the citizens of Isfahan, and some of Timur's tax collectors were killed. This time he showed no mercy and ordered a general massacre. Historians estimate that anywhere between 100,000 and 200,000 citizens of Isfahan were killed.

Following the sack of Isfahan, Timur was again distracted by the conflict with Toqtamish, but in 1392, he commenced another campaign into Persia. He first defeated the formidable Kurdish fighters in the northern region of Persian Kurdistan, then took the southern city of Shiraz in 1393. Its rulers, the Muzaffarid dynasty, initially agreed to become vassals of Timur, but they later revolted. Timur simply annexed the city and region, destroying Muzaffarid power.

In that same year, Timur captured Baghdad for the first time. Timur installed a prince of the Sarbadar tribe as his puppet governor of Baghdad and returned home to Samarkand again, well pleased with the success of his Persian campaigns.

Into India

In 1398, Timur decided to launch a new campaign south into India to attack the Delhi sultanate. At that time, it was ruled by Sultan Nasir-ud-Din Mahmud Shah of the Tughlaq dynasty. Timur took a small handpicked force directly into the mighty Hindu Kush mountains.* By December, Timur and his troops were close to the city and prepared to confront the armies of the sultan.

The decisive battle occurred on the December 17, 1398. The sultan immediately unleashed his most terrifying weapons against the Timurid army: war elephants. The elephants were protected by chain-mail armor and had sharp tusks coated with poison.

Timur's men were initially afraid of these formidable animals, but Timur had heard that elephants were easily spooked. He had his men dig a deep trench in front of their positions so that the elephants could not reach them.

Then, Timur had some of his camels loaded with wood and hay, which was set on fire. The poor camels were goaded to charge at the elephants with their backs on fire. This completely unnerved the elephants, who turned around and charged back toward their own lines, causing havoc as they did so. The Tughlaq forces were thrown into disarray and fled, as did the shah, and Timur had won the Battle of Delhi.

Hundreds of thousands of residents were executed in the sack of Delhi. Timur took an enormous amount of captured treasure out of India and hastened back to his beloved Samarkand, where he used his new resources to further beautify the city.

Back to War in the West

One year after the sack of Delhi, Timur was at war in the west again. This time he was in conflict with Bayezid I, the powerful sultan of the Ottomans, and also with Nasir-ad-Din Faraj, sultan of the Mamluk dynasty in Egypt. The ostensible cause of the war was Bayezid's decision to annex territories in Anatolia that belonged to the Turkmen. As Timur had already claimed sovereignty over the Turkmen, Beyezid's actions were interpreted as encroaching on Timur's imperial domain.

Timur first approached Baghdad, which he had easily captured almost a decade earlier, only to find the city denying him entrance. An enraged Timur was forced to besiege the city for several weeks, and when he finally captured it, he exacted terrible revenge. He ordered that each of his soldiers was to bring him two severed heads until a total of 90,000 dead had been counted and piled up into 120 pyramids.

With Baghdad secure, Timur now returned to the problem of Ottoman sultan Bayezid I. In 1402, Timur invaded Anatolia, confronting Bayezid on July 20 at the Battle of Ankara. Timur's army might have numbered as many as 140,000 men, and it also included more than 30 elephants that Timur

Conquest of Baghdad by Timur

had brought back with him from India. Bayezid was seriously outnumbered, with perhaps 85,000 men. However, Bayezid did have the support of up to 20,000 skilled Serbian and Albanian knights in full harness.

When the two armies confronted each other on that scorching hot July day, Timur's skilled Mongol cavalry immediately galloped toward the enemy. They unleashed volley after volley of arrows that killed thousands of Bayezid's troops in the first assault.

In the midst of battle, the Ottoman forces were desperate for water. Timur diverted a nearby creek away from them, depriving the Ottomans of any opportunity to slake their thirst. At this, many soldiers deserted Bayezid and came over to Timur. The Ottoman army quickly succumbed and was crushed, although Bayezid escaped into nearby mountains with a few hundred horsemen.

Anticipating this possibility, Timur had already stationed men in the mountains, and Bayezid was soon captured. By all accounts, Timur treated his captive well, but the Ottoman ruler died a few weeks later. Timur continued to march westward and devastate Anatolia.

Conclusion

By 1403, Timur was 67 years old and the ruler of a vast empire that included Turkey, Syria, Iraq, Iran, the Caucasus, central Asia, Pakistan, and northern India. It is impossible to know how many people had died in the construction of this empire, but modern demographers have estimated a total death toll approaching 17 million people.

Timur was not quite finished with trying to further expand his empire. There remained one region of Eurasia that was not yet part of the empire: China, which was now under the control of the Ming dynasty. After the Ming founder Hongwu had driven the Mongols back to the steppe in 1368, they had automatically taken up the traditional approach of earlier Chinese imperial dynasties in claiming ownership of much of Inner Eurasia. The Ming emperor assumed the Timurids to be vassals of his tributary empire.

In 1394, Hongwu dispatched Chinese ambassadors to the court of Timur, demanding that he pay homage to Hongwu. When the three ambassadors arrived, they were detained. Hongwu sent another large embassy in 1397, which was treated with similar disdain, as was a third delegation sent to inform Timur that Hongwu was dead and had been succeeded by Yongle as emperor of the Ming.

Ultimately, Timur decided that he simply had to invade China. In preparation for the invasion, Timur made strategic alliances with various Mongol tribes now living back on the Mongolian steppe. One of the most powerful Mongol khans sent his grandson, Oljei Temur, as envoy to Timur, and Persian sources note that the Mongol prince actually converted to Islam while staying in Samarkand.

Although Timur had launched his previous campaigns in the spring, this time he decided to set out in the winter of 1404. The writer Michael Prawdin has posited that Timur made this decision because he thought his time was running out.

Conditions were so severe that many horses perished, and men suffered from frostbite. Early in February, Timur crossed the icy Syr Darya river at Otrar, the same town where Chinggis Khan had launched his Khwarazmian campaign 180 years earlier. Timur immediately became ill with fever and great pain. He died early in the morning of February 18, 1405.

TIMUR'S MAJOR CAMPAIGNS

LECTURE 21 TRANSCRIPT

In the early 1990s, English travel writer Colin Thubron journeyed into central Asia, only recently liberated from the collapsed Soviet Union. In one chapter of the book he subsequently wrote about the experience, he focused on the Uzbek city of Samarkand, a city I have visited on many occasions, and a city whose atmosphere of exoticness still grips the traveler today.

When I first read Thubron's account, I was somewhat irritated by it, because it seemed to dwell on the violence that Chinggis Khan and Timur—Thubron calls them the "world predators"—had unleashed on the region, rather than the extraordinary people of Uzbekistan who had done so well in building their new nation in the post-Soviet era. But at the same time, I couldn't help but be impressed by Thubron's ability to capture the essence of Samarkand, which he describes as a city that "rings with a landlocked strangeness, and was the seat of an empire so remote in its steppe and desert that it only touched Europe to terrorize it."

That remote empire was, of course, the one constructed by Timur, who made Samarkand his capital and turned it into a city rich in magnificent architecture and art. In our next lecture, we will focus on the adornment of Samarkand by Timur and his successors, but in this lecture, we follow Timur on the major campaigns that made the construction of his vast steppe and desert empire possible. These campaigns also financed the construction of Timur's many building projects in Samarkand, because from each of them he returned with masses of booty and treasure. We shall occasionally make use of some of Colin Thubron's compelling descriptions of Timur as we consider the story of these huge campaigns of conquest and the impact his victories had on diverse peoples all over Eurasia.

Thubron, no admirer of Timur but acutely aware of his contradictory and overwhelming personality, introduces him into his story following a discussion of the impact of Chinggis Khan and the Mongols on Samarkand. He writes:

Tamerlane, the Earth Shaker, was the last and perhaps most awesome of these world predators. Born in 1136, 50 miles south of Samarkand, he was the son of a petty chief in a settled Mongol clan. He acquired the name Timur-i Lang or Timur the Lame after arrows maimed his right leg and arm, and passed as Tamerlane into the fearful imagination of the West. By his early-thirties, after years of fighting over the splintered heritage of Genghis Khan, he had become lord of Mavarannah, the Land Beyond the River, and had turned his cold eyes to the conquest of the world.

> Timur had multiple identities that often contradicted each other, particularly his heritage as a nomadic Turko-Mongolian tribal leader, but also his desire to become ruler of the sedentary realm of Islam. These dual intentions provided both opportunities and challenges; Timur, in essence, wanted to re-create the Mongol Empire, but also to rule the Dar al-Islam. The traditions of both worlds influenced even the titles that Timur could claim for himself.

Mongol traditions were very clear that only a descendant of Chinggis could ever use the title khan, so despite the fact that Timur installed various Chinggisid princes on different regional thrones, and also married into the Chinggisid lineage—which meant that he could call himself *gurgan*, or royal son-in-law—he could never claim the title of khan. Instead, Timur used the title emir, which means king, and he was always careful to claim that he was acting on behalf of the Chagatayid rulers of his home region of Transoxiana.

Similarly, although he became a great power in the Muslim world, Timur could never claim the most important Islamic title of caliph, because as a Sunni Muslim, Timur believed that that was reserved exclusively for members of the Quraysh tribe into which the Prophet Muhammad himself had been born. Instead, Timur used his intuition and his personal historians to propagate the myth that he was some sort of a supernatural being who had been ordained by Allah—that he was indeed the "Scourge of God" proclaimed by Christopher Marlowe's *Tamburlaine the Great*.

Timur's continuing and quite astonishing successes as a conqueror only made it easier to support the claim that God was on his side. To most Muslim farmers and merchants, it would have been no stretch at all to believe that Timur was a supernatural being chosen by Allah to rule over them. Having chosen his titles and spun their supporting myths, and having become Lord of the Land Beyond the River, Timur did indeed turn his cold eyes to the conquest of the world, spending most of the remaining decades of his life on near constant military campaigns of conquest.

Timur's success as a conqueror was made possible by the formidable army he constructed and the effective way he used this to topple various regional powers before appointing his sons or other trusted lieutenants to rule their kingdoms. Timur's split nomadic/sedentary identities also influenced the sort of army he constructed. As Beatrice Forbes Manz observes, "Timur's strength lay in his ability to exploit both nomad and settled resources." At the heart of Timur's army was the Mongol cavalry descended from the original hordes that had fought for Chagatai during the era of the Mongol khanates. To these hardened and skilled nomadic horse-riding archers, he added various contingents of foot soldiers and other types of cavalry conscripted from the settled territories he conquered.

Rulers who swore allegiance to Timur, either voluntarily or after being defeated by him, were expected to contribute additional troops for his campaigns, and Timur would also conscript local nomadic contingents into his cavalry as he passed through a region. In addition, when the Mongols had ruled the sedentary populations of Persia and the Middle East during the Ilkhanate era, they had created regional armies called *cherig*, and Timur also made use of these by assigning them to his regional governors to help them quell any uprisings. So much like the army of Ilkhan Hulagu, when Timur set out on campaign, he did so at the head of a huge, multi-ethnic army possessed of a wide range of skills and specialists with the collective ability to defeat any opponent, sedentary or nomadic.

But an army is only as good as its leader, and although Timur certainly gathered around him a group of loyal and skilled officers, he tended to make most major military decisions himself, trusting to his tactical genius and his flair for improvisation. As he set out on a campaign, Timur rode at the head of a single invading army, but as the campaigns developed, he often divided his forces into various contingents and dispatched them in several different directions at once, much as Chinggis Khan had done during the Khwarazmian campaign. This tactical approach, as noted by Beatrice Forbes Manz, "combined overwhelming force with the advantage of unpredictability, which confused his foes."

Timur also maintained tight control over his troops, allowing them to undertake massacres of defeated urban populations only after he had selected specific cities to suffer them, and only after he had given explicit permission for the massacre to commence. His army did pillage various regions, but Timur would sometimes have his men work to restore damaged agricultural lands before they moved on.

Like the Mongols, and indeed all the great nomadic armies since the Xiongnu had first emerged late in the 3rd century BCE, Timur used a decimal system to organize his army. His children and grandchildren, along with trusted loyal companions, became the core commanders of his military contingents. He was always careful to distribute conquered troops and commanders widely throughout his realm to prevent any build-up of power by different families and their personal troops. Often he would destroy the most powerful regional dynasties, but left smaller ones in place to administer the region more diffusely and with less concentration of power, thus creating an effective system of checks and balances in the region.

Timur does not appear to have been interested in establishing any permanent administrative structures, or capitals, in the regions he conquered. His was very much a command center on the move. We know that he did have several skilled Persian administrators travel with him, whose job was to ensure the successful operation of taxation and revenue, and also Turkic scribes whose job was probably to keep records and write accounts of the campaigns, usually in the Uyghur script. Timur also had law specialists accompany him on campaign, whose job may have been to conduct tribunals against any errant officers in the army. He did not always distinguish between military and administrative roles, and it appears that some of his most senior Turkic-Mongolian military commanders were also given responsibilities for tax collection and the supervision of regional bureaucrats.

OK, let's turn now to a consideration of how Timur's approach to the art of war played out on the five major campaigns: two into Persia, one into India against the Delhi Sultanate, another into Anatolia to confront the Ottomans, and his final campaign against the Ming Dynasty in China.

Persia was the heartland of the former Ilkhanate, and Timur's campaigns into that region were sandwiched between his long conflict with Toqtamish. Following the death of the last ilkhan, Abu Said, various factions had moved into the power vacuum in Persia and created a number of regional states. Timur decided to add the Ilkhanate to his burgeoning empire, initially by destroying the states that ruled the eastern portions of the former Ilkhanate, particularly the region of Khurasan and the cities of Kandahar and Herat, which he captured in 1381.

With these regions secure, in 1383, Timur marched west into Persia proper, capturing Tehran, which surrendered to him and so was spared any general massacre. Other towns like Sultaniyeh were not so lucky, and when Khurasan revolted against Timurid rule in 1384, Timur destroyed the town of Isfizar and cemented many of its residents into the walls of the city alive. After completing this phase of the campaign, Timur returned to Samarkand for a year before marching into the Caucasus in pursuit of Toqtamish again, which ended up occupying him for the next several years.

When Timur returned to Persia in the late 1380s, he was pleased to find that the cities and regions he had conquered earlier had generally remained loyal to him, thanks in part to the good work of the generals he had left there and of his son Miran Shah, who Timur had installed as regent. On this second phase of the Persian campaign, Timur first focused on the important southern cities of Isfahan and Shiraz.

As Timur approached Isfahan in 1387, the city sent out emissaries to greet him, and they offered the immediate surrender of the city. Timur accepted the surrender and treated the city with leniency, but soon afterwards, a revolt broke out amongst the citizens of Isfahan, and some of Timur's tax collectors were killed. This time he showed no mercy and ordered a general massacre.

Historians estimate that anywhere between 100,000 and 200,000 citizens of Isfahan were killed, and one source counted more than 28 towers that the Timurid army constructed out of decapitated human heads, each containing 1,500 or more skulls. Like Chinggis Khan, Timur used terror in a systematic way to send messages to other towns that resistance was futile, and they would be much better submitting and avoiding any sort of massacre.

Following the sack of Isfahan, Timur was again distracted by the conflict with Toqtamish, but in 1392, he commenced another campaign into Persia. He first defeated the formidable Kurdish fighters in the northern regions of Persian Kurdistan, then took the southern city of Shiraz in 1393.

Its rulers, the Muzaffarid Dynasty, initially agreed to become vassals of Timur, but they later revolted. So Timur simply annexed the city and region, destroying Muzaffarid power.

In that same year, Timur captured Baghdad for the first time, doing so with relative ease and a small military contingent after a sudden surprise march of just eight days. The ruler of Baghdad, Sultan Ahmad Jalayir, escaped the Timurid forces and fled to Syria where he came under the protection of Mamluk Sultan Barquq. Timur installed a prince of the Sarbadar tribe as his puppet governor of Baghdad and returned home to Samarkand again, well pleased with the success of his Persian campaigns.

As we shall see in a moment, this was not the end of Timur's forays to the west, but in 1398, he decided to launch a new campaign in an entirely different direction, south into India to attack the Delhi Sultanate. At that time, the Delhi Sultanate was ruled by Sultan Nasir-ud-Din Mahmud Shah of the Tughlaq Dynasty. The Tughlaqs were Muslims of Turkic-Indian origin who had first taken control of Delhi in 1320. The founder of the dynasty was Ghiyath al-Din Tughluq, whose father had been a Turkish slave and mother a Hindu.

After marching through Afghanistan, Timur divided his army into three. One contingent of 30,000 soldiers led by his grandson Pir Muhammad was sent south from Kabul into the Punjab. A second wing led by a younger grandson, Muhammad Sultan, march southeast through the foothills of the Himalaya against the city of Lahore.

Timur himself took a small, handpicked force directly into the mighty Hindu Kush Mountains. Historians find it difficult to find any strategic reason for this other than Timur's hubris in wanting to conquer a remote and mountainous region that no other conqueror had ever set foot in. The ascent was steep and icy, and many of the horses could not make their way up the slopes. And when descending from high passes, Timur and his troops were forced to use ropes for men and horses.

Michael Prawdin offers a fascinating description of how the ageing Timur himself was lowered down the slopes: "For Tamerlane they constructed a sort of toboggan fitted with rings through which ropes were passed, and he was lowered to a stage excavated by ice axes where he could stand for a while. By five such stages he was progressively lowered down, until he reached a place where he was able to continue unaided."

The horses were not so lucky, and most had fallen to their deaths by the time the party reached the Indus River, very near the spot where around two centuries earlier, Jalal al-Din, the son of Khwarazmian shah Muhammad, fleeing a pursuing Mongol army, had plunged with his horse into the river and swum to safety on the other side.

Timur and his troops crossed the Indus on September 30th, 1398, and continued southwards towards Delhi, reconnecting the various contingents of his army along the way and easily dealing with sporadic resistance from local rulers. By December, he was close to the city and prepared to confront the armies of Sultan Nasir-ud-Din. The decisive battle occurred on the 17th of December, 1398. The sultan immediately unleashed his most terrifying weapons against the Timurid army: war elephants. The elephants were protected by chain-mail armor and had sharp tusks coated with poison.

Timur's men were initially afraid of these formidable animals, but their ever-resourceful leader, who had heard that elephants were easily spooked, had his men dig a deep trench in front of their positions so that the elephants could not reach them. Then Timur had some of his camels loaded with wood and hay, which was set on fire. The poor camels were goaded to charge at the elephants with their backs on fire. Screaming with pain, the camels were soon amongst the elephants, who, completely unnerved, turned around and charged back towards their own lines, causing all sorts of havoc as they did. The Tughlaq forces were thrown into disarray and fled, as indeed did Shah Nasir-ud-Din, and Timur had won the Battle of Delhi.

Colin Thubron offers his own graphic description of the battle: "On the Ganges plain before Delhi, the Indian sultan's squadrons of mailed elephants, their tusks lashed with poisoned blades, sent a momentary tremor through the Mongol ranks, but the great beasts were routed and the city and all its inhabitants leveled with the earth."

Hundreds of thousands of residents were executed in the sack of Delhi, and the city was said to have reeked of decomposing bodies for weeks afterwards. The dead were decapitated, and again, their heads were piled up into macabre towers that were feasted on by the birds. This was one of Timur's greatest victories, but a disaster for Delhi, which took well over a century to recover from this devastating blow, and also for the great Ganges Plain of India, where perhaps 5 million people died as a result of the invasion.

Timur took an enormous amount of captured booty and treasure out of India and hastened back to his beloved Samarkand, where he used his new resources to further beautify the city.

One year after the sack of Delhi, Timur was at war in the west again, this time with Bayezid I, the powerful sultan of the Ottomans, and also with Nasir-ad-Din Faraj, sultan of the Mamluk Dynasty in Egypt. The ostensible cause of the war was Bayezid's decision to annex territories in Anatolia that belonged to the Turkmen. As Timur had already claimed sovereignty over the Turkmen, Bayezid's actions were interpreted as encroaching upon Timur's imperial domain.

He first approached Baghdad, which he had easily captured almost a decade earlier, but which this time denied him entrance. An enraged Timur was forced to besiege the city for several weeks, and when he finally captured it, he exacted terrible revenge. He ordered that each of his soldiers was to bring him two severed heads, until a total of 90,000 dead had been counted and piled up into 120 pyramids. When the soldiers ran out of citizens to execute, they turned on prisoners of war that had been captured earlier in the campaign. And when these ran out, several sources note that some soldiers beheaded their own wives so as to achieve their quota.

Few cities in word history have suffered the number of brutal invasions and sackings that Baghdad has endured. The city was founded on July 30th, 762, as the purpose-built, carefully designed capital of the Abbasid Caliphate. Baghdad was strategically very well located between the two great rivers of the Tigris and Euphrates and at the center of major trade routes. The outer wall of the Abbasid capital was an impressive 80 feet high and was surrounded by a deep moat. Inside the walls were magnificent gardens, palaces, and mosques, and broad thoroughfares connected the main city gates.

As the imperial capital, it attracted many of the best and brightest minds of the Islamic world, functioning as the intellectual hub of the caliphate through the 9th century. By the beginning of the 9th century, the population of Baghdad was somewhere between 300,000 and 500,000 people. Even as the Abbasid Caliphate began to splinter late in the 10th century, the city remained one of the great commercial and cultural hubs of Eurasia for the next 350 years, until it was sacked by Hulagu and his Mongol army in February 1258, bringing an end to the Golden Age of Islam.

In the aftermath, Baghdad was rebuilt and became an important regional center under the Mongol ilkhans before being sacked again by Timur in 1401. But Baghdad survived Timur and continued to function for centuries afterwards as a regional center under a series of successor states. It was captured again in 1534 by the Ottoman Turks, which led to another period of decline. In 1907, the population of Baghdad was something like 185,000, but by 1950, as the capital of the newly created kingdom of Iraq, the population had climbed back to 600,000.

The city flourished in the 1970s thanks to oil revenue, although its infrastructure was badly damaged by shelling in the first Gulf War of 1991. Baghdad was bombed again in March and April 2003 during the US invasion of Iraq. The city has been under US and allied occupation ever since, although since June 2004, its administration, and that of the entire Iraqi nation, has been under the control of the elected national Iraqi government. Few cities in the world have endured the regular destruction heaped upon Baghdad, but it is still functioning nearly 1,300 years later, a testament to the will and persistence of its people over all those centuries.

With Baghdad secure, Timur now returned to the problem of Ottoman sultan Bayezid I, who had been sending him insulting letters. In 1402, Timur invaded Anatolia, confronting Bayezid on July 20th at the Battle of Ankara. Timur's army might have numbered as many as 140,000 men and also included more than 30 elephants that Timur had brought back with him from India. Bayezid was seriously outnumbered, with perhaps 85,000 men, 25 percent of which were recently conquered Tatars. But Bayezid did have the support of up to 20,000 skilled Serbian and Albanian knights in full harness.

Bayezid had been busy besieging the Byzantine capital of Constantinople at the time of the invasion, but immediately marched back to Ankara when news of Timur's approach reached him. After having been force-marched from Constantinople to Ankara through the summer heat, Bayezid's troops were tired and thirsty. Allowing his men no time to rest and recover, and ignoring the advice of his officers who suggested adopting a defensive strategy against Timur, Bayezid charged onwards in the hope of confronting Timur's army head on. But the crafty Timur found a way of avoiding the Ottoman forces and instead circled back until they were quietly following behind the marching Ottomans, even camping in the same locations the enemy had just left a day or so earlier and making use of Ottoman tents and water.

When the two armies did finally confront each other on that scorching hot July day in 1402, Timur's skilled Mongol cavalry immediately galloped towards the enemy, unleashing volley after volley of arrows that killed thousands of Bayezid's troops in the first assault. Some of the European knights who were allies of Bayezid, protected from the Timurid arrow storm by their heavy armor, fought their way through the Timurid lines and urged Bayezid to follow them, but the Sultan refused.

In the midst of battle, and with the Ottoman forces desperate for water, Timur diverted a nearby creek away from them, depriving the Ottomans of any opportunity to slake their thirst. At this, many Turkmen soldiers deserted Bayezid and came over to Timur. Exhausted and desperate for water, the Ottoman army quickly succumbed and was crushed, although Bayezid escaped into nearby mountains with a few hundred horsemen.

Anticipating this possibility, Timur had already stationed men in the mountains, and Bayezid was soon captured. By all accounts, Timur treated his captive well; after all, as Michael Prawdin notes, "they both belonged to the same race and professed the same religion." But the Ottoman ruler died a few weeks later, and with nothing to stop him, Timur continued his march westwards and devastate Anatolia.

Some Muslim sources describe the Timurid army as almost out of control, acting more like savages than a disciplined invading force. Timur and his army soon reached the Aegean Coast, where he besieged and captured the city of Smyrna, the stronghold of the Christian Knights Hospitallers, and carried out brutal beheadings of many of the inhabitants in the aftermath.

The Battle of Ankara was a disaster for the Ottomans, who now splintered into competing factions and fought a civil war that lasted for the next 12 years. But as students of history, we must remember that even though this was a great victory for Timur that inadvertently gave the city of Constantinople, and indeed the Byzantine Empire, a 50-year reprieve, in the end, Timur's empire crumbled quickly while the Ottomans went on to construct one of the great empires of the early modern world, an empire of global significance that lasted well into the 20th century.

By 1403, the now 67-year-old Timur was ruler of a vast empire that included Turkey, Syria, Iraq, Iran, the Caucasus, central Asia, Pakistan, and northern India. It is impossible to know how many people had died in the construction of this empire, but modern demographers have estimated a total death toll approaching 17 million people. An important Christian source, John, the archbishop of Sultaniyeh, who headed an embassy set to Timur by Charles VI of France and Henry IV of England, wrote in all seriousness that Timur had destroyed three-quarters of the world's Muslim population. For a while, various European courts, as well as the pope, hoped that Timur would become a great ally with the Christians against the Muslim world, but these hopes came to nothing.

Despite the extraordinary success of his campaigns, Timur was not quite finished with trying to further expand his empire. There remained one region of Eurasia that was not yet part of the empire, the most glittering prize of all: China, which was now under the control of the Ming Dynasty. After Ming founder Hongwu had driven the Mongols back to the steppe in 1368, they had automatically taken up the traditional approach of earlier Chinese imperial dynasties in claiming ownership of much of inner Eurasia. It was natural, then, for the Ming emperor to assume the Timurids to be vassals of his tributary empire.

But it wasn't until 1394 that Hongwu actually got around to dispatching Chinese ambassadors to the court of Timur, demanding that he pay homage to Hongwu. When the three ambassadors arrived, they were detained. Hongwu sent another large embassy in 1397, which was treated with similar disdain, as was a third delegation sent to inform Timur that Hongwu was dead and had been succeeded by Yongle as emperor of the Ming.

Ultimately, Timur decided that he simply had to invade China, the wealthiest and most glittering prize sought by all the steppe nomadic conquerors that had preceded him—the Xiongnu, the Turks, the Jurchen, and of course the Mongols. In preparation for the invasion, Timur made strategic alliances with various Mongol tribes now living back on the Mongolian steppe. One of the most powerful Mongol khans sent his grandson, Oljei Temur, as envoy to Timur, and Persian sources note that the Mongol prince actually converted to Islam while staying in Samarkand.

Although Timur had launched his previous campaigns in the spring, this time, he decided to set out in the winter of 1404. Michael Prawdin is convinced that Timur made this decision because he thought time was running out for him. As Prawdin puts it, "There can be little doubt that it was the dread that death would overtake him before he could reach the farthest goal of his ambition which induced Tamerlane to assemble his army in the middle of a severe winter."

Conditions were so severe that many horses perished, and men suffered from frostbite. Early in February, Timur crossed the icy Syr Darya river at Otrar, the same town where Chinggis Khan had launched his Khwarazmian campaign 180 years earlier. Timur immediately became ill with fever and great pain. He died early in the morning of the 18th of February, 1405. As Prawdin puts it, "the Ruler of the World passed away in the seventieth year of his age." Join me next time as we explore the extraordinary city of Samarkand, which under Timur evolved into the splendid capital of the "ruler of the world."

SAMARKAND: TIMUR'S CULTURAL CAPITAL

Although not his hometown, the city of Samarkand captivated the Turko-Mongol conqueror Timur. Early in his reign as emir, he decided to make Samarkand, which is in modern-day Uzbekistan, his capital. This lecture focuses on Timur's impact on Samarkand, though the city already had a rich and lengthy history long before Timur appeared in central Asia. It also touches on Timur's efforts in the town of Kesh.

Samarkand's Timurid Connection

Samarkand was sacked in 1220 during the Mongols' Khwarazmian campaign. It was still somewhat ruined when Timur decided in 1370 to make it the capital of his empire. Over the next 35 years, he returned to the city 19 or 20 times following his campaigns, and he rebuilt the city just to the southwest of the ancient site of Afrasiab. Timur was careful to spare the lives of artists, craftsmen, and architects living in cities he conquered so that he could send them back to improve and beautify his capital.

An accurate eyewitness account of the rebuilding of Samarkand by Timur is available in the form of a journal kept by Castilian envoy Ruy González de Clavijo. For example, he reports that Timur "gave orders that a street should be built to pass right through Samarkand" with "shops opened on either side of it."

Timur would sometimes order that brand-new buildings should be torn down and redone if he was unsatisfied with the results. A classic example of this is the construction of the vast Bibi-Khanum mosque, dedicated to his favorite wife. It was finished in 1404, shortly before Timur's death, and he regarded it as the architectural jewel of his empire.

Timur and Kesh

Although Timur lavished much of his resources and time on his adopted capital, he did not forget his hometown of Kesh, or modern Shahrisabz, 50 miles to the south of Samarkand. Clavijo also visited Kesh and has left us a description of what Timur the builder was attempting to accomplish there, particularly "a magnificent mosque which Timur had ordered to be built."

The mosque is still incredibly beautiful today, but it was not the only building Timur was constructing in Kesh, nor indeed the most imposing. That title surely belongs to the great palace Timur had constructed in his hometown. The palace was known as Ak-Saray.

Mosque Timur, modern day

Visitors to Shahrisabz today will find the great palace of Timur in ruins. All that remains are the pillars that once supported the giant arch at the entrance, but these have a tremendous noble grandeur. The pillars still have sections of beautiful, unrestored mosaics on them.

Gur-Emir

Back in Samarkand, the magnificent Gur-Emir is the final resting place of Timur and his family. It is also a major and influential achievement in the history of Turkic-Persian architecture. In particular, it is the precursor and model for much of the later architecture of the Mughal tombs in India, including the famous Taj Mahal in Agra, which was built by Timur's descendants, the rulers of the Mughal dynasty.

The Gur-Emir was originally a complex of buildings topped with magnificent azure domes. The construction of the actual mausoleum commenced in 1403 under the direction of Timur, following the death of his beloved grandson and intended heir, Muhammad Sultan, for whom the tomb was intended.

Timur had no intention of being personally buried in the Gur-Emir; he had constructed his own tomb in the mosque in Kesh, beside that of his father. But Timur's sudden death in the frigid winter of 1405, early in his campaign against the Ming dynasty, meant that the passes into Kesh were covered in deep snow; the only option was to bring his body back to Samarkand. It was another of Timur's grandsons and successors, Ulugh Beg, who completed the work on the tomb, effectively turning the mausoleum into the family crypt of the Timurid dynasty.

Standing in front of the Gur-Emir mausoleum, one is struck by the apparent simplicity of its design and by the glittering blue dome. The entrance portal into the former complex is exquisitely decorated with carved bricks and mosaics. The main dome, with a diameter of roughly 50 feet and a height of more than 40 feet, is bright blue in color but also decorated with various colored patterns.

Inside the building the mausoleum is a large, high chamber with deep niches in its sides and different motifs on the walls. The lower part of the walls are covered by onyx slabs that blend together to appear as though they are a single panel. Most of the upper walls are decorated with painted plaster and gilded arches.

There are various stories associated with the Gur-i Emir, some legendary, others factual. One story concerns a solid block of dark green jade that Ulugh Beg had placed on the headstone directly above the tomb of Timur.

According to the story, the block of jade had originally been housed in a temple used by Chinese emperors, although in which city this temple was located is unknown. The block later came into the possession of Du'a, the longest-reigning khan of the Chagatayid *ulus*, who ruled from 1282 to 1307.

It is believed to be the largest single block of jade known anywhere in the world. Exactly how it came into the possession of Ulugh Beg is unclear, but he decided that a fitting place for it to reside would be directly above the tomb of his grandfather, where it rests to this day.

SAMARKAND: TIMUR'S CULTURAL CAPITAL
LECTURE 22 TRANSCRIPT

Early in the 20th century, English author and diplomat James Elroy Flecker composed a brief poetic drama in which he attempted to capture the exotic essence of Samarkand, and of central Asia more generally. The work is titled *The Golden Road to Samarkand*.

The dramatic scene, rendered in beautiful poetry, is set at the Gate of the Sun in Baghdad, where a group of merchants, pilgrims, women, camels, camel drivers, and the city watchman have gathered. A caravan is forming and preparing to march out of Baghdad, to head east into the desert towards Samarkand. Each group mentions their reasons for undertaking the journey. The merchants, drapers, and grocers all have goods to trade, but the pilgrims have more esoteric motives. One of the Pilgrims, Ishak, explains himself thus:

> We are the Pilgrims, master; we shall go
>
> Always a little further: it may be
>
> Beyond that last blue mountain barred with snow,
>
> Across that angry or that glimmering sea,
>
> White on a throne or guarded in a cave
>
> There lives a prophet who can understand
>
> Why men were born: but surely we are brave,
>
> Who take the Golden Road to Samarkand.

The watchman and women try to dissuade the members of the caravan from setting out on such a long and perilous journey, but the pilgrims are firm and try to make their case again. The second pilgrim, Hassan, wistfully imagines the journey ahead:

> Sweet to ride forth at evening from the wells
>
> When shadows pass gigantic on the sand,
>
> And softly through the silence beat the bells
>
> Along the Golden Road to Samarkand.

The other pilgrim, Ishak, then articulates the motivation of adventurers and seekers of truth from all times and all places by decrying:

We travel not for trafficking alone:

> By hotter winds our fiery hearts are fanned:
>
> For lust of knowing what should not be known,
>
> We take the Golden Road to Samarkand.

The watchman is finally prevailed upon to open the gate, and the caravan departs. He asks the women what they think of being abandoned like this by the men. One woman replies, "they have their dreams and do not think of us." As the caravan disappears into the desert, its members can be heard singing in the distance: "We take the Golden Road to Samarkand."

Flecker was born in 1884 in London and studied at both Oxford and Cambridge. Before becoming a professional poet, playwright, and novelist, he served in the British consular service in the Eastern Mediterranean. He died of tuberculosis in 1915, aged just 30, a tragic early death mourned as a great loss to British poetry. Although he traveled no further east than Syria, Flecker's brief dramatic poem *The Golden Road to Samarkand* has been acknowledged ever since as capturing the allure of the exotic central Asian city in a way few of the other artists also inspired by the idea of Samarkand were able to do, including Goethe, Keats, and Christopher Marlowe, the author of *Tamburlaine the Great*, to name but a few.

Although not his hometown, the city of Samarkand also captivated the Turko-Mongol conqueror Timur, who early in his reign as emir decided to make Samarkand his capital. The city already had a rich and lengthy history long before Timur appeared in central Asia. The name Samarkand derives from Sogdian and can be translated as "Stone Fort" or "Stone Town." The original settlement was founded sometime around 700 BCE by ethnically Iranian Sogdians, and it evolved into one of the most important centers of Sogdian culture.

Originally farmers, the Sogdians later grew very wealthy through their role as intermediaries in Silk Roads trade. Situated in the Zerafshan River Valley, it had access to good water from melting snows, fertile soil, and abundant sunshine. Early farmers dug an elaborate series of irrigation channels, and the area surrounding the city also provided good pastureland for grazing. With successful agriculture and its location on major trade routes, the city and its population quickly prospered.

In the 6th century BCE, Samarkand was incorporated into the vast Achaemenid Persian Empire constructed by Cyrus the Great, and it was selected by the Persians as the capital of their easternmost province, the Sogdian satrapy. The Persians fortified the city with a citadel and strong walls and encouraged craft production in the suburbs.

In 329, Samarkand, known to the Greeks as Marakanda, was captured by Alexander of Macedon, who famously said something like: "Everything I have heard about Marakanda is true, except that it is even more beautiful than I had imagined." Although the city suffered significant damage in its sacking by Alexander, it quickly recovered and flourished under Hellenistic influence as part of the empire of Alexander's successor in the region, Seleucus Nicator. Seleucid craftsmen introduced classical Greek construction techniques, replacing the traditional oblong bricks of the city with square ones, for example, as well as using superior methods of masonry and plastering.

Once central Asia came under the control of two powerful empires, those of the Parthians and the Kushans, Samarkand prospered as a key commercial city during the first Silk Roads era, between roughly 100 BCE and 250 CE. In the mid-3rd century, Samarkand was incorporated into the expansive realm of the Sasanians and flourished as an important and eclectic religious center. The city facilitated the dissemination of various religions throughout central Asia, including Buddhism, Zoroastrianism, Manichaeism, Judaism, and Nestorian Christianity.

Samarkand was ruled by the nomadic Hephthalites, or White Huns, between 400 and 550, and then was briefly incorporated into various Turkic empires until the 7th century, when the powerful Chinese Tang Dynasty claimed the city, and indeed much of inner Eurasia, as part of its tributary empire. The great Tang Buddhist pilgrim Xuanzang passed through Samarkand in the early 630s and had this to say about the city and its surrounds:

The country of Sa-mo-kien is about 1,600 or 1,700 li in circuit [one li equals about 430 meters]. ... The capital of the country is 20 li or so in circuit. It is completely enclosed by rugged land and very populous. The precious merchandise of many foreign countries is stored up here. The soil is rich and productive, and yields abundant harvests. The forest trees afford a thick vegetation, and flowers and fruits are plentiful. The Shen horses are bred here. The inhabitants are skillful in the arts and trades beyond those of other countries.

Visitors to Samarkand today can find striking evidence of the wealth of Samarkand late in the 7th century by visiting the excellent small museum at Afrasiab, on the sides of a huge hill that marks the site of the ancient city. The museum is built around one of Samarkand's most extraordinary archaeological finds, gorgeous frescoes that were painted on the walls of the palace of a Sogdian king named Varkhouman.

The frescoes depict the king receiving ranks of foreign dignitaries astride elephants, horses, and camels who have come to attend his wedding to the daughter of the governor of another regional power named Chach. The bride leads the procession, riding on a white elephant, accompanied by friends and dignitaries on camels and horses. On the northern wall are scenes of horsemen fighting against various wild beasts, as well as boats with men and women. The eastern wall shows young men swimming in the sea, plus various birds and animals. The wall directly behind the king's throne shows a procession of the ambassadors, including some from China. The frescoes are striking evidence of the wealth and prestige accumulated by Sogdian elites through centuries of trade along the Silk Roads.

Early in the 8th century, the Sogdians lost control of Samarkand after it was captured by the armies of the Islamic Umayyads, but it took several decades before the residents of the city gradually abandoned their diverse religious beliefs and converted to Islam. Legend has it that after the Battle of Talas, which was fought in 751 in nearby Kyrgyzstan between the forces of the Tang Chinese and the Abbasid Caliphate, which had succeeded the Umayyads, the secret of papermaking was obtained from two captured Chinese prisoners. This led to the founding of the first paper mill in the Islamic world, from where the technology gradually spread westwards and eventually on to Europe. If you travel to Samarkand today, you can visit a wonderful paper mill on the outskirts of the city, still producing superb paper by using traditional techniques, including water wheels for energy.

As the Abbasid Caliphate splintered into a series of loosely affiliated Islamic states in the 9th century, control of Samarkand passed to the Iranian Samanids, who ruled the city and the region from 819 to 999 CE. Under the Samanids, Samarkand continued to flourish as a major commercial city at the junction of important trade routes.

At the very end of the first millennium, the Samanids were overthrown by Turkic tribes migrating through the region, and for next 220 years, Samarkand was ruled by a succession of successful Turkic groups, including the Karakhanids, the Seljuqs, and the Khwarazm-Shah. As we have seen, the behavior of Khwarazm-Shah Muhammad in approving of the murder of Chinggis Khan's commercial mission to the city of Otrar so incensed the great Mongol leader that Samarkand was sacked in 1220 during the Mongols' Khwarazmian campaign.

Even by the time Ibn Battuta traveled through the region more than a century later, Samarkand had only partly recovered. He describes it as "one of the greatest and finest of cities, and most perfect of them in beauty." But Ibn Battuta also wrote that "there were formerly great palaces on [the river's] bank, and constructions which bear witness to the lofty aspirations of the townsfolk, but most of this is obliterated, and most of the city itself has also fallen into ruin."

This brings us to Timur, who 150 years after its devastation at the hands of Chinggis decided in 1370 to make the still semi-ruined city of Samarkand the capital of his Timurid Empire. Over the next 35 years, he returned to the city 19 or 20 times following the campaigns and rebuilt the city just to the southwest of the ancient site of Afrasiab. Timur was careful to spare the lives of artists, craftsmen, and architects living in cities he conquered so that he could send them back to improve and beautify his capital.

As Colin Thubron describes it, "At [Timur's] direction a procession of captured scholars, theologians, musicians and craftsmen arrived in the capital with their books and tools and families—so many that they were forced to inhabit caves and orchards in the suburbs." One contemporary observer, Ibn Arabshah, noted that Timur founded new towns around Samarkand, like planets orbiting the sun, to house many of these artisans and their families. He named these towns after the capitals of regions he had conquered. So there was a Damascus and a Cairo, a Baghdad and a Shiraz, and even a Paris, which survives today.

We are fortunate to have an accurate eyewitness account of the rebuilding of Samarkand by Timur in the form of a journal kept by Castilian envoy Ruy González de Clavijo, who was sent as an ambassador to Timur's court by King Henry III of Castile and León in Spain.

Leaving Cádiz in 1403, Clavijo and his party sailed across the Mediterranean to Constantinople, then east through the Black Sea to Trebizond. From here, they traveled overland through Iran, visiting the cities of Tabriz and Sultaniyeh, before eventually reaching Transoxiana and Samarkand. A keen observer, Clavijo provides descriptions of virtually everything he encountered upon his journey, but he is particularly eloquent on the urban renewal that was going on in Samarkand and of Timur's personal supervision of many of the projects.

For example, he reports that Timur "gave orders that a street should be built to pass right through Samarkand, which should have shops opened on either side of it in which every kind of merchandise should be sold, and this new street was to go through to the other side, traversing the heart of the township." Timur wanted this accomplished quickly, and with their heads at risk, the workmen and their supervisors

> began at speed, causing all houses to be thrown down along the line that his highness had indicated for the passage of the new street. No heed was paid to the complaint of persons to whom the property might belong, and those whose houses were demolished suddenly had to quit with no warning, carrying away with them their goods and chattels as best they might.

> Timur would sometimes order that brand-new buildings should be torn down and redone if he was unsatisfied with the results. A classic example of this is the construction of the vast Bibi-Khanum Mosque, dedicated to his favorite wife, although Clavijo thought it was dedicated to the mother of his wife. According to Clavijo:

The Mosque which Timur had caused to be built in memory of the mother of his wife seemed to us the noblest of all those we visited in the city of Samarkand, but no sooner had it been completed than he begun to find fault with its entrance gateway, which he now said was much too low and must forthwith be pulled down.

> Clavijo then describes Timur's impatience in having the entranceway reconstructed. He arranged to have meat and coins thrown down to the masons to encourage them to keep up the work. As Clavijo notes, "thus the building went on day and night until at last a time came when it had perforce to

> stop—as was also the case in the matter of making the street
> [for the new bazaar]—on account of the winter snows which
> now began constantly to fall."

I have wandered through this enormous congregational mosque several times. It was finished in 1404, shortly before Timur's death, and he regarded it as the architectural jewel of his empire. Actually, it was originally decorated with some of the jewels Timur had brought back from his Indian campaign.

But over the decades and centuries that followed, the mosque slowly fell into disuse and crumbled to ruins. Its demise was hastened by the fact that its enormous dimensions pushed the construction techniques of the time to the very limit, and as a result of Timur's impatience, it was built much too quickly. Put simply, Timur's lofty visions for ever larger and grander buildings exceeded the technical abilities of his workers and their materials to realize them.

Still, much of the mosque survived for almost 500 years, until 1897, when it partially collapsed during an earthquake and was completely abandoned. In 1974, the government of the Uzbek Soviet Socialist Republic began to reconstruct the mosque, to the extent that the current mosque is effectively a brand-new building, and no original work remains. But the current Bibi-Khanum Mosque, closely modelled on Timur's original, is nonetheless impressive, measuring 182 yards in length by 119 yards in width. The cupola of the main chamber is 120 feet high, and the entranceway that was originally too low for Timur's tastes now towers 100 feet above the pavement.

Although Timur lavished much of his resources and time on his adopted capital, he did not forget his hometown of Kesh, or modern Shahrisabz, 50 miles to the south of Samarkand. Clavijo also visited Kesh and has left us a description of what Timur the builder was attempting to accomplish there:

> There are throughout the city many fine houses and mosques,
> above all a magnificent mosque which Timur had ordered to
> be built but which was as yet not finished. In this mosque
> is seen the chapel in which his father's burial place has been
> made, and beside this is a second chapel now being built in
> which it is intended that Timur himself shall be interred when
> the time comes.

Although the mosque is still incredibly beautiful today, it was not the only building Timur was constructing in Kesh, nor indeed the most imposing. That title surely belongs to the great palace Timur had constructed in his hometown, the ruins of which remain awesomely impressive even today. Clavijo describes the construction on the palace known as the Ak-Saray, which means the "White" or "Noble Palace," which took place over a period of two decades:

> On the following morning … they came and took us to see another great palace that was being built; and this palace they told us had been thus in hand building for the last twenty years, for though continually thus working day after day the builders were still at their work upon it. This palace had an entry passage constructed to be of considerable length with a high portal before it, and in this entrance gallery to the right and to left there were archways of brickwork encased and patterned with blue tiles. These archways led each one into a small chamber that was open having no door, the flooring being laid in blue tiles. At the end of this gallery stands another gate-way, beyond which is a great courtyard paved with white flagstones and surrounded on the four sides by richly wrought arches. This courtyard indeed may measure some three hundred paces in its width. We were assured that it had been Timur himself who was the builder of this great palace.

Visitors to Shahrisabz today, ancient Kesh, will find the great palace of Timur in ruins. All that remains are the pillars that once supported the giant arch at the entrance of the palace, but these have a tremendous noble grandeur. The pillars still have sections of beautiful, unrestored mosaics upon them.

On one of my first visits to the Ak-Saray, a team of French archaeologists was hard at work excavating the flooring of the entrance gallery, and they had indeed uncovered the magnificent blue tiles that Clavijo described. Near to the palace stands a noble modern statue of Timur. It is a place where people go to have their wedding photographs taken today.

The Ak-Saray was destroyed in the second half of the 16th century by Abdulla-Khan II, ruler of the Persian Shaybanid Dynasty, which took control of Transoxiana. Legend has it that when Abdulla-Khan was visiting the city, he saw the great gleaming palace in the distance, and thinking it closer than it actually was, he started to gallop towards it. The khan rode hard but still did not come close to the city and the palace. He became so enraged that he ordered its destruction. But the Shaybanids could not destroy the great pillars, which have stood the test of time even though the arch that once connected them has long since fallen. Today, the towers are still almost 120 feet high, although they once soared 150 feet into the sky. Inside each is a spiral staircase, now closed to the public, which once took visitors up to lofty toothed parapets.

On the remains of one of the towers is this mosaic inscription: "If you doubt our greatness, look at our constructions," followed by the name of the Iranian master builder of the Ak-Saray, Muhammad Jusuf Tebrizi. As I say, the ruins are tremendously imposing, and the inscription is a powerful testament to the success of Timur both as conqueror and builder. But the irony is not lost on modern visitors who can't but help think of the famous lines in Percy Bysshe Shelley's poem "Ozymandias."

You remember the scene: A traveler in a foreign land comes across two enormous and trunkless legs of stone in the desert, surrounded by the ruins of what had once been a monumental statue. On the pedestal are inscribed the following immortal lines: "My name is Ozymandias, King of Kings; look on my works ye mighty and despair!" Shelley concludes his brief sermon on the long history of once-powerful conquerors and rulers, and on the ephemerality of their empires, with the following ironic lines: "Nothing beside remains. Round the decay of that Colossal Wreck, boundless and bare, the lone and level sands stretch far away."

There is one final building back in Samarkand that we need to discuss before concluding this lecture: the magnificent Gur-i Emir, the Tomb of the King, the final resting place of Timur, his sons Shah Rukh and Miran Shah, his spiritual adviser Sayyd Baraka, and his grandsons Ulugh Beg and Muhammad Sultan. The Gur-i Emir is not only important as the final resting place of Timur and his family; it is also a major and influential achievement in the history of Turkic-Persian architecture. In particular, the Gur-i Emir is the precursor and model for much of the later architecture of the Mughal tombs in India, including the famous Taj Mahal in Agra, which was built by Timur's descendants, the rulers of the Mughal Dynasty of North India.

The Gur-i Emir was originally a complex of buildings topped with magnificent azure domes. The construction of the actual mausoleum commenced in 1403 under the direction of Timur, following the death of his beloved grandson and intended heir, Muhammad Sultan, for whom the tomb was intended. The complex originally included a madrassa and a *khanaka*, a place for pilgrims to stay, but all that remains of the complex today is the entrance portal and one of the four original minarets, as well as the mausoleum.

As we have seen, Timur had no intention of being personally buried in the Gur-i Emir; he had constructed his own tomb in the mosque in Kesh, beside that of his father. But Timur's sudden death in the frigid winter of 1405, early in his campaign against the Ming Dynasty, meant that the passes into Kesh were covered in deep snow, so the only option was to bring his body back to Samarkand. It was another of Timur's grandsons and successors, Ulugh Beg, who completed the work on the tomb, effectively turning the mausoleum into the family crypt of the Timurid Dynasty.

Standing in front of the Gur-i Emir mausoleum for the first time—or for the fifth, sixth, or seventh time, for that matter—one is struck by the apparent simplicity of its design and by the awesome glittering blue dome. The entrance portal into the former complex is exquisitely decorated with carved bricks and mosaics, a masterpiece allegedly completed by master craftsman Muhammad ibn Mahmud Isfahani. The main dome, with a diameter of roughly 50 feet and a height of more than 40 feet, is bright blue in color but also decorated with various colored patterns, and its superb heavy-ribbed fluting gives the cupola both monumentality and beautiful symmetry.

Inside the building, the mausoleum is a large, high chamber with deep niches in its sides and different motifs on the walls. The lower part of the walls are covered by onyx slabs that blend together to appear as though they are a single panel. These panels are beautifully decorated, and above the slabs is a marble stalactite cornice. Most of the upper walls are decorated with painted plaster and gilded arches. On the floor of the mausoleum are ornately carved slabs. These are not the graves themselves but indicators of their location in a crypt directly underneath.

There are various stories associated with the Gur-i Emir, some legendary, others factual. One story concerns a solid block of dark green jade that Ulugh Beg had placed on the headstone directly above the tomb of Timur.

The story has it that the block of jade had originally been housed in a temple used by Chinese emperors, although in which city this temple was located is unknown. The block had later come into the possession of Du'a, the longest-reigning khan of the Chagatayid Ulus, who ruled from 1282 to 1307. It is believed to be the largest single block of jade known anywhere in the world. Exactly how it came into the possession of Ulugh Beg is unclear, but he decided that a fitting place for it to reside would be directly above the tomb of his grandfather, where it rests to this day.

Another story concerns Nader Shah, a powerful Iranian leader who ruled as Shah of Persia from 1736 until his assassination in 1747. Much like his heroes Chinggis Khan and Timur, Nader Shah was a brilliant but cruel military leader who undertook major campaigns of conquest all over Eurasia, including in the Middle East, the Caucasus, central Asia, and south Asia. After invading Transoxiana, Nader tried to carry off Timur's sarcophagus, presumably to take with him back to Persia. But as his men tried to move the sarcophagus, it broke in two, which was interpreted as a very bad sign by the Shah's advisers, who urged him to leave it in its rightful place in the Gur i-Emir. The shah grudgingly concurred.

A third story concerning the tomb of Timur comes from the dark days of World War II. I'm sure it will come as no surprise to you to learn that most of the archaeologists who unlocked the long and complex history of central Asia were Soviet Russians and central Asians, because these desert realms were part of the Soviet Union for nearly seven decades. One such brilliant Soviet archaeologist and anthropologist, Mikhail Mikhaylovich Gerasimov, developed a particular skill at using skulls to reconstruct the faces of ancient peoples, including hominids such as Neanderthals and the so-called Java Man. Gerasimov also gained access to the remains of famous people, such as the Russian ruler Ivan the Terrible and several others, using their skulls to reconstruct their faces.

In June of 1941, Soviet leader Josef Stalin dispatched Gerasimov to Uzbekistan with explicit orders to open the tombs of the Timurids in the Gur-i Emir and reconstruct their faces. On June 19th, 1941, Gerasimov and his team opened the crypt of Timur and removed his remains for detailed examination. In the course of their research, they measured Timur's height as roughly 5 foot 8, which would have made him a rather tall man in his time. Gerasimov also carefully examined Timur's right leg and found that it had indeed been badly damaged, so that Timur the Lame would certainly have walked with a pronounced limp. Examining the other interred bodies, they confirmed the historical account of the execution of Ulugh Beg—more about this in the next lecture—and also the authenticity of the occupants of the other graves. And Gerasimov obtained enough information from Timur's skull to later reconstruct his face.

The local people were not happy with what they saw as a sacrilegious raid on the sacred Muslim crypt. They told the Soviet archaeologists of a legend which claimed that any disturbance of the bodies would lead to a catastrophe. They said that there is an inscription inside the tomb which says "Whomsoever opens my tomb shall unleash an invader more terrible than I." The scientists thought the story ridiculous, but literally three days after Gerasimov opened the tombs, Adolph Hitler launched Operation Barbarossa; that is, on Sunday, June 22nd, 1941, the Nazi invasion of the Soviet Union began.

Gerasimov and his team dismissed this as pure coincidence and continued their examination of the bodies for more than a year. But the legend persists, particularly because just as Timur's remains were being reinterred in the Gur-i Emir in November 1942 as part of a full Islamic burial ritual, the Soviet high command was also unleashing Operation Uranus as part of the Battle of Stalingrad, an operation that has been recognized by historians ever since as one of the turning points of the Second World War.

Historian Svat Soucek succinctly sums up the impact of Timur on Samarkand and Transoxiana by observing that "if the Mongol interlude was a traumatic experience in the history of central Asia, the Timurid period can be viewed as ultimately its most glorious one. Timur endeavored to embellish his capital, Samarkand, with grandiose architectural monuments some of which still constitute the pride of modern Uzbekistan."

Despite the general decline of the region that followed the death of Timur, a story we'll relate in the next lecture, Samarkand still resonates today with the ghostly echoes of Timur's builders, when it became, in the words of Colin Thubron, "the Mirror of the World and the premier city of Asia." If your fiery hearts are indeed fanned by hotter winds, and if you lust to know that which should not be known, then I strongly urge you all to take the Golden Road to Samarkand.

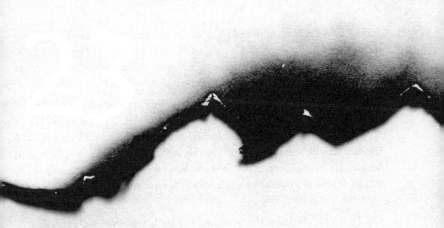

FROM MUGHALS TO SOVIETS: EURASIA AFTER TIMUR

This lecture explores the fortunes of several of Timur's descendants who attempted to rule over the remnants of the vast empire he had built. It also considers the history of inner Eurasia more broadly.

Power Struggles after Timur

Timur's death in February 1405 set off a bitter struggle for succession. His heir apparent, Muhammad Sultan, had died two years earlier. Timur had attempted to divide his empire into four distinct regions, each under the control of the descendants of one of his sons.

Azerbaijan and Iraq were given to the family of Amarinshah, who would die just three years after Timur. The southern and central portions of Iran were bequeathed to the children of Umar Shayk, who had already died more than a decade earlier. The southeastern regions of the empire were given to Pir Muhammad and his descendants. Finally, the northeastern lands of the Timurid empire were given to Shahrukh.

Despite this plan to equitably divide his realm, two different succession struggles erupted immediately following Timur's death. Within each family line, members jostled for regional prestige and authority, while in the heartland of Transoxiana, a larger struggle for control of the overall empire ensued.

Some of the regional states did not last long. Azerbaijan broke away from the Timurids, and Turkmen took control. And in Iran, the descendants of Umar Shayk became bogged down in vicious squabbles between themselves that resulted in the murder of at least one claimant for the throne.

The larger struggle for control of the empire went through several phases. In March of 1405, a month or so after Timur's death, a grandson of Timur named Khalil Sultan boldly marched into Samarkand and claimed the throne. Khalil Sultan restored friendly relations with Ming China, and he and Shahrukh then came to some sort of an agreement to divide the empire between themselves, with Khalil Sultan ruling in Transoxiana and Shahrukh in Khorasan.

Khalil Sultan faced serious opposition to his claims on Transoxiana, both from other descendants of Timur and also from Chagatayid khans. In 1409, Khalil Sultan was captured and handed over to Shahrukh, who immediately marched to Samarkand as the now de facto emir of the Timurids. He installed his son Ulugh Beg as governor there and promptly returned to his capital of Herat.

Shahrukh in Charge

For the next five years, various other contenders challenged Shahrukh's claim to supreme power, but by 1413, his army had defeated the forces of all rival claimants. In 1415, Shahrukh installed another of his sons, Ibrahim Sultan, as governor of Shiraz. Five years after that, he reconquered Azerbaijan, thus more or less reconstituting the entire empire of Timur and cementing himself as supreme leader of the Timurid world. He survived an assassination attempt in January 1427, and two years later defeated various tribes that were attempting to conquer western regions of the Timurid realm, thus further tightening his hold on power.

Shahrukh

Contemporary sources describe Shahrukh as both a great warrior and an intelligent and pragmatic leader. Although generally inclined to peaceful administration, Shahrukh did not hesitate to use his military acumen and powerful army to destroy all pretenders to the throne, including Chinggisid princes.

In 1429, a new threat appeared in the form of a Turkic Jochid khan named Abul Khayr, whose followers were called Uzbeks. They rose up in the region of the Aral Sea and invaded Khwarazm. Shahrukh tried to keep them at bay by stationing garrisons along the northern frontiers of the empire, but from 1431 on, Uzbek contingents were raiding Transoxiana almost at will.

Shahrukh remained a formidable military commander until the end of his life, and he generally maintained the integrity of his borders. Ultimately, his empire unraveled from within as most of his governor sons and senior administrators gradually died. Shahrukh himself became seriously ill in the spring of 1444, although he recovered sufficiently to crush various rebellions that had erupted in the provinces. By now, only one of Shahrukh's sons, Ulugh Beg, was still alive.

The circumstances of Shahrukh's death on March 13, 1447, typified the sort of life he had been forced to lead as emir of the Timurid empire. He succumbed to illness in the midst of a military campaign to the west against yet another pretender to the throne, Sultan Muhammad.

After Shahrukh

Inevitably, Shahrukh's death led to another succession crisis. Ulugh Beg immediately claimed supreme power and began to mint coins in his name, while other rival and often obscure Timurid princes seized power in various quarters of the realm, including the capital, Herat.

Shahrukh's decision to divide the empire of Timur into two distinct regions became a geopolitical reality during this period, even though various claimants for power still hoped that Khorasan and Transoxiana might one day be reunited. By 1454, the rulers in each region were explicitly recognizing the Oxus River as a formal boundary between their states.

The bitter internal struggle that continued between the various descendants of Timur through the mid-15th century facilitated the emergence of three non-Timurid groups who were quick to exploit these fractures: Uzbeks, Turkmen, and resurgent Mongols. Of the three, the Uzbeks were the most dangerous. They repeatedly raided parts of both Transoxiana and Khorasan throughout the late 15th century. Turkmen tribes remained restive further west, and the Mongols raided into the Fergana Valley almost at will.

Later Timurid Rulers

A handful of later Timurid rulers stand out from the pages of history during the second half of the 15th century. Abu Said had genuine ambitions to reunify the Timurid Empire, although he was thwarted by Turkmen and Uzbeks.* His son Sultan Ahmad, who took control of Transoxiana following the death of Abu Said in 1469, managed to keep the Uzbeks and Mongols at bay for a quarter century until his death in 1495.

While these events were unfolding in Transoxiana, a distant relation of Abu Said, Sultan Husayn Bayqara, seized the former capital of Herat and ruled from there until his death in 1506, although he was forced to give up large parts of his empire to Turkmen.

As a military and political leader, Husayn Bayqara seems to have achieved little beyond a brief period of stability, but culturally, his reign was successful. Specifically, two brilliant literary figures flourished in Herat under Husayn Bayqara: 'Abd al-Rahman Jami and 'Ali Shir Nava'i.

Babur

The last memorable Timurid was surely Zahir al-Din Muhammad Babur. His impact was not be felt in central Asia, however, but in India, where he went on to found the mighty Mughal Empire that would rule much of the subcontinent until the arrival of the British in the 18th century. Babur was also a writer, and he has left behind a superb prose memoir in flowing Turkic documenting his life and fortunes as a Timurid prince.

Babur clearly had political ambitions from the beginning, although he was forced to spend much of his early life as a fugitive, fleeing or hiding from more powerful Uzbek and other Timurid rulers. He briefly seized power in Samarkand. After he was driven out, he moved south to take control of Kabul. At one stage he was trapped in the city and, fearing imminent attack from a powerful Uzbek army, he and his retinue decided to flee south into modern Pakistan. Although Babur later returned to Kabul, it was clear that his ambition was now focused on South Asia.

Over the next two decades, Babur gradually assembled a powerful military force. It was probably never more than 7,000 men strong, but this was sufficient for Babur to march into India and win the decisive Battle of Panipat, fought to the north of Delhi in April 1526. Babur's seemingly meager forces were augmented by gunpowder weapons, which had spread from the Ottoman realm into central Asia.

Despite the use of gunpowder weapons, most historians now believe that Babur's success at Panipat and at the following year's Battle of Khanwa was actually because of the effectiveness of Mongol contingents who fought on the extreme left and right wings of Babur's army. More than four centuries after the birth of Chinggis Khan, the mobile archer warriors were still proving their effectiveness in winning battles. However, this moment definitely marked the end of an era: The advent of gunpowder weapons would soon render even the most formidable nomadic cavalry useless.

Battle of Khanw

Babur took control of much of northern India, establishing a formidable late-Timurid state there. Although Babur died in 1530, his successors turned the empire he had established into one of the major Eurasian powers of the early modern world, particularly during the reign of Babur's grandson Akbar, who ruled from 1556 to 1605.

It was one of Akbar's successors, Shah Jahan, who commissioned the construction of the Taj Mahal in 1632 to house the tomb of his wife Mumtaz Mahal. The inspiration for this magnificent mausoleum came directly from the Gur-Emir in Samarkand, the tomb of Timur and some of his family, thus creating a direct cultural link between the founder of the Timurid empire and the Mughals.

FROM MUGHALS TO SOVIETS: EURASIA AFTER TIMUR

LECTURE 23 TRANSCRIPT

Ulugh Beg was one of the grandsons of Timur. His father, Shahrukh, emerged from the messy succession struggles following the death of Timur as ruler of the Timurid Empire, and in 1409, he appointed Ulugh Beg governor of Transoxiana. Ulugh Beg ruled the region for the next four decades from his capital city of Samarkand, until he was executed in October 1449.

Ulugh Beg might not have been a particularly effective ruler, but he was a brilliant scholar with a wide range of academic interests, particularly in mathematics and astronomy. Shahrukh allowed Ulugh Beg considerable autonomy as governor of Transoxiana, which meant that he was largely free to pursue his scholarly interests. Ulugh Beg invited leading scientists and mathematicians from all over the Islamic world to come to Samarkand to conduct their research and to teach, and Samarkand flourished once again as a great cosmopolitan city, home to a large community of intellectuals who worked together in the pursuit of new knowledge.

To house the 60 or 70 illustrious scientists Ulugh Beg brought to the city, and to allow students from all over Transoxiana to study with them, Ulugh Beg had a superb madrassah, essentially an institution of higher education, constructed on the Registan Square in the center of Samarkand. *Registan* means "sandy place" in Persian. It was a large public space where people gathered to hear royal proclamations, usually heralded by blasts on enormous copper trumpets. And it was also the place where public executions were carried out.

Today, the Registan is framed by not one but three spectacular madrassahs, each superb examples of Islamic architecture. Ulugh Beg's madrassah was erected on the west side of the Registan between 1417 and 1420. The other two are more recent, both built in the 17th century. All three have been seriously damaged over the centuries by earthquakes. The fact they are still standing is testament to the quality of their construction, but also the work of the Soviet Union and the modern Uzbek national government in protecting them. For four centuries, the Registan ensemble of madrassahs has provided one of the most awe-inspiring sights in all of Eurasia.

Ulugh Beg's Samarkand madrassah is one of three he had constructed in Transoxiana during his 40-year reign as governor; the other two are in Bukhara. Each of his madrassahs were focused on teaching and research in advanced mathematics, sciences, and literature, and the Registan madrassah was one of the most highly regarded colleges in the entire Muslim world in the 15th century. We know the names of many prominent scholars who worked there, and we also know that Ulugh Beg himself gave lectures there.

The madrassah is tremendously impressive, with an imposing portal facing the square, capped with a lancet arch. This portal is about 100 feet tall and is visible from locations all over Samarkand. Each of the four corners of the building is flanked by tall and beautiful minarets. Above the entrance arch are striking mosaics. Inside the building is a large, square courtyard with entrances off it leading to various rooms, including a mosque, lecture halls, and the dormitory cells where the students lived. The building is topped with a beautiful fluted blue dome decorated with rosettas. Its construction and importance as a major institute of higher education is undoubtedly one of the finest achievements of Ulugh Beg during his reign as Timurid governor of Transoxiana.

But the madrassah was not Ulugh Beg's only contribution to human knowledge, or to his city of Samarkand. What Ulugh Beg and his colleagues most wanted to understand was the stars they observed shining brightly every night above the deserts of Transoxiana. They wanted to measure the distances between stars, and from an observer on earth, essentially to create a sort of mathematical star map. This was 200 years before Galileo invented the telescope in the early 17th century, of course, so Ulugh Beg and his scientists had to come up with some other form of technology to map the stars. They created an effective celestial observatory, all right, but not one that would be familiar to most people in the 21st century.

In 1424, four years after his madrassah had opened, and presumably at the urging of his professors and students, Ulugh Beg began construction of a huge quadrant device. This was a giant sextant 33 feet long that could be used, along with trigonometry, to measure the location of stars relative to other stars and to the earth.

First, an arch was erected that was used to determine midday, and then a trench dug about six feet wide into the hillside under the arch, along the line of the meridian. In this arc-shaped trench the giant sextant was placed, allowing it to move backwards and forwards on tracks over a radius of about 150 feet. Construction took five years, and the entire device was housed underground to protect it from earthquake damage.

As a result of their work at the observatory, Ulugh Beg and his colleagues produced a superb work of astronomy, the Zij-i Gurgani, which, following a theoretical introduction in Persian, catalogues the precise coordinates of exactly 1,018 stars, along with the complex mathematical equations they had used to plot the location of these stars and other celestial phenomena. These astronomical tables, which corrected many errors in previous tables dating all the way back to Ptolemy, were so accurate that they were still highly regarded and in widespread use in Europe well into the 17th century.

Although Ulugh Beg was undoubtedly a brilliant and collegial scientist, he struggled to keep control of his realm during the troubled period following the death of his grandfather Timur. As historian Michael Prawdin describes him, Ulugh Beg was "one of the gentlest rulers in history. But he was far in advance of his time and was not hard-headed enough to be a successful ruler in these days of iron."

In the end, Ulugh Beg was captured and beheaded on either the 25th or 27th of October 1449. As Beatrice Manz Forbes notes, this was "a shocking act, condemned in the Timurid histories." Ulugh Beg was buried in the Gur i-Emir alongside his father Shahrukh and his grandfather Timur. The accuracy of the historical accounts of his decapitation were confirmed when his tomb was opened by Soviet archaeologist Mikhail Gerasimov in 1941.

Soon after the murder of Ulugh Beg, religious fanatics destroyed his observatory, and it was completely lost to history until 1908, when Uzbek-Russian archaeologist V. L. Vyatkin came upon a document describing its location. Vyatkin started digging at the site and soon discovered the arch that had been constructed to determine midday. In the early 21st century, the Uzbek government re-created part of the astronomical instrument at its original location, and tourists today can visit a roofed-over section of the extraordinary quadrant, plus an excellent small museum.

The fate of the Samarkand Observatory is our entrée into this, the final lecture in a series of four on the Timurid Empire. In this lecture, we explore the fortunes of several of Timur's descendants who, like Ulugh Beg, attempted to rule over the remnants of the vast empire his grandfather had built. We also consider the history of inner Eurasia more broadly over a period of more than six centuries, from the early 15th century all the way through to the end of the 20th century. That leaves us with one final lecture to wrap up this course on the impact of the mighty Mongols and Timurids on world history.

Timur's death in February 1405 set off a bitter struggle for succession. His heir apparent, Muhammad Sultan, had died two years earlier, and so, following the example established by Chinggis Khan just before his death, Timur had attempted to divide his empire into four distinct regions, each under the control of the descendants of one of his sons.

Azerbaijan and Iraq were given to the family of Amarinshah, who would die just three years after Timur. The southern and central portions of Iran were bequeathed to the children of Umar Shayk, who had already died more than a decade earlier. The southeastern regions of the empire were given to Pir Muhammad and his descendants, although Pir Muhammad himself would be dead just two years later. Finally, the northeastern lands of the Timurid Empire were given to Shahrukh, who would not only survive for more than another four decades, but also reign as supreme ruler of the Timurid Empire until his death in 1447.

Despite his plan to equitably divide his realm, immediately following Timur's death, two quite different succession struggles erupted. Within each family line, members jostled for regional prestige and authority, while in the heartland of Transoxiana, a larger struggle for control of the overall empire ensued. Some of the regional states did not last long. Azerbaijan broke away from the Timurids, and Turkmen took control. And in Iran, the descendants of Umar Shayk became bogged down in a vicious squabble between themselves that resulted in the murder of at least one claimant for the throne.

The larger struggle for control of empire went through several phases. In March of 1405, just a month or so after Timur's death, a grandson of Timur named Khalil Sultan boldly marched into Samarkand and claimed the throne. Khalil Sultan did have some Mongol blood through his mother's line, and so he emphasized the legitimacy of his claim as a continuation of Chinggisid rule. Khalil Sultan restored friendly relations with Ming China, and he and Shahrukh then came to some sort of an agreement to divide the empire between themselves, with Khalil Sultan ruling in Transoxiana and Shahrukh in Khorasan.

Khalil Sultan immediately faced serious opposition to his claims on Transoxiana, both from other descendants of Timur and also from Chagatayid khans who may have still been hoping to resurrect the old Chagatayid Ulus. In 1409, Khalil Sultan was captured and handed over to Shahrukh, who had managed to stay above these various struggles and keep his treasury in good order. Shahrukh immediately marched to Samarkand as the now de facto emir of the Timurids, installed his son Ulugh Beg as governor there, and promptly returned to his capital of Herat.

For the next five years, various other contenders challenged Shahrukh's claim to supreme power, but by 1413, his army had defeated the forces of all rival claimants. In 1415, Shahrukh installed another of his sons, Ibrahim Sultan, as governor of Shiraz, and five years later, he reconquered Azerbaijan, thus more or less reconstituting the entire empire of Timur and cementing himself as supreme leader of the Timurid world. He survived an assassination attempt in January 1427, and two years later defeated various tribes that were attempting to conquer western regions of the Timurid realm, thus further tightening his hold on power.

Contemporary sources describe Shahrukh as both a great warrior and an intelligent and pragmatic leader. A ruthless military commander, he is reported to have offered the following advice to his soldiers: "The warrior must thrust into the center of the fight and of the blood-bath. If wounded, he must know no other camp than the mane of his steed. Wretched is he who calls himself a man while imploring the mercy of his foe; he deserves to die the death of a dog." Although generally inclined to peaceful administration, Shahrukh did not hesitate to use his military acumen and powerful army to destroy all pretenders to the throne, including Chinggisid princes.

In 1429, a new threat appeared in the form of a Turkic Jochid khan named Abul Khayr, whose followers were called Uzbeks. This is one of the first appearances of that name in the history of inner Eurasia. They rose up in the region of the Aral Sea and invaded Khwarazm. Shahrukh tried to keep them at bay by stationing garrisons along the northern frontiers of the empire, but from 1431 on, Uzbek contingents were raiding Transoxiana almost at will.

Shahrukh remained a formidable military commander until the end of his life, and he generally maintained the integrity of his borders. Ultimately, his empire unraveled from within as most of his governor sons and senior administrators gradually died. Shahrukh himself became seriously ill in the spring of 1444, although he recovered sufficiently to crush various rebellions that had erupted in the provinces. By now, only one of Shahrukh's sons was still alive, Ulugh Beg, the governor of Transoxiana.

The circumstances of Shahrukh's death on March 13th, 1447, typified the sort of life he had been forced to lead as emir of the Timurid Empire. He succumbed to illness in the midst of a military campaign to the west against yet another pretender to the throne, Sultan Muhammad.

Inevitably, Shahrukh's death set off another succession crisis. Ulugh Beg immediately claimed supreme power and began to mint coins in his name, while other rival and often obscure Timurid princes seized power in various quarters of the realm, including the capital, Herat. Shahrukh's decision to divide the empire of Timur into two distinct regions became a geopolitical reality during this period, even though various claimants for power still hoped that Khorasan and Transoxiana might one day be reunited. But by 1454, the rulers in each region were explicitly recognizing the Oxus River as a formal boundary between their states.

The bitter internal struggle that continued between the various descendants of Timur through the mid-15th century facilitated the emergence of three non-Timurid groups who were quick to exploit these fractures: Uzbeks, Turkmen, and resurgent Mongols. Of the three, the Uzbeks were the most dangerous. They repeatedly raided parts of both Transoxiana and Khorasan throughout the later 15th century. Turkmen tribes remained restive further west, and the Mongols raided into the Fergana Valley almost at will, particularly during periods when, as noted late-Timurid historian Stephen Dale puts it, "Timurid princes were actively at each other's throats."

A handful of later Timurid rulers stand out from the pages of history during the second half of the 15th century. Abu Said, whose military power, Dale points out, was the last to depend heavily on militarized nomadic forces, did have genuine ambitions to reunify the Timurid Empire, although he was thwarted by Turkmen and Uzbeks. His son Sultan Ahmad, who took control of Transoxiana following the death of Abu Said in 1469, managed to keep the Uzbeks and Mongols at bay for a quarter century until his death in 1495.

While these events were unfolding in Transoxiana, a distant relation of Abu Said, Sultan Husayn Bayqara, seized the former capital of Herat and ruled from there until his death in 1506, although he was forced to give up large parts of his empire to Turkmen. As a military and political leader,

Husayn Bayqara seems to have achieved little beyond a brief period of stability. But as Stephen Dale puts it, despite the extraordinary scientific achievements of Ulugh Beg, "many contemporary and subsequent Muslim rulers and scholars regarded the artistic and cultural activities of Husayn Bayqara's Herat as the golden cultural moment of the post-Mongol era in the eastern Islamic world."

This reputation rests largely on the work of two brilliant literary figures who flourished in Herat under Husayn Bayqara: Abd al-Rahman Jami and Ali Shir Navai. Navai was a Herat native, the son of bureaucrats, who studied at the same madrassah as Husayn Bayqara and developed into a superb poet. Bayqara gave Navai a government post that essentially left him free to write his superb verse in Turkic. His work was responsible for the elevation of Turkic language to the status of a genuine literary language. Conversely, Navai's colleague Jami is recognized today as one of the last great poets to write in classical Persian language. The deaths of the two poets in 1492 and 1501 were probably recognized then, just as they are today, as the end of a great cultural era.

But this was not yet the end of the Timurids' contribution to world history. The last memorable Timurid was surely Zahir al-Dina Muhammad Babur. His impact was not be felt in central Asia, however, but in India, where he went on to found the mighty Mughal Empire that would rule much of the subcontinent until the arrival of the British in the 18th century. Babur was also a writer, and he has left behind a superb prose memoir in flowing Turkic documenting his life and fortunes as a Timurid prince.

Babur clearly had political ambitions from the beginning, although he was forced to spend much of his early life as a fugitive, fleeing or hiding from other more powerful Uzbek and other Timurid rulers. He briefly seized power in Samarkand, then after he was driven out moved south to take control of Kabul. At one stage, he was trapped in the city, and fearing imminent attack from a powerful Uzbek army, he and his retinue decided to flee south into modern Pakistan. As Dale describes it, they "hastily abandoned Kabul with little more than the shirts on their backs." Although Babur later returned to Kabul, it was clear that his ambition was now focused on South Asia.

Over the next two decades, Babur gradually assembled a powerful military force, although it was probably never more than 7,000 men strong. But this was sufficient for Babur to march into India and win the decisive Battle of Panipat, fought to the north of Delhi in April 1526, 128 years after his predecessor Timur had also won his battle outside Delhi back in 1398. Babur's seemingly meager forces were augmented by gunpowder weapons, which had spread from the Ottoman realm into central Asia. At the Battle of Panipat, Babur's men used mortars, matchlock rifles, even canon under the expert control of Ottoman advisers.

But despite the use of gunpowder weapons, most historians now believe that Babur's success at Panipat, and at the Battle of Khanwa fought the following year, was actually because of the effectiveness of Mongol contingents who fought on the extreme left and right wings of Babur's army. Even now, more than four centuries after the birth of Chinggis Khan, and some 17 centuries since the appearance of the Xiongnu on the stage of world history, the mobile, well-led horse-riding nomadic archer warriors were still proving their effectiveness in winning battles. But this moment definitely marked the end of an era: The advent of gunpowder weapons would soon render even the most formidable nomadic cavalry useless.

Babur took control of much of northern India, establishing a formidable late-Timurid state there. Although Babur died in 1530, his successors turned the Timurid-Mughal Empire he had established into one of the major Eurasian powers of the early modern world, particularly during the reign of Babur's grandson Akbar, who ruled from 1556 to 1605.

It was one of Akbar's successors, Shah Jahan, who commissioned the construction of the Taj Mahal, the Crown of Palaces, in 1632 to house the tomb of his wife Mumtaz Mahal. The inspiration for this magnificent mausoleum came directly from the Gur-i Emir in Samarkand, the tomb of Timur and some of his family, thus creating a direct cultural link between the founder of the Timurid Empire and the Mughals. Stephen Dale reminds us of these connections when he writes:

The [Mughal] lineage absorbed novel traits under the influence of its predominantly Hindu environment but in most respects retained its original characteristics even in decline. It was in fact a late Timurid dynastic artefact with indigenous South Asian overtones that the British discovered when they entered Delhi in the eighteenth century.

Michael Prawdin also has something to say about the character of Babur:

When, a century after his ancestor Tamerlane's death, Babur was definitively expelled from Transoxiana by a new nomadic wave—the Uzbeks under a Khan of the house of Chinggis—he did not bow his head before the bludgeoning of fate, but, inspired by the adventurous tradition of his race, dreamed once more the dream of world conquest. Though he had to flee, he fled to fight for new realms.

> This sounds like a fitting epitaph, not just for Babur, but for Shahrukh, Timur, Batu, Hulagu, Qubilai, all the way back to Chinggis Khan himself.

OK, time is short, so we need to tell the remainder of this story quickly. Back in Transoxiana, an Uzbek khan named Muhammad Shaybani crossed the Syr Darya in 1500 and seized control of Samarkand from a cousin of Babur. Muhammad was distantly related to Chinggis Khan, so in some ways, Shaybanid rule also represented a continuation of Chinggisid rule in central Asia. Although they were of nomadic stock, the Turkic Uzbeks had been well exposed to Arab, Persian, and Islamic culture, so Shaybanid rule also represented a degree of cultural and political continuity in the region. The Shaybanids ruled Transoxiana for the entire 16th century, from 1500 to 1599.

In the western regions of the former Timurid Empire, meanwhile, Shah Ismail defeated rivals in Iran and founded the Safavid Dynasty. Muhammad Shaybani and Shah Ismail were both Turks, but the Shaybanids were Sunni, and the Safavids were Shia. In the inevitable military clash that erupted between them at Merv in 1510, the Safavids defeated the Shaybanids, a victory that has had long-lasting world historical consequences. The ultimate result was a stalemate between the two regions that, as Svat Soucek notes, pitted "schismatic Iran against orthodox central Asia for 300 years, right down to the latter's conquest by Russia in the nineteenth century."

Even as the Shaybanids and Safavids were maintaining order in their respective regions, global geopolitical changes were taking place that were destined to dramatically impact much of Eurasia. Europe and Russia were just beginning a period of sustained innovation and expansion, and as maritime trade completely eclipsed Silk Roads overland trade, landlocked central Asia was poised to slip back into a sort of stagnant provincialism, although this was not so obvious during the 16th century.

But powerful Russian czars like Ivan III and Ivan IV—the so-called Terrible, who ruled for more than 50 years between 1533 and 1584—were busy building an empire that began to compete with other imperial powers like the Ottomans. The Russians initially expanded eastwards and reached the Pacific by 1649, staking out their claim on both Mongolia and Siberia against the Chinese along the way.

As this Russian expansion was occurring, the peoples of central Asia were absorbed in their own political conflicts. In the 17th century, much of Transoxiana, including Bukhara and Samarkand, was brought under the control of the Khanate of Bukhara. Bukharan khans were devout Muslims who adorned the religious establishments of the two cities. Bukhara was the more important city during this period, and the Mir-i Arab madrassah that had been built by Shaybanid khan Abdallah II made the city one of the foremost centers of Sunni learning in the entire Islamic world. The flourishing Sufi sects of the city also made Bukhara a major center of Sufism. But Samarkand was not neglected, and it was Bukharan khans that had two beautiful madrassahs constructed on the Registan, next to the madrassah Ulugh Beg had built two centuries earlier.

Further west, Turkmen tribes gradually took control of the Karakum Desert and the foothills of the Kopet Dag mountains, on the border between modern Turkmenistan and Iran. The Turkmen remained fragmented and restive, but a new dynasty established itself at Khiva in the 17th century, the Khanate of Khiva, which tried to establish control over much of Turkmen realm. During the khanate period, Khiva also became a significant center of learning, a situation that lasted well into the 19th century.

Despite the cultural achievements of the khanates, the fate of central Asia was intimately bound up with that of Imperial Russia. Inevitably, the Russians turned their attention to the south and undertook the conquest of central Asia in two stages.

During the long first phase, from 1730 to 1848, Russia took control of modern Kazakhstan. During the second stage, from 1864 to 1884, Russia captured all the modern territories of Uzbekistan, Kyrgyzstan, Tajikistan, and Turkmenistan. Tashkent was stormed by Russian forces in 1865, the emir of Bukhara was routed in 1868, and the emir of Khiva was defeated in 1873. In 1881, the Russians crushed Turkmen resistance at the Battle of Goktepe, just a few miles north of the modern capital of Ashgabat. And the conquest of central Asia was completed in 1884, when the Russians acquired the remnants of Merv, which had been so brutally sacked by the Mongols six and a half centuries earlier.

This string of Russian victories in central Asia provoked great distrust amongst the Imperial British, leading to the so-called Great Game of espionage and diplomacy that now played out between these two competing imperial powers. An ugly chapter of the Great Game took place in Bukhara when British officers Charles Stoddart and Arthur Conolly were imprisoned in a vermin pit and then publicly beheaded by the emir on June 17th, 1842. But outright war was eventually averted through the work of the Pamir Boundary Commission and the subsequent Anglo-Russian Convention of 1907, which clearly delineated their separate spheres of interest in central Asia.

The Russians introduced an effective imperial administrative system for their new central Asian territories. In some regions, they appointed military governors to rule—in others, civilian governors-general. And they eventually divided central Asia into five regions and two protectorates. Tashkent was the seat of the 11 Russian governors that ruled from 1867 to 1917, and it quickly became the largest and most sophisticated city in all central Asia. Because of the introduction of high-quality educational institutions by the Russians, by 1917, a well-educated central Asian population had emerged, agitating for independence.

After the Bolshevik Revolution in Russia in October 1917, hopes for independence ran high amongst central Asian nationalists. But these hopes were dashed. Within six months, the new Soviet government in Russia had declared Tashkent the capital of the Turkestan Autonomous Soviet Socialist Republic.

The most geopolitically significant effect of Soviet rule was to draw up national borders for five brand new central Asian republics. Before this, as we have seen repeatedly throughout the course, central Asian borders had been fluid, based on Mongol khanate divisions, nomadic or sedentary lifeways, rivers that shifted through the desert, and tribal and religious affiliations. Now five new nations were effectively "invented" as the Kazakhs, Kyrgyz, Tajik, Turkmen, and Uzbek Soviet Socialist Republics.

Moscow then forced collectivization on the five republics in a Five-Year Plan between 1928 and 1932, but the results were disastrous, and millions died of starvation. Anti-Soviet resistance groups emerged, like Alash Orda, and these, along with other outspoken intelligentsia, caused Stalin so much trouble he decided to eliminate all dissenters. This led to purges of untold tens of thousands of central Asians who were killed in mass executions and buried in mass graves.

Heavy industrialization followed in the 1930s, a process that received a tremendous boost during the Second World War when many factories were relocated from western Russia into central Asia to preserve Soviet industrial capacity from the invading Nazis. Millions of central Asian soldiers were conscripted into the Red Army and died fighting the Nazis. The Russian population of the region swelled dramatically during the war, with evacuees from the war zones increasing numbers of Russians to several million. After the war, the five Stans became even more deeply embedded in the political and economic fabric of the USSR.

If you talk with older folks in Uzbekistan or Turkmenistan today, you might be surprised that many of them are ready to list for you some of the benefits of Soviet rule. Health care was dramatically improved with the construction of new hospitals. New industrial plants, mines, and farms employed millions. Education expanded to reach all social levels, and literacy reached 97 percent. Women were given economic equality and maternity leave for the first time. And artistic expression was encouraged so that distinctive national identities were able to emerge.

And let's not forget that it was Soviet archaeologists who unlocked the long and complex history of inner Eurasia. And it was Soviet engineers who saved the crumbling monuments of the region from collapse, like the astonishing madrassah constructed on the Registan in Samarkand by Ulugh Beg, grandson of the last great nomadic conqueror in world history, Timur.

But of course, all this ended in the early 1990s, after Mikhail Gorbachev's well-intentioned policies of glasnost and perestroika shattered the Soviet Union. When Gorbachev resigned as leader of the party on August 24th, 1991, he dissolved the Central Committee, put an end to party control of the military, and told regional party organizations that they would have to fend for themselves. The union of 15 republics simply dissolved overnight as they scrambled to declare their independence. By the end of 1991, the parliaments of all five central Asian republics had voted to declare their sovereignty and were free to forge their own destinies, a story that surely belongs to another course.

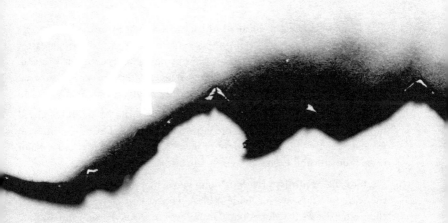

THE MONGOLS
AND THE MAKING OF
THE MODERN WORLD

This lecture examines the heritage of the Mongols from a variety of perspectives, including the consideration of them as conquerors, unifiers, social and political revolutionaries, protectors of commerce, facilitators of the spread of epidemics, and disseminators of crucial technologies that undoubtedly did play a role in the making of the modern world. At the heart of this lecture is a fundamental question: How might the world today be different had the Mongols—and the Timurids, for that matter—never existed?

Mongol Administration

Peerless in conquest, the Mongols had to face the challenge of imperial administration. Once they had destroyed the existing government structures of the countries they conquered, they needed to assume the administration of these countries themselves.

The Mongols turned to local administrators drawn from the bureaucrats who had been running civil government in these cities and states for centuries. Persian and central Asian administrators were particularly valued, and they were often transferred long distances across Eurasia to take up bureaucratic posts in far flung regions of the empire.

This was particularly true of Yuan China, where the Mongols imported hundreds if not thousands of medium- and high-level administrators to work for them. This movement of professional administrators had a major impact on cultural exchange across Eurasia.

Despite the administrative positions given to professional bureaucrats, the Mongol elites always made it clear who was in charge of the courts they established in Mongolia, China, central Asia, Persia, and Russia. The Mongols made sure to maintain a strong military presence in each conquered state, and this gave Mongol rulers the highest status, privilege, and power. But within these same courts, all manner of ideas and religions were allowed to flourish.

The Impact of the Pax Mongolica

After the devastation of initial conquest, the Mongols were able to put in place reasonably effective civil administration across the vast extent of their realm, which led to the establishment of a genuine Pax Mongolica. It is important not to overstate this idea of a Mongol peace: There were extensive periods of conflict within and between the various khanates, but evidence indicates that most economies throughout the empire revived, and transregional trade and cultural exchange flourished.

This was further facilitated by the Mongol practice of transferring talented artists, intellectuals, and craft workers from one part of the empire to another, often thousands of miles away. During the Pax Mongolica, it was inevitable that crucial technologies and ideas would spread from one end of Eurasia to the other. The landmark study on this was done by historian Thomas Allsen in his 2001 publication *Culture and Conquest in Mongol Eurasia*.

Allsen discusses a variety of exchanges in his study. He first focuses on the flow of historical information from China and other parts of the empire to Persia, particularly to the research institute established by the great Persian world historian Rashid al-Din.

Once Rashid al-Din's historical research spread back to China, this considerably increased the knowledge Chinese scholars had about historical events in the Islamic world. Allsen also traces the spread of ideas about geography, topography, and mapmaking across Eurasia, and he points out numerous instances in which Persian and Chinese cartographers learned much from each other's work.

Medical exchanges during the Pax Mongolica were also of considerable consequence for people throughout Eurasia. Although the Mongols had a variety of medical practices of their own prior to expansion, once the empire had been established, Mongol elites gained access to the finest medical treatments available anywhere in Eurasia.

Mongol rulers brought into their service entire retinues of medical professionals, which meant that as they traveled, so too did ideas about medicine. Chinese doctors were transported westward as early as 1219, and both Chagatai and Hulagu had Chinese physicians in their personal retinues. Many of these remained in the Ilkhanate and became physicians to later rulers.

Printing

The argument that the Mongol empire helped create the modern world rests substantially on their role in the spread of two technologies in particular, one of which was printing. The Chinese invented paper in the 2nd century CE, and that this had spread into the Islamic world by the 8th century. By at least the 7th century and perhaps earlier, block printing was in use in China. During the time of the Song dynasty, printing was flourishing all over China, producing a wide range of books, calendars, and government edicts.

Experiments with moveable type printing began in the early 11th century, and the technology was in use in China, Korea, eastern central Asia, and even Tibet by the advent of the Mongols, who quickly became enthusiastic adopters of the technology. In 1236, Ogedai ordered the establishment of a series of regional printing workshops across much of northern China. Because the Mongol script used far fewer characters than classical Chinese script required, the Mongols immediately embraced the use of moveable-type printing even as the Chinese were making tentative steps toward adopting it.

Knowledge of moveable type printing soon spread from the Yuan state to the Ilkhanate. Rashid al-Din includes in his history of the world a detailed account of paper and how it was made, of the technology of the printing press, and of the results of its use.

The precise pathway by which the technology of moveable type printing moved further west and into Europe is difficult to determine. One likely conduit is that western travelers in the Mongol empire must undoubtedly have encountered large numbers of printed books on their travels and perhaps brought some home, which in turn stimulated discussions in Europe.

Gunpowder

Gunpowder was another Chinese invention destined to change the world. There are a few textual references that hint at experiments with gunpowder as early as the Han dynasty, but undoubtedly by the 7th-century Tang dynasty, the Chinese military was using gunpowder weapons of various types. Just before the Mongols turned up in China, the Jin and Song had been using formidable gunpowder weapons in their battles for control of northern China.

Many historians have argued that the Mongols played a major role in the spread of gunpowder technology from China to the Middle East and eventually on to Europe, but others are not so certain. Because of ambiguous textual evidence concerning the Mongols' use of gunpowder outside of China, some scholars downplay their role. Others like Tonio Andrade argue the Mongols used gunpowder weapons effectively and consistently.

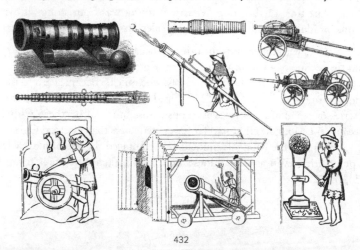

Jin dynasty sources clearly record Mongol bombs raining down on besieged cities. Some evidence also suggests that Mongols armies used gunpowder weapons in the Middle East and Europe, although historians like Tim May are not convinced.

The Spread of Awareness

Perhaps the Mongols' most important contribution was to establish conditions that made it possible for dozens of European merchants, missionaries, and envoys to travel deep into Asia and then return to their home countries. This gave European rulers and intellectuals a new awareness of the world beyond the borders of their small city-states and kingdoms. That in turn acted as a powerful spur to the Renaissance, to subsequent European global exploration, and ultimately to European imperial control of most of the surface of the earth.

It is because of this that some historians, justifiably perhaps, see the Mongols as the architects of the modern world. If there had been no Pax Mongolica, we can only wonder how much longer it would have taken for the medieval world system to have given way to the early modern, and to the emergence of political and economic structures that were soon utterly dominated by European states.

In other words, the interconnected trans-Eurasian system created by the Mongols was the foundation on which the subsequent emergence of capitalism, globalization, and European imperialism was built. That the Mongols did all this in only about a century of control of the largest contiguous empire the world had ever seen was extraordinary.

THE MONGOLS AND THE MAKING
OF THE MODERN WORLD

LECTURE 24 TRANSCRIPT

What, finally, are we to make of the Mongols? Should we think of them as little more than brutal conquerors who brought death and destruction to millions of humans, from Korea to Hungary? Or should we see them as unifiers who brought together for the first time the great variety of cultures, languages, religions, and technologies that existed across Eurasia? Was their impact upon the social, political, and economic structures of all the kingdoms, empires, and caliphates they came to rule fleeting or long-lasting?

Perhaps we should focus on the Mongols' support of commerce and agree that, through their support of land and maritime trade, the Mongols made possible the third great era of the Silk Roads. We should also acknowledge the role of the Mongols in the transfer of technologies from east Asia to Europe, particularly technologies of warfare that were destined to play a profound role in subsequent European and global history.

In trying to sum up the place of the Mongols in world history, should we agree with Jack Weatherford and others that given their political and social impact and their role as facilitators in the dissemination of crucial ideas and technologies, the Mongols truly were the architects of the modern world? Other historians would caution us that this is going too far, however. Tim May, for example, describes Weatherford's argument as "an almost Pollyanna-ish perspective" propagated out of zeal to reverse the long historiographical tradition of treating the Mongols as nothing more than brutal conquerors.

These differences remind us that there have, indeed, been many significant revisions in the way historians have viewed the Mongols over the centuries since they first burst upon the world stage. Michael Prawdin sums this up beautifully when he writes:

The historians of [the Mongols'] day, most of them belonging to subjugated, civilized peoples, could see nothing but that destruction and devastation, misfortune and terror, had been let loose upon mankind. Later generations were able to enjoy the advantages bequeathed by their worldwide empire. To them came the fruits of the fertilizing contact between the great national cultures, which was perhaps the most outstanding requisite for the changes and the unanticipated impetus of Europe during the next few centuries. Now, by the time the Mongolian realms had ceased to exist, the subjugated people were ripe to enter into the heritage.

But this evolution of historical interpretation has been far from uniform. It's too easy to say that historians who were contemporary to the events they described were uniformly critical of the Mongols or focused only on their brutality. Think, for example, of the nuanced assessments offered by some of our most important sources for this course, particularly Ata-Malik Juvaini and Rashid al-Din. Both could be critical of Mongol ferocity but also praise Mongol social egalitarianism and religious tolerance.

It would also be inaccurate to argue that all modern historians have a more positive view of the Mongols. Historian John Boyle, writing in 1970, clearly identified the tensions inherent in considering the Mongols as either destructive or constructive. As Boyle pointed out, the question of which of these interpretations to focus on is often determined by the interests of the historian who is considering them. For some nationalist historians, the conquest of their states by the Mongols was an inherently regressive experience that they use to explain their country's lack of progress or sophistication today. But for world historians and big historians, focused on the larger picture of the impact of the Mongols on Eurasia and eventually on the world, their constructive role as facilitators of exchange is highlighted as the most important consequence of the Mongol era.

Our task in this final lecture is to consider the heritage of the Mongols from a variety of perspectives—as conquerors, unifiers, social and political revolutionaries, as promoters of religious tolerance, protectors of commerce, as facilitators of the spread of deadly disease epidemics across Eurasia, but also as disseminators of crucial technologies that undoubtedly did play a role in the making of the modern world.

We have already had much to say about the Mongols' attitude towards trade and religion, and also their role in the spread of the Black Death across Eurasia and into Europe, with disastrous consequences. So perhaps it makes more sense here to consider other types of exchanges that were equally consequential. At the heart of this lecture is a fundamental question: How might the world today be different had the Mongols, and the Timurids for that matter, never existed?

The Mongols and Timurids were the final great historical efflorescence of the crucial role that militarized pastoral nomads had played in Eurasian history ever since the first galvanizing appearance of the Scythians and the Xiongnu. As part of the eastern steppe world, the Mongols and Timurids were inheritors of the military tactics and political organization of the Xiongnu, innovations introduced late in the 3rd century BCE by their formidable ruler Modu.

But something else emerged with the Xiongnu that would influence all the great steppe empires that followed, an imperial tradition that evolved into an ideology about the destiny of the nomads to rule, an ideology that has been called Tengriism after the great sky god of the steppe, Tengri. The Xiongnu believed they were destined by the gods to create a steppe empire, and so, too, did the rulers of the subsequent Turkic, Uyghur, Khitan, and Jurchen empires. And as we have seen, this was certainly also true of the Mongols, who, particularly following the death of Chinggis, turned this belief into a divine imperative to conquer the world.

Politically, the Xiongnu model of a ruling clan that seized and maintained power over other clans through war and conquest also influenced their imperial successors, including both the Mongols and Timurids. The Xiongnu confederation had included a range of different nomadic and semi-nomadic peoples who probably spoke different languages and followed different cultural traditions, but who had all agreed to follow the powerful Xiongnu *shanyu* and his elite clan. The later Turkic confederation also consisted of many different tribes that agreed to acknowledge a core political elite as their overlords.

After Chinggis Khan carved his way to power over Mongols, Merkit, Keraits, Turks, Uyghurs, and others, thus uniting under his banner a diverse range of peoples speaking different languages, he and his family were similarly acknowledged as the *altan urugh*, the Golden Clan. And as Chinggis then secured victory after astonishing victory, this idea that the khan and his golden family had been chosen by heaven to unite the tribes and lead them to world conquest only strengthened. This belief helps explain the continuing prestige of the Chinggisid lineage over the centuries that followed.

Of course, this divine blessing was something of a two-edged sword, because the prestige of the family and of the khan was utterly dependent on military success. Fortunately, as a military leader, Chinggis Khan was peerless, an undisputed military genius who never lost a battle, but much of this military success can also be traced back to his steppe imperial predecessors. The organization of his military had a clear precedent with the Xiongnu—the use of units of ten, a hundred, a thousand, and ten thousand light and heavy cavalry, for example. His officers were carefully selected from his *nokur*, his household staff, an idea that also had precedence in the steppe world. These were men who had left their home tribes to become the companions of Chinggis Khan, his most trusted advisers and commanders. It didn't matter to the Mongols what ethnicity or tribe these men had come from. If they were loyal, tenacious, and superb leaders of men, they now constituted the new military aristocracy of the Mongol world.

This *nokur* aristocracy, in which every single member had a personal bond with the khan, was then able to militarize millions of pastoral nomads from across a broad region of the steppe and lead them on extraordinary campaigns of expansion. This was true of Chinggis, of course, but also of Ogedai and Hulagu and Qubilai and Timur and Shahrukh and Babur. An initial impetus behind these wars was the acquisition of enormous treasure in the form of booty that could be used to sustain both the aristocracy and also the common soldier. But once the empire had been established, it was necessary to encourage, support, and tax commercial activity in order to maintain a steady stream of income. This explains the Mongols' support, in a variety of ways, of merchants all the way from the Black Sea to China.

Peerless in conquest, the Mongols then had to face the challenge of imperial administration, a problem each of their steppe imperial predecessors also had to deal with. Once they had destroyed the existing government structures of the countries they conquered, they needed to assume the administration of these countries themselves. This was something new for the Mongol elites. Of course, they knew very well how to rule nomads, but having to effectively govern millions of sedentary farmers, merchants, and craft workers who lived in villages, towns, and cities was something else again.

It is hardly surprising, then, that the Mongols turned to local administrators drawn from the bureaucrats who had been running civil government in these cities and states for centuries. Persian and central Asian administrators were particularly valued, and as we have seen, were often transferred long distances across Eurasia to take up bureaucratic posts in far-flung regions of the empire.

This was particularly true in Yuan China, where the Mongols imported hundreds, if not thousands, of medium- and high-level administrators to work for them. This movement of professional administrators had a major impact on cultural exchange across Eurasia. As Thomas Allsen notes:

> The Mongolian rules of China systematically placed peoples of different ethnic, communal, and linguistic backgrounds side by side in the Yuan bureaucracy. There were, in other words, quite literally thousands of agents of cultural transmission and change dispersed throughout the Yuan realm.
>
> But despite the often very senior administrative positions given to professional bureaucrats, the Mongol elites always made it clear who was in charge of the courts they established in Mongolia, China, central Asia, Persia, and Russia. The Mongols made sure to maintain a strong military presence in each conquered state, and this gave Mongol rulers the highest status, privilege, and power. But within these same courts, all manner of ideas and religions were allowed to flourish.

All this meant that after the devastation of initial conquest, the Mongols were able to put in place reasonably effective civil administration across the vast extent of their realm, which led to the establishment of a genuine Pax Mongolica. This is not to overstate this idea of a Mongol peace. Clearly, there were extensive periods of conflict within and between the various khanates, but all the evidence indicates that most economies throughout the empire revived, and transregional trade and cultural exchange flourished.

This was further facilitated by the Mongol practice of transferring not only bureaucrats, but also talented artists, intellectuals, and craft workers from one part of the empire to another, often thousands of miles away. Think of Timur as a classic example of this. He sent so many thousands of builders and craft workers back to beautify his capital of Samarkand that he had to construct entirely new suburbs for them to live in.

In this environment, this century of the Pax Mongolica, it was inevitable that crucial technologies and ideas would spread from one end of Eurasia to the other. The landmark study on this was done by historian Thomas Allsen in his 2001 publication *Culture and Conquest in Mongol Eurasia*. Allsen discusses a variety of exchanges in his study, which essentially traces the spread of material and non-material products between east and west Asia. He first focuses on historiography, on the flow of historical information from China to other parts of the empire to Persia, and particularly to the research institute established by the great Persian world historian and senior administrator of the Ilkhanate, Rashid al-Din.

Once Rashid al-Din's historical research spread back to China, this considerably increased the knowledge Chinese scholars had about historical events in the Islamic world, of which they seem to have been largely ignorant up to that point. But the innovative approach of Rashid al-Din was not emulated in China, where official histories like the *Yuan Shih* continued to follow a stale, formulaic approach, and in any case were later ideologically edited by the Ming, who detested the Mongols.

Allsen also traces the spread of ideas about geography, topography, and map-making across Eurasia and points out numerous instances where Persian and Chinese cartographers learned much from each other's work. The dissemination of this more accurate knowledge of Eurasian geography was of profound importance to subsequent world historical events.

In fact, S. A. M. Adshead has argued that a crucially important step towards the emergence of a modern world system was the diffusion "and integration of geographical knowledge." Once this knowledge of the shape of Eurasia, and of the physical features it contained, came into existence, it became permanent. There were now far fewer blanks on the map. Marco Polo and the hundred or so other Europeans who traveled extensively throughout the Mongol Empire added further details to this geographical knowledge, and there can be no doubt that it was the Pax Mongolica that made its dissemination possible.

In so many other areas, the close relationship between the Yuan Dynasty and the Ilkhanate, particularly during the reign of Ilkhan Ghazan, facilitated the dissemination of knowledge. Allsen has a chapter on agricultural exchanges, for example, both ideas about agronomy, but also actual seed exchanges, so that new crop species were introduced in both east and west Asia. This in turn led to the spread of new ideas about food.

Prior to the Pax Mongolica, Mongol cuisine was decidedly undistinguished, but as the empire evolved, so, too, did the sophistication and variety of foods. Allsen compares the observations by Friar Carpini at the coronation of Guyuk in 1246, who noted that meat in broth was the only food offered at the celebratory feast, with those of William of Rubruck a decade later, who found a much greater variety of food available in the capital of Karakorum.

By the time Marco Polo arrived at the court of Qubilai Khan, he was expressing his astonishment at the great diversity of meat, fish, and bird dishes available, as well as a wide range of alcoholic beverages. All of this indicates the increasing influence of Persian and Islamic ideas about cuisine on those Mongols living in China, which elevated the fare available, at least at the court of Qubilai Khan, to the status of haute cuisine. But this was also a two-way dissemination. Rashid al-Din notes various Chinese food and beverage items that were now available in west Asia, including the increasing importance of rice to Islamic cuisine, along with rice wine and even chopsticks.

Medical exchanges during the Pax Mongolica were also of considerable consequence for people throughout Eurasia. Although the Mongols had a variety of medical practices of their own prior to expansion, once the empire had been established, Mongol elites gained access to the finest medical treatments available anywhere in Eurasia. As part of the same process whereby Mongols conscripted peoples with talents and moved them all over the empire, so Mongol rulers brought into their service entire retinues of medical professionals, which meant that as they traveled, so, too, did ideas about medicine. We know that Chinese doctors were transported westwards as early as 1219, and both Chagatai and Hulagu had Chinese physicians in their personal retinues. Many of these remained in the Ilkhanate and became physicians to later rulers.

And again, this cultural transmission was not one way. For centuries Nestorian Christians had been slowly filtering eastwards from the Mediterranean and settling in locations along the Silk Roads, so that by the time of the Mongols, they had a substantial presence throughout inner Eurasia and China. The Nestorians favored western medical practices, and several Syriac medical treatises have been discovered at Nestorian sites that provide clear evidence of their role in spreading Greco-Roman medical ideas eastwards, particularly those practices championed by 2nd-century Greek physician Galen.

As important as each of these cultural diffusions were, the argument that the Mongol Empire helped create the modern world rests substantially on their role in the spread of two technologies in particular, printing and gunpowder. We know that the Chinese invented paper in the 2nd century CE and that this had spread into the Islamic world by the 8th century. We also have evidence that by at least the 7th century, and perhaps earlier, block printing was in use in China. The world's oldest printed book was discovered near

Dunhuang, a copy of the Buddhist Diamond Sutra dated to 868. Certainly by the Song Dynasty, printing was flourishing all over China, producing a wide range of books, calendars, and government edicts.

Experiments with moveable-type printing began in the early 11th century, and the technology was in use in China, Korea, eastern central Asia, and even Tibet by the advent of the Mongols, who quickly became enthusiastic adopters of the technology. In 1236, Ogedai ordered the establishment of a series of regional printing workshops across much of northern China. And because the Mongol script used far fewer characters than classical Chinese script required, the Mongols immediately embraced the use of moveable-type printing even as the Chinese were making tentative steps towards adopting it.

Knowledge of moveable-type printing soon spread from the Yuan state to the Ilkhanate. We know this because Rashid al-Din includes in his history of the world a detailed account of paper and how it was made, of the technology of the printing press, and of the results of its use. However, the precise pathway by which the technology of moveable-type printing moved further west and into Europe is difficult to determine.

One likely conduit is that western travelers in the Mongol Empire must undoubtedly have encountered large numbers of printed books on their travels, and perhaps brought some of these home, which in turn stimulated discussions in Europe that provided, as Allsen puts it, "an incentive to innovation." Certainly, Marco Polo makes several references to printed materials he encountered. This is hardly conclusive as a channel of dissemination, of course, but the sheer volume of printed material produced by the Mongols undoubtedly helped spread the technology on to Europe.

Gunpowder was another Chinese invention destined to change the world. There are a few textual references that hint at experiments with gunpowder as early as the Han Dynasty, but undoubtedly by the 7th-century Tang Dynasty, the Chinese military was using gunpowder weapons of various types. Just before the Mongols turned up in China, the Jin and Song had been using formidable gunpowder weapons in their battles for control of northern China, including a terrifying shrapnel device called the "thunderbolt-ball" that blasted pottery shards and iron coins to cut a swathe through the enemy whenever the weapon was detonated.

Many historians have argued that the Mongols played a major role in the spread of gunpowder technology from China to the Middle East and eventually on to Europe, but others are not so certain. Because of ambiguous textual evidence concerning the Mongols' use of gunpowder outside of China, some scholars downplay their role. Others, like Tonio Andrade, argue that not only did the Mongols use gunpowder weapons; they used them so effectively and consistently they should be labeled "the first gunpowder empire."

Jin Dynasty sources clearly record Mongol bombs raining down on besieged cities as just one of several types of gunpowder weapons the Mongols employed in their conquest of China. As we saw in an earlier lecture, some evidence also suggests that Mongol armies used gunpowder weapons in the Middle East and Europe, although historians like Tim May are not convinced.

Scholars have labored long and hard to find evidence of a clear dissemination pathway from the Mongols' undoubted use of gunpowder in their wars in China, through their possible use of similar weapons in the Middle East and Eastern Europe, to the adoption of gunpowder weapons by European courts soon afterwards, but the evidence is ambiguous. As Tim May concludes, "Although the spread of gunpowder is directly related to the rise of the Mongols and the Pax Mongolica, it is unclear whether the Mongols themselves contributed to the spread."

OK, after this brief survey of some of the material and non-material exchanges that occurred as a result of the Pax Mongolica, are we any closer to answering the question of how the world might have been different if there had been no Mongol Empire? Perhaps the Mongols' most important contribution was to establish conditions that made it possible for dozens of European merchants, missionaries, and envoys to travel deep into Asia and then return to their home countries. This gave European rulers and intellectuals a new awareness of the world beyond the borders of their own small city-states and kingdoms, which acted as a powerful spur to the Renaissance, to subsequent European global exploration, and ultimately to European imperial control of most of the surface of the earth.

It is because of all this that some historians, justifiably perhaps, see the Mongols as the architects of the modern world. If there had been no Pax Mongolica, we can only wonder how much longer it would have taken for the medieval world system to have given way to the early modern, and to the emergence of political and economic structures that were soon utterly dominated by European states. In other words, the interconnected trans-Eurasian system created by the Mongols was the foundation upon which the subsequent emergence of capitalism, globalization, and European imperialism was built.

That the Mongols did all this in only about a century of control of the largest contiguous empire the world had ever seen was extraordinary. But as we have seen, the logistics of administering such a vast world state were beyond the control of any peoples in the 13th century, let alone rulers from the steppe nomadic tradition. Indeed, in the very nature of the lifeway of steppe nomadic pastoralism lay the seeds of eventual imperial dissolution.

As Michael Prawdin concludes: "During four centuries their hordes wandered over the land, crowding one another out, and engaged in a warfare of mutual destruction. They produced rulers and warriors for conquest or defense, but nowhere did they take root." This was true of the Xiongnu and the Khitan, the Mongols and most of the Timurids, although not of Babur, who established the powerful sedentary empire of the Mughals, nor of the Turks, who built the formidable Ottoman Empire.

And what of the ancient heartland of all these empires, the steppes of Mongolia to which the Mongols returned after their hour upon the stage? Mongols in the region remained restive throughout the 15th century and were an ongoing problem for the Ming, but after that, Mongolia gradually became a quiet backwater.

In the 16th century, the Golden Family of Chinggis Khan converted to Buddhism, which led to the development of a close relationship between Mongol elites and lamas of Tibetan schools of Buddhism. This effectively reduced the political prestige of the Chinggisids, as the leaders of other tribes now established their own relationships with Tibetan Buddhist leaders, whose support became crucial for any claims of leadership to advance.

It was Altan Khan, a direct descendant of Chinggis, who was the first to convert in 1578, and he subsequently bestowed on his Tibetan master Sonam Gyatso the title of Third Dalai Lama. The word *dalai* is actually Mongolian for "ocean." Sonam Gyatso's predecessors were posthumously designated the first and second Dalai Lamas. Mass conversion to Buddhism followed all over Mongolia, and many men joined monasteries.

Ironically, the first Buddhist monastery to be built in Mongolia, Erdene Zuu, or the Hundred Treasures, was constructed right beside the former Mongol capital of Karakorum in the Orkhon Valley. It was partly constructed out of blocks of black stone taken from Karakorum. At its peak, Erdene Zuu contained about 100 temples, had space for 300 *gers* to be erected inside its walls, and was home to about 1,000 monks.

The progression from masters of the world to a people no longer in control of their own destiny happened quickly for the Mongols. During the 17th century, parts of Mongolia were incorporated into the empire of the Chinese Qing Dynasty, successors to the Ming and the last dynasty destined to rule China. When the Qing collapsed in 1911, Mongolia tried to claim its independence under their most prestigious leader, the Jebtzun Damba, or Living Buddha. He was declared both the sacred and secular ruler of the country and given the title Bogd Khan, or Holy King.

But both China and Russia laid claim to parts of Mongolia, and after the Mongolians established a capital at the site of present-day Ulaanbaatar, it was invaded by Chinese nationalists in 1918, and then by Soviet troops in 1921. Mongolian nationalists argued that the best hope for the country was to side with the Soviets, and in July 1921, a people's government was declared in Mongolia. The Bogd Khan was retained as a ceremonial ruler, but the real power behind the throne now lay with a group of communists that headed the Mongolian People's Revolutionary Party.

In the 1930s, Josef Stalin ordered that purges of political opponents should occur in Mongolia, just as they were all over the Soviet Union. Stalin's Mongolian henchman, Khoorloogiin Choibalsan, seized all the pastoralists grazing land and declared private ownership of land illegal. He also ordered the destruction of all religious institutions, which meant that something like 700 monasteries were partially or totally destroyed, including Erdene Zuu. Of an estimated 27,000 people who were executed during these purges, some 17,000 of them were Buddhist monks.

Despite these purges, after the Sino-Soviet split occurred in the 1950s, Mongolia continued to side with the USSR. Through the 1960s and '70s, the influence of the Soviet Union was ubiquitous in Mongolia. Russian food and culture dominated, and young Mongolians went to Moscow to pursue their university studies.

But after communism collapsed in Europe in 1989, and with the USSR on the brink of extinction, huge nationalist demonstrations broke out in Ulaanbaatar in March 1990. Elections were held in July that same year, and a coalition of old communist party bosses and new democratic leaders were elected. The restoration of democracy led to economic collapse. The new government's approach to this challenge was unique; essentially the rapid reprivatization of all lands, animals, and state-owned businesses. But it worked, and Mongolia has gradually become a fully capitalist and democratic modern nation in which freedom of speech, religion, and assembly are all guaranteed by law.

If you ever find yourself in Mongolia, and I sure hope you do, I know you will be impressed by the vibrant modern city of Ulaanbaatar and its larger-than-life symbols of national hero Chinggis Khan. But if you want to experience the real Mongolia, travel out to the steppes, the endless miles of grassland where extended families still live in their *ger* communities, where young men and women demonstrate extraordinary horse-riding skills as they tend vast flocks and herds of up to 1,500 animals, and where wrestling and archery and traditional arts and crafts still flourish in the communities of nomads. Here is where you will find the timeless heart of Mongolia.

Stand still in the midst of these endless vistas and imagine yourself transported 900 years back in time. Over the horizon, a group of Mongol soldiers comes galloping towards you with orders from the great khan that he is putting the army together again for another great campaign of conquest. It is time for the men to restring their bows, tend to their armor and weapons, and reassemble at the great camp in the Orkhon Valley, where the khan will climb the hillside above, raise his bow, and shout, "We ride!"

The echoes of the Mongol era are palpable in the modern nation of Mongolia, an era in which armies of skilled mounted archer warriors under brilliant leadership changed the world forever.

QUIZ 2

13. Following the division of the Mongol empire into four khanates, the central Asian khanate was controlled by descendants of which of the following?

A. Chagatai and Ogedai. **B.** Ogedai and Jochi.

C. Jochi and Tolui. **D.** Tolui and Chagatai.

14. Historian Rashid al-Din also served in which of the following official positions under the ilkhans Ghazan and Oljeitu?

A. Ambassador to the Yuan dynasty court of Qubilai Khan.

B. Grand vizier of the Ilkhanate.

C. Governor of Baghdad.

D. Guide and translator for Marco Polo.

15. The most important consequence of the Mongols firing dead bodies into the city of Kaffa during a siege was:

A. The capture of the city and plundering of an enormous treasure.

B. The exit of Italian merchants from the city, which had grave financial consequences for the Golden Horde.

C. The transmission of the bubonic plague to Europe.

D. The replacement of the Genoan maritime empire by the Venetian republic.

16. How did the extensive Eurasian travels of Rabban Sawma differ from the journeys of most other travelers we are aware of during the Pax Mongolica?

A. Sawma was commissioned by Mongol rulers to visit heads of state in Europe.

B. Sawma was able to convert perhaps 6,000 Chinese individuals to Christianity.

C. Sawma began his journey as a Christian envoy, but he later converted to Islam.

D. Sawma visited every Mongol khanate and their capitals during his travels.

17. **The Mongol Yuan dynasty in China was eventually overthrown by which of the following?**

A. The Song dynasty.   B. The Qing dynasty.

C. The Ming dynasty.   D. The Sui dynasty.

18. **Although Timur was probably born in the 1320s, he later chose the year 1336 as his "official" birth date for which of the following reasons?**

A. He wanted his enemies to think he was younger than he actually was.

B. He wanted to legitimize his claim to power by linking it to the reign of the last ilkhan.

C. According to his Sufi advisers, the year was particularly spiritually propitious.

D. It was exactly 100 years after the death of Chinggis Khan.

19. **Timur became the most powerful ruler of the Muslim world in the 14th century, but he could never claim the title of caliph because:**

A. That title was reserved exclusively for members of the tribe into which the Prophet Muhammad had been born.

B. It was religiously incompatible with the other titles Timur had already claimed for himself, including gurgan and khan.

C. Timur claimed to be a Muslim only to enhance his political power, not out of genuine religious conviction.

D. Timur preferred to rule as the power behind the throne, so he left a figurehead caliph in place.

20. **On which of the following buildings constructed by Timur is there an inscription reading: "If you doubt our greatness, look at our constructions"?**

A. The Bibi-Khanum Mosque dedicated to his mother-in-law in Samarkand.

B. The Ak-Saray palace in Kesh.

C. The Gur-Emir tomb in Samarkand.

D. The elaborate mosque dedicated to his father in Kesh.

21. Timur's grandson Ulugh Beg is best remembered today as:

A. A powerful conqueror who established the Mughal Empire in India.

B. A profoundly spiritual ruler who governed Transoxiana as a theocracy.

C. An intellectual and scientist.

D. A sultan who presided over a cultural golden age in Herat.

22. The Pax Mongolica facilitated a two-way exchange of all of the following trans-Eurasian cultural practices except:

A. Agricultural technologies and seeds.

B. Geographical knowledge and cartography.

C. Medicinal practices and treatments.

D. Chinese philosophies, including Confucianism.

23. Ultimately, the idea that the Mongols deserve to be recognized as the "architects of the modern world" rests on which of the following claims:

A. Their military strategies influenced European attitudes toward warfare.

B. Their egalitarian social structures influenced Chinese attitudes toward the status of women.

C. They established conditions that allowed trans-Eurasia travelers to increase European knowledge of the world.

D. They facilitated the transmission of gunpowder weapons from China to Europe.

Answers:
13:A; 14: B; 15: C; 16: A; 17: C; 18: B; 19: A; 20: B; 21: C; 22: D; 23: C

BIBLIOGRAPHY

Primary Sources

John of Monte Corvino (John of Montecorvino). *Report from China 1305*. Translated by Henri Cordier. London: Hakluyt Society, 1914. Available through Medieval Sourcebook. Important eyewitness account of life in Beijing during the Yuan dynasty in the early 14th century.

John of Pian de Carpini (John of Plano Carpini). *The Journey of Friar John of Pian de Carpini to the Court of Kuyuk Khan, 1245–1247.* Translated by William Woodville Rockhill. Readable translation of the adventures of Carpini during his journey to the court of Guyuk Khan.

Juvaini, Ala-ad-Din Ata-Malik. *Genghis Khan. The History of the World Conqueror.* Translated by J. A. Boyle. Manchester University Press, 1997. Arguably the single most important eyewitness source on the rise of Chinggis Khan and the expansion of the Mongol empire under subsequent khans.

Rabban Sawma. *The History of the Life and Travels of Rabban Sawma.* Translated by Sir E. A. Wallis Budge, London: Harrison and Sons, 1928. A personal account of the travels of Mongol envoy Rabban Sawma to the pope and crowned heads of western Europe in the late 13th century.

Rashid-al-Din Hamadani. *The Compendium of Chronicles.* Crucial eyewitness source history of the Mongols written by the early 14th-century vizier to Mongol ilkhan Gazan.

The Secret History of the Mongols: A Mongolian Epic Chronicle of the Thirteenth Century. Translated by Igor de Rachewiltz. Western Washington University: Western Cedar, 2015. By far the best translation of this crucial anonymous history of Chinggis Khan and his son and successor Ogedai.

William of Rubruck, *The Journey of William of Rubruck to the Eastern Parts of the World, 1253–55.* Translated by W. W. Rockhill. London: Hakluyt Society, 1900. Full of astute observations on the Mongol way of life, Rubruck's travel narrative sheds important life on the Mongol world.

Secondary Sources

Andrade, Tonio. *The Gunpowder Age: China, Military Innovation, and the Rise of the West in World History*. Princeton: Princeton University Press, 2016. A fascinating study of the invention of gunpowder, its military applications, and its evolution under a variety of states and empires.

Allsen, Thomas T. *Culture and Conquest in Modern Eurasia*. Cambridge: Cambridge University Press, 2001. One of the finest books ever written on the Mongols.

Amitai, R. *The Mongols in the Islamic Lands: Studies in the History of the Ilkhante*. Aldershot: Hampshire, 2007. In-depth study of the Mongol Ilkhanate and its interactions with surrounding peoples, written by a specialist in this particular khanate.

Attwood, Christopher. *Encyclopedia of Mongolia and the Mongol Empire*. New York: Facts on File, 2004. Everything you ever wanted to know about the Mongols and the modern nation of Mongolia in convenient, alphabetized encyclopedia form.

Biran, Michael. *Chinggis Khan*. Oxford: OneWorld, 2007. Important biographical study on Chinggis Khan by one of the world's leading Mongol scholars.

———. "The Mongols in Central Asia from Chinggis Khan's Invasion to the Rise of Temur: The Ogodeid and Chaghadaid Realms." In *The Cambridge History of Inner Asia: The Chinggisid Age*. Edited by Nicola di Cosmo, Allen J. Frank, and Peter B. Golden. Cambridge: Cambridge University Press, 2009. Succinct and scholarly account of the Chagatayid *ulus* and its impact on the culture of central Asia.

Broadbridge, Anne F. *Women and the Making of the Mongol Empire*. Cambridge: Cambridge University Press, 2018. This book makes an important contribution to our understanding of the role of women in the Mongol world and their place among Mongol elites.

Chambers, James. *The Devil's Horsemen*. London: Cassell, 1998. Rich details on the Mongol invasion of eastern Europe.

Dale, Stephen. "The Later Timurids c. 1450–1526." In *The Cambridge History of Inner Asia: The Chinggisid Age*. Edited by Nicola di Cosmo, Allen J. Frank, and Peter B. Golden. Cambridge: Cambridge University Press, 2009. Important study of the later years of the Timurid family and empire.

Delgado, James. *Khubilai Khan's Lost Fleet*. London: The Bodley Head, 2009. Fascinating study of the fleets Qubilai Khan assembled for his two thwarted attempts to invade Japan.

Dunn, Ross. *The Adventures of Ibn Battuta. A Muslim Traveler of the 14th Century*. UC Press, 1990. Still the most readable account available of the extensive travels of Ibn Battuta, including throughout the Mongol Empire, by a leading world historian.

Elverskog, Johan. "The Tumu Incident and the Chinggisid Legacy in Inner Asia." *The Silk Road* 15 (2017): 142–152. Fascinating account of the lingering power of the Mongols in central Asia, focused on the 1449 defeat of a Ming army by Mongol Oirat ruler Esen Tumu.

Forbes Manz, Beatrice. "Temur and the Early Timurids to c. 1450." In *The Cambridge History of Inner Asia: The Chinggisid Age*. Edited by Nicola di Cosmo, Allen J. Frank, and Peter B. Golden. Cambridge: Cambridge University Press, 2009. Brief but scholarly introduction to the rise and career of Timur.

———. *The Rise and Rule of Tamerlane*. Cambridge: Cambridge University Press, 1989. Canto edition, 1999. The author's in-depth research and superb scholarship make this still arguably the most reliable and extensive account available of the career of Timur.

Grousset, Rene. *The Empire of the Steppe*. New Brunswick: Rutgers University Press, 1970. An important book in the historiography of nomadic studies that uses translated primary sources to offer the first detailed account of the great steppe empires of Eurasia.

Halperin, Charles. *Russia and the Golden Horde: The Mongol Impact on Medieval Russian History*. Indiana University Press, 1987. A detailed, thorough, and scholarly account of the extent of Mongol influence on Russian history.

History on the Net. "Mongol Empire Timeline." https://www.historyonthenet.com/mongol-empire-timeline. A useful and readily accessible reference timeline on the history of the Mongol Empire.

Jackson, Peter. *The Mongols and the West*. London: Pearson-Longman, 2005. A classic study of the Mongols' impact on Russia and Europe by one of the world's leading Mongol scholars.

Kalta, Prajakti. *The Silk Road and the Political Economy of the Mongol Empire*. London and New York: Routledge, 2018. Focuses on the role of the Mongols in helping revive Silk Roads trade in the 13th to 15th centuries.

Lane, George. *Daily Life in the Mongol Empire*. London: Greenwood Press, 2006. As the name implies, the author offers a vividly realized insight into life in various cities and regions of Eurasia under Mongol rule.

Man, John. *The Mongol Empire: Genghis Khan, His Heirs and the Founding of Modern China*. London: Corgi Press, 2015. A readable and accurate account of the rise and fall of the family of Chinggis Khan.

May, Timothy. *The Mongol Art of War*, 2007. Timothy May demonstrates that the Mongol military developed from a tribal levy into a complex military organization. He describes the makeup of the Mongol army from its inception to the demise of the Mongol empire.

———. *The Mongol Conquests in World History*. Reaktion Books, 2012. A superb account of the conquest of the empire by one of the world's leading specialists.

———. *The Mongol Empire*. Edinburgh: Edinburgh University Press, 2018. Another brilliant (and highly readable) account of the Mongols, with a particular emphasis on their interactions with the Muslim world.

McLynn, Frank. *Genghis Khan: His Conquest, His Empire, His Legacy*. London: DaCapo Press, 2015. Readable and comprehensive study of the rise of Chinggis Khan and how he deserves to be remembered today.

Morgan, David. "Marco Polo in China—or Not*." *Journal of the Royal Asiatic Society* 6, no. 2 (1996). Analyzes evidence for and against the historical accuracy of the journey of Marco Polo to Mongol-controlled China.

———. *The Mongols*. 2nd ed. Oxford: Basil Blackwell, 2007. A superb and surprisingly detailed (for a relatively short book) of the Mongols by one of the world's leading Mongol scholars.

Prawdin, Michael, *The Mongol Empire: Its Rise and Legacy*. Aldine Transaction, 2006. A classic account of the expansion of the Mongols by a brilliant Ukrainian-German scholar, written more than a century ago.

Rossabi, Morris. *Kublai Khan: His Life and Times*. UC Press, 1990. Wonderfully readable yet highly referenced biography of Qubilai Khan.

————. *The Mongols: A Very Short Introduction*, Oxford: Oxford University Press, 2012. As the name implies, a great though concise introduction to the Mongols by a superb scholar of medieval Eurasia; part of the excellent Oxford Very Short Introduction series.

Soucek, Svat. *A History of Inner Asia*. Cambridge: Cambridge University Press, 2000. A wonderful and comprehensive introduction to the long, complex history of inner Eurasia.

Thubron, Colin. *The Lost Heart of Asia*. London: Harper Collins, 1994. Fascinating account of travels in central Asia by one of the world's great travel writers.

Vasary, Istfan. "The Jochid Realm: The Western Steppe and Eastern Europe." In *The Cambridge History of Inner Asia: The Chinggisid Age*. Edited by Nicola di Cosmo, Allen J. Frank, and Peter B. Golden. Cambridge: Cambridge University Press, 2009. Succinct and scholarly account of the history of the Golden Horde by a leading specialist.

Veit, Veronika. "The Eastern Steppe: Mongol Regimes after the Yuan (1368–1636)." In *The Cambridge History of Inner Asia: The Chinggisid Age*. Edited by Nicola di Cosmo, Allen J. Frank, and Peter B. Golden. Cambridge: Cambridge University Press, 2009. Succinct and scholarly account of the history of the Mongols after the collapse of the Yuan dynasty in eastern Asia, written by a leading specialist.

Weatherford, Jack. *Genghis Khan and the Making of the Modern World*. New York: Broadway Books, 2004. A dramatic and readable account that nonetheless makes an important contribution to our interpretation of the Mongols.

————. *The Secret History of Mongol Queens: How the Daughters of Genghis Khan Rescued His Empire*. New York: Crow Publishing, 2010. The first popular book written on the role of elite women in the Mongol empire.

IMAGE CREDITS

NOTES

NOTES

NOTES